MEDIA REFORM

Is there a relationship between a free and independent media and the development of a democratic society? What impact does political change have on the media and how do changing media structures influence political reform?

Media Reform examines a complex process: the reform of media and its role in promoting democratic practices. Using examples of media from a range of countries in Latin America, Europe, Asia, and Africa including Uruguay, Poland, China, Indonesia, Jordan, and Uganda, *Media Reform* considers the social and cultural implications of a free and independent media. Each case study provides a background to political transition and reform and addresses the processes of media liberalization, the growth of civil society, new technology developments as they have affected the media sector, and the different trends found in broadcast media and print media.

Contributors: Joseph Man Chan, Roque Faraone, Nilanjana Gupta, Karol Jakubowicz, Lutfulla Kabirov, Ronald David Kayanja, Monroe E. Price, Jack Linchuan Qiu, Andrei Richter, Beata Rozumilowicz, Naomi Sakr, Krishna Sen, Scott Smith.

Editors: Monroe E. Price, Beata Rozumilowicz, Stefaan G. Verhulst.

ROUTLEDGE RESEARCH IN CULTURAL AND MEDIA STUDIES
Series Advisors: David Morley and James Curran

MEDIA REFORM

Democratizing the media, democratizing the state

Edited by
Monroe E. Price,
Beata Rozumilowicz, and
Stefaan G. Verhulst

Taylor & Francis Group

LONDON AND NEW YORK

First published 2002
by Routledge
11 New Fetter Lane, London EC4P 4EE

Simultaneously published in the USA and Canada
by Routledge
29 West 35th Street, New York, NY 10001

Transferred to Digital Printing 2003

Routledge is an imprint of the Taylor & Francis Group

Typeset in Baskerville by Rosemount Typing Services
Thornhill, Dumfriesshire
Printed and bound in Great Britain by
TJI Digital, Padstow, Cornwall

British Library Cataloguing in Publication Data
A catalogue record for this book is available
from the British Library

Library of Congress Cataloging in Publication Data
Media reform : democratizing the media, democratizing the
state / [edited by] Monroe E. Price, Beata Rozumilowicz,
Stefaan G. Verhulst
p. cm. – (Routledge research in cultural and media studies)
Includes bibliographical references.
1. Mass media–Political aspects. 2. Democracy. I Price, Monroe
Edwin, 1938- II. Rozumilowicz, Beata, 1970- III.
Verhulst, Stefaan (Stefaan G.) IV. Series.
P95.8 .M3935 2002
302.23–dc21   2001034874

ISBN 0–415–24353–X

CONTENTS

CONTENTS

TABLES

CONTRIBUTORS

Joseph Man Chan is Professor in the School of Journalism and Communication, the Chinese University of Hong Kong, where he formerly served as director. His research interests include international communication, political communication, and the social impact of information technology. His most recent books are *World Media Spectacle* (SUNY Press, 2002), and *In Search of Boundaries: Communication, Nation-States and Cultural Identities* (Greenwood Press, 2002).

Roque Faraone has taught at l'École des Hautes Études en Sciences Sociales and at the Sorbonne (Paris), and at Ramapo College (USA). He was Head of the University Communication School (Uruguay) and now holds a Chair of Social Communication Theory. He has published extensively and among his books are *La prensa de Montevideo* (1960), *Mass Communication in Latin America* (1973), *Televisión y Estado* (1998), and *La objetividad en la información* (1999).

Nilanjana Gupta is Reader in English at Jadavpur University, Calcutta, India. Her research interests include contemporary popular culture, television and film studies and she is the author of *Switching Channels: Ideologies of Television in India* (OUP, 1998).

Karol Jakubowicz is Head, Strategic Planning, Polish Television, Expert at the National Broadcasting Council of Poland, the broadcasting regulatory authority, and Lecturer at the Institute of Journalism, University of Warsaw. He has worked as a journalist and executive in the Polish press, radio, and television for many years. He has been involved in policy-making and regulation in the field of broadcasting in Poland and internationally, through his personal contribution to writing Poland's Broadcasting Act of 1992, and its subsequent revisions, and to the revision of the European Convention on Transfrontier Television in 1998. He is a past Chairman of the Committee of Experts on Media Concentrations and Pluralism, and is now Deputy Chairman of the Standing Committee on Transfrontier Television, both at the Council of Europe. His work in the field of media studies, concentrating in recent years on media transformation in Central and Eastern Europe, has been published widely in Poland and internationally.

Lutfulla Kabirov is a graduate of the Faculty of Journalism of Tashkent State University and the Russian Academy of Management. He has defended his dissertation on the problems of culture development and has a Ph.D. in philosophy. He is a member of the Writers' Union of Uzbekistan, and the author of seven books. Kabirov currently heads an independent centre on the development of mass media problems in Uzbekistan.

Ronald David Kayanja is a Ph.D. candidate in Development Studies at the University of Leeds. His research interests are in the models of development cooperation and their impact on poverty eradication. He has worked as a development communication consultant. He also works as Public Affairs Officer of the United Nations Development Programme, and writes commentaries on development, international relations, and the media. He holds an M.A. in journalism studies from the University of Wales, Cardiff, and a B.A. in Mass Communication from Makerere University. He worked in journalism in Uganda for ten years.

Peter Krug is a Professor at the University of Oklahoma College of Law in the United States, where he teaches courses in comparative law and international law. He is the author of a number of publications in the field of comparative news media law, with particular emphasis on the Russian Federation.

Monroe E. Price is the founder and co-director of the Programme in Comparative Media Law and Policy at Oxford University. He is also the Joseph and Sadie Danciger Professor of Law and Director of the Howard M. Squadron Program in Law, Media, and Society at the Benjamin N. Cardozo School of Law, Yeshiva University, of which he was the dean in 1982–1991. A member of the School of Social Science at the Institute for Advanced Study, Princeton, in 2000–2001, he was a Communications Fellow at the John and Mary R. Markle Foundation, a Fellow of the Media Studies Center of the Freedom Forum in New York City, and Professor of Law at UCLA until 1982.

Jack Linchuan Qiu is a Ph.D. candidate at the Annenberg School for Communication at the University of Southern California. He obtained an M.Phil. from the Chinese University of Hong Kong. His current research interests include the social role of the Internet, the development of the public sphere, new capitalism, and China.

Andrei Richter is founder and Director of the Moscow Media Law and Policy Centre, housed at Moscow University School of Journalism. He is the editor of the monthly journal *Zakonodatelstvo i praktika mass media* (Law and Practice of Mass Media). He is author and editor of more than a hundred books and articles, mainly on media law.

Beata Rozumilowicz is currently one of five international members of the Organization for Security and Co-operation in Europe's (OSCE) Advisory and Monitoring Group (AMG) in Belarus, where she heads the section for legal, human rights, NGO, and media issues. Prior to her secondment, Dr Rozumilowicz was research associate to the Programme in Comparative Media Law and Policy at the Centre for Socio-Legal Studies, University of

Oxford. She holds a B.A. degree in Political Science from Rutgers College and M.Phil. and D.Phil. degrees in Politics from the University of Oxford. Her doctoral work focused on the reform of the Polish political party system in the wake of democratization and encompassed the programmatic nature of party institutionalization and the variable influence that party organization and finance have had on this consolidation.

Naomi Sakr is a research associate of the University of Westminster and Middle East consultant to several non-governmental organizations. She is the author of *Satellite Realms: Transitional Television, Globalization and the Middle East* (forthcoming), *Walls of Silence: Media and Censorship in Syria* (1998), and *Women's Rights and the Arab Media* (2000).

Krishna Sen did her Ph.D. in Politics at Monash University and is Associate Professor and coordinator for postgraduate research in the School of Media and Information at Curtin University of Technology, Perth, Australia. She has published extensively on various aspects of Indonesian media and society, including *Indonesian Cinema: Framing the New Order* (Zed, London, 1994) and *Media, Culture and Politics in Indonesia* (co-authored with David Hill, OUP, Melbourne, 2000). She has also published on gender issues, including co-editing (with Maila Stivens) *Gender and Power in Affluent Asia* (Routledge, 1998).

Scott Smith holds a B.A. and M.A. in English from California State University, Chico. From 1996 to 1998 he was a United States Peace Corps volunteer in the Republic of Uzbekistan and subsequently worked as country director of Internews Network Uzbekistan in 1999 and 2000. Currently he works as a newspaper journalist in California.

Stefaan G. Verhulst has been co-director of the Programme in Comparative Media Law and Policy at Oxford University since 1996. Prior to that, he was a lecturer in communications law and policy issues in Belgium before becoming founder and co-director of the International Media and Infocomms Policy and Law Studies Department at the School of Law, University of Glasgow. He continues to serve as consultant and researcher for numerous organizations including the Council of Europe, European Commission, and UNESCO. He holds the UNESCO Chair in Communications Law and Policy, edits the *International Journal of Communications Law and Policy* and the *Communications Law in Transition Newsletter,* and is the UK legal correspondent for the European Audiovisual Observatory. In the fall of 2000, he was a Scholar in Residence at the John and Mary R. Markle Foundation.

ACKNOWLEDGEMENTS

This book began with a roundtable discussion at the Freedom Forum's Media Studies Center in New York City, partly inspired by Ann Hudock, then a Democracy Fellow at the Democracy and Governance Center of USAID.

A number of scholars and participants in the process have been invaluable as the project has gone forward. These include Eric Johnson of Internews, Ad van Loon, who had been at the Audiovisual Observatory of the Council of Europe in Strasbourg, and Peter Krug of the University of Oklahoma, who has been one of the pillars in American scholarship on this subject. We have benefited from the insights of C. Edwin Baker of the University of Pennsylvania, who was generous with his scholarship, and Stephen D. Whitefield of Pembroke College, Oxford, Dr Beata Rozumilowicz's thesis advisor, whose teaching is reflected in the sections on theories of transition.

The various chapter authors have been extremely cooperative and congenial during the process of preparing this manuscript. We wish to thank, particularly, Karol Jakubowicz for his trenchant comments and contributions to the theoretical framework of the book. We wish to thank Mr Hinca Pandjaitan of Internews, who made a valuable contribution to the understanding of media transformations in Indonesia. Christopher Cudmore at Routledge was supportive from the beginning and made useful suggestions about form and organization.

Among those who reviewed manuscripts, we should like to thank Gillian McCormack for her review of the chapter on Ukraine. Nancy Beatty Edlin and Bethany Davis Noll were heroic in managing the manuscript, making wise adjustments and revisions to it, and generally assisting in the editing and publishing process.

The interest of the editors in this subject was prompted by a grant from USAID to the Nation Institute for the study of an enabling environment for media law reform. That grant produced a study by Professor Price and Professor Krug that has been widely distributed (2000). It also resulted in a conference, held at the University of Oxford in 1998, in which a number of the authors participated. The conference and research commissioned under the grant were helpful to the editors, but this book is independent of that contract and not produced in satisfaction of it. It is, nonetheless, fitting to express our thanks to the USAID Center for Democracy and Governance for its consistent support of inquiry in this area.

The home for this project has been the Programme in Comparative Media Law and Policy (PCMLP) at the Centre for Socio-Legal Studies, Oxford University. Professor Denis Galligan, Director of the Centre, and Jenny Dix and John Gray of the Centre staff were called upon for their aid at vital moments in the management of the project. The Benjamin N. Cardozo School of Law and its Squadron Program in Law, Media, and Society also provided support, and thanks are due to Dean Paul Verkuil and Peter Yu, Deputy Director of the Squadron Program.

Preparing this study has been a bit like riding a group of semi-wild horses simultaneously. Transitions are, by definition, not easy to capture. Swirling notions of power, democratic tendencies, national influences, and changing technology make each word, each thought, and each chapter a study in instability itself. It is in that atmosphere that this book has been completed. The research was done before the end of the year 1999 and the book was prepared in 2000.

INTRODUCTION

This book examines a complex process: the impact of political transitions on media structures and the impact of changing media structures on political reform. In particular, the effort was to study the difficult moves toward more democratic institutions in a widely varied set of contexts. The study introduces hypotheses concerning forms of intervention in media law and policy that might assist scholars, government officials, and society in general to render media more plural and diverse. The chapters explore the timing or stages within the overall media reform process. International organizations, entities committed to the building of civil society, regional aggregations, and private corporations are struggling in regard to the shape of media space and its impact on individuals and society. The purpose here is to search for common themes, common approaches, and a greater understanding of the relationship between public actions and social results.

To achieve this goal, the editors and authors sought comparative perspectives. In this book, we have experimented with a relatively novel approach to comparative analysis in the field of media reform, as we shall set forth below. The introduction of competition from the private sector in Poland, the passing of a new press law in Indonesia, and the persecution of journalists for libel and sedition in Uganda seem wholly disconnected from each other and from theories of democratic transformation. But it is the task of a comparativist to try to integrate such phenomena to the greatest extent possible. Here, we believe we have made a start.

Individual cases, while consequential within their societies, must be placed in a context from which they can later be analyzed. One function of such analysis would be to provide guidance to those involved in transitions in overarching processes of media reform and democratization. It is only in comparison with other similar occurrences that change in structure and modifications of law and policy become generally illustrative or informative.

The very concepts of "media reform" and "democratization" have a relative quality. Comparison is integral to building criteria by which to gauge democratization or reform. A comparative framework assists in developing a reasonable assessment of the conditions that represent reform and how these reform processes promote or hinder the development and stabilization of democratic practices. But to say that a comparative approach is desirable leads only to a more complicated set of issues: namely how to select cases to ensure an appropriate comparison.

Numerous strategies exist, each with a concomitant set of strengths and weaknesses. Some scholars have examined individual countries in comparison to previous historical periods or levels of development. Others have undertaken binary assessments in order to underscore similarities and differences at the structural level of comparability. Still others have looked at regional studies that address cases with similar historical and developmental backgrounds to control for these "independent variables" and determine the causal factors influencing the chosen "dependent variable" or question of interest.

In this study, however, the editors and authors have chosen to follow the method of "greatest difference" comparison, which has generally yielded both robust findings and useful levels of generalization. Employing such a framework, the comparativist gains the "optimal view that will permit him to draw reliable and rigorous conclusions" (Dogan and Pelassy 1990: 111). A study structured around the principle of greatest difference allows for meaningful examination among cases with vastly divergent historical backgrounds, levels of development, political institutionalizations, and social, cultural, and ethnic structures. As a result, any commonality found among cases may reasonably be assumed to hold generally. Moreover, assuming that the cases examined are representative of larger conceptual categories, such findings may lead to the development and specification of a general model or theory.

The comparativist, nonetheless, must be careful to ensure the representativeness of the chosen sample groups since national conditions vary widely, making "the hurdle of internationalization ... arduous to cross" (Dogan and Pelassy 1990: 48). In order to avoid spurious conclusions, the analyst must design the comparative framework for application to a selection of cases that are more widely representative of a particular conceptualized group of nations. The utilization of typologies or heuristic categories is often indispensable to a solid research design. The case selection process, outlined in further detail below, reflects extensive use of such categorizations.

The present study has been developed with such considerations in mind. It brings together analyses of vastly divergent nations, each of which has been undergoing political transition and media reform. The country expert investigations presented in Chapters 2 through 11 endeavor to uncover the development of the dual process of transition and reform while exploring the causal link between them. Authors have asked whether media reform promotes democratization and whether democratic rule is a necessary precondition for the development of media, or whether the two processes are mutually exclusive with little to no effect of one upon the other. In addition, the chapters highlight the main aspects of media reform in each case and underscore the individual media sectors that have played key roles within the larger process of transition.

The criteria for case selection

In selecting cases for this study, the editors sought to establish a wide geographical spread along the lines of the "greatest difference" methodology. At the same time, they have ensured comparability by selecting cases based on their relative stage within the political transition process. As a result, patterns found across a variety of disparate nations will be more "generalizable."

The editors realize that placing societies into categories based on their stage of transition is a highly subjective process. Normative, political, and otherwise prejudiced rationales often creep into such assessments and skew the interpretations that follow. Therefore, the editors evaluated transition stages through a series of continuous political dimensions that are relevant to democratic transitions. In each case, the poles represent logical extremes and countries have been arrayed across these political dimensions to determine their relative placement. The editors place those countries that fall on either extreme across most dimensions into either the "pre-transition" or "mature transition" category as indicated. Those in between have been placed into the "primary" or "secondary" stage categories based on the preponderance of the dimensional placements. Table I.1 gives the attributes of a political transition at the two extremes: "pre-transition" and "mature transition."

In making the case selections, the editors also took into account the possibility of the variable impact of factors based on previous regime experience (Linz and Stepan 1996). As Linz and Stepan have argued, the previous regime type has a determinative influence both on the paths open for a transition country and on the tasks that need to be addressed in order to reach democratic consolidation. It is therefore reasonable to assume that the tasks and paths open for the establishment of free and independent media could also be highly dependent upon the previous regime of a country in transition.

As a result, countries have been chosen from each of the theorized non-democratic regimes as well as from each regime subset. Countries that experienced previous authoritarian, totalitarian, post-totalitarian, mature post-totalitarian, or sultanistic regimes are, therefore, represented.[1] Additionally, the editors include three categories important to the structuring of reform processes. The first category included "areas undergoing transformation under the supervision of an international authority" whose transition has included military strife. The second category included "post-colonial" countries that embarked directly on the course of democratization after gaining independence without an interim period of non-democratic rule. The third category included countries under "ethnically segmented authoritarian regimes" that granted access to various resources based upon ethnic divisions.

Each of the cases in the study was selected by the editors both by its previous regime type and by its placement within the larger context of the four stages of political transition.

Pre-transition stage

From the category of pre-transition countries, the editors chose the cases of China and Uzbekistan, two countries that experienced different previous regime types. China has been considered a prime example of a "totalitarian" regime. Uzbekistan has been optimistically described as post-totalitarian but has elements that, as with China, bring it within the borders of transition. It is certainly true, in each case, that transitional elements are strongly present, but this

Table 1.1 Political dimensions of democratic transition

Pre-transition	*Mature transition*
Executive appointed	Executive elected and has effective power to rule
Legislature appointed	Legislature elected and has effective power to rule
No judiciary or judiciary politically controlled	Full judicial autonomy
Bureaucratic posts allocated by association	Bureaucratic posts allocated by merit
No changeover of power between government and opposition	Changeover of power between government and opposition
Restrictions placed on travel	No restrictions placed on travel
No freedom of expression	Freedom of expression
Certain ethnic groups banned from political participation	All ethnic groups legally and effectively granted full political participation
Military domination over state	Complete civilian control over military
Constant threat to citizens of state violence	No threat to citizens of state violence
Right to assembly prohibited	Right to assembly legally and effectively granted
No elections take place	Elections take place regularly
No former democratic experience	Minimum of 10 years of democratic rule
Rule by decree	Rule of law
State control over information	No state control over information
Class of ruling elites	Change of ruling elite classes
No party competition (anti-regime parties banned)	No limits placed on party competition (no parties banned)
No civil liberties	Full civil liberties
Political participation organized by state	High levels of spontaneous political participation
No freedom of religious expression	Freedom of religious expression

demonstrates that our categories, just like most categories, are useful only as a beginning point. Both countries exhibit characteristics that place them within this pre-transition stage of political reform. As a result, these cases provide important insight into the aspects of media reform that come into play during the pre-transition stage.

Primary transition

The editors chose three countries for analysis within the category of the primary transition stage. Again, each case typifies a different previous regime type. The first is Indonesia, which was selected as a country undergoing transition from a "sultanistic" regime type, though not by the chapter authors, Sen and Hill. We include Bosnia-Herzegovina as an area that, at the time of writing, was "undergoing transformation under the supervision of an international authority." Finally, Jordan represents a former "authoritarian" regime and may illuminate important aspects of transition within a country in which religion strongly influences policy.

Secondary stage

Among cases at the secondary stage of transition, the study examines Ukraine, a second example of a "post-totalitarian" regime. We include Uganda as a country that has made the political transition from a previously "authoritarian" regime, and where elements of a colonial past continue to influence the reform process.

Late or mature stage

From the category of a late or mature transition stage, the editors selected three countries. The first is Poland, which made the transition from a "mature post-totalitarian" system. Uruguay is the second case, having emerged from a previously "authoritarian" system of rule. Finally, India represents a purely "post-colonial" transition.

A Freedom House assessment found in Table I.2 categorizes these ten nations and supports our divisions according to transition stage.[2]

Table I.2 Freedom House criteria

Country	Political rights	Civil liberties	Freedom ranking
Poland	1	2	Free
Uruguay	1	2	Free
India	2	3	Free
Ukraine	3	4	Partly free
Uganda	4	4	Partly free
Jordan	4	5	Partly free
Bosnia-Herzegovina	5	5	Partly free
Indonesia	6	4	Partly free
China	7	6	Not free
Uzbekistan	7	6	Not free

In summary, the selection of Bosnia-Herzegovina, China, India, Indonesia, Jordan, Poland, Uganda, Ukraine, Uruguay, and Uzbekistan represents a wide geographical spread. They include the regions of Asia, Central Asia, the Former Soviet Union, Central and Eastern Europe, the Balkans, Africa, and Latin America. They also adequately cover previous regime types and points of transition so that this study may allow for robust levels of generalization.

Other typologies are possible, of course. In September 2000, the United States Agency for International Development (USAID) Office of Democracy and Governance, Bureau of Europe and Central Asia prepared a document that developed a typology, in which categories were assigned to countries. As the paper pointed out, its typologies were "not rigid, nor do they exist on a continuum that leads one to another in a transition to democracy. In a number of instances, there are substantial areas of overlap, where one country may arguably fit into more than one typology." Rather than the four stages used in this book, the USAID model posits five:

- *Consolidating democracies (Estonia, Czech Republic, Hungary, Poland, Latvia, Lithuania, Slovenia)*: A strong political and social consensus exists. There is a relatively high level of government decentralization. Government has passed acceptable media laws; private media flourish; citizens gain access to a variety of different sources of information from both broadcast and print media. Associations lobby on behalf of journalists.
- *Unstable states/divided states (Albania, Armenia, Bulgaria, Croatia,[3] Georgia, Macedonia, Montenegro, Romania)*: Powerful ethnic/clan divisions and loyalties sharply impede nation building and divide citizens at the local level. "Liberal" media laws may exist, but politics still control media regulation. State media are not independent from the governing political party, although reform efforts may have started. Print media are generally plentiful.
- *Weak states/weak societies (Moldova, Russia, Ukraine)*: A stagnant or contracting economy, a lack of proactive support from a generally passive and/or disinterested government, and an increasingly cynical public hamper democratic transition.
- *Consolidating authoritarian states (Azerbaijan, Belarus, Kazakhstan, increasingly Kyrgyzstan, Turkmenistan, and Uzbekistan)*: Elections are used, but increasingly represent little more than plebiscitary endorsements of state power; society remains almost completely state-dependent, with mono-culture economic development (oil, cotton, and so on) and prime businesses in the hands of a political/business elite. National broadcast media are completely controlled by the state; local broadcast media are in the pocket of local politicians. Media laws, even if on the statute books, are not followed, as the government takes extreme measures to control, censure, and even shut down any independent voices.
- *Failed states (Serbia, Tajikistan, international protectorates of Bosnia and Kosovo)*: Economic stagnation and weak governance, civil war and ethnic conflict have interrupted transitions. Basic questions of identity, community, and control of boundaries remain unresolved. Government's capacity to control policy and provide services is limited. The media are either in an embryonic state,

receiving complete support from the international community (for example, Kosovo broadcast media), or professional journalists are working, but are hampered by the authoritarian regime, as in Serbia. Networking among media outlets is essential in defending themselves against powerful state apparatus.

The USAID document sought to establish these categories both as an analytic enterprise and also to assist in the formulation of policy. Its premise was that "a free and independent media, unrestrained by abusive government restrictions, is a key component to building vibrant democracies." As indicated above, one of the functions of the case studies in this book is to probe the extent to which this is a statement that portrays the dynamic of many transitions. The bureau's report also stated that its goal for independent media was to "develop self-sustaining, private (and, at times, public) broadcast and print media." Our case studies are designed, in part, to explore the limitations on the achievement of these goals.

The editors and authors identified a number of elements that they regard as obstacles to reaching the goal of independent media. Such obstacles include:

- weak economies that force media to seek support from political or other actors with narrow interests and away from independence;
- outdated media regulations that impose harsh restrictions on both broadcast and print media;
- politically vulnerable governments that harass, imprison, and sometimes kill dissenting journalists and media managers as a result of their vulnerability;
- substandard equipment that leads to a lack of public acceptance of independent media; and
- isolated journalists who are unable to mount adequate defense of their status.

The chapters which follow will be crucial in examining the various cases to determine the instances of such obstacles and their relationships to different aspects of transition.

Notes

1 For a fuller discussion of categorizing nations into these previous regime types, see Linz and Stepan (1996).
2 The authors do not necessarily support the Freedom House method of ranking countries. These criteria are merely provided as additional illustration. Country rankings are available at http://www.freedomhouse.org/ratings/index.htm. At the time of writing, the latest figures available were those for 1998–1999. Certain country ratings have been adjusted upward or downward in the 1999–2000 Freedom House assessment.
3 Since these typologies were developed, Croatia has experienced a change in government that may result in a change in regime type. It is still too early to tell.

References

Dogan, Mattei and Pelassy, Dominique (1990) *How to Compare Nations: Strategies in Comparative Politics* (2nd edition). Chatham, NJ: Chatham House.

Linz, Juan J. and Stepan, Alfred (1996) *Problems of Democratic Transition and Consolidation: Southern Europe, South America, and Post-Communist Europe*. Baltimore: Johns Hopkins University Press.
Price, Monroe E. and Krug, Peter (2000) Enabling Environment for Free and Independent Media. Study. Oxford University: Programme in Comparative Media Law and Policy. Available at: http://pcmlp.socleg.ox.ac.uk/EnablingEnvironment.pdf.

1

DEMOCRATIC CHANGE
A theoretical perspective

Beata Rozumilowicz

Before proceeding to the individual country analyses, it is necessary to delineate a number of key conceptual tools that underwrite any study of the role of media in its impact on democratic values. This chapter first surveys the definitions of concepts such as "democracy" and "media reform" and explicates the conceptual link between them. Second, it examines the impact of such definitions upon the general framework of the study in order to underscore their normative implications. The chapter then sets out a hypothetical model of media reform and democratization that posits a series of "stages of transition" during which different aspects of the media reform come to the fore and are addressed as primary concerns.

Theoretical background: the impact of media reform upon the process of democratization

What does "democratization" imply?

In order to understand the relationship between media reform and its role in promoting practices which are more democratic, the terms being used must be defined. In particular, the process of "democratization" implies progress toward some ideal of democracy and a clear delineation of the concept must be made.

Any definition of democracy, however, is certain to be contentious. Should the definition be substantive and include factors such as citizen empowerment, inclusiveness, and representativeness or should it be merely procedural (that is, taking account of open and transparent elections, changeover of governments, equal voting rights, and so on)? Further, is democracy a universal principle that allows individuals to generalize cross-culturally or is it an inherently liberal ideal that is unlikely to transfer without problems?

This is not to say, however, that no definition should be attempted. Rather, the difficulty inherent in such an attempt should heighten awareness of the problems encountered by previous studies and provide impetus toward greater precision in defining terms. Choice of terminology should also encompass theoretical and empirical arguments for the favored interpretation. The various interpretations of leading political scientists in their understanding of the term "democracy" are presented in chronological order in Table 1.1.

Table 1.1 Comparative definitions of democracy

Author	Definition
Schumpeter (1987)	Crucial importance of competitive elections to democracy.
Lipset (1960)	"A political system which supplies regular constitutional opportunities for changing governing officials, and a social mechanism which permits the largest part of the population to influence major decisions by choosing among contenders for political office."
Dahl (1971)	"The continued responsiveness of government to the preferences of its citizens, considered as political equals." Public contestation and the right to participate are integral.
Pennock (1979)	Rule by the people (all adult citizens) in which "rule" means that "public policies are determined either directly by vote of the electorate or indirectly by officials freely elected at reasonably frequent intervals by a process [of] one man, one vote and in which a plurality is determinative."
Sartori (1987)	"Democracy is a system in which [...] no one can arrogate to himself unconditional and unlimited power."
Diamond *et al.* (1990)	A strictly political system, rather than an economic or a social one: Meaningful and extensive competition among individuals and organized groups (e.g. political parties) that excludes use of force. Inclusive level of political participation in selections of leaders and policy, at least through regular and fair elections. Civil and political liberties to ensure integrity of political competition and participation, including: (a) freedom of expression; (b) freedom of press; (c) freedom to form and join organizations.
Huntington (1991)	Democracy is a system in which "the most powerful collective decision makers are selected through fair, honest, and periodic elections in which candidates freely compete for votes and in which virtually all the adult population is eligible to vote."
Beetham (1991)	Participation in the decision-making process on collectively binding rules over which the people exercise control.
Hadenius (1992)	"Public policy is to be governed by the freely expressed will of the people whereby all individuals are to be treated as equals."
Parekh (1992)	Democracy defined and structured within limits set by liberalism. Western liberal democracy cannot claim universal validity.

Table 1.1 continues

Table 1.1 (continued)

Vanhanen (1996)	"Democracy is a political system in which different groups are legally entitled to compete for power and in which institutional power holders are elected by [...] and are responsible to the people."
Linz and Stepan (1996)	Sufficient agreement has been reached about political procedures to produce an elected government. A government comes to power that is the direct result of a free and popular vote. Government *de facto* has authority to generate new policies. Executive, legislative, and judicial powers generated by the new democracy do not share power with other bodies *de jure*.

Many authors have remarked upon the fact that civil and political liberties such as freedom of expression, freedom of the press, and freedom to organize are all elements that are necessary to ensure the integrity of political competition. This in turn supports more democratic outcomes (Bollen 1990; Diamond *et al.* 1990; Gastil 1993). Through the use of advanced statistical methodology, however, other authors have shown that these freedoms co-vary and correlate with general levels of democratic competition. As levels of democracy increase, levels of civil and political liberties do so too (Hadenius 1992; Vanhanen 1996). To date, however, the directionality of the causal effect has remained unverified.

Table 1.1 highlights two indispensable aspects of an operational definition of democracy. In the first place, competition among political actors is necessary to ensure a meaningful choice for the electorate and to promote the accountability of representatives after they are elected. In the second place, participation is necessary in order to ensure that those making the choices within a competitive framework are themselves representative of the larger political community.

If democracy is understood as the institutionalized diffusion of political power in a society and its allocation to specified agents via the explicit choices of that society, then both competition and participation are intrinsic to this deliberative process. In light of this definition, for a development to be characterized as a democratizing "media reform," it must contribute to a more competitive or participatory political system as well as to the institutionalized diffusion and fragmentation of political power conferred by the electorate upon a chosen group of representatives.

The role of media should not be restricted to this, however, and a reforming media system can do more than contribute to the advancement of a more democratic political order. It can support economic structures by providing greater information on products and services and promote enhanced societal understanding via access to information regarding myriad societal groups (religious, cultural, and so on). This observation leads to a further quandary regarding the connection between democracy, economics, and society.

The roots of democratization

Since the conclusion of the Second World War, numerous political scientists have explored the prerequisite conditions that contribute to the development and consolidation of democratic political systems. Correlations have emerged that link democracy to capitalist systems, literacy rates, Protestant populations, economic trade with the United States, and military expenditure, among others (Hadenius 1992). By far the clearest correlation which has emerged, however, has been between democracy and economic development or modernization. Although authors generally recognize that additional factors may contribute to explaining residual variation in prospects for democracy, the onus has fallen mainly on economic development and modernization.[1]

This conclusion implies that the prospects are bleak for those hoping to further democratic government with little or no power to influence economic development. The findings of one author, however, lead to the possibility of more optimistic expectations. Tatu Vanhanen (1996) has found that it is not so much economic development, *per se*, which influences the prospects for democracy, but rather the way in which this economic development is distributed. In nations where a variety of social and economic goods were more equitably distributed among a number of social groups or classes, prospects for democracy were greater. In countries where these economic, intellectual, and social "powers" were concentrated in the hands of a single or a few such groups, democracy failed to thrive.

Intuitively, this finding makes sense. Social or class groups which have managed to gain a hegemony of economic or social power are likely to use these advantages to consolidate political power in order to ensure their predominance. This has clear implications for the role that media play in supporting democracy. Before addressing this question, however, the concept of "media reform" must first be examined.

"Free and independent media" and the process of media reform

In the process of media reform, the general assumption is that media should progress ever nearer to an ideal of freedom and independence and away from dependency and control. Scholars generally argue that a media structure that is free of interference from government, business, or dominant social groups is better able to maintain and support the competitive and participative elements that define the concept of democracy and the related process of democratization.

Free and independent media, however, are not a good in themselves, but only in as much as they support other, more intrinsic values and goals (that is, democracy, a particular economic structure, greater cultural understanding, general human development, and so on). In a certain sense, free and independent media buttress these greater societal objectives and are, therefore, subordinate to them.

The development of free and independent media has traditionally been linked to freedom of expression, viewed both in democratic theory and practice as an intrinsic and universal human right. Yet, as T. M. Scanlon has stated, "to analyze the freedom of expression [...] we need to identify the values it seeks to protect" (1990: 335). It is not enough to posit freedom of expression as a teleological good without further examining its function in human life.

In the first place, expression and communication are aspects of "humanness" that require actualization and, in certain ways, a human life is not fully realized unless it can express and communicate its state, concerns, and interests. In media development, this concern has given rise to a dual and dialectic process. On the one hand, the freedom and independence of media are necessary so that individuals can find a public forum in which to express opinions, beliefs, and viewpoints to their fellow humans. On the other hand, the freedom and independence of media are needed to inform, entertain, and thereby enrich human life through the profusion of others' ideas, opinions, and visions.

Both aspects are seen as vitally important to the functioning of democratic government and democratic institutions. Without ample expression of options, choices become limited or stunted and, without adequate information, meaningful decisions cannot be undertaken. A subsidiary issue, however, which arises with the delineation of "free and independent media," is the question of free and independent from whom or what.

In the classical conception of media as the watchdog of democracy, freedom and independence were related directly to governance. In order to provide the public with adequate information to make decisions as well as to ensure a forum for the development of ideas and options, it has been felt that state monopolization of media sources must be limited. Therefore, media have been relegated to the competitive market with the understanding that economic criteria of access should prevent tyranny of opinion. Although some scholars have supported other solutions (such as public ownership models), market mechanisms have predominated in most discussions of democratic transitions.

Yet, many theorists have argued that the market introduces its own prospects of tyranny. Modern technologies have led to circumstances in which media are central to an ever-greater degree, and media monopolization is an increasingly significant threat. Modern societies can reasonably question whether media dominated by the market offer the depth of information and the plurality of options necessary for democratic government to thrive.

Transitional societies may further experience control of their national media by certain social or cultural elites. This can limit the access to these sources for minority social and cultural groups. In this case, to ensure democracy, it is important to ensure access to those less privileged.

How does one support the other?

It seems that the essence of media independence and freedom lies in its non-monopolization, whether by the government, the market, or by dominant social forces. This observation also links into Vanhanen's conclusion cited above. Namely, it is not so much the modernization of societies that leads to democracy as the way in which goods are distributed between different social groups. Consistent concentration of resources in the hands of one group seems to be antithetical to the development and consolidation of democratic forms of government.

If this observation is accepted, the conclusion that follows is that societies should be structured in such a way as to assure a demonopolization of media sources. This will ensure the freedom and independence of media, and thereby promote competitive and participative democracy. For media to become truly free and independent, a nation's legal, institutional, economic, and socio-cultural arenas must all support this diffusion of control and access.

In this context, independence can mean either private or public ownership (or mixed ownership), depending on outlook, predisposition, or predilection as long as demonopolization is assured. This also affects the role of media as government watchdogs. Although some have theorized that media can only be free if there is both a party in power and an effective opposition to provide a useful critique of the government in power, it is possible to accept that independent media exist in a state that has a dominant political party, as long as access and voice are equally distributed both on paper and in practice. This conclusion forms the benchmark of what this study considers "free and independent media." Specifically, free and independent media exist within a structure which is effectively demonopolized of the control of any concentrated social groups or forces and in which access is both equally and effectively guaranteed.

Ensuring this media structure must happen at two levels. On the one hand, the rule of law is necessary to establish effective guarantees of this freedom. Without an adequate legal structure, no examination of media can take place and no recourse for those who find themselves disenfranchised is available. On the other hand, substantive guarantees of this freedom may arise only at the level of civil society where the rule of law is reinforced by the existence of social institutions that ensure its development into something more than just a dead letter. Both of these arenas are explored within the framework of this study.

The methods amenable for achieving these dual ends, however, may also be quite variable. Edwin C. Baker has made the important argument that the tools at the disposal of the political scientist or legal scholar may depend to a large degree upon the particular conception of democracy that is espoused. Baker distinguishes a hybrid that he terms "complex democracy." This term embodies aspects of both the pluralist and republican models; namely competition among interests (taken from the liberal pluralist model) along with attempts at consensus building through participation and discourse within a community (Baker 1998: 335).

Baker analyses how these differing notions imply varying solutions within the legal sector. It is also possible to hypothesize their implications for the civil sector. In consideration of the fact that this study has argued a conception of democracy along the lines of the "complex" model advocated by Baker, the available solutions from this perspective are examined in the section that follows.

Promoting media reform toward free and independent media

As discussed above, the creation of free and independent media is examined in the context of this study on the basis of two types of variables. The first consists of legal-institutional variables, the second socio-cultural variables. Each of these aspects is addressed in turn.

Legal implications

The viewpoint of a "complex" notion of democracy calls for both society-wide media (specified by republican theory), and strong, partisan, and segmented media (advocated by liberal pluralists) to satisfy both criteria of competition and participation. Lee Bollinger who has argued that this justifies different regulatory regimes for different media, has highlighted this point (1991: 116–120). James Curran, however, has pointed out that media should also differ in their internal organizational principles and possibly their economic base (1996: 105–106). It is theorized that this diversity should reduce the threat of corruption of any particular media sector not only by governmental forces but by economic, social, and cultural elites as well.

Curran, in particular, has suggested a "five sector" approach, with each sector addressing a different democratic need. The "core" sector is envisaged as an institutionally centered and revitalized public-service broadcasting system which serves the society as a whole and creates a single forum for the proliferation and development of issues, which would promote democratic participation within society while addressing republican democratic concerns. The "civil" sector, on the other hand, serves the competitive interests of democracy and allays the fears of pluralists. Under this view, a public agency such as a modified Swedish Press Subsidies Board has been mooted as a possible institution that would provide assistance to marginalized groups seeking a voice. This sector would serve a multiplicity of interests through traditional media of newspapers, newsletters, and magazines.

A sector of media "professionals" would be free to pursue their own standards, freed from the control of either governmental or market constraints, and a "private enterprise" sector would account for the interests of the market. Finally, Curran envisages a "social market" sector that would allow the expression of new and not fully voiced interests that may gain importance within a society.

Although quite complex and intricate, Curran's model exemplifies an ideal scenario in which competition and participation are best addressed. In opposition both to the pluralist model of democracy and to the republican model, Curran's vision recognizes that neither aspect of democracy is a zero-sum game. They can be promoted at the same time and an analysis of the media structure in any particular case should seek to identify the area that is most underdeveloped and concentrate reformist energies toward its growth.

In fact, espousing both principles of democracy (competitive and participative) seems to recommend the existence and promotion of at least two media sectors, each with different funding sources, organizational principles, and end goals. Further, this conception recognizes and addresses the important fact that media should, in some sense, be free from the state as well as from the market or a particular cultural monopoly. As John Keane has pointed out, "media [...] should aim to empower a plurality of citizens who are governed neither by undemocratic states nor by undemocratic market forces" (1991: xii). Baker supports this notion when he states:

> There is every reason to expect that market forces, especially advertising, corrupt both common discourse and pluralist segmentation

and, moreover, that the market provides inadequately, whether in amount or quality, for both. Observation should convince most people of this conclusion, but economic theory also predicts it.

(1998: 387)

Since the market tends to underproduce items with positive externalities, government might be held to be responsible for their provision.

A dual sector approach can address these problems. A market-led media sector ensures that economic interests are met, that government oversight is established, and that the competitive principles of democracy are secured. Within this sector, advertisers are free to present their goods to target audiences, programmers can utilize fees provided by these advertisers to draw in audiences, and audiences, presumably, are informed and entertained to the extent that the market would allow. Such a sector demands the presence of anti-trust legislation, ownership laws which limit concentration, licensing laws, rules on advertising, as well as laws that protect media from government interference and audiences from unsubstantiated accusations in such areas as libel and defamation

The second sector, however, ensures that the needs of non-dominant or impoverished groups within a society are met. It also mitigates the corrupting effects of media primarily based on advertising revenue. It ensures that market forces that "could conceivably cripple the press's performance of the checking function" are offset on the basis of the principle that democracy requires intervention when the market fails to perform.[2]

In this sector, such contentious issues as the right to publish and the right to access are ensured and information necessary to democratic decision-making is provided (such as guaranteed airtime for political party platforms). It would also create a society-wide forum in which a common discourse emerges and which allows people more fully to conceptualize themselves and their roles within their greater society.

Complex democracy is concerned not only with the provision of accurate information, but also with encouraging debate within the context of a cultural dialogue. As numerous social groups are often excluded from the market, such a dialogue becomes impossible. A state-funded public access media complements a market-based media by allowing diverse non-dominant groups to discuss, form, and maintain their identity that is "undermined to the extent that mainstream actors control and constantly orient cultural discourse toward presumptively 'common' concerns" (Baker 1998: 407).

This sector would demand more regulatory legislation in content regulation, laws providing for a multiplicity of sources, as well as legislation that would ensure equal coverage for all societal and political interests. The matter of regional versus local balances in coverage needs to be negotiated as well as access for national minorities or disadvantaged social groups. Such laws need to be in place before a social media sector can thrive.

Socio-cultural implications

On the other hand, Baker rightly states that the role of media as government watchdog is "arguably the democratic function least likely to require or benefit from government support. It is instead best guaranteed by a sense of professionalism that exists among journalists" (Baker 1998: 391). This brings us to the second dimension of an "enabling environment"; or a media (and more widely a civic) culture, which promotes information proliferation, competition among views, and tolerance of ideas (Price and Krug 2000).

For such a culture to become ingrained, an educational system must exist that instills values of tolerance within the society. Differences of viewpoint need to be accepted by those inhabiting the system toward which the second media sector would contribute. More specifically, the development of such a culture calls for a number of mechanisms at the level of the media professionals. Among other things, training schemes for journalists could be instituted which would instruct them in the ways of investigative journalism and a sense of professionalism in their craft. A code of ethics could be drawn up to demarcate more clearly the boundary between what is considered acceptable within the profession and what is not.

Seminars that instruct politicians in the workings of this new type of media system should be advocated, teaching tolerance of viewpoints and acceptance of dissent and diversity in viewpoints presented. This would act as a first stage toward development of an acceptance of pluralism that represents part of what democracy stands for.

This conception of a legal-institutional and a socio-cultural aspect of a bi-sectoral media forms a guide to possible alternatives within the transitional process for the purposes of this study. As a result, both of these aspects will be examined by the individual country analyses in context of a hypothesized general model of media reform. This is outlined in greater detail below.

Stages of transition: a model of analysis

In order to organize the wealth of information provided in the individual country cases, a model of analysis has been developed which is structured around the concept of "stages of transition." It is hypothesized that the process of establishing free and independent media in transitional democracies can be broken down into four theoretical stages. These stages closely map those that have been proposed for the democratic transition process in general (Rustow 1970; O'Donnell *et al.* 1986; Linz and Stepan 1996; Ágh 1998).

Pre-transition stage

A preliminary stage of media reform often comes before any political transition process has begun. This pre-transition stage lays the groundwork for a continuation of the media reform process, which becomes possible once a political transition gets under way. In addition, the nature and shape that this pre-transition phase takes may have a direct bearing upon the general process of media reform itself. An analysis of this stage, therefore, is integral to understanding the development of free and independent media.

In many cases, this pre-transition stage is signaled either formally or informally by the regime in place. Signaling often occurs through an "opening" in the regime's previously controlled political, economic, and/or social arenas. At the most basic level, this may involve a greater willingness on the part of the regime to accept open criticism. More significant signals may include the recognition of opposition groups (Solidarity in 1980) or the internal fragmentation of a once cohesive ruling party or elite group (the Soviet Communist Party after Brezhnev).

At any stage, however, backsliding is a distinct possibility and many societies will initially fail to get beyond this pre-transition stage (as happened in Poland until 1989). Yet, once this occurs, the possibility of transition is on the horizon and reformers can take advantage. While the options open to reformers and their allies at this stage may be greatly constrained, certain lines of reform exist which can be pursued or advanced.

In this pre-transition phase of political transition, problems and tasks exist for developing media that are specific to this initial stage. Within different media sectors (which themselves are embedded in political, economic, and social structures) some of these tasks blur into questions of general political reform. They may include some of the following:

- identifying the soft-liners or reformers within the ruling regime and providing them with support (material, informational, moral, and so on) in disseminating their opinions, viewpoints, and criticisms;
- attempting to persuade the regime to recognize an opposition (which may be either structured or unstructured);
- providing an identifiable opposition group with the resources that will supply it with access to means of communication in order to disseminate its opinions and views;
- attempting to persuade the regime to allow more open criticism to emerge and be voiced without fear of reprisal;
- attempting to minimize reprisals when they occur;
- utilizing international broadcasting, where available, as a means of disseminating vital alternative information sources;
- providing constructive media infringement critiques (or more general human rights critiques);
- identifying and actively supporting a future civil society or potentially active civil sector.

The means of achieving these goals and their utility may prove variable depending on the particular characteristics of a country's pre-transition period. During this stage, a balance becomes difficult. Overstepping the norms accepted by the regime may lead to backsliding, even at this early stage. Once, however, the regime agrees to some measure of power-sharing, the country has moved on to the next stage of development – primary transition.

Primary transition

The primary stage of political transition is marked by a period of systematic change within the formerly authoritarian regime. It culminates in the final destruction of the old system and the establishment of new institutional and regulatory structures. The start of this stage is characterized by the regime's willingness to transit. This willingness is signaled by the regime's formal or informal devolution of power (or some portion of it) to the opposition forces within the country. This process may manifest itself in a number of ways.

Internally pacted transition (structured)

In this case, transition occurs as a result of a formal agreement between the former regime and the newly emerging opposition forces. This is most often reflected through the holding of elections or in the codified transfer of positions of authority to the emerging opposition. This form of transition is theorized to be relatively stable because it is a voluntary process that engages both parties.

Externally pacted transition (structured)

An externally pacted transition arises when a third party is formally involved in the transition process. This most often occurs when problems have emerged which have drawn international attention and third party arbitration. In this case, the former regime and the emerging opposition forces agree to a pact in order to prevent possible or continuing violence. They may also agree to external arbitration because, although they desire a transition, they are unable to come to an agreement on its terms.

This form of transition is theorized to be less stable because parties only agree on short-term solutions. Additionally, it is less stable because actors agree to such pacts when they lack other options or when they experience undue external pressures. Once such external pressure is removed or new options arise, the pact ceases to constrain. This form of transition is most prone to backsliding.

Ruptured transitions (unstructured)

Ruptured transitions classically occur through revolutionary overthrow of the previous regime. In most cases, the former regime is either marginalized entirely or eliminated brutally. However, certain elements of it may often wait in the wings to establish renewed control. Regime factionalism should not be mistaken for a ruptured transition; often internal regime rivalries lead to increased control rather than transitional processes. When a ruptured transition does occur, however, it is quite stable. This is as a result of the fact that the former regime forces effectively cease to hold any influence or power.

The defining characteristic of all regime transitions that differentiates this stage from its predecessor is the systematic way in which change begins to take place and the legal, institutional, and/or economic revisions that occur. The enactment of various media legislation (such as statutes on access to information, defamation, ownership, content, and so on) and the establishment of a legislative framework for all media sectors often mark this period. This process occurs within a wider context of efforts to develop a rule of law approach and democratically oriented political institutions and processes within the transitional society.

At the same time, the economic structure of the society in question may also be undergoing revision. Many aspects of media reform are crucially influenced by the changes that are implemented within this sector. As a result, such basic economic questions as those of ownership, taxes and tariffs, and the provision of state subsidies to certain sectors of the economy all influence the degree to which free and independent media are able to develop. This has especially been the case in the countries of Central and Eastern Europe as well as those of the former Soviet Union.

During this period, policy-making and implementation take central stage. Various policy initiatives are codified or otherwise set via precedent. The main focus for media reformers at this stage is hypothesized to lie in the formulation of draft legislation, both within the media arena and also in other more general areas such as political, institutional, or economic structural design. At the same time, reformers, aware of problems that they stand to face at later stages, should formulate their solutions with an eye toward the use and misuse to which these structures could be put in the future.

At this point, it will not only be the particular laws that must be addressed, but also the institutional structure which administers those laws. The structure includes the courts, the regulatory agencies, and the culture of censorship or its absence. In some societies, there is only this environment and precious little effective law. In this case, what is understood as "law" may take the form of legislation that emanates from a parliament as well as the formal (and perhaps informal) orders, decrees, or actions of an executive. Strategies that theoretically should be implemented at this stage of media reform include the following:

- analyzing other legislative media models;
- analyzing how emerging economic legislation will impact the development of media and the formulation of appropriate media law to offset any undesirable effects;
- calling upon the assistance of known media law experts in the drafting of such legislation;
- consulting with experts from other nations that have implemented such models in similar scenarios to enable the greatest degree of trouble-shooting;
- developing skills in lobbying the government effectively for desired legislative solutions;
- keeping abreast of the developing institutional structure in order to understand how it functions and how results can best be achieved;
- issuing state subsidies or tax incentives to both state-owned and private media, with recognition of the fact that reforming economic structures within transitional societies many times cannot support the development of a base, which could sustain truly free and independent media.

In addition, any inconsistencies and imbalances apparent at this time within the institutional or economic structure itself, which may have an important impact on the development of free and independent media law in the future, will also be addressed.

Secondary stage

The interim stage of the media reform process is characterized, in the words of Attila Ágh, by "the mixture of two systems in a creative chaos" (1998). Newly formulated legal, political, economic, and social structures will have been put into place during the initial stage of transition. As a result, this secondary stage focuses upon the fine-tuning of the media legislative framework. During this period, three logical possibilities exist:

- immediate consolidation – the reforming regime accepts the fully functional new legislative framework as it stands and works within it in a "rule of law" mode;
- authoritarian backlash – the reforming regime (or any remnant) abandons the reform process altogether and returns to a period of authoritarian rule;
- institutional revision – the reforming regime attempts to implement the newly instituted media legislative framework in a manner most advantageous to their interests.

This is possible as a result of inappropriate structuring or inappropriate utilization. The possibilities of backlash and consolidation are demonstrated in Figure 1.1.

Immediate consolidation is the least likely. An authoritarian backlash returns the system to a pre-transition phase. The problem, however, most likely to be faced during this phase of transition is that of elite capture of various institutional branches or functions. This can stifle legal functioning or turn legislative development toward non-democratic ends. Two specific problems may exist at this secondary stage of development: inappropriate structuring and inappropriate utilization.

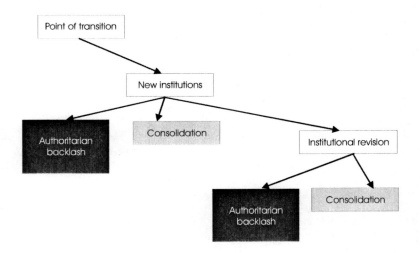

Figure 1.1 Institutional revision in the secondary stage

Inappropriate structuring

The new legal, political, economic, and social structures may be incomplete or may bear the scars of the previous regime (especially if a pacted transition has occurred).

In this case, media reformers have recourse to the approaches offered in the primary stage of transition (see above). Rebalancing and reformulation are necessary and experience will have shown which areas should be constrained to a greater or lesser degree. For instance, one subordinate hypothesis could be that defamation legislation needs to be tightly constrained so as to ensure that government does not overuse it detrimentally. Another is that executive rule by decree should be curtailed in order to allow media breathing space. Efforts should be made to remove harmful remnants of the previous system from the new institutional structures.

Inappropriate utilization

The new legal, political, economic, and social structures may be complete and unscarred, but implemented by dominant groups in a manner inappropriate to their reformist design. Options open to media reformers during this stage include the following strategies:

- seminars and training conferences held for both politicians and journalists to explain and clarify the new institutional and legal order as well as its intended functioning and rationale;
- roundtables that bring together media professionals and policy makers in order to establish personal contacts and to discuss grievances and seek possible solutions;
- networks of media professionals that may lead to more systematized and institutionalized cooperation between those working in similar fields. This can encompass traditional networks, or more technologically advanced electronic networks and communication channels;
- seminars that train media professionals in investigative and responsible journalism, addressing the distinction between uncovering the truth and fabricating it, and establishing a mind frame within which objectivity is stressed and partisan coverage is downplayed. In conjunction, this effort should implement the use of self-regulatory frameworks such as codes of ethics;
- foreign investment may be encouraged in order to bring a measure of independence to various media sectors that suffer from an inadequate domestic economic base.

It is hypothesized that reformers can solve this problem through an iterative game scenario within which actors come to understand the desired function of legislation that has been formulated or adjust laws and institutions to fit more clearly with their particular set of preferences. This period may again result in backsliding if democratic norms and principles are not accepted as structuring mechanisms in the new game of politics. On the other hand, various external stimuli such as international pressure, internal educational programs both for political actors and for society in general, as well as positive feedback loops that encourage compliance may enable a country to progress to the next stage in the democratization process.

Late or mature stage

The late or mature stage of political transition again presents media reformers with three distinct possibilities. Even at these late stages, the threat of renewed authoritarianism remains, especially if the revisions undertaken in the secondary stage have proven unfruitful or overly threaten the previously ruling elite. On the other hand, the fine-tuning process may continue for a lengthy period before consensus on form, content, and application is achieved. As the transitional system approaches a late or mature stage, it becomes defined by the emergence of a coherent new system. Different goals and problems emerge at this stage that need to be addressed in order to safeguard the newly emerged system from backsliding to a previous stage.

By this point, legal and institutional questions have been substantially addressed and most actors that have an impact on media will be relatively comfortable operating within the newly established norms. At this point, the main task is to consolidate commitment to this new system while drawing ever larger segments of society into the forum. This should strengthen democratic commitment through participation.

At this stage, the options that are open to media policy makers and reformers are hypothesized to include some of the following alternatives:[3]

- establishing international "awards" or honors, linked to financial support for paradigm media performers. This creates a certain prestige associated with free and independent media and promotes increasing professionalism;
- creating international training institutes for media regulators in transition societies;
- building or financing libraries and technical assistance units, which can provide the basis for intellectual development and innovation;
- establishing educational programs within primary and secondary schools that discuss and promote the beneficial influences of free and independent media within a democratic society;
- setting up educational funds or scholarships that promote training and education in investigative journalism and in management aspects of media;
- encouraging exchanges of media professionals among countries in order to promote alternative ways of approaching various media problems and to encourage creative solution-seeking while at the same time establishing international networks of media experts;
- providing secondary training and educational seminars, and conferences for media professionals in order to keep them up to date on current developments within their field and to reify commitment to journalistic professionalism;

- addressing newly emerging media technologies as interaction within traditional media sectors (print, radio, television) stabilizes and becomes regularized.

Conclusion

This "stages of transition" model asserts that distinct strategies and approaches are discernible at different stages of the media reform process and within the process of democratization in general. At all stages, tools and solutions taken from subsequent stages are available to media reformers and policy makers. However, each stage is hypothesized to have its own unique focus.

In the pre-transition stage, media actors attempt to widen the level of discourse and room for regime criticism within a society. At the same time, they also attempt to pinpoint reformist tendencies within the authoritarian regime, embryonic opposition groups, or latent sectors of an emerging civil society to lend them support.

During the primary stage of media reform, reformers concentrate their efforts on creating a viable legal and institutional framework within which free and independent media can begin to develop. This stage will also include the formulation and structuring of economic mechanisms in certain case scenarios.

The secondary stage is devoted to the fine-tuning of these institutional mechanisms. Where institutions have been "inappropriately structured" they will need to be reformulated. Media reformers will also attempt to instill a broader consensus in "utilizing" the legal-institutional framework "appropriately" if this has not previously been done.

Finally, the late or mature period of reform attempts to consolidate the commitment of media professionals and policy makers to working within the new institutional system while incorporating larger portions of society into the process in order to broaden the democratic discussion.

In the country cases that follow, this general model of media reform is implicit as the country experts explore its applicability to the process of media reform and its relationship to democratization in the 1990s.

Notes

1 This connection was initially tested and supported by the findings of Lipset (1959) and Lerner (1968) and later validated by Diamond and Marks (1992).

2 As Baker argues, "competitive, profit-oriented pressures could lead media entities to abandon expensive, investigative journalism and replace it with cheaper, routine beat reporting, or even cheaper 'press-release' or wire service journalism. The market could tilt journalism towards stories that are the easiest (that is, the cheapest) to uncover and, even more troubling, the easiest to explain or the most titillating. An effective watchdog would have reported early on about the massive savings and loan scandal, which predictably resulted from deregulation of these financial institutions. The media, however, found that early reporting was simply too difficult or boring" (1998: 390).

3 While allowing the continued development of those solutions offered in the section dealing with "inappropriate utilization."

Bibliography

This list includes suggestions for further reading as well as material specifically cited in the text.

Ágh, Attila (1998) *The Politics of Central Europe*, London: Sage.

Almond, Gabriel A. and Verba, Sidney (1989) *The Civic Culture: Political Attitudes and Democracy in Five Nations*, London: Sage.

Bagdikian, Ben H. (1983) *The Media Monopoly* (fifth edition), Boston: Beacon Press.

Baker, Edwin C. (1998) "The media that citizens need," *University of Pennsylvania Law Review*, 147: 317–408.

Beetham, David (1991) *The Legitimation of Power*, Basingstoke: Macmillan.

Blumer, Jay G., McLeod, Jack M., and Rosengren, Karl Erik (1992) *Comparatively Speaking: Communication and Culture across Space and Time*, London: Sage.

Bollen, Kenneth A (1990) "Political Decocracy and Measurement Traps," *Studies in Comparative International Development*, Vol. 25, No. 1, Spring: 7–24.

Bollinger, Lee C. (1991) *Images of a Free Press*, Chicago: University of Chicago Press.

Chehabi, H. E. and Linz, Juan J. (1998) *Sultanistic Regimes*, Baltimore: Johns Hopkins University Press.

Chehabi, Houchand E., Stepan, Alfred C., and Linz, Juan J. (1995) *Politics, Society, and Democracy: Comparative Studies*, Boulder, CO: Westview.

Corcoran, Farrel and Preston, Paschal (eds) (1995) *Democracy and Communication in the New Europe: Change and Continuity in East and West*, Cresskill, NJ: Hampton Press.

Curran, James (1996) "Mass media and democracy revisited," in James Curran and Michael Gurevitch (eds), *Mass Media and Society*, (second edition), London: Arnold Publishers.

Curran, James and Park, Myung-Jin (eds) (2000) *De-Westernizing Media Studies*, London: Routledge.

Dahl, Robert A. (1971) *Polyarchy: Participation and Opposition*, New Haven: Yale University Press.

Dahlgren, Pete, and Sparks, Colin (1991) *Communication and Citizenship: Journalism and the Public Sphere in the New Media Age*, London: Routledge.

Diamond, Larry (1999) *Developing Democracy: Toward Consolidation*, Baltimore: Johns Hopkins University Press.

Diamond, Larry, Linz, Juan J., and Lipset, Seymour Martin (1990) *Politics in Developing Countries: Comparing Experiences with Democracy*, Boulder, CO: Lynne Rienner Publishers.

Diamond, Larry J. and Marks, Gary Wolfe (1992) *Re-examining Democracy: Essays in Honor of Seymour Martin Lipset*, Newbury Park and London: Sage.

Gastil, John (1993) *Democracy in Small Groups: Participation, Decision Making, and Communication*, Philadelphia: New Society.

Hadenius, Axel (1992) *Democracy and Development*, Cambridge: Cambridge University Press.

Held, David, McGrew Anthony, Goldblatt, David, and Perraton, Jonathan (1999) *Global Transformations: Politics, Economics, and Culture*, Oxford: Polity.

Huntington, Samuel P. (1991) *The Third Wave: Democratization in the Late Twentieth Century*, Norman: University of Oklahoma Press.

Keane, John (1991) *The Media and Democracy*, Oxford: Polity.

—— (1998) *Civil Society: Old Images, New Visions*, Oxford: Polity.

Kowalski, Tadeusz (1999) *Transformation in the Context of Transition: Development of New Information Technologies within Professional, Legal and Political Frameworks*, Montreal: Orbicom.

Lerner, Daniel (1968) *The Passing of Traditional Society: Modernizing the Middle East*, New York: Free Press.

Lichtenberg, Judith (ed.) (1990) *Democracy and the Mass Media*, Cambridge: Cambridge University Press.

Linz, Juan J. and Stepan, Alfred (1996) *Problems of Democratic Transition and Consolidation: Southern Europe, South America, and Post-Communist Europe*, Baltimore: Johns Hopkins University Press.

Lipset, Seymour Martin (1959) *Social Mobility in Industrial Society*, London: Heinemann.

—— (1960) *Political Man: The Social Basis of Politics*, Garden City, NY: Doubleday.

McCormack, Gillian (ed.) (1999) *Media in the CIS: A Study of the Political, Legislative, and Socio-economic Framework*, Brussels: European Commission.

O'Donnell, Guillermo A., Schmitter, Philippe C., and Whitehead, Laurence (1986) *Transitions from Authoritarian Rule: Prospects for Democracy*, Baltimore: Johns Hopkins University Press.

O'Neil, Patrick H. (ed.) (1997) *Post-Communism and the Media in Eastern Europe*, London: Frank Cass.

Parekh, Bhikhu C. (1992) *The Concept of Fundamentalism*, Warwick: Peepal Tree.

Pennock, Roland J. (1979) *Democratic Political Theory*, Princeton: Princeton University Press.

Price, Monroe E. and Krug, Peter (2000) Enabling Environment for Free and Independent Media. Oxford University: Programme in Comparative Media Law and Policy. Available at http://pcmlp.socleg.ox.ac.uk/EnablingEnvironment.pdf.

Przeworski, Adam *et al.* (1995) *Sustainable Democracy*, Cambridge: Cambridge University Press.

Raboy, Marc and Dagenais, Bernard (1992) *Media, Crisis and Democracy: Mass Communication and the Disruption of Social Order*, London: Sage.

Randall, Vicky (ed.) (1998) *Democratization and the Media*, London: Frank Cass.

Rustow, Dunkwart A. (1970) "Transitions to democracy," *Comparative Politics*, 2(3).

Sartori, Giovanni (1987) *The Theory of Democracy Revisited*, Chatham, NJ: Chatham House.

Scanlon, T. M. (1990) "Content regulation reconsidered," in Judith Lichtenberg (ed.) *Democracy and the Mass Media: A Collection of Essays*, Cambridge: Cambridge University Press.

Schumpeter, Joseph (1987) *Capitalism, Socialism, and Democracy* (sixth edition), London: Unwin.

Vanhanen, Tatu (1996) *Prospects of Democracy: A Study of 172 Countries*, London: Routledge.

2

CHINA

Media liberalization under authoritarianism

Joseph Man Chan and Jack Linchuan Qiu

The purpose of this chapter is to examine the factors that have brought about critical changes in the structure of media in the People's Republic of China and to trace the trajectory of media liberalization there. This history serves as an illustration of how media may develop in a society that is moving from totalitarianism to marketized authoritarianism.

The first two parts of the chapter will serve as background to the role of information in Chinese history and of the reforms since 1978. Part three will examine the paths of media reform and their relationship to the economic reforms. Part four will discuss the specific mechanisms of reform and Part five will consider how state corporatism and an emerging civil society will shape the future of media in China. In reviewing China's media development in conjunction with the changing relationship between the state and society, this chapter will help identify enabling conditions that may lead to independent media in a transitional society like China. An analysis of the mechanisms and patterns of China's media reform is critical in understanding the relationship between political reform and media liberalization.

While ideological control persists, the country has shifted its national policy from class struggle to economic construction. Chinese media have both contributed to this shift and formed part of this re-orientation. China's mass media began developing rapidly after Deng Xiaoping initiated reform in 1978. As Table 2.1 shows, the number of daily newspapers doubled between 1985 and 1995 while the number of television stations more than quadrupled. The proliferation of radio stations is even more remarkable, increasing by more than six times. Radio and television now reach over 85 per cent of the population. The number of telephone sets per 100 people has increased from 0.43 in 1980 to 8.11 in 1997 (*China Statistical Yearbook* 1996; 1998).[1] Although computers are far from universally accessible, the growth in the number of Internet users is alarming, skyrocketing from 620,000 in 1997 to about 16.9 million in July 2000 (China Network Information Centre 2000). It is projected that the figure will reach 20 million by the end of 2000 (*Hong Kong Economic Journal* 2000: 12).

In addition to the increase in the number of newspapers and television shows and the penetration of phones and the Internet, new genres are being introduced. These include advertising, lifestyle, sports, stock news,

Table 2.1 Media development in China, 1985–1997

Year	Daily newspapers	Circulation/ 1,000 people	TV stations	Population coverage (%)	Radio stations	Population coverate (%)
1985	231	44.7	202	68.4	213	68.3
1990	282	35.0	509	79.4	635	74.7
1995	560	44.3	837	84.5	1,202	78.7
1997	304[a]	34.0	923	87.6	1,363	86.0

Note

a The number of daily newspapers in 1997 dropped because the 1998 yearbook, unlike its predecessors, excluded newspapers which were published fewer than seven times a week. The figure should be higher than that for 1995.

Sources: The Yearbook of China's Journalism, 1986, 1991, 1996, 1998; *The Yearbook of China Radio and TV*, 1986, 1991, 1996, 1998.

infotainment, Gongfu movies, and Disney cartoons, all of which were previously unavailable. These changes reflect the gradual retreat of communist ideology from people's private lives and are reproduced in the ways people dress and talk, cultivating a popular culture with values that were once condemned.

The role of information in Chinese history

The Chinese leadership's reluctance to endorse free media originates in years of history that emphasized strict control of information as a key to political and social order. According to the feudal tradition, the imperial state orthodoxy, rulers were endowed with the Heavenly Mandate and thereby qualified and obliged to manage the interests of their subjects. Borrowing from Confucianism, this involved maintaining the social order of a unidirectional flow of information within the five filial relationships: from ruler to subject, from parent to child, from teacher to student, from husband to wife, and from elder to younger sibling. When the printing press was developed during the Tang dynasty, the emperor restricted its use mainly to the printing of almanacs, calendars, and dynastic materials (Gellhorn 1987: 9). When the newspaper was introduced to China from the West during the Qing Dynasty, the imperial rulers regarded it as a subversive channel and implemented censorship rules to prevent the publication of dissident opinions (Alford 1993: 8).

Despite its anti-feudal rhetoric, the Chinese Communist Party (CCP) views the mass media as a loyal servant of the state, used to impose ideological hegemony on society (Lee 1990: 5). The CCP subjects the press to strict censorship and controls all printing presses, radio stations, and TV stations. Media authorities are appointed to communicate CCP's policies to all of society and to interpret public events, advising the public as to which events are acceptable or encouraged and which are prohibited or discouraged. Media opposition has been quelled by deeming any criticism of the state an act against the state and, by definition, a crime.

It is wrong to assume that the CCP merely inherited its press from the feudal past. The commandist media system was more a result of the influence of the Soviet model, Marxism-Leninism, and the practical needs for ideological and social control. According to CCP ideology, all media are tools of class struggle. Within the party itself, the major functions of media have been to promote indoctrination, agitation, and mobilization, which were very important during the CCP's long history of armed struggle before it came to power in 1949.

When the CCP became the ruling party, it held on to control of media and suppressed dissent in order to maintain the status quo. Such tight control over the dissemination of information reached its apogee during the Cultural Revolution (1966–1976), when the party line was published daily by the official newspaper of the CCP and then copied verbatim by every other newspaper in the country. Chaos reigned during this period, not only in media, but also in society. It was in response to this chaos that China's next leader, Deng Xiaoping, promulgated reforms that had important implications for all aspects of society, not least of which was media.

The reforms since 1978

The year in which Deng initiated economic reform, 1978, is a watershed in China's media history. Under the leadership of Mao Zedong, programs such as household registration, job allocation, distribution of food coupons, and the commune system served to restrict people's mobility and control their daily life. Meanwhile, official education, media, arts, and literature ensured ideological uniformity. This system of absolute control was discredited, however, by the disasters of the Cultural Revolution. When Mao died in September 1976, Deng Xiaoping launched a series of reforms to regain the CCP's lost legitimacy. Deng could not discard all of Mao's socialist principles and institutions, however, without abdicating political power. Thus, he limited the reform program to a pragmatic one, designed to maintain political power while simultaneously regaining legitimacy (Kuan 1991: 1.3).

Deng's first step was to restore political institutions that had been destroyed during the Cultural Revolution and to reject the notion that political legitimacy could stem from the charismatic personality of one man (Kuan 1991: 1.6). Collective leadership was adopted as the operational rule. The central secretariat was restored in 1979, and a new CCP charter was promulgated in 1981 with detailed regulations governing the scope and structure of the CCP's activities.

Closely tied to the institutionalization of the political process was a lessening of the all-controlling influence of Maoist ideology. Deng initiated an unprecedented discussion on whether Mao's policies centered on class struggle should be rectified, later known as the "Great Debate Concerning the Criterion of Truth." As a result of this debate, traditional Maoist ideology was replaced with pragmatism and empiricism. The new guiding principle of the CCP was to "seek truth from facts" (Polumbaum 1990: 41). However, Deng stated that those scientific principles in the Thought of Mao Zedong that had been proven correct through practice would still guide the CCP leadership in their political struggles.

This focus on pragmatism and empiricism paved the way for a new central policy goal: to satisfy the material aspirations of the people without sacrificing

CCP leadership (Kuan 1991: 1.3). A June 1981 resolution of the central committee of the CCP stated that the major problem facing China was the gap between the increasing need of the people for material goods and the underdevelopment of social production. It declared that the efforts of the CCP and of the state were to be shifted to modernization through economic development, signaling that the absolute societal control of the Maoist era had yielded to the economic imperative of generating wealth. Significantly, this opening in the economic sphere was not accompanied by a similar opening in the political sphere.

To justify the economic imperative and reconcile it with social control, Deng coined the phrase "socialism with Chinese characteristics" (Kuan 1991: 1.6). This phrase gave the leadership flexibility to stress socialism when they worried that development was progressing too quickly and to stress Chinese characteristics when they wanted to depart from the canon encompassing Marxism, Leninism, and Mao Zedong Thought and encourage development. They did this through a three-part reform system consisting of the responsibility system, the transition to a commodity-based economy, and an opening to the international economy.

By January 1983, the responsibility system, whereby individual rural households made contracts with production teams to produce a set quota in return for an allocation of land, was implemented across China. It met with such success that the concept spread to other areas, and in January 1987 a responsibility system was instituted in a limited number of state and collective enterprises.

The second aspect of the economic reforms was the transition from a centrally planned economy to a commodity-based one. State allocations of producer goods were partially liberalized and state controlled prices were partially deregulated, further decentralizing the economy. Economic decision making was decentralized to local governments and primary economic units such as state enterprises and many Chinese started small, privately run enterprises in the service, commercial, and industrial sectors.

The third and final element of the economic reform program was an opening to the international economy. Once a staunch proponent of self-reliance, China set up special economic zones that had flexible policies to attract foreign investment, technology transfer, and tourism.

Until the late 1980s, while certainly dramatic, these reforms did not overhaul the basic Stalinist framework of the economy, but rather rationalized planning within it. They lacked a long-term blueprint. Subsequently, when political control seemed to be in danger, periods of retrenchment followed periods of reform. This also meant that it was never clear when a conservative backlash would follow a period of enthusiastic reform.

Reforms in other areas were therefore cautious at best and economic liberalism was joined by political conservatism. In October 1987, while the thirteenth CCP congress proclaimed that political reforms were important, it narrowly defined political reform as improving government efficiency, strengthening the vitality of the CCP, fighting bureaucracy, and promoting enthusiasm among people. Both economic and political reforms were carried out within the context of the CCP's overall goal of retaining power.

The crackdown on the pro-democracy movement in 1989 was a major setback to China's reforms. The momentum of reform was revived after Deng Xiaoping made his famous southern tour in 1992, and advocated "building a socialist market economy with Chinese characteristics." According to orthodox Marxism, the market, as a capitalist feature, should be restricted and finally eliminated. Deng's deviation from orthodox Marxism was later formally confirmed by the CCP and enshrined in its charter. This policy to develop a "socialist market" not only had important implications for China's economy, but its repercussions were also felt in the social and media spheres.

Paths of media reform

In the wake of reforms in the 1990s such as marketization and privatization, new media genres, programs, and publications flourished (Y. Zhao 1998; Wu 2000). The public demand for these new media outlets opened profitable markets, leading to the gradual growth of professionalism, media commercialization, and media internationalization.[2] The party–state relaxed media control and diversified institutional structure.[3]

Just like economic reform, however, media reform threatens political power, and vestiges of Imperial and Maoist views of information still hold currency. China's present leaders continue to view information media as tools for legal, political, and social manipulation. Thus, just as in pre-1978 China, Leninist press theory, administrative monopoly of news production, political repression of dissent voices, and the absence of journalism laws largely characterize media, with media operation being subject to the ultimate dictates of the party–state.[4] The combination of economic reform pushing media reform with political concerns for ideological control has led to the swing and lack of continuity between reform and retrenchment as well as uneven liberalization across media genres. In this section, we shall examine in turn the economic logic behind media reform, the swing between reform and retrenchment, and the unevenness of media liberalization.

The economic impetus to media reform

The loosening of the CCP's ideological control was crucial to reform in the media industry. After Deng initiated the "Great Debate Concerning the Criterion of Truth," press freedom could be openly discussed and truthfulness became a cherished value of news production (He 1998). Journalists worked to redress the ideological extremes of Cultural Revolution journalism summed up as "falsehood, exaggeration, and empty talk" (Polumbaum 1990: 41). However, economic reforms led to relatively more decentralized and autonomous media, to greater diversity of content, and to higher degrees of predictability and professionalism.

The most significant change has been decentralization. Whereas media used to be centralized under strict CCP control, various social organizations such as the National People's Political Consultative Council, the Women's Association of All China, and the Youth League, are now establishing their own publications (Wu 2000). This diversity does not represent total autonomy since they are still licensed and ideologically supervised by the CCP (Lee 1990: 16). But it does represent a step in the direction of autonomy.

The material contained in China's 1986 General Provisions of Civil Law has encouraged autonomy in many sectors of the economy, including media. These provisions articulate broad guidelines for the regulation of economic and personal transactions with the implicit assumption that society is composed of discrete entities, each of which can individually make contracts to sell, buy, or enter into other obligations. Within broad limits, therefore, individuals have rights to regulate their own affairs. This has been translated into a greater autonomy within the media as contract and joint ventures have introduced some form of indirect private ownership (Chan 1993). In principle, however, the party–state still owns all mass media organizations exclusively.

Economic reforms have had a significant impact on the content of publications and broadcasts, leading media away from exclusive dedication to CCP's political and ideological matters (Chan 1993; He 1998). Since Deng justified marketization in 1992, an overwhelming majority of media organizations have responded to new competitive market forces by turning to entertainment and soft news to stimulate public curiosity. The new variety in content brings previously unheard voices to the public consciousness and leads to a lessening of the previously all-encompassing nature of communist ideology in daily life (Wang 1995).

The advertising market has shown some of the most remarkable changes following from economic impetus. Although advertisements enjoyed a period of rapid growth before the communist takeover in 1949, commercials in China were banned under Mao's planned economy. Media organizations depended on the party–state's subsidies for survival. However, advertisements re-emerged in Shanghai in 1979 and rapidly spread to other cities (Huang 1997). As the 1980s opened, official subsidies turned out to be inadequate to cover the soaring costs of media operation (Chen and Huang 1996). Advertising thus became an indispensable source of revenue, at first as a supplement to and finally as a substitute for subsidy in the 1990s for all but a few national media, such as the *People's Daily*, which are run by the central party authority.

A third way in which the economic reforms have encouraged media liberalization is by fostering predictability and stability in the media. To achieve this stability, the state has established bureaucratic media regulatory agencies such as the State Press and Publication Administration (Cheek 1988; Polumbaum 1994). Certainly, the new administrative measures are not aimed at establishing a democratic rule of law, but they do attempt to regularize the relationship between the state and media, establishing a predictability and stability that encourages business involvement.

A final way in which the economic reforms have encouraged media liberalization is through the market demand for objective and informative reporting leading to a growing sense of professionalism among journalists (Li 1994; Lee 1994). Education for journalists expanded to fill the demand for members of the press corps and the result was an increase in the number of young, more skeptical, and better-educated journalists (Polumbaum 1990: 40). At the end of 1986, a national forum of provincial newspaper editors expressed their desire for greater editorial independence. They argued that the CCP committees should "strengthen and improve leadership" over journalism, but that they should refrain from exercising "excessive and rigid management" and should allow news organizations "a free hand" in covering news (Polumbaum 1990: 41).

In March 1989, *People's Daily* editor Hu Jiwei lobbied for a journalism law that would create a modicum of freedom for reporters and editors. At the National People's Congress in 1989, he argued that press freedom would give people proper channels to air their grievances and could serve to stabilize society rather than be a destabilizing factor feared by the authorities. He concluded, "freedom of the press not only contributes to social justice but also facilitates the construction of democratic authority by the Chinese leadership" (Lee 1990).

Development of a professional consciousness and appreciation of the value of a free press reached its height during the 1989 pro-democracy movement, when hundreds of media workers marched on the streets of Beijing for a free press and faster pace of reform. These workers were from the New China News Agency, China News Service, *People's Daily*, *China Youth Daily*, and Central People's Broadcasting, among other influential media organizations. However, this call for a free press was suppressed during the bloody crackdown on the pro-democracy movement in 1989. Hu himself fell from the CCP's favor and was blacklisted.

By pushing media toward autonomy and decentralization, allowing diversity of content, and fostering predictability and professionalism, economic reforms have both allowed for and encouraged media reform. The road has not been smooth, however. As the next section will show, periods of progress toward a liberal and independent media have frequently been followed by periods of retrenchment, as the leadership worried that its authority was being eroded.

The pattern of reform and retrenchment

The official line on media reform has been that mass media should be allowed to change and develop in order to promote economic modernization. In reality, however, this does not entail significant change because it means that media should promote a stable environment where CCP's political power is not questioned. The CCP leadership has expressed great hostility toward the concept of press freedom, fearing that it will lead to a loss of political power. Even Hu Yaobang, one of the most liberal post-Mao leaders, referred to the press as "the CCP's mouthpiece." The main task of journalists, he said, was "to use a vast quantity of vivid facts and speeches promptly and accurately [to promote...] the ideas of the CCP" (Lee 1990: 8). Hu's comments are indicative of CCP's sentiment toward media liberalization. Like the economic reforms, media reform is characterized by alternating periods of progress and retrenchment, "oscillating between left and right as political struggles take sudden turns" (Chan 1993).

Thus, the relatively relaxed media environment created by the debate on the criterion of truth which encouraged "seeking truth from facts" and first opened the doors to media reform was interrupted by the "Anti-spiritual pollution campaign" in 1983. As this campaign fizzled out, reform gained momentum again with CCP leadership tolerating and at times even encouraging ideas such as diversity in content, openness of information, and editorial autonomy. Veteran journalists criticized Leninist press theory and discontent was prevalent among journalists.[5] Government subsidy decreased, whereas imported programs were on the rise (Chan 1994a; Hong 1998).

This openness is evidenced in the official response to the call of the 1986 national editors' forum for editorial independence. Teng Teng, the deputy head of the CCP propaganda department, agreed with the forum's conclusion that more informative news was needed, saying, "Newspapers should not carry stories without news value" (*People's Daily* 1986). Further, reformers got support from the top when Zhao Ziyang called for media transparency and openness in his speech at the CCP's Thirteenth National Congress in 1987. He demanded that the work and conduct of political leaders should be under the surveillance of public opinion; that the people should be informed of important events; and that the people should participate in discussions of important issues (Zhao 1987).

The 1987 'Anti-bourgeois liberalization campaign' and the political backlash that followed economic retrenchment in late 1988, however, quelled this momentum. In conjunction with a backtracking on economic reform measures that were causing inflation, the CCP leadership shifted from encouraging media openness to encouraging media to paint a positive picture, bolstering confidence among the people and creating an environment of "stability and unity" (Polumbaum 1990: 43). In December 1988, Hu Qili, the Politburo member in charge of propaganda, said that journalists must "publicize the tremendous achievements of our construction and reform convincingly and with perfect assurance." The government should not be subject to "supervision by public opinion," he said, rather the press should "correctly guide public opinion" (*New China News* 1988).

Media reformers were not completely dissuaded, however. During the 1989 pro-democracy movement, independent views were published, talks between protesters and party leaders were broadcast live, and the national propaganda machine was temporarily paralyzed. Journalists took to the streets with the banner, "Don't force us to lie," demanding further reforms. Brief as the period was, China's media have never been so close to freedom and independence.

Media development closely reflected the dramatic leftward turn of national politics in general (Lam 1991). And during the 1989 crackdown, numerous journalists were "purged" and the government banned 13 per cent of all publications (Feir 1997). Terms such as transparency, editorial autonomy, and press freedom became taboo and political controls were reasserted. Zhao Ziyang, the CCP leader pushing for reform, was ousted and media reform seemed to have been forgotten (Wu 1997; Lam 1991). In January 1991, at a meeting of the executive council of the All-China Journalists' Association, a member of the Political Bureau Standing Committee, Li Ruihuan, promised media reform, stating "we must further implement journalistic reform so that news reporting can be more mass oriented, and that it will be what readers like to read and hear" (*South China Morning Post* 1991). Little action backed these words, and soon thereafter President Jiang Zemin promulgated the "Strike hard" campaign in response to a perceived proliferation of "spiritual pollution" in media (*The Economist* 1996: 41).

Uneven patterns of liberalization

Media reform has clearly followed the swing of the political pendulum. Press freedom has gained ground when economic reform surged ahead, but lost momentum when it retreated. Overall, however, when we survey the state of media in China today, it is clear that the gains outweigh the losses. The magnitudes of the political-ideological oscillations appear to have been decreasing over the years.

In drawing such conclusions, it is crucial to survey the entire field. A look at a particular genre in a particular locale could easily lead to a differing conclusion, since a variety of political, economic, and geographic factors have encouraged liberalization in some areas, while slowing it in others. Specifically, media content that is political is far more controlled than that which is apolitical. Genres that are traditionally close to the center of political power enjoy less freedom of expression than those at the political periphery. And media organizations in Beijing are under tighter control than those in the outlying provinces and districts. These individual patterns combine to form a complex and uneven pattern of liberalization throughout China's media establishment.

Content is the most decisive factor in this uneven pattern of liberalization. Direct political coverage is the least liberalized genre. The Xinhua News Agency writes official daily reports of political events that are then reproduced in the most prominent position on the front pages of newspapers and in prime-time broadcasting news programs (Lu 1994). All means of public political communication play the role of "mouth-piece" for the CCP and a centralized agency operates on a daily basis to ensure that media organizations do not step beyond ideological boundaries (Su 1994). Although reports of corrupt conduct of political figures are not unusual today, it is still forbidden for lower level media organizations to criticize cadres at higher official posts without the prior consent of their supervisory bodies (Y. Zhao 1998).

In less sensitive genres like entertainment, sports, and art, however, content control is relaxed as long as the program is not considered politically offensive. This gives rise to the proliferation of media topics such as lifestyle, sports, and technology that are subject to little official censorship. Other genres that operate with a higher relative autonomy include information about finance, real estate, and technology. Advertising, the most lucrative part of the entire media industry, is the most internationalized genre. In 1998, eight out of the ten largest advertisement producers in China were international 4A companies which had been allowed to enter China only since 1994. The advertising industry in China may be regarded as a foreign capitalist concession that sharply contrasts with political coverage, the ideological bastion of the CCP.

A second factor contributing to patterns of uneven liberalization is media type. Media that have been traditionally controlled by the political center of power, such as newspapers and television, enjoy less autonomy than media at the political periphery, such as film and theater or internationalized media, such as advertising and the Internet (Chen and Huang 1996). Newspapers and television are still largely regulated by the CCP's propaganda departments and are considered by the CCP to be the main conduit of ideological control. The Central Propaganda Department of the CCP is still at the pinnacle of the administrative pyramid and private ownership of newspapers and broadcasting stations is still officially banned.

In the pre-reform period, the ideological control by the CCP of film and theater was also considered to be crucial. Movie-going was a collective activity organized by work-units for their members to receive "public education." Now, however, the movies are regarded as a leisure activity in the private sphere and there is a major retreat of communist propagandists from these realms (Chu and Pan 1999; Wang 1995). This decline of ideological control has allowed the importation of programs from Hong Kong, Taiwan, Europe, and Hollywood (Chan 1994a). The most liberalized media are the ones that are most influenced by the international scene (Ma 1999). Advertising, the most international genre, is under little ideological control.

A final factor contributing to the uneven patterns of media liberalization is the location of the media organization. Although, in principle, policies should be carried out nationwide, they often meet with local resistance or adaptation when they are implemented, exhibiting differences between Beijing and other cities, the center and periphery, the urban and the rural areas, the coastal area and the interior.

The pirating of prohibited media products is a very profitable industry. Some officials in small towns and rural areas show tolerance to those who reproduce banned books, magazines, and audio-visual products and sell them in black markets. In doing so, they forgo standardized political principles in the hope of economic returns. This creates a gap between official policies of media control and their implementation, further contributing to uneven liberalization (He 2000). Moreover, in the spirit of reform experimentation, local cadres sometimes try new methods without approval from above, widening the discrepancies.

The present mediascape of China can be characterized as a partially liberalized authoritarian media system. The tightness of political control varies across media, genre, and geographical locations. Specifically, the controls are more relaxed in non-official media, apolitical information, and locations that are relatively far from the power centers.

Processes of media liberalization

Liberalization in the context of China is the transformation of the commandist Chinese media system into one that enjoys greater relative autonomy from the party–state. It encompasses several processes that do not work alone but in combination, including commercialization, improvisation, bureaucratization, internationalization, and technologization. This section discusses how each mode operates.

Commercialization

Commercialization refers to the process by which media come to respond to the profit motive as a driving force and to depend on advertising and other business activities for revenue (Chan 1993). In 1992, commercialization gained momentum after Deng's speeches justifying marketization sparked the growth of advertising, "infotainment," "weekend supplements," and even "paid journalism"

(Y. Zhao 1998; Chan 1993; Chu 1994; He and Chen 1998). These sources of revenue allowed media organizations to survive despite decreasing subsidies from the Chinese government. However, the profit motive did not necessarily lead to the media's dissociation from the party–state. Some media organizations have successfully satisfied the propaganda needs of the CCP while also making a profit (Pan 2000). The most recent trend is toward conglomeration, which includes the merger of media outlets and the diversification of media's business activities (Lee 2000a; 2000b). This rapid change reflects not only the nationwide shift from a planned to a market economy, but also the declining ability of the party–state to finance the media system (Chan 1993). It also represents redistribution of organizational resources – administrative, economic, and symbolic – in the hope of achieving institutional integrity to balance the fragmentary power of commercialization. However, the party–state keeps a careful eye on such experimentation and reasserts its control whenever media organizations go too far (Chan 1995).

Although outright private ownership is not allowed, various social or non-official organizations have established their own media organizations, leading to a relatively decentralized media structure (Wu 2000). The publications run by these social organizations can print less ideological news and take a more relaxed editorial line. Within media organizations, divisions for advertisement, public relations, and other market-related activities are increasingly influential, as media operation becomes more commercialized (Chen and Huang 1996).

A crucial indicator of commercialization is the growth of the advertising industry. Table 2.2 shows that national advertising revenue has been growing by leaps and bounds, especially for television broadcasting which increased by about 165 per cent between 1985 and 1997. The annual growth rates for television, newspaper, and radio are generally in double figures.

Table 2.2 Advertising revenue by type of media in China, 1985–1997

Year	Newspapers	TV million Yuan	Radio
1985	22,011.6	6,869.6	2,670.7
(%)[a]	(+85.5)	(+102.2)	(+15)
1990	67,710.5	56,136.8	8,641.6
(%)[a]	(+7.6)	(+55.1)	(+15.8)
1995	645,800.0	649,800.0	73,800.0
(%)[a]	(+28)	(+45.2)	(+48.85)
1997	968,265.0	1,144,105.0	105,776.0
(%)[a]	(+24.6)	(+26)	(+21.2)

Note
a Growth rate as compared to the advertising revenue of the previous year.

Sources: Modern Advertising (xiandai guanggao), No. 3, 1995; No. 3, 1996; No. 3, 1997; No. 3, 1999.

This shift in income source has immense implications for media content, media function, and the relationship between media organizations. Advertisements not only constitute a new form of information, but also embody a new media role – to reach the consumers and serve the market. In the heat of competition for target audiences, advertisers are sometimes tempted to test ideological bounds (Lee 1990: 17).

All this testifies to the importance of economic development for liberalizing a communication system. Although commercialization may not immediately lead to democratization, the abundance of apolitical content fostered in the process marks the transformation of China's media from total reliance on the political center to limited but increasing autonomy, from a propaganda instrument serving the party–state exclusively to one rendering multiple social functions (He 1998; Lee 2000a).

Improvisation

It is in the context of this trend toward commercialization that three other processes of media change introduce new and sometimes liberalizing practices in the Chinese media system. The first of these processes is improvisation, the way in which "journalists design, implement, and justify their non-routine journalistic practices that are functioning to weaken, circumvent, and erode the hegemony of the commandist system associated with the communist ideology" (Pan 2000). Improvisation is necessary because of the tension between the conflicting roles journalists are supposed to play, serving both the political elite and the market, a tension for which no existing routine provides an adequate solution (Polumbaum 1990).

Although the goal of such activities is not change at the macro level but the temporary legitimization of specific non-routine practices, the accumulation of improvisation effects can demonstrate that journalists are not only the mouthpiece of the party–state but also active reformers who extend the ideological boundaries in an *ad hoc* manner. In so doing, they exert their own influence on media content, on the perceived role of media, on journalistic values, and even on managerial norms.

In this sense, the concept of improvisation can be extended to include all those who participate in media production at grassroots level such as producers of entertainment programs, advertising agencies, and low-level managers/regulators. By moving away from the routine, most of them engage in setting up their "webs of subsidies" as alternative sources of information, interpersonal relations, and financial return that are not formally available within the authoritarian media system (Pan 2000). This leads to greater autonomy in their work.

Bureaucratization

Building a media market entails new rules of the game, rules that differ from those of the commandist model and allow regulators, competitors, and consumers to be co-oriented in a system with increasing stability. The new administrative measures do not aim to establish a system of rule *of* law as in democratic societies but a system of rule *by* law that regularizes the relationship between the powerful state and the media organizations based on the political bottom line.

In the 1980s, especially during the period of political reform under Zhao Ziyang (1986–1989), various experiments were conducted to reduce direct political manipulation of media production, including the system of apportioning responsibility to the editor-in-chief, the establishment of state agencies that took away part of CCP's regulatory power, and the drafting of a comprehensive journalistic law (He 1998). Although many of these experiments have been suspended since the pro-democracy movement in 1989, the general trend toward bureaucratization continues.

The power of specialized governmental regulatory agencies such as the State Press and Publication Administration has been consolidated in a more standardized and predictable manner. This contrasts with the use of traditional and less predictable control mechanisms through the voice of day-to-day documents by the sole authority of CCP's Central Propaganda Department (Cheek 1988; Polumbaum 1994). Technocrats, rather than ideologues, are becoming increasingly important in the process of media regulation. The rules of the game in the mediascape start to be gradually stabilized, reflecting the rationalization of the state bureaucracy in the Weberian sense. These changes are positively related to liberalization because the new rules, albeit politically conservative, are shaped, at least in part, by market logic.

While improvisation describes liberalization among low-level journalists and media managers, bureaucratization takes place at higher administrative levels. However, improvisation and bureaucratization do not operate at two completely separated levels. In certain cases such as media conglomeration, the line between improvisation and bureaucratization is vague because interactions, negotiations, and compromises among forces at various administrative levels are involved. It may also be difficult to tell whether the changes are temporary or long-term, opportunistic or strategic, ideologically particularized or structurally oriented. It is thus more appropriate to conceive of improvisation and bureaucratization as interconnected. If a lower level experiment is economically successful and politically tolerable, it will be more likely to be institutionalized at a higher level of the media system.

Internationalization

Before the reform era, the Chinese media system was dissociated from counterparts in other parts of the world. As China opened up, however, it showed growing tolerance toward foreign media, resulting in some level of media internationalization (Chan 1994a). Media internationalization can be the consequence of regulated trade or of infiltration, a process by which foreign media products are distributed in China without the consent of the authority. Infiltration can be the result of spillover, black market activity, and the sheer force of technological advances.

Spillover refers to the liberalizing power of certain technologies. Specifically, when media programs that are produced overseas are distributed among the domestic audience, a media source not controlled by the CCP is accessible throughout the country. For example, radio signals are received from Hong Kong and Taiwan in their adjacent mainland provinces, Guangdong and Fujian. Many listeners are attracted to these signals from outside mainland China, thus exerting competitive pressure on the local radio stations, which have responded by imitating the foreign formats and styles.

The consequences of spillover have been dispersed to inland areas and carried onto the levels of programming, content format, and media management through demonstration and market competition. Such impact is not restricted to radio but also affects the audio-visual industry. For instance, television programs from Hong Kong and other parts of the world have exerted strong influence over Chinese media, especially in the vicinity of Hong Kong (Chan 1994b; Chan 2000). The effects of terrestrial and satellite television are even more profound, because of the prominence of television in the everyday life of ordinary people (Chan 1994b). Regardless of whether spillover is intentional or not, the Chinese government, successfully or not, reacts by jamming signals in the case of radio and television and banning reception devices in the case of terrestrial and satellite television.

The black market also plays a significant role in the internationalization of Chinese media. Foreign books, magazines, VCDs, and politically sensitive materials that have a wide appeal are smuggled into China. The black market serves internal piracy as well. Unlike spillover, which relies on technological factors, black market activity is highly dependent upon an underground network that connects various social forces in an organized manner. It is very difficult to eliminate the black market because of the size of China and the infamous corruption of Chinese officials.

Technological advancements have also made it easier for foreign media to reach the Chinese public. In addition to traditional international broadcasting, China is covered by satellite television originating from abroad. Internet is the latest medium that can bring a wide variety of information and entertainment to China. The party–state has subsequently introduced measures to restrict the inflow of sensitive information. As the Internet can easily evade national boundaries and bureaucratic controls, it poses unprecedented challenges for the Chinese bureaucrats who are eager to maintain the CCP's tight information controls.

As China opens to the world and China's policies fluctuate, the influence of foreign media may wane. However, according to the agreement between China and the United States signed in late 1999, China is to join the World Trade Organization (WTO) in the early 2000s. China is scheduled to open its market to more foreign media productions and to allow up to 50 per cent foreign ownership of telecommunications operations. Coupled with the rapid growth of Internet accessibility, the impact of globalization will become more visible in the years to come. Cultural influence from outside as well as the presence of foreign interests will add to the pluralism of China that will be conducive to further media liberalization.

Technologization

As used here, technologization refers to the process by which new media are introduced and socially affect the culture. It is increasingly recognized that new media, especially the Internet, play an important role in China's media liberalization (Chen and Chan 1998; Qiu 1999; Lee 2000a). Even before the Internet became publicly accessible in the late 1990s, technologies such as cassette tapes, compact disks, VCD, satellite, and cable television constituted an effective force that made the country's media system more open to the world and freer from the monopoly of the party–state (Chan 1994a). This trend continues with the Internet, whose liberalizing power is enhanced by its global accessibility, channel capacity, interactivity, and decentralized structure.

Though usually less effective than with the political censorship of the traditional mass media, the CCP is quick to set rules to control new media such as satellite television and the Internet. For instance, the State Council banned the unauthorized reception of satellite television in 1993. However, the ban was not effectively enforced throughout the country, resulting in a pattern of uneven blockage.

With the Internet, restrictive measures taken by the government include the registration of users, access, and service providers, as well as the establishment of a national firewall to prohibit access, and the utilization of Internet surveillance technologies (Qiu 1999/2000). In order to limit the breadth of online political discussion, a hierarchical administrative structure has been set up under the Ministry of Public Security, which is staffed by mid-level technocrats and low-level sysops (Qiu 1999/2000). Consequently, online messages are systematically cleansed, oppositional sites banned, and a few rule-breakers detained for leaking "state secrets" (*The Economist* 2000: 24–28). These regulatory efforts may not be able to control the new medium as effectively as they could mass media. However, they nevertheless establish an institutional process by which the liberalizing potential of the Internet is mediated, thus dampening the liberalization impact (Qiu 1999).

Although these control measures are indeed confining in many regards, the liberalizing power of new technologies should not be underestimated. It is true that no technical innovation can sweep away the nation's system of media control overnight. But compared to traditional mass media, greater autonomy and content diversity are tied to the Internet's relative openness, higher accessibility, interactivity, and international connectivity. Another important factor of change lies in China's ambitions in technological achievements. Although the CCP's ideological departments are concerned over the liberalizing effects of new media, they find it difficult to persuade their colleagues in the technology and economic departments to slow down or to abide by the traditional forms of censorship, resulting in an institutional schism between the country's ideological apparatus and the telecommunications industry. The notion of the information superhighway is indeed contested at national, regional, and local levels under the shadow of international capital, a promise that comes with China's ascension to the WTO (Y. Zhao 2000).

The tension between the ideological imperative, the economic logic, and the increasingly competitive organizational environment has led to reduced effectiveness in policy implementation, as borne out by the diversifying content on the Internet and the prosperity of media black markets on the street. It is not easy to predict whether the liberalizing impact of the new media will be finally absorbed or will force the authorities to give up their tight control. If the past speaks for the future, technological developments such as the Internet and satellite television will boost media liberalization in China.

Civil society and state corporatism

The above review shows that China has attained remarkable achievements in liberalization, but is still far from having free and independent media. New media actors have emerged, including entrepreneurs, media professionals, entertainers, advertisers, and some semi-official interest groups. Ideological indoctrination is no longer the sole purpose of media, as it now fulfils multiple functions and interests, including the connection of producers with consumers, the supervision of social ills and the bureaucracy, and the establishment of a controlled forum for the public.

The pluralistic nature of the audience is increasingly recognized, as reflected in the multiplication of apolitical information and entertainment. Criticism of the ruling authority and the dominant ideology is still limited, and democratic discussion is even rarer. In sum, media reform in China represents liberalization under authoritarianism, marked by the limited growth and diversification of alternative cultural and information resources.

Before the reforms, the CCP had control over every aspect of society, from birth control to marriage to leisure activities. As China opens up, people are beginning to enjoy professional autonomy and personal freedom. The gradual withdrawal of the state from society creates space for the development of China's civil society, with economic ties among ordinary members of society and private commercial organizations forming its base. Non-official organizations of various kinds are increasing in number. Religious groups, for instance, are exerting growing influence among various social strata, including intellectuals and government officials. But many of the non-official groups are still subject to institutional constraints.

The civil society of China is filled with ambiguities and uncertainties, and in its embryonic form civil society does not necessarily spell the end of authoritarian rule there. Economic policies in China are still highly dependent on central decision-making agencies with little grassroots participation and scanty public debate. Most critically, the profits of the emerging market usually find their way back to the power elite either formally as taxes, tariffs, and toll fees or through underground channels of corruption, thus reinforcing their dominant status.

Indeed, the social groups and organizations are still state-licensed and must turn to the state for protection. Through administrative agencies, the state continues to intervene in the operation of the media market, thus blurring the boundaries between the state and the market (Pan 2000). This particular mode of interface between state and market is characteristic of "state corporatism" (Schmitter 1974; Cawson 1986; Bell 1995).

State corporatism, a feature of a transitional society moving from totalitarianism to market-based authoritarianism, is the collaboration between the party–state and the market as well as the interpenetration of political and financial interests (Zhang 1994). In Chinese media, a symbiosis is emerging between the state and the market economy, exemplified by the policy allowing conglomeration (Pan 2000). Through give and take, media organizations are affecting the creation of state policy by representing their own economic interests in terms of general public interests and by performing the public functions imposed by the state. Meanwhile, the state continues to maintain its strategic control over the media market through licensing, regulating, and allocating resources such as personnel and funding. The emergence of corporatism is the state's response to and an indication of increasing development of the Chinese society.

Conclusion

All societies are transitional in the sense that they are in a state of flux, with the old being replaced by the new. Many societies have come to share some common features. Without assuming a linear model of media development, a question often asked by students of Chinese media is whether marketization will eventually lead to a free press. Attested by the case of China, economic growth and marketization are two important enabling conditions for the development of a more liberal press. Without them, media will have little chance of economic independence, a precondition for a free and independent press. However, in the absence of democratization, economic development and marketization will not necessarily lead to a free press.

This is borne out by the case of Singapore whose tight press control contrasts strongly with its advanced economic status (Chan 1997). If the brief period of freedom the Chinese press enjoyed during the 1989 pro-democracy movement and the cases of Taiwan and Korea are anything to go by, democracy is the very foundation of a free press. Democracy represents socio-political pluralism, an equitable distribution of power, and the existence of checks and balances. Only democratization is capable of ending the party–state's existing monopoly over media ownership, appointment of key personnel, and political information. Media commercialization with the endorsement of the state may give rise to a symbiosis between money and power, resulting in state corporatism.

Meanwhile, there is no denying that civil society in China is growing. Frictions between the ideological and economic logics will intensify while other kinds of social tensions will abound. How far the CCP can cope with such contradictions without a more equitable redistribution of political power is an important question for the years to come.

Notes

1 Since 1990, the number of telephones has included mobile phones.
2 On "professionalism" see Li 1994; Lee 1994. On "media commercialization" see Chan 1993; Chu 1994; Lee 2000b. On "media internationalization" see Chan 1994a and Hong 1998.
3 Chu, 1994; Chen and Chan, 1998; He, 2000.

4   On "Leninist press theory" see Lee 1990. On "monopoly of news production" see Su
    1994. On "repression of dissent voices" see Su 1994 and Lu 1994. On "media operation
    under dictates of party–state" see Wu 1994: 137.
5   On Leninist press theory see Y. Zhao 1998 and He 1998. On discontent see Polumbaum
    1990.

References

Alford, W. (1993) "Don't stop thinking about ... yesterday: why there was no indigenous
    counterpart to intellectual property law in imperial China," *Journal of Chinese Law*,
    7(3): 8.
Bell, D. (1995) "Communications, corporatism, and dependent development in Ireland,"
    Journal of Communication, 34 (July): 207–224.
Cawson, A. (1986) *Corporatism and Political Theory*, Oxford: Basil Blackwell.
Chan, J. M. (1993) "Commercialisation without independence: trends and tensions of
    media development in China," *China Review*, J. Cheng and M. Brossean (eds), Hong
    Kong: Chinese University of Hong Kong Press.
—— (1994a) "Media internationalization in China: processes and tensions," *Journal of
    Communication*, 44(3): 70–88.
—— (1994b) "National responses and accessibility to STAR TV in Asia," *Journal of
    Communication*, 44(3): 112–131.
—— (1995) "Calling the tune without paying the piper: the reassertion of media controls
    in China," in L. C. Kin, S. Pepper, and T. K. Yuen (eds) *China Review 1995* (pp. 5.1–5.16),
    Hong Kong: Chinese University Press.
—— (1997) "Power structure, economic development, and press freedom: A comparative
    study of Hong Kong and Singapore," *Journal of Journalism and Communication* (Beijing)
    (in Chinese).
—— (2000) "When capitalist and socialist television clash: the impact of Hong Kong TV on
    Guangzhou residents," in C. C. Lee (ed.) *Money, Power and Media: Communication Patterns
    and Bureaucratic Control in Cultural China*, Evanston, IL: Northwestern University Press:
    245–270.
Cheek, T. (1988) "Redefining propaganda: debates on the role of journalism," *Issues and
    Studies*, 25: 47–74.
Chen, C. S., Zhu, J. H., and Wu, W. (1998) "The Chinese journalist," in D. Weaver (ed.) *The
    Global Journalist*, Caskill, NJ: Hampton Press.
Chen, H. L. and Huang, Y. (1996) "Uneven development of mass media commercialisation
    in mainland China: the case of the press," *Journal Studies Mass Communication Research* (in
    Chinese), 53: 192–208.
Chen, H. L. and He, Z. (1998) *The Chinese Media: A New perspective*, Hong Kong: Pacific
    Century Press (in Chinese).
Chen, H. and Chan, J. M. (1998) "Bird-caged press freedom in China," in J. Cheng (ed.)
    China in the Post-Deng Era, Hong Kong: Chinese University Press.
China Network Information Centre, "Report of Internet Development in China," July
    2000. Available at http://www.cnnic.net.cn/develst/cnnic200007.shtml
China Statistical Yearbook, 1996 and 1998.
Chu, J. L. and Pan, Z. D. (1999) "The time race and time signification in the reform era: a
    study of changing movie theatres in urban China," *International Journal of Cultural
    Studies*, 2(1): 33–57.
Chu, L. L. (1994) "Continuity and change in China's media reform," *Journal of
    Communication*, 44(3): 4–21.
The Economist. (1996) "Publish and be ideologically damned," 26 October: 41.
The Economist. (2000) "Wired China," 22 July: 24–28.
Feir, Scott (1997) "Regulations restricting Internet access: attempted repair of rupture in
    China's great wall restraining the free exchange of ideas," *Pacific Rim Law and Policy
    Journal* 6: 376.
Gellhorn, W. (1987) "China's quest for legal modernity," *Journal of Chinese Law* 1(1): 9.

He, Z. (1998) "Press freedom in mainland China: past, present and future," in Z. He and H. L. Chen, *The Chinese Media: A New Perspective* (in Chinese), Hong Kong: The Pacific Century Press.

—— (2000) "Chinese Communist Party press in a tug of war: a political economy analysis of the *Shenzhen Special Zone Daily*," in C. C. Lee (ed.) *Money, Power and Media: Communication Patterns and Bureaucratic Control in Cultural China*, Evanston, IL: Northwestern University Press.

Hong, J. H. (1998) *The Internationalization of Television in China: the Evolution of Ideology, Society, and Media since the Reform*, Westport, CN: Praeger.

Hong Kong Economic Journal. (2000) "Internet users number about 9 million," 19 January, p. 12 (in Chinese).

Huang, Shengmin (1997) "The demise and revival of China's advertising industry," in Joseph Chan, Leonard Chu and Zhongdang Pan, (eds) *Mass Communication and Market Economy*, Hong Kong: Lufeng Press: 347–358.

National Statistical Bureau (1999), *China Statistical Yearbook*, Beijing: National Statistics Press.

Kuan, Hsin-chi (1991) "Introduction," in Hsin-chi Kuan and Maurice Brosseau (eds) *China Review 1991*. Hong Kong: Chinese University Press.

Lam, W. W. (1991) "The media: the party's tongue and throat defend the faith," in Hsin-chi Kuan and Maurice Brosseau (eds) *China Review 1991*. Hong Kong: Chinese University Press.

Lee, C. C. (1990) "Mass media: of China, about China," in C. C. Lee (ed.) *Voices of China: The Interplay of Politics and Journalism*, New York: Guilford Press: 3–32.

—— (1994) "Ambiguities and contradiction: issues in China's changing political communication," *Gazette*, 53: 7-21.

—— (2000a) "Chinese communication: prisms, trajectories, and modes of understanding," in C. C. Lee (ed.) *Money, Power and Media: Communication Patterns and Bureaucratic Control in Cultural China*, Evanston, IL: Northwestern University Press: 3–44.

—— (2000b) "Servants of the state or the market? Media and journalists in China," in J. Tunstall (ed.) *Media Occupations*, London: Oxford University Press.

Li, L. R. (1994) "The historical fate of 'objective reporting' in China," in C. C. Lee (ed.) *China's Media, Media's China*, Boulder: Westview Press: 225–238.

Lu, K. (1994) "Press control in 'new China' and 'old China,' " in C. C. Lee (ed.) *China's Media, Media's China*, Boulder: Westview Press: 147–162.

Ma, E. K. (1999) "Rethinking media theories: the case of China," in J. Curran and M. Park (eds) *De-Westernising Media Studies*, London: Routledge.

New China News (1988) 23 December.

Pan, Z. D. (2000a) "Improvising reform activities: the changing reality of journalistic practice in China," in C. C. Lee (ed.) *Money, Power and Media: Communication Patterns and Bureaucratic Control in Cultural China*, Evanston, IL: Northwestern University Press: 68–111.

—— (2000b) "The structure of historical narratives and their construction: the case of Chinese media coverage of the Hong Kong handover," in Tao Dongfengt and Gao Binzhong (eds) *Cultural Studies*, Vol. 1, Tianjing: Tianjing Social Science Press: (in Chinese).

People's Daily (1986) 20 August: 3.

Polumbaum, J. (1990) "The tribulations of China's journalists after a decade of reform," in C. C. Lee (ed.) *Voices of China: The Interplay of Politics and Journalism*, New York: Guilford Press: 33–68.

—— (1994) "Striving for predictability: the bureaucratization of media management in China," in C. C. Lee (ed.) *China's Media, Media's China*, Boulder: Westview Press: 113–128.

Qili, Hu. (1988) *New China News*, 23 December .

Qiu, J. L. (1999) *Mediating the political impacts of the Internet: the case of China*, unpublished master's thesis, Chinese University of Hong Kong.

—— (1999/2000) "Virtual censorship in China: keeping the gate between the cyberspaces," *The International Journal of Communications Law and Policy*, winter, 4: 1–25.

Schmitter, P. (1974) "Democratic theory and neocorporate practice," *Social Research*, 50: 885–928.

South China Morning Post (1991) 17 January.

Su, S. Z. (1994) "Chinese communist ideology and media control," in C. C. Lee (ed.) *China's Media, Media's China*, Boulder: Westview Press: 75–88.

Teng, Teng (1986) *People's Daily*, 20 August: 3.

Yu, X. (1994) "Professionalization without guarantees: changes of the Chinese press in post-1989 years," *Gazette*, 53, 1–2: 23–41.

Wang, S. G. (1995) "Private time and politics: Changes of leisure time in urban China," *Chinese Social Science Quarterly*, summer: 108–125 (in Chinese).

Wu, G. G. (1994) "Command communication: the politics of editorial formulation in the *People's Daily*," *China Quarterly*, summer: 197–211.

—— (1997) *The Political Reform of Zhao Ziyang*, Hong Kong: Pacific Century Press (in Chinese).

—— (2000) "One head, many mouths: diversifying press structures in reform China," in C. C. Lee (ed.) *Money, Power and Media: Communication Patterns and Bureaucratic Control in Cultural China*, Evanston, IL: Northwestern University Press:45–67.

Wu, J. (1995) *The Road of a Decade*, Hong Kong: Jing Bao Culture Press (in Chinese).

Zhang, B. H. (1994) "Corporatism, totalitarianism, and transitions to democracy," *Comparative Political Studies*, 27: 108–126.

Zhao, Y. (1998) *Media, Market, and Democracy in China*, Urbana: University of Illinois Press.

—— (2000) "Caught in the Web: the public interest and the battle for control of China's information superhighway," *Info*, 2(1): 5–30.

Zhao, Z. (1987) "Advancing along the road of socialism with Chinese characteristics (*yanzhe you zhongguo tese de shehuizhuyi daolu qianjin*)." Report to CCP's Thirteenth National Congress, 25 October (in Chinese).

3

UZBEKISTAN

Lutfulla Kabirov and Scott Smith

Introduction

Since the fall of the Soviet Union in 1991, Uzbekistan, like its former Soviet neighbors, has struggled to define itself as an independent country. This period has been marked by a considerable amount of political speech promising transition to a more democratic society with efforts to reform and stimulate a market economy. In reality, the Republic of Uzbekistan has earned a reputation for consistently imposing stricter control in the spheres of human rights, politics, and the economy.

Approaching the end of the republic's first decade of independence, government control likewise has prohibited mass media in Uzbekistan from playing a significant role in the country's transformation and developing into a vital part of its political and social reform. At times indirect forces, including the depressed economy, hinder mass media development and in other instances the government of Uzbekistan directly impedes media participation in the democratic transition. The government controls the mass media with instruments of censorship still intact from the Soviet period and newly created forms to match media's growing attempts to participate in public discourse.

Democratically oriented legislation often does not work in parallel with long instituted power structures and is therefore seldom adhered to in practice. This chapter examines the role of mass media in the early stages of Uzbekistan's transition from Soviet rule to independence and provides an example of forces that have significantly limited mass media development in the last years of the Soviet Union and through the first nine years of independence.

An overview of the democratization process

The process of democratization in Uzbekistan is shaped by the country's long-Central Asian heritage, seventy years of Soviet rule, and another 130 years prior to that of Russia's imperialist presence. The totalitarian Soviet Uzbek state did not aspire to democracy but rather inherited independence from imperialist rule as a result of the Soviet Union's collapse. The exact starting point of the democratic transition in Uzbekistan is a contentious issue. Some believe that democratic reform in Uzbekistan began prior to independence, during the Soviet period. Change initiated in 1985 with the coming to power of Soviet leader Mikhail

Gorbachev and the resultant reforms of perestroika, or "restructuring," transformed the Uzbek Communist Party.

Others say that the transition process began on 1 September 1991, the day the Republic of Uzbekistan proclaimed its independence from the collapsing Soviet Union. In the same month, many state decrees that furthered democratic reforms were introduced. On 14 September the Uzbek Communist Party was dissolved, and on 17 September an act banning political party activism or organization within state employers (factories, unions, and so on) was passed, removing their political affiliation. At almost the same time, as a symbol of transition, the European Convention for the Protection of Human Rights and Fundamental Freedoms was ratified.

One possible starting point for the current transition is June 1989, the time of conflict between the Uzbeks and Turkish Meskheds. During this period, a national opposition movement, Birlik (Unity), which was not officially registered with the state, became a recognized and accepted aspect of the nascent civil society. The movement entered into dialogue with the Uzbek government, reminiscent of the pattern in Poland. By the end of 1989, Birlik, led by Abdurakhim Polatov, and Erk (Freedom), led by Mukhammad Solikh, both now in political exile, had set a strong example and other opposition parties and movements had begun to organize within Uzbekistan. Another opposition group emerging there, Interfront, began to unite the Russian-speaking populations of the republic. The government granted official permission to these groups to hold meetings, legalizing free assembly. The people and the regime seemed to move in tandem toward democratic reforms. On the one hand, citizens' groups exercised their right to self-expression; on the other, the regime began to understand the necessity of abandoning the administrative-command management system and embarking on true democratic reform.

In 1990, the main principles for transition toward democracy were formulated. Through discussion between groups such as Birlik and the state, policies were formulated to guide the sharing of state power among different branches of government, and the Erk opposition party was officially registered.[1] Following independence, the people of Uzbekistan experienced an explosion of interest in national self-determination, culture, history, and language. The ban on religion was finally removed, and in 1990 alone more than 300 mosques and religious schools were constructed for immediate use. In autumn 1990, the first contested elections to the Uzbek parliament were held with the participation of a newly emerging opposition party. The process culminated in a presidential system of government. In 1990, the parliament elected Islam Abdughanievich Karimov, leader of the People's Democratic Party, to the presidency.

The next move toward democratic reform began on 31 August 1991 when parliament legislated a change of name for the country. The Uzbek Socialist Republic officially became the Republic of Uzbekistan. Instead of the "shock therapy" plan for a shift to a market economy following Russia's example, the new republic and its president opted for layering economic reforms. This layering meant that the government would be strongly involved in the reforms, while maintaining goals such as the construction of legal and economic rights, the modernization of economic structures, and the reorientation of the national outlook and culture based on democratic principles.

Despite the democratic steps, including the establishment of a national human rights agency, Uzbekistan was laying the foundations for the development of a new "absolute" rule, with power concentrated in the hands of the new president. On the one hand, there was a formal decentralization and local mayors were given the task of managing the territories. On the other, these mayors were made directly accountable to the president. Though constitutional norms and national legislation were outwardly respected, they were implemented only in coordination with the president. This state of affairs was justified by the argument that presidential oversight would bring about the consolidation of civil society while preserving the country's unity and stability. Stability and order were achieved at the expense of infringements of democratic standards.

One of the most blatant infringements during this proposed transformation to democratic standards has been the presidential election of 9 January 2000. Roundly criticized by Western embassies and international organizations for not representing a genuinely democratic process, President Islam Karimov won an overwhelming 91.9 per cent of the votes. The OSCE was most outspoken about election violations and issued a statement afterward saying that the presidential election in Uzbekistan fell far short of OSCE standard requirements and therefore it "could not justify observing these elections" (Office for Democratic Institutions and Human Rights 2000). Then US State Department spokesman, James Rubin, said at a press conference that, "The United States government believes that this election was neither free nor fair and offered Uzbekistan's voters no true choice." Rubin added that the government had refused to register bona fide opposition parties and would not allow members of those parties to stand for president.[2]

Toward the end of its first decade of independence, the government of Uzbekistan began egregiously to disregard individual human rights in the name of national security. Threats from unstable neighboring countries to the south, Tajikistan and Afghanistan, and terrorist bombings allegedly targeting President Karimov on 16 February 1998 provided convenient rationales for decreased adherence to international human rights standards. Following those five bomb blasts which killed sixteen and injured another 130, a serious crackdown on suspected terrorist groups with possible ties to the assassination attempt began. One Human Rights Watch report on Uzbekistan opens, "Human rights protections in Uzbekistan deteriorated rapidly and dramatically in 1999" (2000). The report goes on to explain that the police had detained thousands of men suspected of being associated with political opposition groups or independent Muslims who proclaimed they were, or were suspected of being, members of sects not registered with the government.

As it happens, of the citizens the government has targeted as terrorist threats, few have been journalists. The government of Uzbekistan prefers indirectly to target journalists critical of officials. Two cases have had international notoriety. One instance of a journalist being jailed for his criticism of a government official is S. Yalgashev who wrote for the paper funded by and named after the political party Adolat (Justice). After publishing critical material about the regional mayor, Yalgashev was arrested for possession of narcotics. Another reporter for the state paper *Khalq Suzi* (The Word of the People), Polat Gadaev, was arrested for allegedly taking a bribe after having published critical material about the government. Gadaev served less than one year of his sentence before being granted an amnesty because of his age and declining health (Smith 1999).

Journalist and former member of the Uzbekistani parliament, Karim Bakhriev has claimed that finding other ways of targeting a journalist who writes to voice opposition to the strong government's ideology discredits the journalist and prevents the start of a public debate on freedom of speech issues in Uzbekistan (Smith 1999). To other practising journalists the message is clear that even the appearance of opposing the strong government could have consequences for their personal safety. Indirect censorship by entrapping journalists for criminal activities has a chilling effect on others who must decide on a daily basis either to reveal corruption and civic dishonesty, or ignore it.

Another important factor that limits media ability to function is the republic's economic instability. Uzbekistani entrepreneurs acknowledge that there has been slight progress in starting small capitalist ventures since independence, but for foreign investors who have experienced the difficult business climate of independent Uzbekistan, the transformation to a free market economy is far from realized. Most of the medium-sized and small investors who saw Uzbekistan as a newly opened market have been greatly disappointed, leaving only a few big companies such as Coca-Cola and the Korean auto manufacturer Daewoo which are able to hold out for better times (EIU 1999: 36).

For Uzbekistan's media, already stifled by the controlling government, a stagnant economy means that it is impossible to take advantage of advertising revenues of foreign companies working in their communities, and local businesses are not prosperous enough to invest in advertisements. Consequently, Uzbekistan's media are not financially independent enough to wean themselves off the state budgets and thus away from state control. A weak economy cannot be cited as an instance of censorship through which the government directly limits the mass media, but economic forces function as a daunting barrier to state and private media alike, whose staff find themselves continually dependent upon state budgets and sponsorship.

Media reform during democratization

In the early 1980s, media in different territories of the USSR experienced varying levels of freedom. During Soviet times, mass media in Uzbekistan were rigidly tied to the dominant power structures. Newspapers were funded, and therefore controlled, by government organs like ministries and city governments. In the late 1980s, reforms began to occur, including the expansion of broadcasting and press in languages other than Russian. However, despite the acceptance in the republics of glasnost, or openness, and Gorbachev's support of different opinions in the media, Uzbekistan's local party functionaries outlined clear boundaries to freedom of speech.

As glasnost progressed, it became possible to organize public demonstrations and meetings, and opposition newspapers printed opinions not passed down from controlling government organs. But most outstanding was the change in public attitude; people were not afraid openly to express their thoughts, as would previously have been considered dangerous. Yet, no mechanism existed to allow the development of new mass media technologies or new television channels.

Limited means of distribution remained under the control of the party in its various incarnations. Each newspaper edition carried party committee commentary arguing for the renewed implementation of strict communist ideology.

In 1989, the Communist Party quickly lost authority and effective control over mass media. A short period of extensive freedom of speech for the Uzbekistan media ensued. In 1988, there were 196 newspapers and magazines in Uzbekistan; by 1990 their number had almost tripled (State Registry of the Press Committee 1991). Former Soviet newspapers were renamed. In 1990, a new government newspaper, *Khalq Suzi* (The Word of the People) was published in both Uzbek and Russian and was free from censorship. Other newspapers were transferred from governmental control to that of their editors or staff. For example, the largest Russian-language newspaper, *Pravda Vostoka* (Truth of the East), previously the domain of the Communist Party, was taken over by its editors. For the first time in the history of Uzbek mass media, newspapers became commercial ventures. Editors of newspapers were no longer appointed by the state, but were to be selected by journalists' collectives, the staff of the publication.

The circulation of uncensored independent newspapers sharply increased. For example, the circulation of the intelligentsia newspaper, *Uzbekiston Adabiyoti* (Literature of Uzbekistan) increased from 30,000 to 94,000. The youth newspaper *Turkestan*'s circulation tripled and it published the charter of the national opposition movement, Birlik. For the first time, religious newspapers and purely commercial papers that did not carry political commentary appeared.

At the same time, this period was marked by the appearance of extremist publications, particularly ethnic papers calling for the overthrow of the existing order. The editors of certain publications demanded that reforms should benefit Uzbeks only, or that languages other than Uzbek be prohibited. The newspaper *Munosabat*, which declared itself independent, espoused such views, and a leaflet calling for the expatriation of ethnic Russians was widely circulated. Some mosques advocated the formation of an Islamic state.

In addition, the period saw plans to decentralize mass media. In 1994, all local (regional, urban, district) newspapers were removed from the control of the state committee for the press and transferred to the direct control of local authorities and founders (a familiar Soviet vehicle akin to publisher) who could publish without permission from the center. Shortly after independence, the founders of local mass media may have differed slightly in their views from the local authority, but not greatly. However, in contrast to developments in the printed press, television and radio broadcasting remained under strict government control.

The period of unbridled freedom ended in 1991. Between then and 1996 formal legal structures for the press were introduced. On 14 June 1991 a new law codified the role of the state toward mass media and created the beginning of a legal system governing media activity. Censorship was prohibited, but the state retained the power to protect state secrets from disclosure. Internal censorship or self-censorship by journalists trained in Soviet journalism continued and the democratic policy that allowed editors to be elected by the staff declined as the government began to appoint the editors-in-chief again.

Under the Soviet system, all newspapers and magazines were obliged to provide advance copies to the state censors, who had the right to remove any material. Separate censors existed within the broadcasting media as well as in each regional area with regard to printing. After 1991, though officially abolished by the passage of Article 4 of the law on mass media which clearly states that "Censorship of the mass media is inadmissible in the Republic of Uzbekistan," censorship continued at the state printing committee. Its members' control over printing gave them the ability to remove unacceptable material. This control was embodied in the authority of government officials to fire any editor-in-chief or force the firing of his/her staff members. Another means of censoring was to stop financial support, paper delivery, and access to state publishing houses for printing.

The government agency that edited out or rejected unacceptable text during the Soviet era was, as of 2000, still located on the second floor of the building that housed the republic's major editorial offices in Tashkent. This institution, the Inspection Agency of State Secrets, has remained intact and unaffected by any reforms in print journalism. Journalists' articles must receive a stamp of approval from the agency, which for over twenty years has been directed by the same individual, before they may be published.

Journalist and Uzbekistani mass media law specialist, Karim Bakhriev, has noted that few cases regarding print journalists have been heard in the courts. This is so primarily because the state censors weed out critical material so thoroughly that there are no published facts on which to incriminate journalists. Besides, in the years since the confirmation of Uzbekistan's constitution there have been no instances of a print journalist suing for his or her rights; a likely explanation is that they do not believe their rights will be respected in the courts where every judge is appointed by the president and serves a short, five-year term. Specialists like Bakhriev believe that the Uzbek mass media laws are good on paper, but no public debate on issues concerning freedom of speech is allowed to exist (Smith 1999).

In 1997, new laws began to provide for a democratic structure in the media. Three media laws were ratified: "On the protection of the professional work of journalists," "On safeguards and the freedom of access to information," and "On the mass media."[3] According to these laws any kind of censorship was prohibited, protection for journalists was provided, and journalists were also allowed access to any information they needed. These new laws met international standards, with the exception of the law "On the mass media" which gave the state the right to dissolve any mass media company. This right of dissolution in effect nullified other beneficial legal pronouncements because the protections and freedoms given in the other laws could not prevent the state from arbitrarily closing a newspaper. The post-1997 laws were ineffective for another reason: financial control remained in the hands of the local governmental bodies. These laws were created with little or no input from the journalists; their passage did not inspire enthusiasm, as skepticism regarding practical and effective implementation was rampant.

According to the law "On the mass media," newspapers were obliged to publish not only official communiqués of government bodies, but also other materials issued by the state information agency. In addition, laws "On publishing" and "On copyright and related rights" had been ratified on 30 August 1996. A television and radio corporation code was instituted by a presidential decree on 7 May 1996, according to which television and radio broadcasting in Uzbekistan was granted numerous independent rights. Broadcasting companies were created for the regions.

An especially important provision of the code was the introduction of competition into the field of broadcast media. Alternative stations began to emerge through the involvement of private individuals. By August 1999, twenty-two non-governmental television stations operated across a number of small cities in addition to five non-governmental radio stations. At a national level, thirty non-governmental television channels were broadcasting successfully. Much of this output was formal, not driven from below by the mass media itself but resulting primarily from state initiatives.

While these laws seemed to signal a transition toward democratic media practices, the government continued maneuvering for control. In 1996, it dissolved the Independent Union of Journalists. Formed in 1957 with branches throughout the USSR, the journalists' union functioned to defend its members and provide services for them. The union assisted journalists in finding a position, facilitating retirement benefits, organizing annual vacations, as well as publishing a professional monthly journal.

The official reason for dissolving the union in December 1996 was the formation of the Political Fund for the Democratization and Support of the Mass Media. The government claimed that this new fund made the previous journalists' union obsolete because the two organizations fulfilled the same obligations. The union was forced to relinquish its registration and bank account to the new fund. Although the founders declared the fund independent, they were closely connected to the state administration. Journalists do not see the fund as a source of defense or any other service associated with the previous union.

Outside of the union, efforts of journalists who wished for greater freedom of speech have been frustrated. For example, the editor-in-chief of *Khurriyat* (Freedom), Karim Bakhriev, in 1996–1997 printed a series of articles critical of the lack of freedom of speech in the country. He was attacked verbally and editorially for these articles, and forced to step down from his position after the republic's first independent paper had printed only five issues. His fate was widely analyzed in journalistic circles and has served as an additional reason for self-censorship. Overwhelmingly, editors and print media owners feared the presence of objectionable materials in their publications. An anti-democratic tradition of caution was stronger than any newly crafted legislative rights.

Reforms within state broadcast media

During the Soviet period, television reached nearly 100 per cent of the population and was an important tool for the formation of opinion and control of information. Broadcast media continue to play an extensive role in the life of Uzbek society. Watching television during the evening meal and into the night is part of Uzbek culture. Since market economics has limited the operation of print media and reduced their impact, television and radio broadcasting have continued to be important tools for state propaganda. Since independence in 1991, the state has controlled broadcasting media. In 1992, a state company for television and radio broadcasting was founded through which the government has supervised the broadcasting media.

In the past few years, as greater amounts of information have reached Uzbekistan from the West, and the content of Moscow programs transmitted on Uzbek television has improved, the population has become increasingly disappointed by the lack of quality programming and information relevant to viewers. In response, the president issued a decree on 7 May 1996, "On the rise of the role of television and radio in the public life of Uzbekistan." With this decree Uzbek television was transformed into a national television and radio company, UzTeleRadio, and additional rights and creative possibilities were delegated to it. The organizational structure of the television and radio company is based on the eleven regional television companies, the radio network, and the "TeleFilm" studios.

According to this decree, UzTeleRadio was to become financially independent from the state budget by 2000. No clear terms outlining privatization or financial sustainability were established, and as a result the company remained dependent on the state budget and control. By order of the ministerial cabinet, an independent governing board of founders was to assume control. The chairman of the television and radio company had the status of a government minister and his deputies and political commentators were appointed by a decree of the president. The company's executives have all the rights and privileges of high government officials, benefits which themselves may cause these officials to adhere strictly to state policies. UzTeleRadio remains largely funded from the state budget; nearly 60 per cent of the funds allocated are spent on hardware, and the company must earn the remaining 40 per cent through advertising or other commercial activity. These resources are then channeled into more creative purposes. Television programming is transmitted over four channels: 1-National, 2-Youth, 3-Regional, and 4-Urban. The total volume of programming across all four channels is sixty-four hours per day. In-house production accounts for forty-nine of these hours.

The government has failed to move away from its totalitarian control over television and radio broadcasting content and maintains the right to regulate informational programming. The right to report political events in the republic is granted to relatively few commentators. In Uzbekistan political comments can only be made by specially appointed journalists and commentators who have work experience and training in the central governmental bodies; from these positions they are deemed qualified to speak on behalf of the government and assigned to TV. Journalists of state TV who do not follow this career path are allowed to read only comments prepared by governmental information agencies.

The freedom to make political comments faces certain important obstacles. Across the common grid of television broadcasting, one channel that transmits for eighteen hours will broadcast informational programs in four blocks of thirty minutes each for a total of two hours. These four blocks, however, are absolutely identical. Within each of the informational blocks, the political events are reduced to releases, which have been provided to the station by governmental sources. Additional comments and the expression of political views by the commentator are prohibited.

The structure of radio broadcasting mimics the organization of Uzbek television. For instance, 80 per cent of the radio network is open to inspection by the state. There are eight radio stations registered with the designated state committee. Five are state-run while three are non-governmental. In addition to these, there are about twenty state radio studios registered in the regions.

The low popularity of print media in Uzbekistan has led to a recent increase in the number of radio listeners. At the same time, the radio audience has decreased since Soviet times because people prefer to watch television. In addition, Uzbek radio often directly transmits news that was printed in the newspaper and may also have been transmitted by television because Uzbek radio does not possess its own information service. In the regions, private radio stations are not registered. In Tashkent, three non-governmental radio stations are in operation: Grand, Sezam, and Uzbegim Taronaci. The majority of the transmissions of these three stations are musical broadcasts. When they do broadcast "news," they very cautiously refer to political news and keep to neutral subjects.

The emergence of private broadcasters

During the same Soviet perestroika period that saw unbridled freedoms among print journalism in Uzbekistan, small, private TV broadcasters also gradually emerged in regional towns throughout the country. In the year 2000, about thirty non-governmental stations were registered with the government and broadcast with varying levels of regularity and programming quality; approximately fifteen of these stations produce local news programs. The first stations which started operating in the spring of 1991 were Mulokot TV in Kokand, Orbita TV in Angren, and STV in Samarkand; new stations continue to emerge as a result of individual entrepreneurial inspiration or family efforts, an example being Turtkul TV in the Karalpakstan region which began to broadcast in February 2000 (Anarbaeva 2000).

Contrary to the opinions of certain Western experts, the appearance of the first non-governmental television stations in Uzbekistan did not represent effective competition to Uzbek state TV in the first years of independence. In 1992, non-governmental television represented a commercial service developed for the state's benefit. The main activity was showing family celebrations, broadcasting birthday greetings, or airing pirated films from the West. News programs were not on the programming agenda. In the early 1990s it was not appropriate to use the term "independent" to describe these stations since the programming and news content did not distinguish them from state owned and controlled stations. The role of these non-governmental stations has changed steadily since the first couple of years, frequently to the anger of government authorities which prefer to maintain control of broadcast information.

The success of the individual station lies largely in the director's ability to maintain constructive relations with local government officials who hold the power to prevent a station from being re-registered. Some TV stations under the leadership of financially minded individuals have tended toward pro-government ideology, and the stations' programming reflects this stance. Founders of these stations have used their media companies to advance their political and financial careers, paying less attention to raising community issues and promoting social change through program content and more to appeasing influential government officials with apolitical reports.

Two examples of such companies are STV in Samarkand and MTV in Andizhan. Owners of both stations have successfully achieved high places in the republic's government in Tashkent while building media companies comprising TV, radio, and tabloid newspapers. Despite having established media companies with technical facilities on a level with their Western counterparts, little can be said for the journalists' freedom to practice balanced or critical reporting. Tasked with propagating the government ideology, journalists at these pro-government independent stations are allowed to produce only news stories devoid of critical material, and other programming largely includes cultural events, films, Latin American soaps, and retransmitted Russian channels.

Yet other non-governmental stations have concentrated on building businesses while equally upholding journalistic integrity. This has caused them considerable trouble with the government. With training and technical support from international donor and development organizations, these companies number about thirteen, the best examples being Orbita TV in Angren, Aloka-AK in Gulistan, ALC TV in Urgench, and Kaldirgoch TV in Guzar.[4] Non-governmental stations are founded either by shareholders or by private individuals. The others are organized jointly by state and public structures in addition to their private individual or corporate base. Not forming a cohesive network throughout the republic, the capacity of each station to reach the population of its city or region depends on the power of its transmitter.

These stations have also not flourished financially. Their annual budgets range from US$5,000 to US$12,000. The financial difficulties of these broadcasters are indicative of the general economic depression the country faces. The pro-government stations STV and MTV have become profitable ventures with estimated annual incomes in the range of US$20,000 to US$25,000.[5] The weekly quantity of locally produced programming varies from zero to two hours, and the range of total airtime each week is from twelve to ninety hours. Employee turnover plagues typical independent stations because they are paid poorly and irregularly. A journalist typically making about US$10 a month is easily lured to a slightly higher salary at a local state affiliate where there is less freedom or to non-media work that is more profitable. Many promising journalists cannot afford to develop their craft and to reach professional maturity because of the pressure to increase their salary.

Another factor prohibiting non-governmental stations from prospering is the bureaucratic interference the government invents to distract stations from trying to present balanced opinions, expose corruption, and form media associations. The government first began taking serious notice of small, independent stations in the regions when these stations attempted to form an independent electronic mass media association (ANESMI) in spring 1998. An initial initiative of Unesco, ANESMI was designed to be an association of electronic broadcasters in four of the Central Asian former Soviet republics: Kazakhstan, the Kyrgyz Republic, Tajikistan, and Uzbekistan. The primary mission of the association was to lobby in support of media interests. The Uzbekistani government felt threatened by having to vie for control of independent TV, radio, and cable companies which held ties with numerous independent stations throughout the Central Asian region and had the backing of international organizations. In an attempt to control the association, the presidential apparatus of Uzbekistan sent its own candidate to contest the presidential seat, but members unanimously elected the director of a non-state radio station, Ulugbek Ergashev. Because the attempts of the apparatus at controlling Anesmi were unsuccessful through these means, the government subsequently refused to register the association and has maintained this position since 1998.

In further answer to the directors' attempt at organizing, in 1998 the Cabinet of Ministries formed a new broadcast commission to oversee a newly established annual re-registration process required of all TV stations. This commission, called the Interagency Coordination Commission to Improve and Increase Effectiveness of Informational Activities and the Spread of Data (MKK), is made up of nineteen representatives, including two deputy prime ministers for the Republic of Uzbekistan, the deputy-minister of the National Security Service (NSS, former KGB), and the minister of justice. The head of the state TV company, a competitor of non-state stations, also holds a seat on the MKK. No representatives of non-state TV stations are present, creating a monopoly of state control over non-governmental broadcasters.

The MKK is a complex organization which, for example, conducts technical inspections of non-state stations. Stations not meeting minimum technical standards (which rise each year) are often banned from broadcasting until costly equipment upgrades are made. The MKK also has a branch in each region administering stations locally. Made up of city and regional representatives of the mayor's office, police, and NSS, each local MKK branch functions as a locus of control over the private station in its jurisdiction. Each member of the local MKK has the authority to refuse or approve his recommendation to the republic level MKK for a station's re-registration. If the mayor, for example, feels threatened by the station's news reports, he may use his authority as an MKK representative to intimidate the station director (Smith 1999; Anarbaeva 2000).

In 1998, the first year in which the MKK imposed annual re-registration, the process took four months. Non-governmental stations were subjected to rigorous technical and programming inspections and required to submit massive amounts of documents at short notice. During the second year of annual re-registration, the process lasted six months during which time the licenses of twelve stations lapsed and the government ordered two stations to be closed. The official reason for closure was the fact that both stations possessed expired licenses. This moment of tension between private stations and the MKK came during the parliamentary and presidential election season. Stations waiting for the MKK to decide on re-registrations practiced strict self-censorship. They feared they might fail re-registration tests and even be closed indefinitely if they reported material objectionable to the local or republic government.

One of the stations the government closed, Aloka-AK in Gulistan, quietly lobbied local officials and was allowed to begin broadcasting after nine months of being off the air. The second, ALC TV in Urgench, became the first private TV station in the history of the Uzbekistani mass media to sue the government over licensing issues. The station lost its appeal, first at the city court and then at the regional court and remained closed pending decisions about further litigation.

Nonetheless, nearly a decade after the start of independent broadcasting, signs of progress are beginning to be noticed. In contrast to the government's constant attempts to stop the operation of private stations, there have been encouraging gestures of cooperation. Perhaps certain government officials are sympathetic to the regional independent broadcasters, or officials are beginning to understand that these established broadcasters cannot be intimidated out of existence. Senior government officials increasingly engage journalists and directors in dialogues about their roles as independent broadcasters.

The most significant sign of improved relations with the government was the new law effective 1 September 2000 increasing the term of broadcast licenses from one year to a minimum of five (Anarbaeva 2000). This important step forward may release stations from the constant fear that independent reporting may jeopardize the government's willingness to approve their annual re-registration. In fact, directors will not be required to participate in the costly and time-consuming annual bureaucratic process, which could take four to six months.

Re-registration for station directors often means paying bribes to a number of officials for their signature and stamp of approval and also involves constant travel between their regional city and Tashkent to submit these packages to the Republic MKK. Causing the process to recur each five years rather than annually will allow station directors to invest more financial and administrative resources into developing their stations. The ameliorating effect of the new law has yet to be measured. The unfortunate void between writing good legislation in Tashkent and realizing it as a new bureaucratic process is a serious problem in Uzbekistan. And other forms of bureaucratic interference could be substituted if private broadcasters were seen to constitute an apparent threat to authority.

The question of independence

Of the 495 newspapers and 113 magazines registered in 1999, 377 newspapers and sixty-nine magazines are state-run. Thus, the majority of information space continues to belong to government organizations. By the end of the first decade of independence, there were only three daily national newspapers in Uzbekistan, and all of them were state-run: *Narodnoye Slovo* (The Word of the People), *Khalq Suzi* (The Word of the People), and *Pravda Vostoka* (The Truth of the East). In these newspapers, there was a conspicuous absence of independent thought regarding significant events such as disasters. In 1998, there was a natural disaster in the Fergana region. International news agencies managed to transmit this information on the day of the disaster. In Uzbekistan, however, this news did not reach the papers until two days later through the state news agency. Although Uzbek journalists knew of the disaster because it was shown on Russian television, no one attempted to report the event. In this case, it seems that the journalists demonstrated a desire to wait for the official point of view before reporting independently.

Direct management of the mass media occurs through their founding bodies. In many cases, the state and local *khokimiyat* (government) form these bodies. This relationship is then formalized in an agreement drafted between the newspaper and its founding members and registered with the local authorities. The agreement may determine the overall character of a publication because it establishes the core principles by which the publication will operate. The newspaper is obliged to cover a certain subject and to each type of content is allocated a certain amount of information space. For example, the national literary newspaper *Uzbekistan Adabiyoti va San'ati* (Literature and Arts of Uzbekistan), organized by the Ministry of Culture, is limited to issues of art and culture. The national agricultural newspaper *Qishloq Khayoti* (Province Life), organized by the Ministry of Agriculture, is limited to reporting on issues related to village life, and so on.

The state's influence over publishing is compounded by the fact that most newspapers are published at state printing houses. In 2000, no semi-private printing houses existed. In addition, nearly 80 per cent of newsprint is supplied through the state or its agents. The publication of newspapers and magazines is very expensive in relation to available income in a depressed economy. Up to 95 per cent of the state newspapers in Uzbekistan are unprofitable and continue to be published at the state's expense. For example, the amount of 100 million soms (equivalent to US$125,000) is transferred from the state budget annually to subsidize three of the republic's national papers. Regional newspapers are likewise subsidized through their local governments.[6]

Thus, in addition to legal and political codification of the role of media in society, financial concerns affect media. In the early 1990s, many foreign experts came to Tashkent and conferences publicized the benefits and technical needs of a free and independent press. The transformation of the mass media into a series of commercial firms was occurring, but the consequence of wider dependence on advertising had a marked effect on television. It had become dependent on foreign films and cheap soap operas. The new independent and small alternative stations were marked especially by their dependence on marginal forms of external revenue. Programming was often organized around special orders for such events as weddings or birthdays. The news and public affairs element of programming found it hard to compete.

In the press, the large financial resources required to publish constituted an effective barrier to media freedom. In contrast to the growth in the quantity of titles, which tripled to nearly 500 by 1997, the medium experienced a decline in the circulation of practically all newspapers and magazines (Freedom House Country Report 1998). From 1992 to 1995, the total circulation of newspapers fell by ten times. Half of the district newspapers altered their publishing frequency so that they appeared only once a week or once every ten days.

There is very little entrepreneurial experience in creating semi-private newspapers. In 1999, the semi-private print media market in Uzbekistan consisted of two mixed forms of ownership: private concerns in association with a state body (twelve newspapers) and private concerns in association with one of a number of non-governmental organizations, such as funds, creative unions, or public organizations (seven newspapers). These newspapers are weeklies and are oriented toward advertising, purchased content, or entertainment topics. They are published in narrow geographical areas and target specific cities with specific populations and businesses. Such narrow geographical focus allows the papers to maintain stable circulation and to increase their profit; however, this profit covers only about 50 per cent of expenditure.

In order to make up for the shortage, semi-private newspapers become involved in economic ventures – in other words, commercial firms engage in unrelated business activities. The profits of these firms are then invested in the newspaper. Part of the profit is spent on infrastructure, including computers and communication facilities. The rest is generally used to increase the size of the edition rather than to promote circulation. The extra space is used for advertising which currently fills 70 per cent of newspaper space. For instance, *Biznes Vestnik Voztoka* was initially published in 1991 with only four pages. In 1999, it took up sixty-four pages though it has since been reduced (see the section on Assessment). An informal analysis of ten issues of *Biznes Vestnik Vostoka* (Business Herald of the East) showed that advertisements occupy about fifty-three pages of sixty-four.

The legal status of semi-private and of state newspapers is practically identical. Both need to pass through two registration processes. The state press committee administers the first, in which prospective papers must obtain a license to print, and local authorities which register newspapers as legal entities administer the second. The only difference between the processes lies in the "type" of registration: a semi-private newspaper registers as a business concern while a state newspaper registers as a non-commercial firm. Aside from the licensing process, differences exist in financing the two types of newspapers. Semi-private firms aspire to increase their incomes and extend their market share. Interviews conducted with the editors-in-chief of state newspapers, however, have shown that 75 per cent are not interested in profit and insist on state financing, while only 25 per cent support complete independence and autonomy. These unofficial indicators show that journalists are accustomed to the stability of government funding and are only mildly concerned about then having to conform to government control. Nonetheless, there is a generational segmentation within this sample. Of the 25 per cent favoring greater independence, all editors fall below the age of 30 and have only entered the field recently.

Democratization: international influence on Uzbek print media reform

Foreign investment in the mass media is prohibited in Uzbekistan. Foreign individuals or organizations are forbidden to set up mass media outlets. A unique form of foreign investment comes from grants given to newspapers by foreign foundations, such as the Eurasia Fund, the Soros Foundation, and the Konrad Adenauer Foundation. These grants are targeted mainly at the development of newspapers and the training of journalists in modern methods of operation with civil society reform in mind, not profits.

The foreign development community sponsored by Western governments is primarily interested in having non-governmental media take a greater role in Uzbekistan's civil society. Little foreign aid is channeled to the vast majority of newspapers in the republic which are government-owned. International information and news is very poorly represented on the pages of the Uzbek printed press. Before 1991, all international information was delivered by TASS or APN and occupied up to 40 per cent of newsprint space. In 1999, it comprised only about 5 per cent. In addition, this information is mainly reprinted from

Russian newspapers and from information drawn from foreign embassies in Tashkent.

According to the Master-Press corporation catalog, there are 235 Russian and 195 foreign publications available in Uzbekistan (1999). However, there were only 452 subscriptions in Tashkent and these were primarily placed by organizations and corporations. Private persons constituted only 5 per cent of the subscribers. There is no information available on subscription rates to foreign publications in other regions of Uzbekistan, but subscribers are believed to be very few in number because of the high costs of such subscriptions. For instance, in June 1999 the minimum wage in Uzbekistan was 1,750 soms a month, which is roughly equivalent to US$4; the biannual subscription to Russian newspapers (including *Trud*, *Izvestiya*, and *Komsomolskaya Pravda*) cost 12,000 soms (US$30), more than seven times the minimum wage.

Aside from this factor, language barriers contribute to the low level of subscriptions to the foreign press, except in the case of the Russian language papers, where the subscription level exceeds that of subscriptions to national papers. Two Russian newspapers, *Trud* and *Argumenti i Facti*, are published in Tashkent at the expense of the republic. The circulation of each of these publications is five times that of national publications.

Since 1995, news correspondents from foreign countries have been working throughout Uzbekistan. Before that date, the foreign contingent was mainly Russian since visa exchanges with other countries did not exist and a foreign journalist could work in Uzbekistan only on the basis of an intergovernmental agreement between the host and sender countries. This changed with the ratification of the law "On the protection of the professional work of journalists" in 1997. However, a Chinese news correspondent in Tashkent still works on the basis of a bilateral agreement, "On cultural co-operation," concluded between China and Uzbekistan.

Western media staff interested in collecting and broadcasting news about and throughout Uzbekistan have encountered problems. In 1998, the Uzbekistani government revoked the BBC's medium-wave radio frequency on which were broadcast Uzbek, Russian, and English services. Left with only UKV frequency between 2:00 a.m. and 5:00 a.m., BBC broadcasts are almost impossible to receive within Uzbekistan. According to Yuri Goligorsky of the BBC in London, a sizeable quantity of the BBC's audience was lost when the corporation's 1996 contract was not extended. The government of Uzbekistan blamed technical facilities for the change, but Goligorsky says that the "technical reason does not stand up to scrutiny" (interview, 18 October 2000 by Scott Smith). Radio Free Europe–Radio Liberty (RFE/RL) has experienced similar complications in Uzbekistan (Aziz Djuraev interview, 10 October 2000 by Scott Smith).

Foreign and local investment in Uzbek broadcasting

Aside from advertising income, there have also been direct investments in media. The government does not make public its own budgets and internal allocations, but there have been moderately significant financial investments on the government's part and these have been matched by external donors. In 1999, there was unconfirmed talk of a DM100 million (US$50 million) investment into top-line equipment for thirteen regional state-owned TV stations. Half was directly funded from government budgets while the remainder was said to be donated by a major German company.

In 1997, the state implemented a complex assistance program for the technical restructuring of the national television and radio companies. The funding for this program amounted to US$10 million. Sony Corporation donated US$7 million in broadcasting equipment to Uzbekistan. These figures are significant in terms of bolstering the media's technical infrastructure which was in dire need of modernization; it is likely, however, that, even more than equipment, state-owned media companies are in need of training if their content is to resemble that of modern news, information, or entertainment broadcasters.

An Egyptian television company serialized the film *Prophet* during 1997–1998 as well as a number of other feature films. Since 1992, daily transmissions of Turkish television are broadcast in one and one-half hour slots. Transmissions averaging thirty-five hours per week of Russian informational programs have also been retained. In 1993, the national television and radio company signed an agreement with the Indian television company, Doordarshan, for the exchange of programs that are now delivered weekly in three-hour slots. Doordarshan, as technical provider, has helped to install the satellite antennas for reception of these transmissions.

Since 1996, the US Worldnet television company has been presenting news from the BBC and from CNN and has provided technical assistance to help install satellite antennae. The German television company Deutsche Welle delivers German language learning programs such as "Made in Germany," an economic program with innovative business information, free of charge (*BBC Summary of World Broadcasts* 1999). International broadcast exchanges are less frequent. Uzbekistan is unique among the republics in the CIS because it is not included in the international Mir Interstate Television and Radio Broadcasting Company, established in 1993 in an attempt to unite most of the television companies of the former Soviet republics with the exception of the Baltic states (*BBC Summary of World Broadcasts* 1993). In 1998, the transmission of Kazakh television was terminated. This transmission had been broadcast for four years and for five hours daily on a separate channel. Kazakh journalists provided a more liberated presentation of opinions and the termination may have been a disappointment to many Uzbek viewers.

Uzbek national television is not valued highly by Uzbek society in general. Interview polls carried out in 1997 among editors of regional, district, and urban newspapers show that while 92 per cent of those interviewed watched television, more than half of this sample (65 per cent) preferred to watch Russian television or foreign films.[7] Of those interviewed, 52 per cent stated that although they watched information programs, they watched only the official segments and only if this was connected to their journalistic activities. Eighty-nine per cent expressed a desire for change within Uzbek television.

Cultural diversity and religion: its impact on print media

The largest national minority in Uzbekistan is Russian: 5.5 per cent of a population of over 24 million.[8] In Tashkent, Russians number 37 per cent of the 2.6 million city dwellers. Uzbek print media are published in three languages: Uzbek (88 per cent), Russian (10 per cent), and Tadjik or Kazakh (2 per cent). Up to 80 per cent of national television broadcasts are presented in the Uzbek language. At the regional level, this figure is even greater. Nonetheless, 19 per cent of broadcasts are in Russian.[9]

The main religion in Uzbekistan is Islam. Religion is officially separated from the state. However, the "Islamic renaissance" has had an effect on the development of Uzbekistan during the 1990s. Until 1990, it was generally forbidden to address issues of faith in a broadcast. The demise of the former system of Soviet ideology left a vacuum that has to some extent been filled by religion. The Muslim religion presented a unique mechanism for the protection and transmission of the universal and spiritual values of the national culture. A surge in religious self-consciousness came about during 1990 to 1992 when media considered it necessary to publish material on religious subjects and the number of television and radio broadcasts devoted to religion increased dramatically. In 1992, up to 10 per cent of all national television broadcasts were oriented toward religion.

Assessment

Despite setbacks, reform of mass media has started in Uzbekistan. Until 1987, only 162 newspapers and magazines and two national television channels existed in the republic. As of August 1999, these figures had increased to 495 newspapers, 113 magazines, forty-five television stations, five radio stations, and three separate information agencies. Since independence, a private mass media sector has emerged. Journalists have been released from the control of the totalitarian Soviet system. A wide field of legal resources has developed for mass media, and international contacts between journalists have increased. International organizations have begun to work actively to assist the democratization of the mass media. However, this does not mean that democracy, itself, has been achieved. Qualitative changes in the mass media have proceeded with difficulty. The decline in circulation of periodicals continues. In 1990, the aggregate circulation of all newspapers in Uzbekistan constituted more than 5 million. By 1999, this number had decreased to fewer than 500,000 copies throughout the republic.

The dynamics of the circulation patterns of the main national newspapers are presented in Table 3.1.

While circulation has declined, publishing costs have risen annually by 40–50 per cent. The cost of a national newspaper subscription in the year 2000 is projected to be eight times higher than the standard living wage. One of the most popular semi-independent papers, *Biznes Vestnik Voztoka* (BVV), which used to run to sixty-four pages, has been reduced to sixteen pages. The number of working journalists has also decreased during the period of transition. In 1992,

Table 3.1 Circulation patterns for the six main national Uzbek papers

Papers	1992	1993	1994	1995	1996	1997	1998	1999
Khalq Suzi	85,600	67,305	38,748	31,633	28,263	34,044	34,044	29,161
Pravda Vostoka	85,900	77,200	36,253	21,928	17,133	13,236	12,384	10,500
Uzbekiston Adabiyoti	98,000	86,000	36,597	10,182	6,388	5,646	5,120	6,600
Narodnoye Slovo	25,000	16,400	12,020	11,225	10,100	9,120	8,600	7,680
Turkeston	78,000	51,700	27,428	10,807	9,000	8,500	7,600	7,029
Molodyezh Uzbekistana	15,000	9,400	4,679	3,322	3,100	3,200	2,870	2,190
Uzbekiston Ovozi	148,000	144,200	70,833	34,227	3,100	27,520	21,400	18,554

more than 7,000 were working throughout the republic, in 1999, there were only 4,500. The cause of this decline may be the cuts in staff as well as the declining prestige of the profession and the low pay. Most significantly, however, interest in the print media has declined among readers over the past ten years. An analysis of four Tashkent newspapers has shown that individual subscriptions accounted for approximately 50 per cent of circulation. This indicates that the other 50 per cent are institutional subscriptions which are usually compulsory.

In 1997, the computer retraining center for journalists, Ilkhom, conducted public opinion surveys concerning mass media. In one of the regions of Tashkent interviewers spoke with 1,000 people.[10] These surveys showed that only 12 per cent of those interviewed subscribed to a newspaper and 23 per cent regularly read the press. Of these, more than half read Russian newspapers published in Tashkent.[11] Among those interviewed, 86 per cent stated that they were not interested in reading local newspapers though they were interested in local news as discussed below. These publications are very similar because they are obliged to use the same information source, the state information agency, which dispatches identical reports to all newspapers. Other sources of information simply do not exist because journalists lack the resources to travel. For example, in 1998, only three Uzbek journalists were able to travel abroad in connection with their work.

In 1996, the Ilkhom center conducted an opinion poll of 200 newspaper editors-in-chief regarding the decline in newspaper circulation. An overwhelming majority (97 per cent) considered the cause of the crisis to lie in the absence of mass media financing. In 1999, the opinions of journalists have changed. In informal conversations, they expressed the view that even the strongest financial injections are not capable of making a newspaper modern or interesting.

Within the context of troubled media the situation in the regions is especially of note. Seventy per cent of mass media output originates in the regions, which consist of twelve oblasts in addition to the autonomous Republic of Karakalpakstan. The regions also experienced an initial decline in circulation, but by 1997 the circulation of most newspapers stabilized and even began to grow. For example, in the Namangan area, circulation had fallen to 50 per cent by 1997. Currently, however, more than half of the newspapers produced in this area are now economically viable and no longer require grants. In addition, 100 per cent of circulation consists of individual subscriptions solicited on a voluntary basis, instead of by order of government officials.

An analysis of these newspapers has shown that journalists in the regions have refused to use materials published by the national papers and have, instead, started to utilize concrete information concerning life in their own locale. They have come to the understanding that their market is more interested in local news and events than in national happenings.

There are a number of primary reasons underlying the current media crisis. The government continues to control print and most broadcast media. Practically all newspapers are government owned, and so is state TV which acts as a tool of distributing state propaganda and has no freedom to report independently of government ideology.

Censorship exists institutionally. Both the constitution of the Republic of Uzbekistan and the law on media explicitly state that censorship is not allowed, but the Inspection Agency of State Secrets must approve every article published in all newspapers before publication.

Mass media laws are generally considered well written, but the rule of law is not enforced. Many journalists are not made aware of their legal rights to collect information and write stories critical of the government. Journalists do not appeal to the courts when their professional legal rights are violated because they have no faith in the effectiveness of the legal system to defend them.

No comprehensive system exists for preparing journalists to work according to international standards of professionalism. Those working already continue to practice the same Soviet style of reporting. Aside from the contribution of international donor organizations, the universities training the next generation of journalists are poor in terms of qualified instructors and technical facilities.

Monopolization and a lack of transparent governance significantly impede independent broadcasters from fulfilling their role and conducting business. No representative of non-governmental broadcasters is allowed to hold a seat on the Republic's broadcast commission, the MKK. A representative of state TV does hold a seat, thus creating a monopoly because state TV directly competes with non-governmental TV and radio stations. Furthermore, the MKK does not hold regular sessions and does not announce its closed meetings. Only after meetings are station directors, who must get their licensing approved by the MKK, notified of results. Irregularity and secrecy do not allow for long-term planning and business practices.

The government allows the broadcast licenses of non-governmental TV and radio stations to lapse for a period of several months annually. During this period, stations practice extreme self-censorship for fear that they will not be re-registered or that they may even be closed when the MKK does meet to decide on re-registrations. The consequence of the new law extending re-registration requirements to five years will not be known for a long period of time.

The government does not permit the existence of journalist's unions or media associations that are independent of its control. The union of journalists in Uzbekistan was dissolved in 1996 for playing too active a role in the creation of free speech, and since 1998 the government has refused to register an association of independent electronic mass media (Anesmi). The government created the Political Fund for the Democratization and Support of the Mass Media, but it is not active and as a government creation is more inclined to adhere to government ideology.

Tight restriction on currency conversion makes investment unprofitable to foreign companies which would otherwise buy advertising time on Uzbekistani media. The lack of advertising income means media companies are dependent upon government sponsorship and therefore they are subject to government control. The same restrictions on convertibility prohibit local media companies from transferring hard currency out of the country to purchase modern broadcast and printing equipment. Conversion restrictions impose limits on the import of paper for magazines and newspapers and make broadcast equipment very expensive.

All editors-in-chiefs of national or party and local newspapers are appointed with the approval of the presidential apparatus. Editors of district and urban newspapers are appointed with the approval of local governmental authorities. While it would be incorrect to conclude that this practice always has negative results, it is true in general terms that journalists are selected not for their professional qualities but for their loyalty to the authorities. Furthermore, the guaranteed salaries of journalists negate any stimuli toward independent action.

A law making state TV a company separate from the government has been passed, in theory privatizing it and making it independent of central governmental control. However, no progress in this transformation had been made by the deadline in 2000. The directors of the UzTeleRadio Company are appointed by the presidential apparatus making them answerable to the government.

Technical insufficiencies make Internet and e-mail access nearly impossible for media workers. No foreign magazines and newspapers are made available because of government control of incoming printed materials and their high cost. The result is that journalists in Uzbekistan are isolated from international discourse and have no model for improving their professional standards.

Recommended measures

The overarching problem integral to each point discussed in this chapter is the government's tendency to control information. The leaders of independent Uzbekistan have intensified the Soviet tendency to control information while verbally espousing democratic reform. In light of the long period of Soviet rule and the anti-democratic social system which had prevailed earlier in Uzbekistan and Central Asia, a long-term perspective needs to concentrate on changing this concept, allowing media to play a role as instruments of creating civil society and facilitating the democratic process.

Democracy is a novel concept in Uzbekistan. As important as the cultivation of a media sector consisting of professional journalists and media workers is the education of government administrators whose jurisdiction oversees those media workers. Currently media are not part of the social and governmental system. Authorities do not understand the role of media as functioning to create positive change but rather see media personnel as a threat to their political positions and livelihoods. Attention must be given to changing the concept of the role of media in society among the current cadre of leaders as well as the future leaders and general society. This is a process of reform on which Uzbekistan is just embarking.

Notes

1 Erk held its inaugural constituent assembly in Tashkent on 27 February 1990. The platform included human rights advocacy, the republic's autonomy within the Soviet Union, and inter-ethnic cooperation and friendship (*BBC Summary of World Broadcasts* 1990).
2 Rubin broke into laughter when he mentioned that the only candidate permitted to run against Karimov had said he was going to vote for the incumbent.
3 "On the protection of the professional work of journalists" and "On safeguards and the freedom of access to information" were ratified on 24 April 1997. "On the mass media" was ratified on 26 December 1997.
4 A number of other privately owned stations registered with the government operate irregularly and primarily broadcast pirated programs as well as retransmission of Russian channels. We note their existence, but their role in the transition to a democratic society is marginal. One such station, Channel 30, is the only non-governmental TV station broadcasting in Tashkent that exclusively shows concerts, films and announcements.
5 These estimated figures are calculated at the unofficial exchange rate of US$1 = 800 Uzbek som as of October 2000. There are no official statistics available and station owners will not disclose such information.
6 This and other data in this work were obtained unofficially through the authors' experience and contacts with key officials or informal polling. Official government statistics are typically not made public and, more frequently, no scientifically valid statistics are generated.
7 The Ilkhom Center interviewed 220 people.
8 The population of Uzbekistan is broken down as follows: Uzbek 80%, Russian 5.5%, Tajik 5%, Kazakh 3%, Karakalpak 2.5%, Tatar 1.5%, other 2.5% (*CIA World Factbook* 2000 [1996 estimate]).
9 Until 1992, there was a separate channel for Russian language broadcasts even though another channel provided Russian television translations.
10 The population of Tashkent is over 2 million.
11 *Trud, Argumenti i Facti.*

References

Ahmedova, E. and Saidaminova, Z. (1998) *The Republic of Uzbekistan: A Brief Reference.* Tashkent: Publishing House "Uzbekistan."
Anarbaeva, Khalida (2000) "TV in Every City. Private TV of Uzbekistan," *Central Asian Media Electronic Bulletin*, No. 6, October. Available at: http//:www.camsp.osh.kg.
BBC Summary of World Broadcasts (1990) "New Public Organization in Uzbekistan," 28 February, Wednesday.
—— (1993) "Government Decision on Mir Television and Radio Company," 28 July, for text of the decree No. 642 of the Russian Federation Council of Ministers as published in *Rossiyskaya Gazeta*, Moscow, first edition 24 July 1993 which created the company.
—— (1999) "DW-TV Business Programs reach 'Millions' Worldwide," 24 September, Source: Deutsche Welle press release, Cologne, in German, 20 September.
CIA World Factbook (2000) Washington DC: Central Intelligence Agency. Available at: http://www.odci.gov/cia/publications/factbook/geos/uz.html (cited 13 February 2001).
Commission of Policy of Radio and Television (1995) *Digests of Articles.* Moscow.
Economist Intelligence Unit (EIU) (1999) Business Operations Report, Central Asia; 4th quarter; Chapter 6: Sales and Marketing: 36.
Freedom House Country Report (1998) "Nations in Transit 1998: Uzbekistan." Available at: http://www.freedomhouse.org/nit98/uzbek.html.

Golishev, V. *et al*. (1998) *Reports on Human Measurement: Uzbekistan, 1998*. Tashkent.

Human Rights Watch (2000) "Uzbekistan Human Rights Developments." Paragraphs 1 and 2. Available at: http://www.hrw.org/wr2k/Eca-23.htm (cited 10 October).

Master-Press (1999) Agency catalogue on the press. Tashkent.

Norov, V. (1997) *International Cooperation and the Development of Legislative Bases in the Field of Human Rights*. Tashkent: Jahon.

Office for Democratic Institutions and Human Rights: Organization for Security and Co-operation in Europe (OSCE) (2000) Press Release: "OSCE/ODIHR on Presidential Election in Uzbekistan." Paragraph 2. 11 January. Available at: http://www.osce.org/news/generate.php3?news_id=136 (cited 10 October).

Razzakov, D. (1998) *Digests of Laws on Mass Media: The Fourth Power*. Tashkent: "Uzbekistan."

Republic of Uzbekistan (1995–1997), *Decrees and Governmental Orders*. Tashkent: "Uzbekistan."

Smith, S. (1999) *Uzbekistan: Commentary*: 1999 World Freedom Review Paragraph 4. Available at: http://www.freemedia.at/archive97/uzbekist. htm (cited 13 October 2000).

State Registry of the Press Committee (1991) Uzbekistan Mass Media. State Committee of Press Data. Tashkent.

Tadjikhanov, U. (1997) *Constitutions of the World*. Tashkent.

Tyurikov, V. (1997) *Independent Republic of Uzbekistan*.

Umarakhunov, I. (1998) *The Republic of Uzbekistan and International Contract Law*. Tashkent: Encyclopaedia.

Other material

International Centre for Journalistic Staff Retraining of the "Eurasia" Foundation, "Ilkhom" Creative Center.

Discussions

Special thanks to the following individuals who provided the authors with information and insights into the media in Uzbekistan:

Babajanov, Shukrat, founder and director, ALC TV Urgench.
Djuraev, Aziz, bureau chief, RFE/RL, Tashkent.
Goligorsky, Yuri, BBC London.
Kadisheva, Helen, official, UzPAK (Electronic connection company).
Khakimov, Zafar.
Miralimov, Shavkat, Tashkent administration of the press.
Muminov, Faizulla, Professor and Journalism Faculty Dean, Tashkent State University.

4

INDONESIA

Media and the end of authoritarian rule[1]

Krishna Sen

It is widely acknowledged that "the conduct of democratic (or undemocratic) politics nationally and internationally, depends more and more" on media (McQuail 1994: 1). What is much more contested is exactly how media and political transformation are related, how one phenomenon shapes the other, and what else needs to be taken into account to answer questions about the role of media in the process of democratization.

The question of media and democratization has taken on a certain political urgency as Indonesia emerges from thirty-two years of military domination under General Raden Suharto's *New Order*. This authoritarian regime was established in 1965 and collapsed in May 1998 with the live international telecast of President Suharto's dramatic resignation. Freed from the constraints of state censorship and propaganda, media have moved quickly toward diversity and pluralism. But the end of authoritarianism did not translate into a pluralist democracy as understood in the West.

This account of Indonesia in transition raises questions about how we should understand the role of media in the fall of the New Order and in the chaotic transitional politics of post-New Order Indonesia. In this chapter we can address only the first part: the place of media in the long survival and relatively rapid unraveling of the Suharto regime. This examination will go some distance in explaining what kind of media institutions were inherited from that regime and in what ways media enable and hinder the process of democratization in Indonesia.

Political transition

In 1968, after gradually consolidating his power since the 1965 coup and counter-attack, Suharto replaced Achmed Sukarno as Indonesia's president. Suharto's New Order was established in the place of Sukarno's populist Guided Democracy, which was characterized by charismatic leadership and intense ideological debates. After the turbulent events in the mid-1960s, the New Order effectively barred political activism and even political debates in the name of restoration of order and stability. Western governments and liberal democrats in Indonesia welcomed the end of Sukarno's radical nationalist regime, which had increasingly aligned itself with the Eastern Bloc in the Cold War and isolated itself from the West. In light of this, Suharto legitimized his rule by claiming to save

Indonesia from communism. He also embraced the doctrine of economic development, and ushered Indonesia into a period of remarkable growth and increasing engagement with the Western capitalist economy.

At exactlywhat point the New Order's system of political control began to crack it is difficult to say. From the point of view of economists the decline clearly dates from the Asian financial collapse in 1997, which severely affected Indonesia. The value of the rupiah plummeted against the US dollar, leaving few companies able to service foreign debts, particularly on short-term loans (Hal Hill 1998: 93–103). The domestic financial system was unable to cope and public confidence was undermined by the closure of sixteen banks on 1 November 1997. Suharto agreed to several bail-out packages with the IMF, and then reneged.

However, for political scientists the end of the New Order started somewhat earlier with the banning of three popular news magazines, *Detik*, *Tempo*, and *Editor*, in June 1994. Bans on publications in one form or another had been used throughout the New Order as one of its weapons against free speech. But the 1994 bans generated a sustained, organized campaign of vocal criticism against the government. In an unprecedented drawn-out legal battle, the editor of the most prestigious of the three proscribed publications, *Tempo*, won two court cases challenging the Minister of Information's authority to impose the ban, though finally defeated in the minister's Supreme Court appeal. From this point on, the media were not merely reporting or reflecting political opposition to the New Order, they were in many instances driving the dissent.

In 1996, the downfall of the New Order continued when the government intervened in the activities of one of two so-called opposition parties, the Partai Demokrasi Indonesia (Indonesian Democratic Party, PDI). They ousted the elected leader, Megawati Sukarnoputri, and replaced her with a government appointee. On 27 July, a group reportedly organized by the army attacked the PDI's Jakarta headquarters to recover it from Megawati's supporters. The attack unleashed a public outpouring of anger and resentment at the New Order on a scale unseen since 1974. The resulting looting and havoc spilled down the main boulevards of the capital, and was graphically captured by both domestic and international media.

In the face of this political unrest and in the midst of the worst economic crisis since his accession to power, Suharto was re-elected president for a seventh term in March 1998, by the People's Consultative Council (MPR), also called the "upper house." Both the re-election of Suharto and the make-up of his new cabinet were unacceptable to international markets and Indonesian dissidents because, as always, the MPR had done little more than ritually re-anoint Suharto and the cabinet included his daughter, long-time cronies, and his protégé B. J. Habibie as vice-president. Student protests increased in frequency and intensity. The mood for reform had spread to usually politically conservative professionals and was dramatically demonstrated when hundreds of bankers, entrepreneurs, and financial managers from the Jakarta Stock Exchange took to the streets on 19 May calling for the president to stand aside (*Jawa Pos Online* 1998). The professional middle class created by the New Order's economics was now openly opposed to its politics of cronyism, arbitrariness, authoritarianism, and, above all, financial mismanagement.

Most authors see the transformation that culminated in Suharto's resignation as sudden, as if dissidence suddenly broke through dictatorship. However, in the media sector it is clear that global technological changes on the one hand and the contradictions within the New Order's own policies of political control versus economic growth on the other, increasingly put media beyond state control.

The contradictions became visible with the weakening of the Department of Information, which oversaw anything defined by the Indonesian government as "media". By the end of the New Order "media" meant enormous print media conglomerates, over 700 radio, and five national television channels in addition to the state broadcasters and the newly emerging Internet. As Indonesian scholar Daniel Dhakidae pointed out, the Department of Information was one of the most powerful of the New Order's "state apparati [sic] [...] because of its double role as an *information apparatus* and an economic apparatus" (Dhakidae 1991: 432).

The key tools of the Department of Information's control of media were developed by the early 1970s, and until the mid-1980s the two most important instruments were formal and informal censorship and corporate organization imposed on owners of and workers in the media industry. During the 1980s, however, the Suharto family and cronies bought up large sectors of the Indonesian media industry and thereby exercised control through ownership. The New Order's own policy initiatives eroded the economic facet of the department to such an extent that in the final years of the New Order it could no longer perform its function as an information apparatus. By the end of the New Order, the department, once central to legitimizing the nation and the state, had grown so irrelevant that it was eliminated from the new administrative structures of the post-Suharto government of President Abdurrahman Wahid.

To understand the relationship between media and Indonesia's transition from authoritarianism, we must go beyond the media-specific policies and practices of the government and its functionaries and understand what some media theorists have called the "media ecology" or "mediascape." In brief, this means that we need to take into account the overall national and global context in which media operated in Indonesia, that is, the total policy framework of the national government and the massive shifts in global media technology. The transformation of media under the New Order eventually placed media institutions, technologies, and content beyond the control of the government.

Ordered press

The long and influential history of Indonesia's newspapers and news magazines (compared to the more recently introduced electronic media) and the national requirement that consumers be literate have often enabled the press to set the political agenda more than any other medium.[2] The print media employ more journalists and concentrate more on newsgathering and dissemination than any other medium. In Indonesia, radio and TV newsgathering had been, until recently, primarily the job of the government networks, Radio of the Republic of Indonesia (RRI) and Television of the Republic of Indonesia (TVRI). Despite having a smaller consumer base than the electronic media since at least the 1970s, and more recently without the immediacy of the Internet, the print media have continued to determine what news *is*.[3]

While historically the press in Indonesia played a highly significant political role, this role was not identical to the role of the press in Western democracies. The notion of a non-partisan "fourth estate" press never was persuasive in Indonesia. At the beginning of the twentieth century, with the emergence of a nascent nationalism, the papers critical of the colonial Dutch quickly became the "press of political struggle" (*pers perjuangan*), a collective with a partisan commitment to independence. During the early years of independence President Sukarno dubbed the press a "tool of the Revolution," responsible for energizing and mobilizing public opinion. Political parties became obvious sponsors of the medium. By the early 1960s, most papers were linked with political parties, an arrangement that was formalized by the Ministerial Decision No. 29/SK/M/65, "the Basic Norms for Press Enterprises within the Context of the Promotion of the Indonesian Press," of the Information Minister in March 1965. According to the decision all newspapers were instructed to affiliate formally with a political party, a "functional group," or mass organization.

With the political transition after the coup of 1 October 1965, the New Order government dropped the "revolutionary" rhetoric and charged the press with safeguarding national security against internal and external threats. It was to be the "guardian" of the *Pancasila*, or Five Principles, that formed the foundation of state ideology. The Five Principles are belief in the one and only God, in just and civilized humanity, in the unity of Indonesia, in democracy guided by the inner wisdom of deliberations of representatives, and in social justice for all the Indonesian people.[4] As the "guardian of the *Pancasila*," the press was to be "free but responsible," in contrast to the "liberal" Western press that was seen as libertine and "irresponsible." The forced reduction of all political parties into two uneasy amalgams, the Indonesian Democratic Party (PDI) and the United Development Party (PPP), in 1973 effectively removed political party influence from the press, although the Golkar, the government's electoral organization, retained its *Suara Karya* daily. Instead of representing party interests, the government urged the press to be its "partner" in accelerating development, which meant, in effect, either supporting the government or eschewing political debates. To a large extent editors complied. The few who did not, risked being banned.

The New Order inherited a system of press permits and controls from the closing years of Sukarno's Guided Democracy.[5] Such permits and controls were extended after 1965 to ensure the government had, at all times, the authority to remove publications deemed a threat to security and order. Forty-three of the country's 163 newspapers were banned in the wake of Suharto's rise to power in 1965 (Atmakusumah 1981: 169, fn. 3). In 1974 after the riots of 15 January, twelve publications were banned and several journalists were arrested. Dozens of journalists were blacklisted by the government and barred from subsequent employment in the industry. Similarly, in 1978, after an increasingly truculent press gave sympathetic coverage to student-led protests against the New Order, seven Jakarta dailies and seven student publications were banned as part of a crackdown against students and intellectuals (David Hill 1994: 37–39).

By comparison to the two previous decades there were very few bans or withdrawals in the 1980s of publishing permits, Surat Izin Usaha Penerbitan Pers (SIUPP). Devoid of a political party based readership, papers moved away from political journalism aimed at a particular readership and sought to increase their audiences across all political spectrums. Mass readerships, needed to attract substantial advertising, turned the press from a "message-based" medium into an "audience-based" one (Dhakidae 1991: 74). The persona of the "crusading journalist," the journalist as activist, spawned by nationalism and bred in the open political conflicts of the 1950s and 1960s, receded in the New Order. In any case, partisan politics, except of the distinctly pro-government variety, had itself been de-legitimized during the 1970s through a series of restrictions on students and political parties (Cribb and Brown 1995: ch. 9). The relative absence of media bans contributed to a growing assumption by the beginning of the 1990s that the government was fostering a new political "openness" (keterbukaan), which analysts compared to the Soviet glasnost. But the June 1994 closure of Tempo, Detik, and Editor stood in dramatic contrast to such an idea. Intimidation continued throughout the preparations for the 1997 general election, and in December 1997 the new Minister of Information, Hartono, issued "stern warnings" to fifteen publications during the lead-up to the March 1998 general session of the parliament (MPR) to elect the president for the next five-year term (Jawa Pos 1997).

The bans, sackings, and other forms of government intimidation operated together with a great quantity of formal regulation and the grid of New Order institutions, which monitored and administered the day-to-day functioning of the media industry to minimize the expression of dissent in the content of publications and in the organization of the industry's workforce.

Open markets

Robison, in his now classic Indonesia: the Rise of Capital, analyzed the growth of capitalism in Indonesia under the New Order, including the protection for national capital in particular sectors. The 1966 Basic Press Law (No. 11, Article 13) stated, "The capital of press companies has to be entirely national capital, and all founders and managers have to be Indonesian citizens." The law further stated, "Press companies are prohibited from giving or receiving services, help or contributions to or from foreign interests, except with the agreement of the Government after hearing the opinion of the Press Council." As with every other industry, the emasculation of any form of labor organization further aided the development of corporate structures. Under a 1969 Department of Information ministerial decree, Indonesian journalists were "obliged to become members of an Indonesian Journalists Organization which is authorized (disahkan) by the Government" (Department of Information 1969: ch. 1, article 3). Until June 1998, only one organization, the Indonesian Journalists Association (PWI), was so recognized. The government tightly regulated it, and its leadership often consisted of serving or retired military officers, Golkar functionaries, senior members of the profession who enjoy cordial working relations with the Government, and even owners of publishing houses (David Hill 1994: 67–73). In this context, Dhakidae (1991) and David Hill (1994) have detailed the rise of a

73

"news industry" consisting of large conglomerate press holdings with cross-media ownership and significant investments in other sectors of the economy.

In the mid-1980s, the government began to embrace the rhetoric of deregulation and "market openness" for the Indonesian economy as a whole. Such a move exposed a schism between the Department of Information's long-established practice of regulating the press for ideological reasons and the economic ministries, such as the Department of Industry and Trade, which increasingly recognized the press as a domestic "industry." One key illustration of the tussle between government departments was over the management of newsprint. The regulation of newsprint had been the responsibility of the Department of Information's Press Guidance Directorate, and was implemented in consultation with the Newspapers Publishers' Association (SPS).

Indonesia does not produce much of its own newsprint, and until 1985 regulatory authority over it primarily involved overseeing imports. PT Inpers, a commercial arm of the SPS, exclusively handled newsprint distribution under an agreement between the Department of Industry and Trade and the Department of Information. However, when the Minister for Industry supported domestic newsprint production and the joint venture Korean firm Aspex Paper commenced production in 1985, the Information Department lost some of its hold over the press.[6] Newsprint, the most vital raw material for the press, lost its government subsidies and monopoly distribution and fell increasingly within the purview of the Department of Industry. Thus ideological control in the hands of the Department of Information was being separated from the economics of the industry under a different department.

The policy gap between economic expansion and ideological control became wider in the early 1990s as the free market argument was pitched against the foreign investment prohibitions in the Basic Press Law. Entrepreneurs, who had invested heavily in the press in the early 1990s, desired capitalization, deregulation, and technological sophistication (Bachir 1992).[7] They also called for a relaxation of the SIUPP restrictions to allow the market, not the Department of Information, to determine the viability of their publications.

On 2 June 1994, Government Regulation No. 20, initiated by the key economic ministries, opened up various restricted sectors of the economy, including the media to foreign investment and majority foreign ownership. The Information Minister (then Harmoko), having been excluded from negotiations that affected his portfolio, dissociated himself from the new regulation, asserting that it contradicted superior Indonesian legislation (notably the 1966 Basic Press Law), which explicitly prohibited foreign investment or intervention in the press. For several days, the press reported extensively on the split and inconsistencies between the various acts and regulations concerning foreign investment in media.[8] Eventually Harmoko received President Suharto's support to exclude media from the new policy. On the policy front the Department of Information and content control won, for the moment, over economic ministries and open markets.

The Department of Information faced a more enigmatic and fluid national and international mediascape than it did in the 1960s when it attempted to cordon off the domestic media in the 1990s. The market was blurring national frontiers as media content and capital moved more freely throughout the world.

Powerful financial interests, particularly members and associates of Suharto's own family with investments in television networks and associated satellite technology, managed to evade restrictions on foreign investment in the media through transfers between media and non-media branches within these conglomerates.

In 1997, Hearst Magazines International, part of the giant American-based Hearst Corporation and publishers of the international women's magazine *Cosmopolitan*, started an Indonesian-language edition, *Kosmopolitan*. The new glossy magazine piggy-backed on the publication permit of a languishing health magazine, *Higina*. In a formal adherence to the 1966 Basic Press Law, there were reportedly no foreign shares in the publishing company PT Higina Alhadin, half of which is held by *Suara Pembaruan* (Indonesia's largest evening paper), the other half by Hard Rock Café franchise owners in Indonesia. Instead, PT Higina Alhadin paid Hearst an undisclosed "copyright" fee. *Cosmopolitan*'s English edition had long been on sale in Jakarta (for Rp.21,000 in early 1998), where an estimated 250,000 copies of foreign magazines sold each week.[9] Introduction of the Indonesian edition (at Rp.7,500) meant the world's best known women's magazine, published in thirty-two countries and seventeen languages, had broken financial and language barriers into another populous market (*Wall Street Journal Interactive Edition* 1997; Gatra 1997; Antara 1997).

Openness of the market was not just a one-way move of Western investment and media content into Indonesia. New regional markets were coming into existence. In 1996, the Jawa Pos Group's *Manado Post* began publishing a bilingual English and Indonesian weekly insert, *Polygon News*, targeted at the East ASEAN Growth Area encompassing Brunei, Indonesia, Malaysia, and the Philippines (Haryanto 1997: 54). In 1998, *The Peak*, a Singapore-based English-language bi-monthly magazine regularly targeted the Indonesian business community as readers and sources for advertising revenue. It included Indonesian-language advertising and widespread coverage of Indonesian business and political figures (Media Indonesia Minggu Special 1996: 23). The emergence throughout Southeast Asia of such economic sub-regions provided a more variegated market for newspapers catering to these linguistic and geo-political border zones at the fringes of the nation states.

However, the conflicts between political control and economic expansion were much sharper in the newer audio-visual media, where technology was eroding national borders and making obsolete the mechanisms of censorship and propaganda developed in early years of the New Order.

Broadcast media

When Suharto became president in 1966, radio and television broadcasting in Indonesia were under state control. Television was politically marginal, having been established in 1962 and still available only to a small, wealthy minority in the capital for just a few hours in the evenings. In a nation with high levels of illiteracy, with the film industry in tatters, and television still in its infancy, the incoming government treated radio as its most potent medium for publicity. But over the next decade, television overtook radio as the state's primary ideological medium. There were two primary forces at play. First, television viewership expanded rapidly through the 1970s due both to rising national prosperity and to specific government initiatives. Secondly, radio was privatized and became redefined from its earlier status as the vector of national politics to a local medium of entertainment. Government policies and practices of the 1970s left radio largely outside state control, and the New Order's bid for a state-based televisual cover over the citizenry ultimately failed.

Radio

In the broad sweep of modern Indonesian history, arguably, there have been three moments of dramatic political watershed: independence in 1949, establishment of the military dominated New Order in 1965, and in 1998 the end of the New Order. In each of these moments, radio was a technology of ideological guerrilla warfare. Indeed, in the first two it was *the* medium of resistance.

The Indonesian republican government, first established in Yogyakarta in 1945, with Jakarta still under the control of the Dutch, opted for the Japanese occupation model of radio. Under the Dutch colonial regime, radio broadcast had been in private hands, mainly Dutch, but also Chinese and indigenous. In 1945, however, the state radio network, Radio Republik Indonesia (RRI), was established as a consortium of eight local stations formerly in the Japanese-controlled network. RRI would remain the only broadcaster until the mid-1960s. In its early years RRI played a major role in keeping the nation and the international community informed about the struggle for independence.

Domestically, radio remained a vital communication tool for the young nation as figures for radio ownership rose rapidly to about half a million licensed sets by the mid-1950s. Radio was used extensively in education, especially political education, such as preparing the electorate for the country's first general elections in 1955. By 1965 there were thirty-nine RRI stations around the country, broadcasting to more than a million licensed radios (McDaniel 1994: 218).[10] Major towns received both national and regional programming of the RRI. News and other designated special broadcasts were compulsorily relayed to all RRI stations around the country from Jakarta. But beyond this, regional stations were able to accommodate programming both in local languages and of local origin. With no television (until 1962), low literacy levels, and a relatively diverse and free press, the RRI was the state's primary and most centralized medium for mobilizing public opinion.

The influence of RRI must have been clear to all sides in the coup and counter-coup of 1965. In the early hours of 1 October, a small group of young officers under the leadership of Lieutenant-Colonel Untung kidnapped six generals and set in motion momentous changes that brought Suharto to power. The first public buildings occupied by Untung's troops on 1 October were the RRI and the telecommunications centers on Jakarta's central Merdeka Square. Untung's first public action was a radio broadcast announcing that a plot by the "Council of Generals" to overthrow the president had been foiled. When, less than twenty-four hours later, Major-General Suharto's forces recaptured RRI's Jakarta studios, he too broadcast his assumption of personal command over the army on RRI.

Radio, not just RRI, was significant in legitimating Suharto's rise to power in 1965. The political instability and dissatisfaction with government radio had fostered the growth of a bevy of hobby radio stations in the early 1960s, sometimes little more than a handful of individuals operating from a private residence. Some of these became more directly politicized after the incidents of 1 October 1965 and were staffed round-the-clock by bands of student activists opposed to President Sukarno. While technically illegal, such anti-communist and anti-Sukarno broadcasts were not just condoned but also actively aided by ascendant factions of the military. Despite low transmission power and very limited audience reach, the existence of "hundreds of 'unofficial' stations ... on the air in the vicinity of the capital alone" (McDaniel 1994: 223) effectively broke RRI's monopoly control over broadcast information and interpretation of the fluid politics of the time. For instance, one of the well-known student stations, Radio Ampera, chose to broadcast its leading news commentaries at 7 pm, precisely the time of the RRI evening news, thereby forcing listeners to choose. The student stations also flaunted RRI's ban on certain types of Western pop music by broadcasting popular songs from prohibited Western bands like the Beatles and the Rolling Stones. The strategy drew young listeners to the fledgling non-government radio in droves. RRI never regained its monopoly of the airwaves.

As Indonesian politics was transformed during the late 1960s, so was radio, as an industry and a cultural and political medium. In 1967, the New Order tried to regularize the non-government broadcasters by separating small hobby stations from those that were by now more formally established broadcasters. In 1968, soon after being confirmed in power as full president, and no longer needing the support of students, Suharto ordered a crackdown to limit campus-based and other student stations. But given the active role private radio had played in the anti-Sukarno propaganda, the New Order had little option but to allow their continuation in some form. In 1970, private radio stations were legalized. The following year the New Order government attempted to curb their political role by obliging the now legalized private broadcasters to relay RRI newscasts and by restricting permissible transmission area and broadcast content.

During the 1970s there was strong growth in commercial stations, so that, over the next decade or so, non-government broadcasting became synonymous with commercial stations. Local governments were also permitted to set up their own stations outside the central government's control. While the monopoly of the Jakarta government over the airwaves was thus broken, with hindsight, many of the former student activists came to see the legalization of private radio as a means of controlling and restricting the function of radio by defining it as an apolitical, entertainment medium.

As part of legalizing private radio, the 1970 government regulation on Non-Government Radio Broadcasting laid out the criteria for establishing a non-government radio broadcasting enterprise and provided the framework for the New Order's radio policy. The "social function" of radio was described as "education, information, and entertainment" and programs were "not to be used . . . for political activities." Foreign investment (or donation) was prohibited. Station owners had to be Indonesian citizens who had not been involved in the banned Communist Party of Indonesia (PKI), and were not office-bearers in any political party or mass organization. More contentiously (and ignored in practice), broadcasts had to be based on written script, held as documentation and noted in a daily log. Licenses were issued for one year and were renewable. Initially, the Department of Communications, and since 1983 the Department of Tourism, Post, and Telecommunications, had responsibility for the technical aspects of broadcast, particularly the allocation of frequencies.[11] The monitoring of content to ensure "security and public order" was the responsibility of the military's Command for the Restoration of Security and Order (KOPKAMTIB) and the Department of Information. Over the years, however, the Department of Information came to be seen as principally responsible for all aspects of radio other than the allocation of broadcast frequency.

A Directive of the Minister of Information No. 39/KEP/MENPEN/1971 issued in 1971 emphasized the local moorings of radio, stating, "a broadcast is local, not national, in character," and that the "nature, content and purpose of a broadcast reflects the local relationship with the conditions and growth of the area reached by the broadcast."[12] After 1982 shortwave broadcast by private radio was phased out. Stations opted increasingly for the AM and, from 1987, FM bands, with clearer transmission over shorter distances.[13] Government regulation stipulated maximum transmitter power, which limited the broadcast area to about 100 kilometers for FM and approximately 30–400 kilometers for AM stations (Lindsay 1997: 105–123, particularly p. 114, fn. 40).[14]

The governance of these local and private stations also increasingly fell within the purview of provincial governments, which, by the end of the 1970s, through Ministerial Directive SK No. 24/KEP/MENPEN/1978 and the Appendix, had the authority to vet any foreign-sourced broadcast material and to determine which of the broadcasts from RRI Jakarta had to be relayed by private stations in accordance with the interests of the region concerned. Further government regulations, such as Instruction of the Director General of Radio, Television, and Film, No. 09/INSTRK/DIRJEN/RTF/78, emphasized that non-government stations should give priority to programs "whose materials are drawn from local regional cultures" and "whose broadcast materials originate domestically and are appropriate to local conditions." The overall effect of such regulation was to emphasize that private radio was a *local* medium, over which provincial authorities, armed with the capacity to terminate licenses, held considerable power.

In the early 1980s a number of measures eroded the control that provincial governments held over private stations within their regions. In 1984, the Department of Information specified the exact amount of news that private stations across Indonesia were obliged to relay and the provincial government was required to enforce a "prevailing code of ethics in accordance with the etiquette and values of the *national* character" (emphasis added). Moreover, "the use of materials which originate from abroad, in whatever form" had to be centrally approved by the Director General of Radio, Television, and Film (in this case, the Director of Radio) in Jakarta.[15] After 1987, annual license renewals for private stations had to be approved centrally by the Directorate General of Radio, Television, and Film of the Department of Information. Many small, private stations tried to operate without a license, mainly because annual renewal was expensive, but also for political reasons. In 1996, over half of the private stations in Aceh, a location experiencing a separatist war since the early 1990s, were found to be operating without a proper license.

By the 1990s, despite explicit government bans on both of these activities, powerful business houses in Jakarta, particularly those of the members of the president's family, were attempting to create radio networks and forging conglomerate cross-media ownerships. The first family's hold over radio was also extended through manipulation of the industry organization, the Commercial Radio Broadcasters' Association (PRSSNI), which was established in 1974. As was the common New Order practice with industry bodies, in 1977 the Minister of Information formally declared PRSSNI the sole recognized association for private radio stations, and all private stations were obliged to join.[16] In 1985, a Directive from the Minister of Information SK No. 245/KEP/MENPEN/1985 explicitly stated that the organization was to "assist the Government in the development and supervision/surveillance (*pengawasan*) of Private Radio Broadcasters in Indonesia." In 1989, in a further step to ensure its responsiveness to the regime, President Suharto's daughter Siti Hardiyanti Rukmana ("Tutut") was elected Chairperson of the PRSSNI. She was appointed in defiance of existing legislation forbidding office bearers in political parties from owning private stations and therefore playing any role in the industry organization. Her position was legalized in 1997 with passage of the Broadcast Bill that superseded previous legislative restrictions in this matter. Tutut relinquished her control of the PRSSNI only in October 1998 after her father's fall from power. Also, in the 1990s Tutut and Bambang, the main media players among the Suharto children, started to acquire radio stations, although their holdings (about half a dozen between them) remained necessarily small in the highly diverse radio industry.

Despite such increased reach of Jakarta's governmental and commercial arm in the last decade of the New Order, in practice and in government policy radio remained a much more "local" medium than either film or television. On the whole, unlike television, commercial radio licenses were issued largely on a commercial basis and without centralized political interventions. The 1997 Broadcast Bill, while noting the different spans of broadcast (local, provincial, regional, national) that were permissible for private television stations, re-stated that radio broadcast was always restricted to the area in the vicinity of the station.

National or local government censorship and surveillance of broadcast was not particularly effective. With little capacity to monitor directly the highly diverse products of a regionally and financially dispersed industry, the government depended on the industry's self-restraint, and the capacity of PRSSNI to ensure this self-censorship particularly at moments of political crisis. The organization frequently acted as the conduit of government instructions and restrictions regarding broadcast content to the radio stations. But such attempts at propaganda and censorship, which could not be backed up with surveillance, were never fully heeded by every station. Even the general ban on private stations producing "news" was avoided under the guise of broadcasting "information programs." Student demonstrations could get reported under the cover of local traffic reports (for example, a report announcing that demonstrators had blocked off certain roads). Nor did the stations keep records of their broadcasts though repeatedly instructed in a variety of government regulations to do so. Such defiance and the immediacy and transience of radio broadcast made both pre-censorship (which was effectively used in the film industry) and post-publication censorship (used with some effect in the publishing industry) ineffective as means of controlling radio.

Pursuing popular ratings and hard-won advertising money, many radio stations by the mid-1990s had started "talkback" programs. Such programming was illegal since radio stations were prohibited from transmitting anything from outside the studios. All kinds of live broadcasts, including talkback, became very popular. In some instances the local military commanders actively protected and encouraged the illegal talkback broadcasts as they perceived these to be one of the few means they had of access to popular opinion. In the final few weeks of Suharto's reign many of the popular stations constantly monitored public opinion by encouraging listeners to ring in and offer views of the political mood of their immediate surroundings. Three days prior to Suharto's resignation, one Bandung radio station, for instance, asked its listeners to wear a white ribbon to indicate their demand for Suharto's resignation. Within hours a listener delivered meters of ribbon to the station and for the next few days the station was inundated with phoned-in accounts of white ribbons around the city.

In 1965, radio as an extension of popular opinion among students helped legitimate the New Order in its early years. In 1998, radio had become far more widespread and had remained a conduit for the expression of opinion from the streets, campuses, middle-class suburbs, small towns, and even slums against an isolated regime in Jakarta. The simplicity of the technology, the relatively low rate of investment needed and profit generated, and the New Order's policy of keeping radio bound to localized communities (thereby restricting both political reach and economic potential) colluded to make this the medium least susceptible to centralized control from the government or the business elite in Jakarta.

Television

The first independent government of Indonesia had depended on state-owned radio as its primary means of communication with the population. The break-up of that singular broadcast voice in the multiplicity of private radio was a symptom, if not a cause, of the end of Sukarno's populist but authoritarian rule. For the Suharto period, television played a similar role. For most of the New Order the state invested in the extension of state-owned monopoly television into the far corners of the nation. In the last decade of its rule the state's domination of the audio-visual landscape was to be seriously challenged in part due to changing technology, but ironically also due to the corrupt practices of Suharto's own family.

Though television was established in 1962, it became significant in Indonesian culture and politics only in the early years of the New Order, beginning in 1965. That year, TVRI was broadcasting for only about three hours in the evenings with only one relay station outside Jakarta, in Yogyakarta. The real growth in television in Indonesia started in the 1970s. New regional stations were added rapidly, mainly relaying Jakarta programs. In 1976, with the help of American technology, Indonesia launched a domestic broadcast satellite, Palapa, followed in 1983 by the more powerful "Generation B" Palapa. The satellite reduced "variations in the broadcast of news and information programs between the regional stations of the TVRI" (Pusat Penelitian Dan Pengembangan Media Massa 1980–1981: 8). It also speeded up, expanded, and regularized the flow of information throughout the Indonesian territory. In 1983, an Integrated Programming Pattern (*Pola Acara Terpadu*) was instituted with all programming for all stations annually pre-determined in the Jakarta headquarters of TVRI. In effect, regional stations became relay stations for TVRI Jakarta. The "obligatory relay" (*wajib* relay) category constituted only about two or three hours a day (a decreasing proportion as the broadcast hours increased). But the budgets of regional stations rarely allowed their programming to exceed 15 to 20 per cent of total airtime. A very small amount of regional programming circulated nationally, and this was always mediated through Jakarta and never exchanged directly between regional stations. Since the mid-1970s all regional stations had a local news segment, but hardly any of this programming ever got into national circulation. Jakarta, not just state television, had the monopoly over the most universally watched and most overtly political part of television broadcast – news.

As in many other parts of Asia, individual ownership of television sets expanded rapidly. By the time the second satellite was launched, the overwhelming majority of the urban population had access to television. The television system, which the New Order state attempted to create on the back of the expansion of the new satellite technology, was highly centralized. As Kitley has suggested: "The fragmented, far-flung archipelago [was] unified in a seamless electronic net which annihilates space and imposes its own time, drawing the vastness and diversity of Indonesia into a whole, structuring for the periphery a clear and constant fix on the center" (Kitley 1997: 92).

However, even after the launch of the more powerful satellite in 1983 and with over 100 relay stations, TVRI broadcast, by its own estimates, covered only about 35 per cent of the nation's land mass and some 65 per cent of the population. Even on the small densely populated island of Java, there were "blind-spots" where TVRI signals could not reach.

In the early 1980s the parabola antennae arrived in Indonesia and created a new problem for Indonesia's television policy. From around 1983 parabola antennae for receiving satellite television broadcasts mushroomed across the skyline of Jakarta's wealthy suburbs, and started spreading to other metropolitan cities. Everywhere in Asia, the coming of satellite-transmitted television programs had generated a new bout of anxiety about Western cultural imperialism. While neighboring states like Singapore and Malaysia moved quickly to ban domestic use of parabola antennae, the decision was much more complicated for Indonesia. The same parabola antennae that threatened to allow foreign broadcasts to permeate national boundaries also held the promise of extending Indonesian national television broadcasts to the corners and pockets of the archipelago, beyond TVRI's terrestrial signal range. In 1986, the government officially declared an "open sky" policy, permitting private and residential use of parabola antennae, which were in any case already in use in many cities by this time. The Department of Information and some regional military commands proceeded to provide isolated rural communities with parabola antennae to enable them to pick up TVRI signals. The Decree of the Minister for Tourism, Post, and Telecommunications, Republic of Indonesia, No. KM 49 Year 1986, on Parabola Antenna Reception of Television Broadcast legalizing parabola antennae also instructed that this use be restricted to receiving broadcasts from the national Palapa satellite.[17] But no one pretended that the angle of the antennae could actually be policed. In any case, foreign programming was available on Palapa itself. By the late 1980s fifteen transponders were in use for non-Indonesian channels including Southeast Asian public broadcasts and international operations like NBC, STAR and CNN broadcasting to Southeast Asia, earning the Indonesian government substantial revenues (Atkins 1995: 25).

Indeed, even without a parabolic device, residents on the east coast of North Sumatra and in West Kalimantan received spillover broadcasts from Singapore and Malaysia. There are no definitive estimates of the proportion of population that had access to these broadcasts, but internal research by the Department of Information produced worrying data that "in one province only forty-one per cent of the respondents watched TVRI, while fifty-eight and one-half per cent watched broadcasts from Malaysian television" (Gayatri 1996). Jakarta's televisual monopoly over Indonesia was under threat.

More importantly, by the mid-1980s the large business conglomerates, created by rapid economic growth, international factors, and corrupt political promotion of particular groups of capitalists, were jockeying for a share of the potentially lucrative Indonesian television market. Ideological interests of the New Order may well have required a government monopoly over television. But the economic interests of the first family demanded privatization of television.

The first private station, RCTI, belonged to Bambang Trihatmojo, President Suharto's third child, at the helm of the powerful Bimantara business group, which held extensive interests in primary and manufacturing industries. RCTI started in 1987 as pay television, but in August 1990 it was permitted to broadcast free to air. Television quickly became the most prominent of Bimantara's wider moves into communication hardware (electronics and telecommunications) and software (newspaper, magazines, television programming). In 1989, Surya Citra Televisi (SCTV), the second private channel, went to air from Surabaya, the capital of East Java and Indonesia's second largest city, and soon afterward opened a second station in Bali. Henri Pribadi, an ethnic Chinese businessman with a long association with Suharto's cousin, Sudwikatmono, who owned the remaining 20 per cent, reportedly controlled 80 per cent of the company shares. The third private channel, Televisi Pendidikan Indonesia (Indonesian Education Television, TPI), was launched in December 1990, renting TVRI transmission facilities. Initially it was restricted to a four-and-a-half hour educational broadcast in the morning, but quickly expanded to eight hours, with only 38 per cent educational content (P. T. Cipta Televisi Pendidikan Indonesia n.d. possibly 1992: 4). Suharto's eldest daughter Tutut owned most of TPI.

TPI's declared profile as an educational channel, run by a purportedly non-profit organization, had allowed it to claim national broadcast via TVRI stations, whereas the other two channels, RCTI and SCTV, were initially restricted to Jakarta and Surabaya. Within a year of going to air, TPI's advertising revenue had overtaken RCTI's organization. TPI's national access and consequent advertising advantage quickly became another element in the public family business rivalry. In 1993, a further deregulation allowed private channels to broadcast throughout Indonesia via the Palapa satellite, so that they could henceforth be received throughout the country and beyond by parabola antennae.

The last two stations, AN-TeVe (which started broadcasting in 1993) and Indosiar (in 1995) were national networks as soon as they were launched. Indosiar was part of the Salim group, one of the largest ethnic Chinese business conglomerates, headed by Lim Sioe Liong, President Suharto's longest standing Chinese associate. AN-TeVe (Cakrawala Andalas Televisi) was to be restricted to West Sumatra according to its initial permit, but in fact, like all the other stations, operated from Jakarta. It was owned in part by the Bakrie group (whose business fortunes pre-date the New Order) and partly by Agung Laksono, closely associated with the Golkar, the New Order's political and organizational vehicle for winning elections.

This powerful group of entrepreneurs resisted all attempts by the Department of Information to restrict their reach in any way at all. This tension was clearest in 1996–1997 as the Parliament completed Indonesia's first Broadcast Bill, which the president refused to sign. This was the first time that the president returned a bill for reconsideration. It was widely reported that the key contention was the bill's requirement that no station transmit to any more than 50 per cent of the national population, which was unacceptable to the industry. Some months later, Harmoko, the long-serving Minister of Information (1983–1997) was replaced. The new minister, Hartono, a close political associate of Tutut, criticized this restrictive provision of the bill, and Parliament obliged by removing the offending clause. Suharto finally signed the bill in October 1997, his last important intervention in the formation of media institutions in Indonesia.

State television, without the financial resources of the private sector, and habituated to an unimaginative didactic programming, rapidly lost its audience to private television. Some surveys showed that, apart from the three evening news bulletins, which were relayed by all of the stations, usually simultaneously, TVRI's audience share had fallen to 6 per cent in the major cities.

Controlling content

The Department of Information tried to control the content of private television partly through a series of regulations obliging the stations to promote various aspects of the New Order's ideology and partly by extending to television the system of film censorship inherited from colonial rule and made more draconian under Suharto. In 1990, a Ministerial Decree required that television programming should support the 1945 Constitution and Pancasila, the state ideology, and "avoid issues that might give rise to SARA conflicts." The term SARA was coined to refer to anything likely to exacerbate tensions based on ethnicity (*suku*), religion (*agama*), race (*ras*) or between social groups or classes (*antar golongan*). Further, all programs were obliged to "support national development plans in accordance with government policy, both domestic and foreign" and they must "be arranged with full regard to good manners and in Indonesian language that is true and correct (*baik dan benar*)." Finally, according to Ministry of Information Decree No. 111 from 1990, programming must avoid "all possibility of becoming a channel for the spread of foreign ideology or culture which could weaken the national character and national defense."

As with the film industry, the government's Board of Film Censorship (BSF) was responsible for ensuring the implementation of content regulations. In 1993, the Board of Film Censorship, was recast as an autonomous body, the Institute of Film Censorship (Lembaga Sensor Film, LSF), ostensibly to be more open and accountable to the community, but in effect became a dumping ground for retired bureaucrats.[18] The LSF had two viewing rooms in operation for six hours each, five days a week, for staff to look at all film, video, and television broadcast material. The massive task would have involved reviewing, on average, about eighteen hours of broadcast from each private station (not including approximately two hours of TVRI relay) seven days a week, plus annually around 300 films and videos of various types and lengths.[19] Clearly this censorship institution created for an older medium and not supported with additional resources was simply not up to the task, given the enormous increases in the amount of audio-visual material. Many television programs (such as game shows or talk shows) were almost impossible to pre-censor in any case. Also, unlike films, which are re-checked by provincial authorities before release in each province, it was impossible to re-check in the provinces television signals that were relayed simultaneously throughout the country.

The government was most concerned that it maintain the ability to dictate the content of television news. As with private radio stations, private television broadcasters were not only barred from producing news, but were obliged to relay TVRI's national news broadcast from Jakarta. The central TVRI produces four half-hour news programs daily. The national news at 19:00 and the international news at 21:00 had to be relayed at the same hour on all channels, barring exceptional circumstances such as ongoing direct telecast of a major event via satellite. The TVRI late news, which closes its daily program, was generally relayed with a few hours' delay by the commercial stations.

Commercial stations quickly started to follow the practice of private radio in casting their own news under the guise of "information." All commercial stations had at least one such evening bulletin, before the news at 19:00, some with high ratings. In 1995, the private stations were formally permitted to produce their own news. Sen and Hill have argued that the nature of the private station bulletins, while in content remaining supportive of the New Order government, nonetheless began to transform the nature of the television news bulletin in Indonesia (Sen and Hill 2000). Such differences in news style became politically significant in the final weeks of Suharto's rule in the private channels' drive for good footage of demonstrations. Sections of the government were anxious about the constant moving images of student campuses in city after city, close-ups of the faces and banners of the protesters, letting students on one campus know what was going on in another, and letting rioters in one city know what could be achieved in another. The army clearly read the private stations' coverage of the events as unacceptable. On 16 May, the week before Suharto's resignation, the office of General Wiranto (then commander-in-chief) informed the Minister of Information that the army would shut down all private television stations unless their news coverage of the protesters could be brought into line. The Director General of Radio, Television, and Film moved to impose the TVRI model on all television. Private stations were instructed not to send their cameras to cover riots and student demonstrations, except as part of a team led by a TVRI camera crew.

It was a final and ineffective attempt to displace close-up pictures of chaos with modulated longshots taken by the national broadcaster.

The New Order government's grip over television and its audiences had been eroding since the 1980s, through a variety of technological and economic factors. Privatization, under the control of a few hand-picked from around the presidential palace, had been expected to deliver to the regime an audience that was tuning out of state television. But the very expansion of the televisual sphere loosened the hold of the state over it. Born in an atmosphere of competition, not only against each other, but in part also against international providers such as CNN, the BBC and so on, private television's programming was honed to a quite different purpose: getting audiences to advertisers. In a time when political dissent against the Suharto leadership was increasingly fashionable among the middle classes, including media professionals, economics dictated distance from official voices, notwithstanding the owners' closeness to the regime.

Conclusion

This account of the media in Indonesia suggests some clear directions in its development in the New Order during 1965–1998. The media was commercialized and its products grew both in quantity and in variation. By the 1990s, the amount of media images and messages and the variety of sources were simply enormous compared to what had been available in 1965. The situation had arisen partly through the New Order's own policy of economic growth and partly through global technological changes. While the New Order government needed to keep a tight rein on the political discourse in the media, it was also under growing pressure for both internal and external reasons to open the lucrative media business to private investment. The content on the vast, and commercialized, technologically diversified media was eventually beyond the state's control. The media chased audiences, who by the late 1990s were the disenchanted citizens of a state in financial ruin. Deliberately depoliticized in the early years of the New Order, the Indonesian media ironically returned to politics largely for commercial reasons of giving the consumers what they wanted. In the sense that commercialism and technological developments in the end colluded against state censorship, the Indonesian media in the 1990s contributed to the fall of a dictatorship which had lasted for three decades.

However, the end of authoritarianism has not translated into a stable electoral pluralist democracy. Freed from constraints of censorship, with the legal bases of a democratic system not yet laid, the new freedoms of the media are being interpreted as a license to have a say and make a profit. In a travesty of the very idea of a free press, one of Indonesia's most successful media companies is publishing two dailies in the war-torn Maluku province – one for each religious side in the civil war. In this context, optimistic projections about cultural diversity and political democracy founded on privately owned, politically unfettered media, need to be tempered.

Notes

1 The arguments and data in this chapter are taken from Sen and Hill (2000). Thanks to David Hill also for editing this piece.

2 For histories of the Indonesian press, see Ahmat (1995); Smith (1969); Lee (1971); David Hill (1994); and Hanazaki and Terjebak (1998).

3 In 1996, there were 283 newspapers and magazines of all kinds in Indonesia, with a total circulation per edition of about 13.5 million copies, of which the 165 daily and weekly newspapers amounted to about 8.5 million copies. There were an estimated 40 million radio sets, and 20 million televisions, the latter reaching an estimated audience of 100 million (Subakti and Katoppo 1996: 27–29). One recent Minister of Information appeared to believe the discrepancy was even greater, having stated in early 1997 that radio reaches 95% of the population and "electronic media" (in this context, presumably meaning "television") reaches 75–80% (*Kompas Online* 1997a)

4 Paraphrased slightly from Department of Information 1992: 38. For a partial translation of Sukarno's initial formulation, "The Birth of the Panca Sila," see Feith and Castles (1970: 40–49). For a discussion of the "New Order" reinterpretation, see Morfit (1981: 838–851).

5 Under its powers after the martial law declaration of 14 March 1957, the Supreme War Command (Peperti) issued Regulation No. 10 (Peraturan Peperti No. 10/1960) in 1960 specifying the obligations of press publications. These were reinforced in a 1963 Presidential Directive (Penpres No. 6/1963), which required papers and magazines to hold a publication permit. This directive was only withdrawn with the passing of the 1966 Basic Press Law (UU No. 11), which stated (in Article 20) that "for a transitional period" publishers required a Publication Permit (Surat Izin Terbit, SIT), obtainable from the Department of Information. In 1982, legislation was passed to replace the SIT with a Press Publication Enterprise Permit (Surat Izin Usaha Penerbitan Pers, SIUPP); this change was implemented two years later. From 1965 until 1977 an additional Printing Permit (Surat Izin Cetak, SIC) had to be obtained from the military security authority, KOPKAMTIB.

6 When Aspex Paper was established, 20% of the shares were held by PT Aspek, with the remainder held by Tecwin Trading Co Ltd, Hong Kong (Dhakidae, "The state, the rise of capital ... , p. 509, fn. 145, citing Tambahan Berita Negara RI, 25-10-1985, No. 86). Industry observers believe that Yoga Soegama, former head of the military intelligence body BAKIN, was originally the figure behind the Indonesian shareholding, but that timber magnate and Suharto confidante, Mohammad "Bob" Hasan, subsequently obtained the Indonesian interest (confidential interview, 13 January 1998), Suryana, Sekretaris Tim Kertas Koran SPS, telephone conversation Perth–Jakarta.

7 On Soetrisno Bachir's media interests, see David Hill (1994: 97–98).

8 On Government Regulation No. 20 and the media coverage, see for example, *Detik* (1994: 4–12); *Tempo* (1994: 28–30); and *Kompas* (1994: various articles).

9 Foreign magazine sales estimate by Leo Batubara, Secretary-General of the Indonesian Publishers Association (SPS), cited in Dwidowijoto (1997).

10 McDaniel makes the point that statistics on licensed radios considerably underestimate actual usage since many owners may seek to avoid paying the license fee.

11 In 1982, the responsibility for allocation of broadcast frequency was devolved to the Director General of Post and Telecommunications. In the new cabinet formed in 1983 that directorate was moved from the Department of Communications to the Department of Tourism, Post, and Telecommunications.

12 Surat Keputsan Menteri Penerangan Republik Indonesia Nomor 39/KEP/MENPEN/ 1971 tentang Petunjuk-Petunjuk Umum tentang kebijaksanaan penyelenggaraan acara serta isi siaran bagi radio siaran non-pemerintah, Bab II Ketentuan-Ketentuan Khusus, Pasal 4, Sifat Siaran, paragraphs (1) and (2).

13 Laws and regulations concerning radio broadcasting appear in PRSSNI 1995 and PRSSNI 1992.

14 These stipulations are widely disregarded, with Lindsay noting that, while FM transmitters should be no more than 100 watts, "most FM stations broadcast with at least 5 kilowatt transmitters, and some as much as 20 kilowatt."

15 In 1987 the Director General of Radio, Television, and Film, in an attempt to stem the establishment of national radio networks, ruled that "bodies operating non-government radio stations are not permitted to open branches or agencies, whether using the same company name or a different company name." In addition, perhaps to stop stations being linked into larger non-radio conglomerates, he ruled, in SK No. 226/KEP/MENPEN/1984, Article 6.3, that "bodies operating non-government radio stations are not permitted to engage in other types of businesses apart from activities linked to the social function of broadcast radio itself."

16 At this time the name of the organization was slightly changed, with "Niaga" (Commercial) being replaced by "Nasional" (National).

17 Like radio and the Internet, responsibility for the television broadcast system lay with the Department of Tourism, Post, and Telecommunications (Deparpostel).

18 In its 1996 membership there was not one person born since 1955, and several born in 1925!

19 In the financial year 1996–1997, the Institute claimed to have "censored 68 national commercial films and 184 imported commercial films, 78 national non-commercial films and 58 imported non-commercial films" plus "6,865 national commercial and non-commercial video films, and 10,478 imported commercial and non-commercial videos" (Department of Information 1998: 223).

References

Ahmat, B. Adam (1995) *The Vernacular Press and the Emergence of Modern Indonesian Consciousness* (1855–1913), Southeast Asia Program, Cornell University.

Antara (1997) "Ada kemungkinan artikel Indonesia terbit di luar negeri," 6 August, posted on Indonesia-p on 6 August.

Article 19, Indonesia: Freedom of Expression and the 1997 Elections (1997) Article 19/Forum-Asia, London: 11–16.

Atkins, William (1995) *Satellite Television and State Power in Southeast Asia: New Issues in Discourse and Control*, Centre for Asian Communication, Media and Cultural Studies, Edith Cowan University, Perth: 25.

Atmakusumah (1981) Kebebasan Pers dan Arus Informasi di Indonesia, Jakarta: Lembaga Studi Pembangunan: 169, fn. 3.

Bachir, Soetrisno (1992) "Bisnis Pers di Tengah Arus Globalisasi," *Kompas*, 10 February.

Cribb, Robert and Brown, Colin (1995) *Modern Indonesia: A History since 1945*, Longman, London and New York: Chapter 9.

Department of Information (1969) Ministerial decree No. 02/PER/MENPEN/1969, chapter 1, article 3.

—— (1992) *Indonesia: An Official Handbook*, Indonesian Department of Information, Jakarta: 38.

—— (1998) *Indonesia 1998: An Official Handbook*, Jakarta: 223.

Detik (1994) 8–14 June: 4–12.

Dhakidae, Daniel (1991) "The state, the rise of capital and the fall of political journalism: Political economy of Indonesian news industry," Unpublished doctoral dissertation, Cornell University, Ithaca: 432.

Dwidowijoto, Riant Nugroho (1997) "Pers Indonesia 2020," *Kompas Online*, 23 April (posted on indonesia-p@indopubs.com, 22 April).

Feith, Herbert and Castles, Lance (eds) (1970) *Indonesian Political Thinking 1945–1965* (partial translation of "The Birth of Panca Sila"), Cornell University, Ithaca: 40–49.

Gatra.com (1997) "Cosmopolitan: Gaya Helen Brown di Higina," No. 41/III, 30 August (posted on Indonesia-p, 31 August).

Gayatri, Gati (1996) Apresiasi Masyarakat Terhadap Siaran TVRI, paper presented on behalf of the Research and Development section of the Department of Information at the "Seminar Membangun Citra Acara Seni dan Budaya Media Televisi," Yogyakarta, 21–22 August.

Hanazaki, Yasuo and Terjebak, Pers (1998) *Institut Studi Arus Informasi*, Jakarta (Indonesian translation by Danang Kukuh Wardoyo and Tim Cipinang of "The Indonesian press in the era of Keterbukaan: A force for democratization," doctoral dissertation, Monash University, 1996).

Haryanto, Ign[atius] (ed.) (1997) Laporan Akhir Tahun: Pers Indonesia Terus di-Pres, Aliansi Jurnalis Independen and Lembaga Studi Pers dan Pembangunan, Jakarta: 54.

Hill, David T. (1994) *The Press in New Order Indonesia*, University of Western Australia, Perth: Press/ARCOSPEC.

Hill, Hal (1994) "The Economy" in *Indonesia's New Order: The Dynamics of Socio-economic Transformation*, (ed.) Hal Hill, Allen and Unwin, St Leonards.

—— (1998) "The Indonesian Economy: The strange and sudden death of a tiger" (pp. 93–103) in Geoff Forrester and R. J. May (eds) *The Fall of Soeharto*, Crawford House Publishing, Bathurst.

Jawa Pos (1997) "Hartono: 15 Media Kena Peringatan," 21 December Internet edition, posted on <indonesia-p@indopubs.com> on 20 December from <http://www.jawapos.co.id/21desember/dep21d1.htm>.

Jawa Pos Online (1998) "Broker BEJ pun Berdemo," 20 May. Available at: http://202.149.241.231/jplalu/mei98/20mei/de20mi4.htm (consulted 30 January 1999).

Kitley, Philip (1997) "Television, nation and culture in Indonesia," unpublished PhD thesis, Murdoch University: 92.

Kompas (1994) various articles, 3–4 June.

Kompas Online (1997a) "Deppen Kembangkan 'Community Newspaper," 28 January. Available posted KdP Net <kdpnet@usa.net>.

—— (1997b) Riant Nugroho Dwidowijoto, "Pers Indonesia 2020," 23 April (posted on indonesia-p@indopubs.com, 22 April)

Lee, Oey Hong (1971) *Indonesian Government and Press During Guided Democracy*, Centre for Southeast Asian Studies, University of Hull/Inter Documentation Co, Zug.

Lindsay, Jennifer (1997) "Making Waves: Private radio and local identities in Indonesia," *Indonesia*, No. 64, October: 105–23, particularly 114, fn 40.

McDaniel, Drew O. (1994) *Broadcasting in the Malay World: Radio, Television, and Video in Brunei, Indonesia, Malaysia, and Singapore*, Ablex, Norwood: 218.

McQuail, Denis (1994) *Mass Communication Theory: An Introduction*, Sage, London, third edition.

Media Indonesia Minggu Special (1996) "Iklan di 'The Peak' Berbahasa Indonesia," "Komunikasi and Bisnis" Supplement, 18 August: 23.

Morfit, Michael (1981) "Pancasila: The Indonesian State Ideology according to the New Order Government," *Asian Survey*, Vol. XXI, No. 8, August: 838–851.

Petunjuk Radio Siaran Swasta Nasional (PRSSNI) (1992) "Sekretariat Pengurus Pusat PRSSNI, Kumpulan Peraturan tentang Radio Siaran Swasta di Indonesia: Tahun 1970 s/d 1992," PRSSNI, Jakarta.

—— (1995) "Pengurus Pusat," PRSSNI, Jakarta.

P. T. Cipta Televisi Pendidikan Indonesia. [no date, possibly 1992] Company profile of Televisi Pendidikan Indonesia: 4.

Pusat Penelitian Dan Pengembangan Media Massa (1980–1981) Laporan Pengembangan Siaran Nasional TVRI (1980–1981) (based on several government funded research reports on television after 1976), Jakarta: 8.

Robinson, Richard (1987) *Indonesia: The Rise of Capital*, Allen & Unwin, London.

Sen, Krishna and Hill, David (2000) *Culture and Politics in Indonesia*, Oxford University Press, Melbourne.

Smith, Edward C. (1969) "A history of newspaper suppression in Indonesia 1949–1965," doctoral dissertation, University of Iowa.

Subakti, Baty, and Katoppo, Ernst (eds) (1996) *Media Scene 1995–1996 Indonesia: The Official Guide to Advertising Media in Indonesia*, PPPI, Jakarta: 27–29.

Tempo (1994) 11 June: 28–30

The Wall Street Journal Interactive Edition (1997) "Advertising: Cosmopolitan Girl Dresses up for Summer Debut in Indonesia," 9 April, posted on "soc.culture.indonesia" and "alt.culture.indonesia" newsgroups on 9 April.

5

BOSNIA-HERCEGOVINA AND POST-CONFLICT MEDIA RESTRUCTURING

Monroe E. Price

Few studies of transitions to democracy examine the abrupt, post-conflict mode of change that has become more prominent in recent years. The norm of transition, if there is such a thing, involves media systems in which domestic pressures are the predominant agents for transformation. At most, there is an interaction between the domestic and those external forces that seek to encourage change. The coercive agent is the state itself, and opportunities for transition are subject to its resistance.

There is a specific class of states, however, where the form of intervention and dynamic for change is quite different. These are states undergoing transformation under the supervision of an international authority or an occupying state. The rate of change, the mode of change, and the role of media in its relationship to change are subject to an authority outside the state. Kosovo, a protectorate of the United Nations, and Bosnia-Hercegovina, subject to the authority of the Office of the High Representative (OHR) under the Dayton Accords, provide examples of this type of change. East Timor and Sierra Leone are also regulated or rehabilitated through actions of the international community.

In recent years, a surprising number of states have been within this category as "peacekeeping" becomes a modern device for international intervention. There are precedents, though not exact ones. After the Second World War, Germany and Japan were states in which, though internal political structures were obviously of key importance, the capacity of the occupier unilaterally to alter the legal system and impose, as it were, democratic approaches, was the defining element of political reality.

These states offer an unusual opportunity to study the relationship between media change and political reform. Entire systems are invented and put in place. While they must be filtered through local realities and political processes, the methods of doing so are totally different from what exists in the other transitions. Political transition is implemented almost by force. An open field exists for the use of subsidies, often from external sources, to encourage particular kinds of media, including those that are "free and independent." Rules concerning media are imposed when elections are held, presumably to make the elections fair, but sometimes to help ensure victory for the candidate favored by the external supervisor. Censorship can be imposed in the interests of producing a more stable and enduring democratic future. The directors of broadcast entities can be hired and fired by the international community. The transitions are "global" because forces outside the state itself determine them.

Global context

After Rwanda, when the seeds of hate were cast in Yugoslavia, there were increased voices contending that the world community's failure to halt the genocide in Rwanda exposed the weakness of an international system that forces states to choose between the extremes of massive, armed humanitarian intervention and mere symbolic action. In response, proposals on the role of the international community in local media during conflicts seemed to search for intermediary options that the UN, NATO, or the United States might use in preventing conflicts. These proposals also reflected the growing acknowledgement that media play a substantial role before, during, and after conflict. They focused on the need for concerted action by the international community to forestall genocidal use of broadcast media that promotes or accentuates devastating conflict.

One intermediary option recommended was a United Nations "information intervention unit" designed to respond to broadcasting efforts that might be used to incite violence in troubled areas. Such a unit would have three primary functions: monitoring, peace broadcasting, and, in extreme cases, jamming radio and television broadcasts. The proponents pointed to the explosive mobilizing role that Radio-Television Libre des Milles Collines (RTLM) had in Rwanda with its repetitive and explicit incitement for Hutu to slaughter Tutsi. Advocates of information intervention did not consider movement toward democracy the immediate goal, but merely desired to avoid conflict or local genocides. Given the rise in the potential for conflict-fostering and genocidal media, the development, refinement, and institutionalization of information-based responses to what Jamie Metzl called "incendiary mass communications" was necessary (1997: 16).

The problem of what to do when the flames of conflict were temporarily under control and when the effort at reconstruction began posed a different set of problems. As a result of the 1991 Paris Agreements, the United Nations Transitional Authority in Cambodia (UNTAC) sought techniques and approaches to alter the structure and practice of information distribution prior to the 1993 elections. Shortly thereafter, under the Dayton Accords, Sfor, the Office of High Representative, together with the Office of Security and Cooperation in Europe (OSCE) and a wide variety of non-governmental organizations (NGOs), took steps to reshape and reform the media space in Bosnia-Hercegovina, recognizing the critical relationship of altering the media as part of reconstructing society.

It became clear that a new approach by the international community was emerging, with vastly important constitutional, political, and structural implications. Administrative machinery was put in place to restructure media, a system which had not been imposed by the international community for almost half a century. While avoidance of conflict (or avoidance of the resumption of conflict) remained a primary goal, the democracy-building function of peacekeeping became significant. In Bosnia-Hercegovina, for example, the OSCE assumed administrative responsibilities for establishing elections and, as part of that, the responsibility for ensuring a media that was consistent with fairness in the voting process.

In addition to the international governmental organizations (IGOs), a variety of NGOs entered the post-conflict peacekeeping field, intent on building a media system that would contribute to a more stable, plural, democratic society. Often, the NGOs had a more explicit agenda of promoting pluralism, as compared to controlling the potential for resumption of conflict. However, these two approaches were not completely dichotomous, but in some ways complementary. If there was a division, it was because IGOs tended to create alternative media outlets that were, at least initially, under IGO control. More plural-oriented NGOs tended to consider that these modes pre-empted independent or existing media outlets, even those associated with belligerents or opposing ethnic factions. The logic of the international governmental organizations was simple: to achieve content that is neutral and peace-oriented. The IGOs often accomplished this through the use of electronic media, which were, at the outset, managed by the IGO itself.

The case of Bosnia-Hercegovina

This chapter concentrates on the use of external power to affect media in Bosnia-Hercegovina, and implications of intervention in the implementation of political change. Because of space and other constraints, the essay focuses primarily on the occupation of television transmitters by NATO during 1997 as an example of the transformation of broadcasting space to enhance a certain movement toward democratic traditions.

While there is a wide-ranging debate about whether and how media reform helps engender political reform in the more standard transitions, similar doubts do not exist in the post-conflict context. It is virtually assumed that shaping media is a necessary part of controlling and building a future democratic state. Indeed, one of the paradoxes of the post-conflict media restructuring is contained in this policy. Control (and often censorship) is considered a prerequisite for a successful transition from war and authority to democracy and stability.

Because the style and circumstance of transition in the post-conflict environment are different from the norm, the method of this chapter will be different from others in the volume. In the non-conflict transition, the shift from pre-transition to or through the primary and secondary phase and to a consolidated transition is deemed progressive (even if it is not always directly sequential). In the post-conflict transition, the shift is abrupt and coerced. It is, to be sure, conditioned by what has gone before (in legislation and profile of the press), but by its very suddenness and completeness, the past plays a different role.

The narrative of control over information in Bosnia is part of a history of efforts by one state, or a group of states, to influence the articulation or suppression of particular narratives within the borders of another state. More than that, it is the precursor of a fairly radical and important area of potential change, given new media technologies, in the way governments treat the information space of other countries in times of crisis. Already, "information warfare" is the subject of increased focus by military strategists.[1] Increasingly, there are examples of media restructuring in the wake of conflict, part of the general effort to alter forces tied to historical animosities reflected in narratives of identity. In this respect, information warfare includes "public diplomacy measures, propaganda and psychological campaigns, political and cultural subversion, deception of or interference with local media, infiltration of computer networks and databases, and efforts to promote dissident or opposition movements across computer networks" (Arquilla and Ronfeldt 1993: 141, 144).

For more than six months in late 1997 and 1998, the NATO troops playing the peacekeeping role in Bosnia (called Sfor) held key broadcast transmitters under "security protection" to ensure that information transmitted to Bosnian Serbs avoided the signals of conflict deemed dangerous by the IGOs' so-called Contact Group, the United States, the United Kingdom, France, Italy, Russia, and Germany. Sfor also used its control of media space to promote a more positive image of itself and the Dayton Accords. Members of the Contact Group sought to create an entire new mechanism for the licensing of radio and television stations throughout Bosnia, establishing standards for their operation and providing enforcement mechanisms (including fines and closures) against what the Office of High Representative deemed transmissions of propaganda undermining the peace process.

This active, directed, and explicit intervention in Bosnia, including the seizure of transmitters, has raised the international debate about the appropriate role of media policy in the prevention of ethnic conflict and preservation of peacekeeping processes to a new level. Studying the seizure of television transmitters in Bosnia through the Office of High Representative in 1997 helps in exploring what role law has in affecting the adjustment of power.

In Bosnia-Hercegovina, the international governmental organizations that used military authority to structure the space of memory contended that they were acting pursuant to law. There can, of course, be efforts to shape memory by the use of force alone without legal justification. That was not, however, what the Office of High Representative and NATO contended as they sought to limit Serbian television's broadcasts, promulgations of memory-prodding rhetoric which had been deemed destructive to the peace process.

The case of Bosnia, like other similar cases, demonstrates how those in power, faced with the opportunity or need for propaganda, use electronic media to play on memories, sometimes to contrast the painful present with a glorious past, sometimes to create or reinterpret a past to justify aggressiveness in the present, often to change perceptions of the present through manipulation of a sense of history. These events demonstrate problems in the way legal systems authorize or prohibit particular modes of invoking, controlling, or inventing memory.

Role of media before the conflict

Media were used to spread terror and fan the flames of war in the former Yugoslavia. Several months before anyone in the region outwardly bore arms, nationalist leaders in the various Yugoslav republics began laying the groundwork for war by planning media campaigns. Slobodan Milosevic, then president of Serbia, who is widely blamed for waging and instigating the war in

Bosnia-Hercegovina, sent paramilitary troops and technicians to seize a dozen television transmitters in the northern and eastern parts of Bosnia-Hercegovina in the spring of 1992. These areas are close to Serbia and had substantial Serb populations. As a result, more than half the people in the territory of Bosnia-Hercegovina began receiving the television signal controlled by Belgrade rather than the usual television from Sarajevo. The idea of a unified Bosnia-Hercegovina information space, with a national signal emanating from Sarajevo, was immediately fractured, and the stage was set to wage a fierce propaganda war that preceded actual fighting.

With Serbian and half of the Bosnia-Hercegovinan airwaves firmly in his hands, Milosevic's television broadcast fictitious reports that Croat militiamen were massacring Serbs in Croatia and Bosnia-Hercegovina. According to the news stories these Croats drained the blood of Serb civilians before murdering them and the main Muslim political party in Bosnia-Hercegovina executed five of its own members for leaking word of a genocidal conspiracy against Serbs in the town of Bosanski Samac.

Of course, neither individual nor collective memory is necessarily uniform in its ideological significance. Mobilization of one powerful memory often requires the suppression of others. In this case, Milosevic's broadcasts emphasized conflict while obscuring fifty years of peaceful co-existence by Muslims, Croats, and Serbs. Widespread Serbian embrace of this bellicose propaganda was particularly remarkable given the 30 per cent intermarriage rate in Bosnia.

There are varying, though unsatisfactory, interpretations of the problem as to why the propaganda was so effective. Some commentators point to historic ethnic divides arising out of the two World Wars; others to the tradition of media controlled by the state. False reports drew heavily on collective memories and suspicions. They were laden with Serb symbolism and historical references to Serb struggles against Ottoman Turks and the Bosnian Muslims who cooperated with them, as well as against German Nazis and Croat fascist collaborators. This appealed to many Serbs on an emotional level; for some, even questioning the truthfulness of the news reports was seen almost as treason against Serb culture.

Some independent journalists in Belgrade wrote about the pernicious and dangerous potential of Milosevic-controlled television, but their publications did not have mass readership and could hardly combat the powerful nationalist television. Whatever the reason, the nationalist and inflammatory propaganda struck fear into the Serb population. So, when Belgrade television encouraged Serbs to arm themselves against the "enemies of the Serb people," many Serbs in both Bosnia and Croatia did as they were told.

The Serbs were not alone in wielding the power and influence of television. Well before any fighting began in Bosnia-Hercegovina, Croatian television, like Serbian, was airing nationalist broadcasts discussing how the Serbs intended to exterminate the Croat population in order to form a "Greater Serbia." These incendiary programs suggested to Croats that they were in mortal danger from the Serbs and that they should arm themselves before it was too late.

In early 1992, the Bosnian Serb leadership left Sarajevo. Soon thereafter, the village of Pale became their self-styled capital. Almost immediately, in April 1992, they began broadcasting their own television channel, Serb Radio and Television (SRT). Firmly under the control of the nationalist leaders who would lead the subsequent war, SRT used the same tactics as those pioneered by Belgrade television. Falsified reports of Serbs being slaughtered by Islamic fundamentalists (Turks) and Croatian fascists (Ustashe) were the norm, as were false reports about Western conspiracies against the Serb nation.

During the first year of the war, the Muslims and Croats were allied together against the Serbs. However, after the Serbs were pushed back from Croat territory in 1993, the Croats turned against their former Muslim allies. Again, television played a key role. The Croats, like the Serbs, wanted to carve out a piece of Bosnia-Hercegovina for themselves to create a "Greater Croatia." Croatian television from Zagreb began broadcasting reports claiming that Islamic fundamentalists were trying to create a state where Catholic Croats would be oppressed and subjugated. The broadcasts portrayed Muslims as dirty anti-Christians, who were intent on depriving the Catholics of their religion and heritage. The strategy encouraged a sufficient number of Croats to fight against their Muslim neighbors. In Hercog-Bosna, the Croat-controlled section of Bosnia-Hercegovina, there was virtually no alternative press. The options were Croatian TV (HRT), Mostar TV, which was even more nationalistic and provocative than HRT, Radio Mostar, and newspapers loyal to the ruling Croatian Democratic Party (HDZ).[2]

The Dayton Accords

The war in Bosnia was a brutal combination of psychological manipulation and physical violence, which ended with the 1996 United States-brokered Dayton Peace Accords. Bosnian President Alija Izetbegovic, Serbian President Slobodan Milosevic, and Croatian President Franjo Tudjman were summoned to Dayton, Ohio, where diplomats worked to hammer out a compromise and redraw the boundary lines on the map. It was finally agreed that Bosnia would remain one country, but divided into two entities: Republika Srpska and the Muslim–Croat Federation.

That structure satisfied the Serbs because they were, in a sense, given their republic, even though it was an "entity," not a state. The agreement satisfied the Muslims because it kept Bosnia whole. It offered less to the Croats, except that, as part of the Muslim–Croat Federation, they were able to form special ties with neighboring Croatia. Critical questions included who would control the information space, which would determine which memories were repeated and reinforced, and what narratives of the future would be created. How history was presented, including the very recent history, would affect the elections, the potential for resettlement of refugees, and the success, if that word were possible, of the Dayton Accords themselves.

The civilian aspects of Dayton were not as well thought out as its military provisions and led to divided and complex sources of authority. The Accords stipulated that the OSCE would organize elections, that the United Nations would create an unarmed civilian police force to supervise the entities' police forces, and that the United Nations High Commissioner for Refugees would oversee the return or resettlement of displaced peoples or refugees. A High Representative chosen by the Contact Group would coordinate the activities of the different organizations.

Together, these organizations aimed to reconstitute Bosnia's former multi-ethnic nature and create a Bosnian national identity against a backdrop of continuing ethnic hatred and loyalties. Each element – elections, domestic security, and the return of refugees – implied a kind of reconstruction of consciousness. Each element, if it were to be perceived as organic and evolved, and not as an artificial creation of an alien occupation, had to find part of its justification in a practice or ethos of the past. The elections, which were designed to reverse ethnic cleansing, would be the IGOs' most crucial task and also the most rigorous test of Dayton's success in altering the relationship of past to future.

In January 1996, the Accords were signed in Paris and immediately put into force. It was not possible, as part of the initial Accords, to dislodge the recently conflicting entities from control over media; Serb and Croat leaders clung to their party-controlled television and radio outlets to maintain and extend existing power. The Serb-held parts of Bosnia were still strictly under the influence of the rabidly nationalist SRT and the Croat-held parts of Bosnia under the equally nationalist influence of Croatian Radio and Television. The Bosniak-controlled part of the country received broadcasts from Bosnia-Hercegovina Radio and Television, which had become increasingly nationalistic over time, though committed to the cause of integration and the success of the Dayton experiment.

All three groups vied for use and control of the airwaves both within and beyond their geographic spheres of influence. Croats, Serbs, and Muslims set about repairing war-damaged television transmitters on mountains within their respective territories, seeking the means to broadcast as far and wide as possible. Belgrade set up a television transmitter in Serbia, near the border with the newly created entity of Republika Srpska, to broadcast Serbian television throughout Serb-controlled territory, and also aided the Bosnian Serbs in repairing transmitters damaged by NATO bombing. Zagreb put up additional transmitters in Croatia, near the border with Bosnia, to broadcast Croatian television into Bosnian territory, and aided the Bosnian Croats in repairing existing transmitters, as well as adding transmitters to increase the coverage of Bosnian Croat television. The Bosnian government received outside assistance from the Norwegian government to renovate and repair some twenty-one television transmitters to enhance the multi-ethnic voice intended to facilitate reconciliation.

Dayton implementation and media

Just days after the Dayton Agreement was signed in Paris, Ambassador Robert Frowick, the American who headed the OSCE mission in Bosnia, arrived in Sarajevo to begin planning for the elections. Frowick and the other European and American diplomats who were implementing the Dayton Accords were keenly aware of the role media played in the war and the role it would continue to play in peace. As long as rival broadcasters saturated the airwaves with invocations of divisive memories and tropes of conflict, the diplomats feared, the unified country envisioned by Dayton could not be realized. If alternative sources of information were not provided across the country, the same nationalist leaders who waged the war and controlled the airwaves were sure to be voted back into power.

The refashioning of narrative became part of the context of administrative vocabulary as it was translated into the field of bureaucratic operation. The template for election reform demanded objectivity and impartiality (as defined by the IGOs); failure to sustain this perspective in representations of past and present issues rendered political parties and broadcasters vulnerable to official complaint. The OSCE established a Media Experts Commission within the Provisional Electoral Commission. It issued a set of rules and regulations, charging the media with duties including "providing true and accurate information," "refraining from broadcasting incendiary programming," and running OSCE and international election-related statements and advertisements.[3] It also set up a monitoring group that could cite violations of these rules. Truth and accuracy could have reference to the past as well as to the present.

In addition to rules designed to restrain the existing media, the OSCE pioneered another technique of intervention, helping to finance a special broadcast network that would positively influence the mix of narratives and images transmitted to the public. The Free Elections Radio Network (FERN) was initially started by the Swiss government to provide "objective and timely information on the elections" to the people of Bosnia-Hercegovina in all entities (Radio Hajat 1996). This project provided a less incendiary news source, avoiding the national broadcasters' constant emphasis on recent hostilities and tragedies, content that OSCE found inconsistent with the reconciliation and democratic process envisioned by Dayton.

Seizure of transmitters and post-seizure details

The existence of a highly polarized and intensely focused ethnically based political party, coupled with a virtual media monopoly, posed a threat to the Office of High Representative and the operation of the Dayton bureaucracy as it went about its rebuilding efforts. In the spring of 1997, in spite of all the efforts to create alternative sources of information across Bosnia-Hercegovina, media remained divided into three mutually antagonistic components in Republika Srpska, Bosniak-controlled Federation territory, and Croat-controlled Federation territory. The party-controlled television stations remained the most influential media outlets and the main source of news for all of Bosnia's ethnic groups.

Other, internationally sponsored, efforts to break a tradition of dependence on official programming were not sufficiently successful. Clearly, the attempts by international governmental organizations to create an alternative to party-controlled media had not been sufficient to combat the nationalist television stations, which continued to stir up hostility, not only toward each other, but also toward the IGOs themselves. Sfor and the OHR felt that much of the work of Sfor and of the other international organizations toward reconciliation was jeopardized by the news and propaganda of nationalist television and radio.

Over the summer of 1997, conflict over the content and control of broadcast media intensified. The Steering Board of the Peace Implementation Council of the Contact Group, distressed by the continuing divisiveness of party-controlled media, issued the Sintra Declaration, a document considered by OHR to be an extension of the Dayton Accords, though neither Bosnian signatories of Dayton nor current elected Bosnian officials signed the Declaration. This instrument dramatically asserted OHR's right both to demand airtime for its own broadcasts and to suspend broadcasts which contravened the letter or spirit of Dayton. The Sintra Declaration was later cited in justification of Sfor's seizure of broadcasting towers.

Within Republika Srpska, struggles for media control intensified as United States-backed Biljana Plavsic announced that the SRT station in her power base of Banja Luka would cut ties with the central SRT Pale station, broadcasting from the seat of rival Radovan Karadzic. The Pale broadcast, sponsored by Karadzic, had drawn heavily on viewers' memories and associations of conflict, openly comparing Sfor to the occupying Nazi forces of a generation before. The broadcast played on recollections of previous atrocities and featured alternating images of Sfor soldiers and Nazi storm troopers.

On 22 August, twenty-two United States troops acted upon the Sintra Declaration and, claiming that they moved to prevent possible clashes between Plavsic and Karadzic, seized the SRT broadcast tower in the northeastern town of Udrigovo. This move cut off SRT Pale broadcasts to the region, temporarily suspending the flood of inflammatory invocations. Ten days later, American soldiers guarding the tower were attacked by a mob of 300 Serbs, presumed to be supporters of Karadzic. Pale radio broadcast that Sfor had "occupied" the SRT transmitter and claimed Sfor was a "heavily-armed military force threatening courageous unarmed citizens" (Bosnian Serb Radio 1997).

The resulting negotiation between the Sfor and the Pale authorities produced a document that became known as the Udrigovo Agreement. Sfor handed back the tower to the SRT authorities in Pale, and in return the Pale authorities agreed to certain conditions for resumed broadcasting. Pursuant to the Agreement, the media of the Serb Republic would stop producing inflammatory reports against Sfor and the other international organizations implementing the Dayton Accords, SRT would regularly provide an hour of prime-time programming to air political views other than those of the ruling party, and SRT would provide the Office of High Representative with a half hour of prime-time programming daily.

The Agreement required SRT to transmit alternate representations both of current events and of the history that had led up to them. In the wake of the Udrigovo Agreement and the formation of the international Media Support Advisory Group (MSAG),[4] the Serb leadership appeared to take a more conciliatory tone toward the Western diplomats implementing Dayton. But that cooperation was short-lived. On 8 September, the OHR and Sfor sent a letter to SRT in Pale, demanding ninety minutes of airtime to broadcast an OHR program that same evening and an hour of airtime the following day, among other time demands. SRT Pale refused to broadcast the material, and instead, further angering international officials, charged OHR and Sfor with violating "freedom and human rights." The SRT Pale newscaster read a statement from the station's editorial board stating:

> We publicly announce that under no conditions would we implement these requests. By doing this, we would trample on our moral integrity

97

and our profession. In our radio and TV broadcast, we shall continue to ridicule orders like the one saying that video material must be broadcast in its entirety and with no changes.

(Radio B92 1997)

Against this background of increased conflict on the airwaves of Republika Srpska, and raised stakes for political control of the entity as the election drew nearer, United States government opinion increasingly favored jamming SRT Pale's broadcast. In fact, the United States dispatched three Air Force EC-130 Commando Solo planes capable both of broadcasting information and jamming existing radio and television signals. United States officials claimed that the primary role of the electronic warfare planes would be to "broadcast fair and balanced news and information to the local population" (Voice of America 1997). However, Voice of America (VOA) broadcasts to Bosnia-Hercegovina also stated that the planes had the capability to jam pro-Karadzic transmissions. VOA reported the American belief that supporters of Karadzic had violated the Udrigovo Agreement's mandate that they soften their rhetoric against Plavsic and NATO peacekeeping troops and broadcast a Pentagon spokesman's claim of Sfor's legal authority to block broadcasts.

Western diplomats feared the media conflict could lead to more violence. Serbian President Slobodan Milosevic was urged to summon Plavsic and rival leader and broadcaster Momcilo Krajisnik to the bargaining table in Belgrade, where the internationally brokered Belgrade Agreement was hammered out. Finalized on 24 September 1997, this document established a "fairness doctrine" for SRT Banja Luka and SRT Pale, in which the two leaders agreed that the unified media environment of the Republika Srpska and free access to media by all participants in elections is "vital" for a democratic process. In point 3, they agreed that news programs be broadcast daily from studios in Pale and Banja Luka alternately.

Hopes for a harmonious implementation of the agreement were immediately dashed. Only a day after it was signed, a news release by the OHR stated that the Media Support Advisory Group (MSAG) had "expressed concern about the editorial policies" of SRT Pale and stated that SRT Pale was continuing to broadcast political announcements as news, "devoid of any balance or alternative opinion." SRT Pale might have taken the news release as a warning. But, characteristically, SRT Pale refused to soften its editorial content, and continued to structure its representations of both Sfor and domestic rivals to invoke memories of conflict, and sustain ongoing hostilities.

On the following day, 26 September, the chief prosecutor of the International Criminal Tribunal for the Former Yugoslavia, Louise Arbour, gave a press conference in Sarajevo, which was covered by SRT. In commentary, the SRT Pale announcer reiterated the Bosnian Serb leaders' long-held position that the tribunal was a political instrument and that it was prejudiced against the Serbs.

The United Nations, a member of the MSAG, considered this a breach of prior understandings, including the Udrigovo Agreement, and demanded that SRT Pale make a public apology on television. On 30 September, SRT Pale did so, stating:

Serb-Radio-TV in this way wishes to apologize unreservedly for its misrepresentation of a news conference given by the prosecutor of The Hague Tribunal, Louise Arbour. We will read out a statement to this effect made by the prosecutor. The statement will be followed by the complete and unedited footage of the news conference given by Judge Arbour last Friday, during her visit to Bosnia-Hercegovina.

(Beta News Agency 1997a)

In spite of SRT Pale's apology, Sfor troops seized control of four SRT transmitters the next day (1 October), thereby preventing SRT Pale from transmitting (Bosnian Serb Television 1997). In addition to asserting that SRT Pale's blunder was a violation of the Sintra Declaration, Western governments also claimed that the station's repeated broadcast comparing Sfor troops to Nazis constituted a threat to the safety of the Sfor soldiers and, therefore, needed to be silenced. SRT Pale's appeal to memories of oppressive occupation, these governments recognized, could have very real consequences in the responses of viewers.

Sensitive to the potential for condemnation of the seizure, Sfor and OHR announced that SRT Pale could regain access to the transmission network and resume operations, but only if strict conditions were met. SRT Pale would be obliged to agree to "criteria for its reconstruction and reorganization, as well as for editorial control of broadcasting, as suggested by the Office of the High Representative in Bosnia-Hercegovina and the international community" (Radio Bosnia-Hercegovina 1997).

On 6 October, several days after NATO seized the transmitters, the major international power broker, United States special envoy for the Balkans, Robert Gelbard, appeared in the region. In a statement two days later, the High Representative said that a "transitory international director-general" and two deputies would be appointed by the OHR to head SRT Pale, that the OHR would draft a statute and editorial charter for the station, that SRT Pale would be obliged to broadcast programs requested by officials from other international organizations without editing or commentary, and that a team of journalists and editors would be brought in to train personnel and supervise the programming of SRT Pale. He added further that international representatives would evaluate the SRT journalists and editors and that "only those who are positively evaluated will be able to get a job again" (Beta News Agency 1997b). This was an extraordinary assertion of power by the High Representative and it infuriated the Bosnian Serb leadership in Pale.

At the Peace Implementation Council's meeting in Bonn in December 1997, the Contact Group members agreed to reinforce efforts to "break the political control of the media," and restructure the media landscape "according to internationally recognized standards." The Office of High Representative said the idea was to create an interim media regulation board to intervene in editorial content, restructure media, and regulate content. The board would provide training to journalists, but it would also have the power to shut down media and decide who could and could not work as a journalist.

OHR would establish two commissions, one to "ensure that media standards are respected and would issue licenses. The other would be of an appellate nature and would deal with complaints on media treatment or media behavior in the communications process" (Dnevni Avaz 1997). In a neat reversal of SRT Pale's Nazi comparisons, the officials noted that the foundation for the new media strategy in Bosnia-Hercegovina was based on the Allies' postwar experience in Germany. Here, the power of the Second World War memories was mobilized against the broadcasters, rather than against the Western powers.

Comprehensive media reform

Ultimately, the OHR recognized the peril of failing to provide clear and consistent guidelines to the media actors in Bosnia. Intervening on a case-by-case basis would not contribute to the rule of law or a legacy of respect for law. They decided on a comprehensive effort to reform the entire regulatory media regime in Bosnia. The OHR, relying on outside experts and, initially, on externally recruited administrators, created an entire framework with objective standards and a mechanism to determine whether a media violation occurred and the proper sanction for each violation.

Such a reform might be considered far more radical than isolated transmitter seizures. The seizures were episodic responses to unique and specific circumstances. The reform sought to put into place a new legal system with tribunals, enforcement mechanisms, and licensing agencies. It attempted to reshape the entire broadcasting system in Bosnia. This was a pattern that would be followed in Kosovo, though with distinctions that were based on contextual factors and styles of exercise of power.

The international governmental organizations saw that the control of media by individual political parties was an obstacle that "bedevil[ed...] efforts to re-establish civil society in Bosnia" and therefore hampered OHR's long-term political reforms. The OHR needed to construct a fundamentally altered architecture in which media were not "ethnically based and directly or indirectly associated to the main mono-ethnic political parties." The result of a structure based on ethnicity had been that "enmities which precipitated the war are now fought out over the airwaves." "[R]eform of the whole media landscape in [Bosnia-Hercegovina] [was] a vital prerequisite for progress in the implementation of Dayton."[5]

The OHR statements provide a sense of the aims of the international community and the aims of the parties to the Dayton Accords for this type of intervention. According to one document (2 October), the aims of the OHR included:

> *To establish, countrywide, a regulatory regime equating to models operating in other democratic, plural societies*. This will be responsible for establishing and enforcing arrangements for fair and equitable access to the electronic media for the full range of opinion. This will be a transitional arrangement, and will remain in place until the [Bosnia-Hercegovina] common institutions establish a satisfactory regulatory regime to replace it under the Media Law, now under consideration.

With respect to the wholesale reform, the OHR wanted to create a "single regulatory body," chaired by an international judge and composed of representatives of the principal international agencies. This body was granted the power to recommend sanctions, to be implemented by the Media Support Advisory Group, and the power to issue and withdraw licenses for all existing broadcasting entities. In early 1998, the concept of wholesale reform was set forth in further detail by the OHR when the international community sought assistance in implementing the Bosnian media reform package.

The OHR announced that it wanted to build an Intermediate Media Standards and Licensing Commission with the power to regulate all media in Bosnia. This commission, later made permanent and turned over to representatives of the communities, was to absorb the election-related functions of the Media Experts Commission and would require all broadcasters to meet a set of "internationally recognized standards of broadcasting" in order to obtain a license. The OHR expected to create a judicial body with "powers of sanction to ensure compliance" with the rulings of the Commission.[6] International experts and Bosnian representatives from both the Federation and Republika Srpska would staff the commission.

This new reform was based on a December 1997 proposal to the OHR. According to this proposal, the intermediate commission would remain in operation until institutions that could perform its functions were in place at the national level, the entity level, or the canton levels. The proposal justified this comprehensive action because "monolithic control allowed broadcasting in Bosnia to be used as a means to divide the ethnic communities." Not only was it true that "the distribution of poisonous propaganda was a major contributor to the war," but "it is still used to indoctrinate the communities." The OHR considered the commission and comprehensive legal reform necessary to avoid a situation where the media "emphasiz[ed] separatism" and thus "h[eld] back the peace process."

Since the OHR felt that the systemic and architectural problems of the existing media model in Bosnia were so pervasive, it observed that restructuring all media, particularly broadcast media, in accordance with internationally accepted standards was the only way to achieve "pluralism and inter-entity broadcasting." The new system would include "codes of conduct for program content," modeled on "the established practice[s] in Western European democracies and in North America" (Proposal 1997: 2). The proposal provided that these codes would also apply to the press and the Internet. Until state agencies were established (and approved), the intermediate commission would establish, regulate, and enforce the codes.

The commission was to have three divisions. The first was an "all-media" complaints commission. It would affirmatively monitor the press and broadcast media, investigate complaints regarding violations of the codes of practice, and recommend action on those complaints if it found them valid. The second division was a licensing sub-commission that would "establish" and administer structural and editorial licensing standards. All broadcasters seeking a license would have to conform to the licensing commission's standards. The third division was an intervention tribunal that would rule on disciplinary procedures and impose sanctions and penalties when appropriate.

The tribunal would have the authority to require "one or more on-screen apologies," or "one or more apologies to be published in the press and on radio." It could prohibit rebroadcast of an "offending program or its content" and temporarily withdraw a license for access to the transmission system (Proposal 1997: 2). Additionally, it was empowered to curtail a license or revoke a license entirely. Finally, it had the power to impose financial penalties on either the station or the directors or principals of the station regardless of whether the station was owned by the government. Under the commission, as it came into being, all broadcast stations in Bosnia-Hercegovina had to be re-licensed, a process that, in some cases, particularly for the retransmission of programming from Croatia, gave rise to significant controversy.

Legal and policy analysis

Bosnia-Hercegovina presents an institutionally and legally complex case study of the phenomenon newly termed "information intervention." In the world of ethnic and regional conflict, whether it involves Zapatistas in Mexico, Kurds in Turkey, separatists in Angola, or Tamils in Sri Lanka, terrestrial transmitters and signals direct from satellites can serve to shape public perception of current events, often drawing on collective memory of previous conflict or injustice. These resurgent memories can fuel campaigns of violence by or against the state and among communities with different views of the public order, often shaped by their different versions of past events. The international community as a whole increasingly sees potential for countervailing media use as a therapeutic tool, including the affirmative use of more pluralistic media to reduce or prevent conflict or increase the possibility of democracy.

Because of the importance of this phenomenon of information intervention, it is important to understand the basis for the international community to intervene in a way that, on one level, seems violative of free speech principles, and that had such a comprehensive effect on media and information space in Bosnia. If the intervening international parties are not acting pursuant to legal authority themselves, their moral claim that those in conflict follow the rule of law loses some of its credibility.

NATO, OSCE, and the Office of High Representative acted as law makers and enforcers; they required that their statements be broadcast, established standards for existing stations, closed stations down, and put a mechanism into operation wholly to revise the licensing and administration of radio and television. What occurred was one of the most comprehensive possible catalogues of the exercise of authority. Various groups within Bosnia questioned whether the UN, NATO, or others had valid power to engage in these activities, and outside groups, including the World Press Freedom Committee, expressed grave reservations as to whether these steps were consistent with international norms.

The law of media intervention in Bosnia is nowhere clearly stated, and it is not necessarily true that the United States and other parties sought a legal justification at each step as it responded to practical realities. But the source of law matters. For example, if the United States and its Western allies were acting as occupiers, then a particular body of international norms would govern their powers and the limits on them.[7] If they were acting, on the other hand, under a consent regime, then the shape of their authority would be governed, in large part, by the conditions of their entry.

Under current norms (norms that, themselves, are subject to debate), "occupation," and certainly "belligerent occupation," does not best describe the status of the international presence in Bosnia. This is important because *occupiers* have the capacity to act in lieu of a sovereign, though those actions are constrained by the duty to serve as a surrogate for the local sovereign and to do so in accordance with internationally established standards (Benvenisti 1992).[8]

On the other hand, in the Dayton Accords the Republic of Bosnia and Hercegovina, the Republic of Croatia, and the Federal Republic of Yugoslavia essentially consented to let the international community enter Bosnia. In other words, the powers of NATO, the OSCE, and the Office of High Representative, to the extent they arose from the Dayton Accords, come from the Parties to the Accord, not from the use of force or from other international doctrines.

Annex 6 of the Dayton Accords provides that the Parties "shall secure to all persons within their jurisdiction the highest level of internationally recognized human rights and fundamental freedoms," including freedom of expression. Restructuring media, including displacing some media outlets and building new ones, might be termed, in a radical sense, the securing of freedom of expression.

Annex 10 of the Accords recognizes that fulfillment of each party's obligation under the terms of the treaty requires "a wide range of activities" including "the establishment of political and constitutional institutions in Bosnia and Hercegovina." It also provides for the creation of a High Representative whose duties are "to facilitate the Parties' own efforts and [...] coordinate the activities of the organizations and agencies involved in the civilian aspects of the peace settlement." This general architectural commitment could be read to include the kinds of powers that Sfor and NATO exercised in reshaping Bosnian media.

In Annex 1-A, the Agreement on the Military Aspects of the Peace Settlements, each party recognized that NATO would establish a multinational military implementation force (first known as IFOR and then as Sfor) "composed of ground, air and maritime units from NATO and non-NATO nations, deployed in Bosnia [...] to help ensure compliance" with the Accords. The Annex authorized IFOR to "take such actions as required, including the use of necessary force [...] to ensure its own protection." In Annex 3 the Parties agreed to ensure "free and fair elections in [...] a politically neutral environment" and, in that connection, they ensured "freedom of expression and of the press." Additionally, the Parties invited the OSCE to "supervise, in a manner to be determined by the OSCE and in cooperation with other international organizations the OSCE deems necessary, the preparation and conduct" for specific elections, including the elections involved in the post-Dayton media disputes.

The Accords, then, are a charter of authority, a specific and bounded invitation, to particular actors in the international community to participate in the peace process in explicitly limited ways. They grant the international community three important fonts of power. The first font is election-specific and flows from Annex 3 of the Dayton Accords (Fulbrook 1992; Foster 1993).

Many of the aspirations embodied in the Dayton Accords and much of the international community's involvement in Bosnia concerned the political process and the indispensable involvement of the media in this process. The authority of the international community in this area lay with the OSCE. On the other hand, the High Representative, with its powers to "coordinate" and to "facilitate" had power, derivatively, to deal with media questions relating to elections.

For example, in the Bonn statement, the Peace Implementation Council supported a comprehensive OHR media strategy because of "the importance of the role of objective media in the run-up to the 1998 elections" (Bonn Peace Implementation Conference 1997: Conclusions, Art. V, para. 1). If a plural, multi-party Bosnia-Hercegovina was to emerge from Dayton, then, at least in the eyes of the OHR, a morphological unity between political party, ethnic group and dominant channel had to be broken. The OHR saw the Bosnian media structure as antithetical to a multi-ethnic future polity. The seizure of the transmitters that serviced SRT Pale was therefore part of a strategic plan to break the hold of the SDS on the media and the electorate.

Perhaps at the heart of the Dayton Accords was an understanding, at least by the Parties, that memory and its exploitation formed as important an element of peacekeeping as more traditional military and quasi-military undertakings. The maintenance of an intensely partisan, politically controlled, monopoly media, strongly contesting the integrity, goals, and competing narrative of Sfor and the IGOs could not have long been tolerated. If a plural, multi-party Bosnia-Hercegovina was to emerge from Dayton, then, at least in the eyes of the OHR, a morphological unity between political party, ethnic group, and dominant channel had to be broken. The media structure symbolized a Bosnia that was seen as antithetical to a multi-ethnic future polity. Breaking the Bosnian Serb nationalist party's hold on media and the electorate was part of the basis for seizing the transmitters that serviced SRT Pale. In establishing the machinery for elections, the Parties agreed to the placement of a set of election principles and a mechanism for deciding when those principles were violated.

Notes

1   Information warfare has been defined as: "Action taken in support of national security strategy to seize and maintain a decisive advantage by attacking an adversary's information infrastructure through exploitation, denial, and influence, while protecting friendly information systems" (Office of the Chief of Naval Operations 1995).
2   Material for this chapter is taken from news accounts reported by the BBC Monitoring Service, available on the BBC Web Site, www.monitor.bbc.co.uk.
3   The Organization for Security and Cooperation in Europe Media Experts Commission main page is online. Available at: http://www.oscebih.org/mec/mecexperts.htm (viewed 19 February 2001).
4   The Media Support Advisory Group (MSAG) consists of the OHR, Sfor, the OSCE and the UN, the four principal organizations responsible for the implementation of Dayton. Established in late September 1997, its function was essentially to monitor and govern media in Bosnia-Hercegovina to the extent that it could according to the Sintra Declaration and the OSCE's MEC. The MSAG declared itself "the body that provided the executive mechanism to demand the level and type of access required in an outlet deemed in violation of the [...] MEC." If such demands were not complied with, the MSAG would then recommend escalation "as necessary" using the paragraph 70 powers of the Sintra Declaration giving the High Representative authority to "curtail or suspend" any media network or program whose output is in violation of the Dayton Accords.
5   Quotes are from internal documents of the Office of High Representative.

6   The Commission was proposed at the Peace Implementation Conference in Bonn (1997).
7   Another source of law, either authorizing the actions of NATO and the OHR or establishing limits to those actions, involves what might be called the law of Occupation. There has been a debate about the use of the term "occupation" in describing the activities of the international community in Bosnia and a debate, also, over the use of the power of the occupier to justify media and information intervention there. After the Second World War, the United States and its allies made it a major objective to refashion totally the radio broadcasting systems in Germany and Japan. One of the important elements of the Occupation was to construct or reconstruct a democratic society. To do that required a transition and an imposed architecture that would have transformative capabilities. A focus on changes in radio seemed especially appropriate given the key role of propaganda in fueling the war, both at home and abroad.

In Germany, the future structure of broadcasting was changed for ever by the Allies, who forced a splitting up and decentralization so as to prevent a dominant national voice. In Japan, the United States government sought to eradicate all elements of militarism and nationalism, as it was there understood. The first Memorandum of the Allies, in somewhat Orwellian phrases that are invited by this kind of situation, claimed to be re-establishing freedom of speech and of the press, but at the same time required that news be true to facts, be faithful to the policies of the Allied Powers, and refrain from skeptical criticisms of the Allied Forces. None of this history, of course, necessarily serves to justify the actions of the Office of High Representative or NATO's Stabilization Force (Sfor). Bosnia is not Japan or Germany and the accoutrements of Occupation are not exactly present there.

In Japan and Germany, the Allies were "belligerent occupiers," and a framework of international law has developed to articulate standards for such an Occupation. Less well developed is what might be called a "non-belligerent occupation," one that is more characteristic of the Bosnian context. (The question of whether there is such a status as non-belligerent occupier and what powers such an occupier has comes down to consent. And in that sense, the issue of the powers and limitations of this non-belligerent occupier are governed by the Dayton Accords since that is the foundational consent of that agreement).
8   Benvenisti traces the evolution of occupation and outlines its role in modern warfare.

References

Arquilla, John and Ronfeldt, David (1993) "Cyberwar is coming!" *Comparative Strategy*, issue 12.

Belgrade Agreement (1997) Belgrade, 24 September.

Benvenisti, Eyal (1992) *The International Law of Occupation*. Princeton, NJ: Princeton University Press.

Beta News Agency (1997a) "Serb Radio–TV apologizes for 'misrepresentation,' " Belgrade, in Serbo-Croat, broadcast 30 September, 14:46 GMT. Reprinted in *BBC Summary of World Broadcasts*, 3 October. Section: World Broadcast Information; other reports; WBI/0040/WB.

—— (1997b) "High Representative to appoint new Serb Radio–TV head," Belgrade, in Serbo-Croat, broadcast 9 October, 13:25 GMT. Reprinted in *BBC Summary of World Broadcasts*, 17 October, Friday. Section: World Broadcast Information; Bosnia-Hercegovina; WBI/0042/WB.

Bonn Peace Implementation Conference (1997) Bonn, Germany, 10 December. Available at: http://www.ohr.int/docu/d971210a.htm (viewed 4 April 1999).

Bosnian Serb Radio (1997) "Serb broadcasts resume in north after Sfor handover," Pale, in Serbo-Croat, broadcast 1 September, 14:00 GMT. Reprinted in *BBC Summary of World Broadcasts*, 5 September. Section: World Broadcast Information; Bosnia-Hercegovina; WBI/0036/WB.

Bosnian Serb Television (1997) Banja Luka, in Serbo-Croat, broadcast 1 October, 14:35 GMT. Reprinted in *BBC Summary of World Broadcasts*, "High Representative's office issues statement on transmitter seizure," 4 October, Saturday. Section: Part 2 Central Europe, the Balkans; Bosnia-Hercegovina; Bosnian Serbs; EE/D3041/A.

Dnevni Avaz (1997) "High Representative's plans to reorganize media," Sarajevo, in Serbo-Croat, broadcast 30 October. Reprinted in *BBC Summary of World Broadcasts*, 7 November. Section: World Broadcast Information; Bosnia-Hercegovina; WBI/0045/WB.

Foster, Nigel G. (1993) *German Legal System and Laws*. Holmes Beach, FL: Wm. Gaunt and Sons.

Fulbrook, Mary (1992) *The Divided Nation: A History of Germany, 1918–1990*. Oxford, UK: Oxford University Press.

Metzl, Jamie F. (1997) "Information intervention: When switching channels isn't enough," *Foreign Affairs*, Nov./Dec.

Office of High Representative (OHR) (1997) Media strategy paper, April.

—— (1997) Media Support Advisory Group (MSAG) press release. Available at: http://www.ohr.int/press/p970925a.htm. (viewed 17 February 2001).

Office of the Chief of Naval Operations (1995) Department of the Navy, OPNAVINST 3430.26 1, 18 January.

Peace Implementation Conference: Bosnia and Herzegovina 1998: Self-sustaining Structures (1997): Bonn, Germany, V. Media, 2a. 10 December. Available at: http://www.ohr.int/docu/d971210a.htm (viewed 17 January 2001).

Radio B92 (1997) "Serbs sever links with international envoys," Belgrade, in Serbo-Croat, broadcast 8 September, 20:00 GMT. Reprinted in *BBC Summary of World Broadcasts*, 12 September. Section: World Broadcast Information; Bosnia-Hercegovina; WBI/0037/WB.

Radio Bosnia-Hercegovina (1997) "SRT Pale studio staff strike over seized transmitters," Sarajevo, in Serbo-Croat, broadcast 3 October, 13:00 GMT. Reprinted in *BBC Summary of World Broadcasts*, 10 October, Friday. Section: World Broadcast Information; Bosnia-Hercegovina; WBI/0041/WB.

Radio Hajat (1996) "OSCE to launch radio network for free elections in Bosnia," broadcast 15 July (available on LEXIS, ALLWRD Library, BBCSWB File).

Snyder, Timothy (forthcoming) "Memory of sovereignty and sovereignty over memory: Poland, Lithuania, and Ukraine, 1939–1999," in Jan-Werner Muller (ed.) *Memory and Power in Post-war Europe: Studies in the Presence of the Past*, Cambridge, UK: Cambridge University Press.

Voice of America (1997) Washington, in English, broadcast 13 September, 17:30 GMT. Reprinted in *BBC Summary of World Broadcasts*, "Arrival of United States 'jamming' aircraft raises controversy," 19 September, Friday. Section: World Broadcast Information; Brazil/Portugal; WBI/0038/WB.

6

MEDIA REFORM IN JORDAN

The stop–go transition

Naomi Sakr

Introduction

Geopolitical considerations have been, and will remain, highly influential in the evolution of Jordanian legislation affecting media. Since the state of Israel was created in Palestine in 1948, the histories of Jordan and the Palestinians have been closely linked. Waves of Palestinian refugees fled to Jordan in 1948 and again in 1967, when Israel occupied Arab territories during the Arab–Israeli war. Today a large proportion of Jordan's population is of Palestinian origin. The changing status of the West Bank, the Jordanian–Israeli peace treaty of 1994, and a history of unstable relations between the Jordanian and Palestinian leaderships form a prominent backdrop to the struggle over Jordanian media law reform.

Overview of media reform

Milestones in the democratization process

"Two steps forwards, two steps back" is how a local journalist described Jordanian public perceptions of democratic achievements in the kingdom, nearly a decade after the landmark parliamentary elections of 1989 (Henderson 1998a). Jordan University's Center for Strategic Studies (CSS), putting democratization into practice, started polling people across the country in 1993 to gauge their satisfaction with the progress of democratic reforms. In the CSS survey for 1998, the last conducted during the lifetime of King Hussein, participants gave Jordan's democracy a score of 4.91 on a scale of one to ten.[1] Comparing this result to those of previous years, the then director of CSS, Mustafa Hamarneh, said the country clearly felt there had been no fundamental progress toward democratization since 1993.[2] In February 1999, a few months after the CSS poll, King Hussein died, having reigned for forty-seven years, and the throne passed to his son. Aged 37 on his accession and with the mindset of a different generation, King Abdullah immediately called for further democratic reforms. Yet Jordan's protracted transition to democracy had too many false starts for these statements to be viewed optimistically and without reserve.

Lively parliamentary elections first took place in Jordan half a century ago. An important early milestone on the road to political participation was reached in

1952 during the brief reign of Hussein's father, King Talal, whose mental illness forced him to abdicate that same year. Under Talal's constitutional changes, the king retained the absolute right to dissolve parliament and appoint the prime minister but the cabinet was made responsible to the elected parliament. This change, combined with the influx into Jordan of Palestinians displaced by the Arab–Israeli war of 1948, enlivened the kingdom's political parties. In the general election of October 1956, leftist parties won seventeen out of forty seats. They formed a government and took actions such as allowing the Communist Party to publish its newspaper, *Al-Jamaheer*, which had been banned by the Anti-Communism Act of 1953 (Snow 1972: 102). The 21-year-old king was alarmed. With the republican movement growing in Jordan in response to events in the wider Arab world, Hussein used the royal prerogative to dismiss the country's first democratically elected government, declare martial law, ban political parties, and order the Cairo-based radio station, Voice of the Arabs, to be jammed (Snow 1972: 114). From April 1957, the cabinet was appointed by the king and responsible to him, not to parliament.

A fresh attempt at political liberalization occurred in the early 1960s. October 1961 saw elections to a new sixty-seat parliament, with equal representation for the East and West Banks of the Jordan River. Party political activity resumed, expressing mounting opposition to domestic repression and to the government's reluctance to make common cause with other Arab states. Once again, Hussein dissolved parliament. When Israel occupied the West Bank in the Arab–Israeli war of 1967, Hussein shored up his legitimacy by creating a nine-man Consultative Council and a thirty-member Senate, comprising fifteen representatives each from the East and West Banks. But rivalry escalated between the Jordanian authorities and Palestinian guerrilla groups inside Jordan. In September 1970, it erupted into full-scale civil war. The Palestinian groups were crushed and martial law was tightened. Hussein's only gesture toward political participation at this stage was to create a National Union as the country's sole legal political organization. He appointed himself as head of this body and his brother as head of a council of sheikhs and notables dealing with tribal affairs.

The next landmark in Jordan's political evolution was the 1974 Arab summit conference in Rabat. There, Arab leaders recognized the Palestine Liberation Organization (PLO) as the "sole legitimate representative of the Palestinian people," forcing Jordan to cede its claim to the (Israeli-occupied) West Bank. With the East Bank–West Bank composition of Jordan's political institutions now in question, Hussein had the constitution amended to allow elections to be suspended indefinitely. In the longer term, however, this suspension was not tenable. A façade of national consensus was achieved through the drafting of five-year economic development plans. By 1979, pressure for formal East Bank representation persuaded the king to appoint a seventy-five-member National Consultative Council as a substitute for parliament (Yorke 1988: 80). In March 1984, he dissolved this body and ordered elections to a National Assembly. Although political parties remained banned, the 1984 elections (in which women could vote for the first time) were widely regarded as relatively free (Kramer 1994: 220). Nevertheless, the new parliament remained subject to the controls imposed by Hussein during the previous two decades.

As the 1980s progressed, a combination of political and economic factors, both internal and external, contributed to mounting public dissatisfaction.[3] During the 1980s, Jordan had turned to the IMF because it was unable to service the foreign debt it had built up to finance its budget deficits, heavy military spending, and extravagant public sector companies (EIU 1999a: 28). In April 1989, the built-up tension burst forth and resulted in protest riots over price rises on fuel and sugar.[4] The 1989 riots broke out among East Bank Bedouin, normally loyal to the crown. Shaken, King Hussein and his brother, Crown Prince Hassan, cast about urgently for advice. When democratization presented itself as the most viable solution, parliamentary elections were arranged and held in November 1989.[5] A National Charter was drafted pledging respect for citizens' "basic rights and public freedoms." Thereafter, the Anti-Communism Act of 1953 was repealed, martial law was lifted, and the power of the intelligence services was curbed (Kramer 1994: 221).

Further elections followed in 1993 and 1997, with the 1993 general election setting a precedent as the first multi-party election since the 1967 Arab–Israeli war. Political parties had little time to prepare for this event, however, having been legalized only in September 1992. Moreover, political party activity was not the only feature that differentiated Jordan in 1993 from Jordan in 1989. When Iraq invaded Kuwait in August 1990, Jordan's government refused to join the US-led coalition against Iraq. This stance and the war itself caused waves of Palestinian and Jordanian expatriates to leave their homes and jobs in the Gulf and to return to Jordan. In all, an estimated 300,000 migrated between 1991 and 1996 (Hourani 1999: 16). Local conditions, including high unemployment, were consequently a major issue in the 1993 electoral campaign. In the absence of established party platforms, independents won forty-five of the eighty seats, followed by the Islamic Action Front, dominated by the Muslim Brotherhood, with sixteen.

As noted at the beginning of this section, 1993 marked a high point of Jordan's democratic reforms. By 2000, it could be said that the country was enjoying the longest continuous period of political opening in its short and turbulent history. However, the achievements of 1989–1993, which bore the hallmarks of preliminary steps toward a structured transition, were not enhanced during the period from 1994 to 1999. On the contrary, the electoral law was changed to favor tribal candidates over political activists and the law governing municipal elections was also modified in 1995 to give the cabinet power to appoint the mayor of the capital, Amman, as well as half of Amman's forty-member municipal council (Kamal 1999a: 14). Jordan's peace treaty with Israel of October 1994, while beneficial in triggering debt cancellation from the United States and other Western creditors, was sufficiently controversial internally to frighten the government into taking new measures to suppress dissent.

Hopes that peace would bring instant economic prosperity proved to be unfounded; instead, bread riots took place in August 1996. As the 1997 general election approached, the government slammed the democratization process into reverse. In May 1997, it clamped down on freedoms conceded in 1993. Opposition groups boycotted the 1997 election in protest at this reversal, leaving the new parliament toothless and quiescent. More rioting flared up in February 1998 and, as King Hussein's health deteriorated, the absence of political direction became increasingly acute. With King Abdullah's accession, the climate improved enough for groups that had boycotted the 1995 municipal elections and 1997 general election to end their boycott and take part in the municipal elections of July 1999. As regards media freedom, however, the situation remained clouded by the rapid sequence of media law advances and retreats experienced since 1993.

Milestones of media law reform

Ironically, the Press and Publications Law in force in Jordan at the end of King Hussein's reign was effectively less liberal than the one in force at the start of it (Hassanat 1998). Despite some relaxation of the law in 1999 and the promise of a "free media zone," the overall thrust of change after 1993 was to restore and even increase curbs on free speech rather than remove them.

The 1953 Press and Publications Law, modified in 1955 and 1973, instituted a licensing regime for the press. It authorized the government to withdraw the license of any publication deemed to threaten national security, contravene the constitution, harm the "national feeling," or offend against public decency. It forbade publication of unofficial news about the royal family or unauthorized military information. In the early years, these powers were used sparingly, achieving the desired effect mainly through deterrence and personal contacts between government officials and newspaper editors (Rugh 1987: 78). As Jordan's conflict with Palestinian guerrilla groups intensified, however, the government reinforced its control on the press. The 1973 version of the law stated that cabinet decisions on licensing were not subject to review from any quarter. It prohibited criticism of heads of friendly states and placed restrictions on publishing information supplied by foreign envoys.[6]

The 1980s saw little in the way of media reform. Layla Sharaf, appointed Minister of Information in 1985, quickly resigned on discovering that her job was to curb the press, not defend press freedom (Najjar 1998: 27). Within days of the outbreak of the Palestinian intifada in December 1987, efforts to silence government critics (by detaining them) were in full swing. In November 1988, the government took shares in the leading daily newspapers from their private owners.

Judged against the previous twenty years, the 1993 Press and Publications Law marked a major milestone of media law reform (*Official Gazette* 1993). It followed on the heels of the 1991 National Charter, which promised media freedom (see below), the 1991 lifting of martial law, the 1992 legalization of political parties, and the 1992 law allowing citizens to have recourse to the High Court of Justice to contest government decisions. Applied in conjunction with these other checks on government power, the 1993 press law helped to unlock the door to many new, more outspoken, publications. It did this mainly by making the licensing system subject to judicial review. It also ordered the government to reduce its newspaper shareholdings to 30 per cent.

In many other respects, the 1993 law was illiberal, repeating earlier prohibitions on items deemed to contravene vaguely worded injunctions relating to the dignity of the royal family, heads of state, and diplomats, the need to protect national unity, public morals, and so on. Large numbers of journalists and publications were penalized under these provisions. Yet striking contrasts between the licensing regime in Jordan and that in other Arab states contributed to a feeling that the climate for media activity had changed. This was reinforced when a former *Jordan Times* columnist, Marwan Muasher, became Minister of Information and announced in 1996 that he planned to end the government's monopoly over broadcasting.

Muasher's plans made no headway, however. In May 1997, a Provisional Law amending the 1993 press law changed the situation so dramatically that one member of parliament described it as the "Law for Nationalizing Thought" (*Al-Ra'i* 1997).[7] It gave newspapers three months to comply with a twelve-fold increase in capital requirements. It made the existing prohibitions on content even stiffer, quadrupled the fines for contravening them, authorized the government to close publications permanently, and reinstated the 1973 requirement that newspaper editors should have worked full-time in the press for ten years.

Although the High Court ruled in 1998 that the 1997 law was unconstitutional, the regime had by then achieved the desired effect of intimidating publishers into practising self-censorship. Moreover, it responded to the High Court ruling by pushing a tough new Press and Publications Law through parliament in August 1998. A year later this was softened somewhat, at the bidding of King Abdullah, but the amendments were not so sweeping as to compensate for the setbacks to date. With free speech still criminalized under Jordan's Penal Code, the press law amendments of 1999 were widely criticized as cosmetic. In early 2000, when the cabinet put the finishing touches to its plan for a free media zone, offering offshore status to private investors in publishing and broadcasting, skeptics were united in questioning the government's definition of "free."

Impact of the legal and institutional framework on media law reform

Jordan is variously described as a constitutional monarchy and a benevolent autocracy. The ambiguity arises from the king's extensive powers, which limit the scope for real political participation by ordinary citizens. Under the constitution, the king appoints the prime minister, supervises the appointment of cabinet ministers, and appoints members of the upper chamber of parliament, the Senate. He has the power to dissolve parliament, call new elections, and declare martial law. As recounted above, these powers have been used frequently. There are no constitutional provisions to make respect for freedom of expression binding on the executive, the legislature, or the judiciary. For this reason, references to freedom of expression in the constitution merely reflect aspirations and official discourse rather than any legal constraint on government power (Article 19 1997: 15).

The most resounding royally endorsed sentiments in favor of free and public political dialogue are those contained in the National Charter. It was devised by a Royal Commission set up in April 1990 in the wake of the riots and elections of 1989. Article 5 of the charter requires the state to draw up policies to ensure that individual citizens and social and political groups may exercise their right to "use the national mass media to state their opinions." The problem with the charter, however, is that its legal status remains unclear and the provisions of subsequent royal decrees have contradicted its pledges.[8] As a forty-page document, the charter could never be put to a referendum. Neither was it passed by parliament.

The separation of executive, legislative, and judicial powers in Jordan is blurred by the king's everyday involvement in the formulation of domestic and foreign policy, his powers of patronage, and his power to issue royal decrees. Whether or not a prime minister asserts his constitutional right to select his own cabinet and make ministers accountable to parliament depends in practice on the individual occupying the post. Jordanian prime ministers rarely stay long in office and, according to one estimate, in the fifteen years prior to 1999, only three prime ministers were "strong" (Interview, Amman, 23 November 1998). Moreover, the prime minister is potentially locked in a power struggle with the chief of the royal court.

Although the September 1992 Political Parties Law No. 32 permitted political parties to contest elections to the lower house of parliament (the eighty-member National Assembly), subsequent curbs on political activity and an election boycott in 1997 served to undermine the legislature's legitimacy and independence. Calls mounted in 1999 for the house to be enlarged to 100 or 120 seats in time for the 2001 elections and for the electoral law to be changed in order to enable voters to return political activists as well as tribal elders to parliament.[9] In the meantime, and pending other legal changes that would liberalize the holding of political meetings and the publishing of party newspapers, campaigning by the kingdom's twenty-one parties would remain highly constrained.[10] Whereas the 1992 law exempted party newspapers from being liable to suspension, the 1997 press law amendments removed this exemption.[11] Meanwhile, the 1992 law itself placed strict curbs on party resources by prohibiting civil society organizations to undertake any activity deemed to be partisan. It forbade "associations, charitable organizations, and clubs" to allow their "premises, instrumentalities, and assets" to be used "for the benefit of any partisan organization."[12]

Similarly, while the High Court of Justice Law of 1992 marked an important step toward strengthening the power of the judiciary vis-à-vis the executive, many further changes were needed to enhance the judiciary's independence.[13] The High Court's ten judges overturned numerous misapplications of the 1993 press law, clearing the way for publication of new political papers and a book on Jordan's observance of human rights (Najjar 1998: 31). In January 1998, importantly, they agreed with newspaper editors that the 1997 press law amendments failed to satisfy the necessary criteria for temporary laws. In December 1999, the High Court overturned the Jordan Press Association's refusal to grant membership to a journalist of eight years' standing (Hamzeh 1999c). For the Jordan Bar Association, however, as for many other observers, these checks on government authority were insufficient. They called for the creation of a constitutional court and an independent body to assess the performance of judges. They also sought the limitation or cancellation of special courts, such as the State Security Court. Draft legislation to this effect went before parliament in late 1999 (EIU 1999b: 16). The draft also proposed replacing the Ministry of Justice with a Higher Judiciary Council that would be responsible for appointing judges (Jordan Times 1999).

Media reform by sector

Reform in print media

Government controls over the press are numerous and heavy-handed, but have failed to stifle completely the vibrancy of newspapers born when short-lived political liberalization measures were introduced during 1991–1993.

State regulation and ownership

Press laws underwent a series of changes during the 1990s, some serving the cause of press freedom and others working against it. For example, the so-called "amendments" made in 1997 to the Press and Publications Law (No. 10) of 1993 actually transformed the spirit of that law from one respecting the separation of powers between the executive and judiciary to one intended to close all possible "loopholes" for free speech.[14] Officials at the time pointed out that the 1997 version of the law abolished prison sentences for publication "crimes," replacing them with fines, and cited this as evidence of greater freedom. They also stressed that the judiciary, not the government, would oversee the law's application. However, the law's numerous strict requirements greatly increased the scope for possible violations and decreased the leeway available to the courts for dealing with them. At the same time, prison sentences could still be imposed for publication crimes under Jordan's Penal Code.

The press enjoyed just a few months of relative respite between January 1998, when the High Court threw out the 1997 amendments, and August 1998, when parliament endorsed the 1998 Press and Publications Law which reinstated most of the 1997 restrictions and added new ones (Article 19: *Memorandum* 1997). During this period, the regime may have concluded that it had acted against its own interests, given the enormous amount of adverse publicity surrounding both the 1997 and 1998 laws. Both sets of legislation provoked a sustained uproar from newspapers and local and international human rights groups. Moreover, the 1998 law was introduced while members of the private press were actively demonstrating to the public the merits of investigative journalism. On the other hand, anticipating a relaunch of the stalled Middle East peace process following the Israeli election scheduled for 1999, the regime evidently judged that the risks attached to allowing unfettered press comment on highly sensitive Israeli–Palestinian negotiations were too high.[15] Its compromise was to pledge that the 1998 law, the most restrictive in the kingdom's history, would be applied with a light touch (Henderson 1998d). Cabinet ministers associated with the law's introduction were replaced and a conciliatory gesture was made toward the press camp with the appointment of Nasser Judeh, until then head of Jordan Radio and Television, as Minister of Information.

In the event, the 1998 press law was invoked on several occasions, while other laws (such as those relating to company registration) were also used to similar effect. Having been primed to pursue journalists, the security apparatus continued a campaign of harassment even after the February 1999 accession of King Abdullah, who surrounded himself with officials believed, rightly or wrongly, to be reasonably broadminded about the press.[16] October 1999 saw the introduction of yet another version of the Press and Publications Law with several of the most repressive articles of the 1998 law formally dropped.[17] It lowered the capital requirements for newspapers, reduced the scale of fines for journalists, and, importantly, cancelled fourteen contentious and vaguely worded restrictions on content. Indeed, the 1999 press law may eventually come to be seen in retrospect as marking a milestone in Jordan's democratization process. Judged against other criteria, however, the apparently less oppressive 1999 law did not seem to be such an innovation. The authorities could still rely on the Penal Code to take journalists, writers, and politicians to court for the crimes of lese-majesty (insulting the king or royal family), inciting sectarianism, or disparaging a foreign country.[18] Meanwhile, the 1999 version of the law still restricted the right to publish to those who could put up the necessary capital (to exceed US$700,000 for a daily and US$70,000 for a weekly) and maintained sanctions for journalists failing to meet government-determined standards of reasonableness and objectivity.

The task of deciding whether press material is reasonable and objective falls to the Press and Publications Department (PPD) within the Ministry of Information. The choice of director for this department consequently sends a clear signal about the government's intentions with regard to application of the current Press and Publications Law. When the harsh law of 1998 came into effect, the authorities backed up their promise to use it sparingly by appointing a known human rights campaigner, Iyad Qattan, to head the PPD.[19] In October 1999, his successor, Abdullah Etoum, defended the 1999 press law amendments by stressing that the PPD had dropped all pending court cases against journalists and had brought no new ones for the past six months (Hattar 1999). He omitted to mention that the security forces were continuing to apprehend journalists. Staff of the independent daily *Al-Arab al-Yawm* (Arabs of Today) were repeatedly questioned by intelligence officers during 1999 and in September, just one month before Etoum's statement, the paper's editor-in-chief, Riyad Hroub, was arrested under the Companies Law on embezzlement charges. It seemed to be no coincidence that amendments to the 1997 Companies Law were rushed through parliament in August 1999, increasing government powers over private entrepreneurs.

Journalists hopeful that 2000 would see the first steps toward the dismantling of Jordan's state censorship apparatus were offered confusing signs. On one hand they remained suspicious that cases brought against colleagues for non-editorial offences simply amounted to PPD harassment and intimidation by the back door. They did not doubt that the Penal Code would be used to charge journalists with offences no longer listed in the Press and Publications Law. On the other hand, they were optimistic that the promised ending of PPD censorship of foreign publications (discussed below) could ultimately lead to the PPD's transformation from a censorship body to a bureau of information and research (Hattar 1999).

Meanwhile, there was little obvious prospect of an imminent reduction of state ownership of the press. State ownership of three daily newspapers was maintained in the wake of press law changes in 1998–1999, as the 1997 amendments cancelled the time limit set by the 1993 law for state shareholdings to be reduced to 30 per cent. The most widely distributed national daily, *Al-Ra'i*, with circulation of around 70,000 per day is 62 per cent state owned. The same applies to the English-language daily, *Jordan Times*, which is produced along with *Al-Ra'i* by the Jordan Press Foundation but has a much smaller circulation of around 8,000. The government stake in the third daily, *Al-Destour*, stands at 35 per cent and its circulation at 50,000. The government's interest in their profitability ensures that these papers have priority for advertising from state-owned enterprises, news stories from the state news agency, Petra, and favorable publicity on state-owned television and radio.

Ownership and regulation of the private press

Whereas the government-backed *Al-Ra'i* has been in existence since the early 1970s, the privately owned and more self-assertive daily *Al-Arab al-Yawm* managed to attract a loyal following within months of its launch in April 1997. Its circulation was estimated at 70,000 in 1999 (Associated Press 1999b). The other privately owned daily, *Al-Aswaq* (Markets), started as a business weekly in April 1993 but began to publish daily later that year. By late 1999, its low circulation (around 7,000 copies) had forced it to reduce the number of pages to cut costs (Hussein 2000).

One of the biggest breakthroughs in the recent history of the Jordanian print media was the explosion of privately owned weekly newspapers that followed ratification of the Press and Publications Law of 1993. The number of weekly titles increased more than three-fold to about eighteen, not counting papers published by political parties.[20] However, the papers licensed under the 1993 law were kept on a short leash. The exact number of court cases brought against the weeklies between the press laws of 1993 and 1997 is not known but appears to be very high. The Ministry of Information figure is sixty-two cases against all papers during the period, including fifty-eight against weeklies. Yet one publisher told Human Rights Watch that thirty cases had been brought against his paper alone (1997: 12). The culture of litigation was intensified and entrenched by the 1997 press law amendments, which imposed tough capital requirements, steep fines, and the threat of permanent closure. All of a sudden, proprietors of weekly papers were forced to find capital of JD300,000 (US$422,750), be prepared to pay fines of up to JD25,000 (US$35,225), and, even then, risked having their publication suspended or closed for violating vaguely worded restrictions on content.[21] Inevitably, mergers and "voluntary" closures followed, but the stronger papers resisted and the government grew impatient. Nine days before the November 1997 election, it stepped in again and suspended thirteen publications, most of them weeklies, for failing to increase their capital to the required amount.

For those private papers that survived the government's heaviest onslaught against the press in 1997–1998, the struggle was far from over. Al-Dar al-Wataniya (National House for Publishing and Distribution), the publishing group responsible for the bold daily *Al-Arab al-Yawm*, the Amman evening paper *Al-Massaiya*, and the successful weekly *Shihan*, is partly owned by Jordan's National Bank and Engineering Association. It became subject to a vicious circle of harassment in which obstacles created by formal and informal state regulation of the press played a major part in the group's mounting financial difficulties; these in turn have increased its vulnerability to state intervention.

June and July 1999 saw attacks of various kinds against journalists connected with the *Al-Arab al-Yawm* publishing group. Shaker al-Jawhari, a regular columnist for the paper, was arrested by the General Intelligence Department, held for thirty-six hours and questioned about his writing.[22] Abdel-Hadi Raji Majali, a journalist with the same paper, was assaulted by unknown assailants and hospitalized for three days after receiving threatening phone calls telling him to stop criticizing the government. Then Sinan Shaqdih of *Al-Massaiya* was detained by intelligence forces for what the State Security Court described as harming relations with brotherly countries. He was released only after King Abdullah personally intervened (Kamal 1999b: 12–13).

Meanwhile, the services of Petra were withdrawn from *Al-Arab al-Yawm* in July 1999 on grounds of "unethical reporting" (Associated Press 1999b).[23] Being ostracized in this way compounded the effects of two years during which state-owned enterprises placed virtually no advertising with the paper (Ayoub 1999). As the group's financial situation deteriorated, staff laid off in 1999 filed lawsuits saying their salaries had not been paid and a board member accused the group's chairman, Riyad Hroub, of financial mismanagement. Hroub was arrested and released on bail equivalent to US$84,500 in September (Fairouz 1999c). Coming perilously close to compulsory liquidation under the terms of Jordan's recently amended Companies Law, the paper moved to avoid this in November by halting publication temporarily while the group's finances were restructured.[24] In December 1999, however, its assets were frozen when the Social Security Department raised a case against it for unpaid fees (Hamzeh 1999b). The case concerned the sum of JD186,000, a rather small amount compared to those reportedly owed by some other Jordanian institutions.

The weekly *Al-Majd* was another prominent publication to experience continued government obstruction after King Abdullah took the throne. In February, its editor-in-chief, Fahd al-Rimawi, was detained for a few hours and his paper suspended for two weeks when he printed a report about an exchange said to have taken place between King Hussein and his brother Prince Hassan. *Al-Majd*'s first edition when it reappeared on news-stands in March 1999 contained a lead story that was deliberately left incomplete to avoid legal risks.[25] The 60-year-old editor of the weekly *Al-Bilad*, Abdel-Karim al-Barghouti, was detained for fourteen days in August 1999 when the prime minister's son, Issam Rawabdeh, took exception to the paper's report that he had "chatted up nurses" outside a hospital in Amman.[26] Requests for Barghouti to be released on bail because of his heart problems were refused.

Diversity within print media

Muted criticism of certain aspects of government has long been permitted in Jordanian newspapers. Rugh, writing in the 1970s and characterizing Jordan's press as "loyalist," noted that negative coverage of public services and economic policies was accepted, provided it cast no doubt on the top leadership (Rugh 1987: 75). The emergence of non-government dailies and weeklies in the 1990s obliged papers in government ownership to sharpen their coverage to maintain market share. Corruption stories appearing in *Al-Arab al-Yawm*, in particular, would tend to be covered by *Al-Ra'i* after an interval of three to four days. Unlike their private competitors, reporters on *Al-Ra'i* and its English-language companion, the *Jordan Times*, would be required to obtain a comment from a government representative before reporting on government affairs. With officials unaccustomed to making themselves available for comment at short notice, these papers' coverage of breaking stories is often delayed. Apart from this constraint, the *Jordan Times* has tended to enjoy more leeway than *Al-Ra'i* because of its predominantly expatriate and foreign readership and because, inside Jordan, its distribution is limited mainly to Amman and the Red Sea tourist resort of Aqaba. *Jordan Times* staff are proud that their paper pushed the limits of government censorship even before the vaunted liberalization process began in 1989.

Nevertheless, human rights and democratization issues started to make headlines in the private press on a regular basis only in the mid-1990s. Some weeklies gained a reputation for unprofessional sensationalism, but others such as *Shihan* and *Al-Majd* came to be regarded as serious and valued forums for news on public affairs. In 1997, the daily *Al-Arab al-Yawm* broke the story of an assassination attempt by the Israeli secret service, Mossad, against Khaled Mishaal of the Palestinian resistance group, Hamas, in Amman. In 1998, it investigated a water pollution scandal that hit Amman during its hottest summer for half a century and exposed malpractice in the sale of an oil pipeline, prompting the government to halt the sale. In 1999, an editor and cartoonist at *Al-Arab al-Yawm* received a court summons for printing a cartoon showing members of parliament on board a truck following an arrow pointing to "the 21st century." The speaker of the lower house apparently took offence because the cartoon suggested MPs had acted with undue haste in passing certain legislation (*Jordan Times* staff, 1999b).

The mid-1990s also saw the birth of political satire in the Jordanian press, with the launch of *Abed Rabbo* in August 1996. This weekly's first issue sold 10,000 copies, with sales subsequently reaching 26,000 at their peak. A few months into its existence, *Abed Rabbo* published a photograph of members of the security forces beating up journalists protesting outside the prime minister's office, juxtaposing it with a denial from the Minister of Information that this had taken place (Najjar 1998: 33). Faced with the capital requirements and fines of the 1997 press law, *Abed Rabbo* closed in June 1997, making a brief reappearance on the news-stands in the spring of 1998.

Al-Jamaheer, the Communist Party newspaper banned in the 1950s, was revived in the wake of the 1993 law, along with papers such as *Al-Ahali* (Democratic People's Party), *Al-Masira* (Democratic Progressive Party), *Al-Fajr al-Jadid* (Socialist Democratic Party), *Al-Nahda* (National Constitutional Party), and so on. Given the fragmentation of the country's opposition, this section of Jordan's press generally failed to build up a large following even before the 1997 clampdown. The exception was *Al-Sabeel*, the Islamist weekly established in 1993 and owned by members of the Muslim Brotherhood. Ironically, frequent criticism by *Al-Sabeel* of what it called "indecent and obscene" material in other newspapers provided the government with ammunition in its attempts to justify the tough curbs of the 1997 and 1998 press laws. Ministers claimed that sections of the press were themselves in favor of tighter laws.

As preparations were made to soften the Press and Publications Law in 1999 and as the government sought to stock its arsenal with alternative weapons against the private press, the government-backed media used ever stronger invective against their rivals. Petra put out an unsigned editorial stating that:

> The media and journalism will always be a target for the petty and envious sector, which works according to its own interests, narrow calculations and murky objectives. They have managed to infiltrate this sacred profession to spew their poison through the institutions they have managed to get hold of through dirty money. It is our duty to condemn this hateful bunch.
>
> (Fairouz 1999b)

Internationalization of print media

Jordan is a state party to the International Covenant on Civil and Political Rights (ICCPR), and, therefore, has committed itself to upholding the right of freedom of expression "regardless of frontiers" found in Article 19 (2) of the ICCPR. In practice, however, it makes ample use of the ICCPR provisos in Article 19 (3) that allow certain restrictions in the interests of respecting reputations, protecting national security, public order, and public health and morals. There are thus very few openings for foreign press activity in Jordan. Article 19 of the 1993 Press and Publications Law forbade non-Jordanians to secure ownership of press companies within Jordan, while Article 19A (1) of the 1992 Political Parties Law stated that parties should depend only on "Jordanian, local, known and specified sources" for their financial resources. The 1998 Press and Publications Law maintained these restrictions and they remained in force after other articles of the 1998 law had been amended. Directors, owners, and editors of press institutions are required to be Jordanian nationals living in Jordan.[27] In Articles 46, 9, and 11 of the law, press institutions and individuals working for them are prohibited from receiving unauthorized financial support from non-Jordanian sources, while accreditation for foreign journalists and foreign news agencies is allowed only on the basis of reciprocity and only if the bureau chief is Jordanian.

The Press and Publications Department controls the entry of foreign publications into the kingdom. Its director announced in February 1999, less than a fortnight after King Abdullah's accession, that Palestinian newspapers and magazines would be allowed into Jordan for the first time since 1967, provided they respected the 1998 Press and Publications Law (Associated Press 1999a). In October 1999, after the law was amended, the new PPD director pledged to lift all obstacles hindering the entry of books, periodicals, and newspapers, enabling them to go from the airport straight to the news-stands (Hattar 1999). With this move, the PPD implicitly acknowledged that its previous attempts to ban the entry of London-based pan-Arab dailies, notably *Al-Quds al-Arabi* and *Al-Hayat*, had not prevented would-be readers from accessing these papers' websites.

International organizations have played a significant role in publicizing the twists and turns of press law in Jordan, both inside and outside the country. The United Kingdom-based Article 19, the US-based Committee to Protect Journalists and Human Rights Watch, and Reporters sans Frontières, based in France, have had a particularly high profile in this respect. In October 1997, a month before Jordan's general election, Article 19 joined with local bodies to hold a seminar in Amman to discuss the May 1997 press amendments. An Article 19 report, funded by the European Commission and entitled "Blaming the Press: Jordan's Democratization Process in Crisis," was presented at the seminar by Saïd Essoulami, who said that Jordan had "slipped out of the top league" in terms of press freedom in the Arab world (Borger 1997). December 1999 saw the opening of a Human Rights Office in Jordan's Prime Ministry under the auspices of the United Nations Development Programme (UNDP). Its aim was to draft a national plan, over a period of two to three years, to develop Jordanian state authorities' understanding of human rights protection and promotion, including protecting and promoting the mass media (*Jordan Times* staff 1999c).

Self-regulation in the print media

The Jordan Press Association (JPA), formed by the Jordan Press Association Law of 1983 during the period of martial law, officially decides who may and who may not practice print journalism in the kingdom. Journalists working for newspapers owned by political parties are excluded from the JPA but for other journalists who wish to be recognized as such, membership of the association is mandatory according to a JPA resolution passed in July 1993. It is a condition of membership that journalists swear an oath in front of the Minister of Information and the Secretary-General of the JPA pledging to respect the country's Press and Publications Law. Members are also required in articles 15, 18, and 20 of the 1993 law to have a university degree or three years' training from a Jordanian publication and they must be working full-time. This stipulation precludes many freelancers and correspondents of foreign publications from joining the JPA. Those who practice their profession in contravention of these rules know that they could be prosecuted at any time. Nevertheless, the growth of non-government papers in the 1990s and the prospect that their journalists would outnumber pro-government members of the JPA prompted the government to open JPA membership to employees of the state-owned Jordan Radio and Television Corporation. An amendment to this effect passed through parliament in August 1998 (Henderson 1998c).

In 1999, the JPA's most public activity was to expel three members for visiting Israel in September of that year. Their visit was said to have violated the JPA's ban on normalization with Israel. The expulsion created serious dilemmas for all concerned; not least the three members who all worked for government-owned papers and who would have to quit their jobs if denied JPA membership.[28] As the controversy raged, the three were given the option to apologize, which they duly took, allowing the expulsion order to be reversed (Hamzeh 1999a). Soon afterward, in another incident, the Higher Court of Justice forced the JPA to reverse its decision to deny membership to Shaker al-Jawhari, a consultant for *Al-Arab al-Yawm* and a columnist with a Gulf newspaper. The Higher Court's ruling was based on the fact that the JPA council had failed to respond to Jawhari's application within the prescribed deadline of thirty days (Hamzeh 1999d).

Civil society and the press

Among the many highly restrictive provisions of the 1998 Press and Publications Law was Article 41, which prohibited publishing institutions, including study and research centers, from receiving financial assistance from abroad without permission from the government (via the Press and Publications Department). This provided yet another mechanism capable of hampering the work of the few academic and non-governmental organizations campaigning openly for press law reform. In most cases, such groups are dependent on a mixture of external funding and the motivation and tenacity of one or two individuals.

Reflecting another aspect of civil society, the opinion polls on democratization, conducted by the Center for Strategic Studies under Mustafa Hamarneh, have already been mentioned. Another notable voice within Jordanian civil society has been that of the Al-Urdun al-Jadid (New Jordan) Research Center, run by a former dissident, Hani Hourani. This center translated and distributed the Article 19 report on Jordan, *Blaming the Press*. The Arab Media Institute, established by George Hawatmeh, a former editor of the *Jordan Times*, also made its mark at the time of the 1997 press law amendments by launching the monthly media journal, *Al-Mashreq al-I'lami*, containing politicized analysis of issues related mainly to the Jordanian press. Rami Khouri, another former *Jordan Times* editor and widely read Amman-based syndicated columnist, joined the chorus of condemnation over the 1997 clampdown on the press (Khouri 1997). The first female member of the lower house of parliament, Toujan al-Faisal, was an outspoken critic of the 1997 press laws.

Abdullah Hassanat, the editor of the *Jordan Times* at the time of the 1998 Press and Publications Law, gave one of the most candid presentations heard at a conference on "Culture and Communication: A Global Information Society," held in Amman in November 1998. With very few exceptions, he said, local universities and newspapers had failed to help "create a breed of free-minded intelligentsia capable of defending the country at crucial junctures" (Hassanat 1998). While apparently not changing the government's mind about proceeding with the press law alterations, opposition by Hassanat, Hourani, and others served to complement critical comments from international press freedom groups and to challenge the authorities to present a more liberal face to Jordan's western financiers.

The MacBride Roundtable and the Jordan Institute of Diplomacy, in conjunction with the Amman-based media-training group for the East Mediterranean area, Jemstone, financed at that point by the European Union, jointly organized the 1998 conference on Culture and Communication. Subsequently reincarnated as the Jemstone Network, with a remit to run courses in independent journalism and create networks of communications specialists across the Middle East region, Jemstone, under the leadership of former BBC journalist Tudor Lomas, demonstrated that such work could be undertaken from Amman.

Broadcasting reform

State ownership and regulation

The state's monopoly over radio and television broadcasting from Amman is exercised through the Jordan Radio and Television Corporation (JRTV), which is under the administrative and financial control of the Ministry of Information and run by government employees. By this means, the government controls what is broadcast. Moves to amend the 1985 law banning private ownership of Jordanian broadcasting stations were signaled in 1996 but had yet to bear fruit by early 2000. The intention in 1996 was to end the government's monopoly, set up an autonomous radio and television entity, and establish a new, more independent status for Petra (*Al-Ra'i* 1996). Such liberalization was ruled out by the hardline stance on the media adopted by the new government in 1997. Nevertheless, the government did allow a non-commercial radio station run by an Iraqi opposition group, the Iraqi National Accord, to operate from a mobile studio near Amman during a period of strained relations between Jordan and the Iraqi government (*Al-Quds al-Arabi* 1997: 16).

In late 1999, plans to reform Jordanian broadcasting resurfaced and a ten-member committee, headed by the Minister of Information, was set up to consider ways of transforming JRTV and Petra into commercial entities with joint public–private sector ownership (*Jordan Times* staff 1999a). A technical team was appointed by the committee to draw up the necessary legislation and was scheduled to complete its work in early 2000, with subsequent government deliberations expected to take a few months. Questions remained as to how much actual change the restructuring would bring. Employees of both JRTV and Petra were reassured that they would not lose their jobs but would be re-appointed to the new organizations. At the same time, it seemed likely that the regulatory body expected to replace the Ministry of Information in overseeing the broadcasting sector would have fairly extensive powers for formulating media policies and monitoring adherence to a prescribed code of ethics (Hamzeh 2000a).

Private enterprise and internationalization

As a first step toward opening Jordan's broadcasting sector to private enterprise, the government formally announced at the beginning of 2000 that it planned to create what was initially called a "media free zone" and subsequently, with a slight shift of emphasis, a "free media zone." King Abdullah espoused the free zone concept, instructing the government in October 1999 to draft a law that would provide tax and customs exemptions and support services and residence permits to attract private satellite broadcasters and production companies to Jordan. In this he seemed to be developing an idea first hinted at in 1998 (*Cable and Satellite Europe* 1998). The free zone, to be established on a tract of land near the premises of JRTV, was deemed to have a promising future because Arab satellite companies based in London and Rome were looking to cut costs by relocating to the Arab world. With Egypt having already established a Media Production City near Cairo, and with Lebanon and Dubai (in the United Arab Emirates) likely to join the competition to attract the Arab satellite firms, Jordan beat Egypt by a few days in announcing the creation of its free media zone (Feuilherade 2000: 13). It was hoped that the project would alleviate local unemployment by creating 10,000 jobs and boost foreign direct investment into the kingdom (Hamzeh 2000b).

It was not clear, however, exactly how much freedom private broadcasters and production companies operating in the Jordanian "free zone" would enjoy. For a start, it appeared that they would be free only to transmit outside Jordan, as the alternative would mean competing with local media on unequal terms. The Prime Minister, Abdel-Raouf Rawabdeh, said that investors, whether Jordanian, Arab or foreign, would have "absolute freedom of expression" and would be free to hire anyone they chose without having to abide by Jordanian laws. Yet the twenty-one articles in the draft law published by Petra on 17 January 2000 indicated that the prime minister would appoint the chairman and six-member board of the entity running the free zone and that contracts signed between this entity and investors would require the latter to observe a code of ethics. Details of the code were not disclosed (Hamzeh 2000b). Previously Ayman Majali, speaking as Deputy Prime Minister and Minister of Information in October 1999, had said that the code would ensure that broadcast material did not undermine Jordan's cultural traditions or criticize religion (Hamzeh and Henderson 1999).

Some potential investors doubted the Jordanian authorities' commitment to freedom of expression. They assumed that Jordan would not want to risk being blamed for programs likely to offend the Saudi, Kuwaiti, or other rich Arab regimes. There were also questions about what foreign broadcasters operating from Amman would be allowed to report about Jordan itself. In October 1999, while the idea of the media zone project was taking shape, Jordanian police attacked and injured Saad Selawi, a correspondent for the London-based, Saudi-owned satellite broadcaster, MBC. They seized him, allegedly broke his camera, and held him for two hours, despite his injuries. Selawi had been trying to film the scene of an armed bank robbery the previous day (Hussein 1999).

In an earlier incident demonstrating the limits of official tolerance, the government closed the Amman office of Qatar's *Al-Jazeera* Satellite Channel in protest at a discussion program, which was said to have slandered Jordan and its people. The program, carried on 3 November 1998 as part of *Al-Jazeera*'s weekly series *Al-Itijah al-Mu'akis* (The Opposite Direction) and chaired by its Syrian presenter, Faisal al-Qassim, dealt with the peace treaty between Jordan and Israel. It contained remarks by another Syrian, Mohammed Khalifa, to the effect that Jordan had been established to serve the "Zionist entity" (Israel) and that Jordan was plotting with Israel to deprive Syria of water resources. Jordan was represented in the discussion by a former foreign minister, Kamel Abu Jaber (*BBC Summary of World Broadcasts* 1998). Citing Article 9 of the 1998 Press and Publications Law, the Director General of Jordan's Press and Publications Department (part of the Ministry of Information) cancelled the accreditation of Jordanian and non-Jordanian correspondents for *Al-Jazeera* in Jordan. The PPD justified this action by saying that the management of *Al-Jazeera* had deliberately insulted Jordan's people and its political system (Arabicnews.com 1998).[29]

There are no bans or controls on reception of satellite broadcasting inside Jordan and more than 15 per cent of the population has access to satellite television (Eutelsat 1998). A wireless cable (MMDS) service was introduced in parts of Amman in 1995, managed by JRTV and rebroadcasting channels from the Saudi-owned pay-TV company ART (Arab Radio and Television), along with BBC World, CNN, and others. Competition from free-to-air direct-to-home satellite television kept subscriptions to the MMDS service very low. Controls on satellite broadcasting have hitherto been exercised by JRTV, as the authority required to approve other companies' satellite uplinks from Jordan for transmission abroad. The free media zone project was expected to remove this bottleneck.

Diversity in broadcasting

For reasons of geography, Jordanians in certain parts of the country can receive terrestrial television transmissions from neighboring states, notably Israel and Syria. Some Israeli programming is subtitled in Arabic. JRTV has, itself, undertaken to broadcast some programming produced by the Palestine Television Corporation based in Gaza and to provide Hebrew soundtracks for television current affairs programs and political talk shows in an effort to familiarize Israelis with Jordanian thinking on the Middle East peace process.[30] Plans also emerged in early 2000 for the eventual creation of local radio and television stations with private sector participation (*Middle East Broadcast and Satellite* 2000: 4). Pending such diversification, JRTV programming remained limited to government-controlled radio broadcasts in Arabic and English, two terrestrial television channels broadcasting in Arabic, English, and French, and the JRTV-operated Jordan Satellite Channel.

Some new approaches to programming were developed within JRTV in 1996 but were not sustained. One innovation was a weekly satirical show on television called *Ahlan Hukouma* (Hallo Government), which annoyed political figures to such an extent that it was taken off the air. The same fate befell a talk show entitled *Hadeeth al-Nas* (People's Talk), which provided ordinary people with a chance to call senior officials to account for their actions and decisions.

Self-regulation in the broadcast media

Appointments within Jordan's state broadcasting sector are subject to a mix of regulation and market forces. This mix has an inevitable impact on the quality and dynamism of work produced inside JRTV. Even before the idea of a free zone for foreign media was floated, the proliferation of Arab satellite broadcasters helped to boost the market for private production companies in Amman. Given the imbalance between JRTV monthly salaries (JD200–250 at most for a reporter or technician), those of companies like ART with facilities in Amman (JD600–800), and those offered by broadcasters in the Gulf (JD1,800–2,000), the trend has been for successful and ambitious JRTV trainees to seek higher-paid jobs elsewhere (Hamzeh and Henderson 1999). There were fears that the free zone would exacerbate this trend.

Pending the arrival of broadcasters in the free zone, it remained to be seen whether the Jordan Press Association would accept an influx of private sector broadcast journalists. The government's purpose in pushing the 1998 Jordan

Press Association law appeared to be to tilt the balance inside the JPA in favor of government employees (Henderson 1998b).

Reform in the field of emerging technologies

State involvement and regulation

By 1999, the kingdom had an estimated 20,000 to 30,000 Internet subscribers. According to calculations by Human Rights Watch, this number was kept artificially low by high prices charged by Internet Service Providers (ISPs) (Human Rights Watch 1999: 45). These in turn are obliged to get their lines from the Jordan Telecommunications Company (JTC) which is due to retain exclusive responsibility for the provision of fixed lines in Jordan until 2002 (Middle East Economic Digest 1997: 7).

JTC was converted from a government agency to a fully government-owned public share holding company at the beginning of 1997. However, its long-standing commitment to sell a 40 per cent stake to a strategic partner ran into problems in 1998 and it was not until late 1999 that formal bids were received. Major investment has yet to be made to increase teledensity in Jordan from the very low level of under six telephone lines per 100 inhabitants in 1996.[31] At the start of 2000, it seemed likely that funding pressures would prolong the situation in which ISP pricing policies would be dictated by JTC, with JTC continuing to demand a share of ISP revenues (Weiner 1997: 77).

It remained to be seen whether this approach would be compatible with the government's so-called "Reach Initiative," spearheaded by King Abdullah, to develop Jordanian information technology (IT) capabilities with the aim of exporting software and attracting high-tech investment.[32] Prerequisites for the initiative to work included scrapping import duties on computer equipment, reviewing censorship procedures, and punishing software piracy. Initial steps along these lines were taken during the second half of 1999 and the twin projects of creating an IT park and free media zone (see above) were promoted by King Abdullah and Jordanian ministers attending the Davos international forum in Switzerland at the beginning of 2000 (Jordan Times staff 2000).

Private service provision

While censorship of the mass media was tightened in 1997–1998, users of privately run Internet news groups took advantage of the anonymity and greater latitude available to them online to air their personal views on political subjects (Henderson 1996: 42–43; Albrecht 1996: 20). Access and National Equipment and Technological Services (NETS), the first two private ISPs, set up bulletin board services. NETS established a forum called "Ask the Government," enabling subscribers to post comments and questions to participating government officials. Barriers of language, cost, and access reserved use to members of the Jordanian elite, many of whom were already familiar with uncensored exchanges in other, non-Jordanian, environments. Weiner points out that, far from adding to domestic pressure for democratization in Jordan, the practice of online political debate may have helped the establishment to take the pulse of opposition and elite aspirations and consider how to meet these within a framework of political continuity (1997: 91–93).

The online chat groups were not, in fact, free from surveillance. Self-censorship flourished after at least two people were summoned for questioning by the intelligence services in 1996 in connection with political comments posted on bulletin boards or chat groups. A NETS spokesman told Human Rights Watch that his company complies with local censorship laws on its users' behalf. Article 2 of the 1998 Press and Publications Law defined "publication" to include "any media in which meanings, words, or ideas are expressed in any way," while Article 5 ordered publications to "refrain from publishing anything that conflicts with the principles of freedom and national responsibility." For these reasons, NETS reportedly reads messages and censors them accordingly (Human Rights Watch 1999: 47–48). Nevertheless, Internet cafés proliferated across the kingdom during the second half of the 1990s. By the end of the decade, there were thought to be fourteen or fifteen such cafés in Amman and twenty in other towns and cities (Human Rights Watch 1999: 45).

Assessment

A holistic approach is needed to understand and assess the net effect of forward and backward steps in the development of Jordanian politics and the media since the late 1980s. First, the significance of media laws rests on a whole body of legislation determining everything from the independence of the judiciary to the solvency of commercial companies. At the same time, a dynamic exists between the liveliness of parliamentary politics and the professionalism of the press. Third, repeated setbacks in the Arab–Israeli "peace process" have been polarizing and distracting in the struggle for and against reform.

Cross-media tendencies

At the end of the 1990s, eleven years after the 1989 elections and seven to eight years after the political reforms of 1992–1993, terrestrial broadcasting in Jordan remained a government-owned monopoly. Proposals for ending the monopoly, aired in 1996 and then frozen, were not put back on the government's agenda until the closing months of 1999. Although it might have been expected that the press liberalization of 1993 would logically lead to similar measures for radio and television, it seemed instead as if the proliferation of non-government newspapers had actually raised the broadcasting ownership stakes, making the government more determined to retain control over radio and television as an antidote to criticism of government policies in the press. In keeping a grip on broadcasting, the Jordanian government remained in step with the predominant practice across the Middle East and North Africa. This was the case despite the emergence of pan-Arab satellite channels that appeared to contest individual government broadcasting monopolies. Whatever their outward appearance, these channels could all be traced to ruling elites (Sakr 1999).

In late 1999, when the government finally turned its attention to ways of restructuring the Ministry of Information and opening the broadcasting sector to private sector involvement, the principal factor influencing its policy reappraisal seemed to be the state of the economy. With unemployment running as high as 25 per cent, the government urgently needed to initiate job-creation schemes in sectors that could accommodate local university graduates (EIU 1999a: 15). A prolonged period of policy paralysis during the final months of King Hussein's illness and hospitalization in 1998–1999 meant that King Abdullah and his new government had to act quickly. In pushing forward the free media zone project in 1999 they, like local media professionals, were aware that introducing different standards for media companies inside and outside the free zone would focus attention on the anomalous status of the government-controlled broadcaster, JRTV. The free zone, if successful in attracting foreign direct investment, would attract employees away from JRTV to take better-paid jobs that might also enjoy relative freedom from Jordanian government censorship. At the same time, by enabling pan-Arab satellite companies to operate more profitably inside Jordan, the free zone would help the satellite channels in their bid to woo Jordanian viewers away from JRTV. In these circumstances, revitalization of JRTV through partial privatization might at least give it a chance to compete.

At the time when the media zone project was hitting the headlines, Jordan's government-owned newspapers continued to dominate the country's print media sector. Non-government media were still struggling for survival, under the weight of financial difficulties brought about by the government's ability to limit their access to information and advertising. However, while not necessarily instrumental in directly triggering broadcasting reform, the non-government press that emerged in 1993–1997 did radically alter the climate for political activity and journalism in Jordan. It did this by creating numerous precedents for calling the government to account. The simple fact of the Higher Court of Justice repeatedly overruling the government in allowing newspapers to be licensed had the dual effect of increasing the diversity of titles on the news-stands and publicly demonstrating the limits that could be set on government power.

Yet, the proliferation of titles also had its roots in wider socio-economic changes. It was driven to a considerable extent by the influx of experienced journalists returning to Jordan from the Gulf as a result of the 1990–1991 Gulf crisis. In 1994, George Hawatmeh noted that the number of licensed journalists in the kingdom increased from 150 before 1989 to 260 five years later (*Middle East International* 1994: 19). Hawatmeh also pointed out that improvements in the quality of Jordanian journalism in this period were linked to improvements in Jordanian politics, based on the existence of recently legalized political parties and, since 1989, a relatively active parliament (*Middle East International* 1994: 19). As the 1990s progressed, the arrival of the Internet helped to sustain the robustness of Jordan's press. Cross-border access to information and advice gave Jordanian journalists ammunition and moral support in their campaigns against the government press curbs of 1997–1998, even if these campaigns alone did not achieve obvious instant success in terms of their own immediate objectives.

Civil society's role in media reform

There is a commonly held belief among Western supporters of civil society development in the Middle East that civil society organizations must, automatically and almost by definition, favor pluralism, freedom of association, and freedom of expression. Studies conducted among these organizations show that this is not necessarily the case (Abdel-Rahman 1999). Interest groups may well seek freedom of expression for themselves but not for others. Thus, sensationalist articles about the private lives of individuals, published by attention-seeking weeklies in Jordan before the 1997 clampdown, attracted calls from other publishers for controls on editorial content. The government used these calls to justify curbs on media. Similar anomalies can be seen in the activities of the Jordanian lobby opposed to normalization with Israel on the terms laid out in the Jordan–Israel peace treaty of 1994. By penalizing media professionals for visiting Israel or meeting Israelis, the Jordanian Press Association and Jordanian Writers' Association have attempted to assert freedom for one viewpoint at the expense of another. Writing in 1998, one observer concluded that Jordanian groups with different political ideologies had yet to learn to cooperate: "Various constituencies for freedom have to stop calling on the government to intervene every time they read something that offends them" (Najjar 1998: 37).

The normalization issue is potentially highly divisive for Jordanian society and goes a long way in explaining why the regime that signed the 1994 peace treaty is so anxious to contain opposition to it by muzzling the media. Proponents of media freedom argue that these efforts are misplaced. They say that the brief interludes of free expression experienced in Jordan in recent years have shown the press to be a "moderating medium," precisely because it allows all sides to have their say (Hassanat 1998). As it is, some civil society organizations – such as the professional associations – expend energy and resources in making their views on normalization known through non-media channels. This distracts their attention from campaigning for more fundamental legislative reforms. Another barrier to such campaigning exists in the form of laws artificially separating political from cultural activism. As explained above, the 1992 law on political parties forbids voluntary or cultural organizations from engaging in what the government defines as political activity. This prohibition reinforces the earlier Law on Societies and Social Organizations 33 of 1966 which bars them from seeking political gain.[33] With these restrictions in place, whether the government chooses to enforce them or whether it turns a blind eye, civil society organizations will be limited in their ability to campaign for, let alone benefit from, media law reform. The 1997 reminders that the authorities should have two days' prior notice of public meetings, together with the 1998 ruling making foreign support for local research centers subject to government approval, further obstructed civil society activity in this regard.

Media and democratization

Various epithets have been applied to Jordan's limited reforms since 1989. They have been described as "defensive" or "pre-emptive" democratization, initiated to "forestall more serious challenges to the political order" (Robinson 1997: 74). These epithets demonstrate that the reforms did not forcibly curtail the regime's freedom of action. Similarly, it may be said, the 1989–1993 reforms in Jordan attracted attention, not because they represented an irreversible breakthrough in political participation but because there was so little progress on this front in other Arab states. Bearing this in mind, it is possible to look at media reform and its relation to Jordan's transition to democracy either optimistically or pessimistically.

Optimistically, one could say that the genie of political liberalization, once out of the bottle, cannot be put back. The effect of experiencing freedoms is incremental. Editors and journalists, having sampled certain press freedoms, will not surrender them again. Any attempts, such as those in 1997 and 1998, to take away such freedoms will ultimately backfire. The public outcry provoked by the press law changes in 1997–1998 can be cited in support of this interpretation, as can the persistent efforts of experienced journalists even in government-owned newspapers to push back the boundaries of censorship.

Pessimistically, one asks whether the 1999 press law changes represent a net benefit to media freedom when judged against the path of reform expected in the early 1990s. Those who think not, point to the government's entrenched broadcasting monopoly and the raft of legislation, from the Penal Code to the 1999 amendments to the Companies Law, that remains available to the authorities to obstruct the activities of non-government media. The frustration, resignation, and (in some cases) emigration of certain reform-minded people also support the pessimistic outlook. According to this position, Jordan's transition to democracy has barely begun. After eleven years of faltering and piecemeal political liberalization, the best that could be said about media reform is that media practitioners have learned to put early judicial reform to good use in pursuing their objectives through the courts.

What follows from both the optimistic and pessimistic readings of media liberalization in Jordan is that comprehensive legal change is a prerequisite for media law reform to have a real impact. Tinkering with individual articles of individual laws may give the impression of change, but it is only an impression. Democratization depends on laws that allow freedom of association and freedom of information alongside freedom of expression. For as long as the government can use its dominant position in the media to squeeze the competition, draw artificial dividing lines between political and cultural activity, block the funding of civil society groups, prevent them from meeting, and so on, democratization remains a distant prospect.

The priority for Jordan is to press ahead with wholesale legal and institutional reform. The priority for foreign interests desirous of promoting media freedom in Jordan is to empower working journalists through local, work-based, training programs. Arab journalists who have worked in democratic contexts, in Europe or the United States, are potentially well equipped to train Jordanian colleagues to undertake credible reporting that they feel inspired and motivated to defend. A prototype for such a training program was tested in Amman during November 1999. Organized by the Jemstone Network, with Arab tutors and funding from the Dutch Ministry of Development and Co-operation, it involved training reporters in investigative journalism skills. Despite pockets of local resistance to such programs, more are needed.

Notes

1 A score of ten represented a fully democratic society.
2 Mustafa Hamarneh resigned as CSS director in July 1999. The previous month he had been quoted in *Newsweek* as describing King Abdullah as the "kid who came from nowhere" (Fairouz 1999b).
3 For example, oil prices crashed in 1986, reducing aid from Arab oil exporters, and the eight-year Iran–Iraq war ended in 1988, lessening Iraq's dependence on the Jordanian port of Aqaba.
4 Introduced as part of an economic adjustment package agreed upon with the IMF.
5 The Egyptian sociology professor, Saadeddin Ibrahim, a democracy campaigner and trustee of the Jordan-based Arab Thought Forum, was one of those using the "D-word" in talks with King Hussein and Crown Prince Hassan. (Dr Ibrahim, interview Cairo, 6 September 1998.)
6 Articles 36, 38, and 44.
7 The MP was parliament's first woman MP, Toujan al-Faisal (Najjar 1998: 133).
8 The controversial and restrictive 1997 press law amendments were passed by royal decree.
9 The Jordan news agency, Petra, reported in November 1999 that nearly 60 per cent of people it had polled supported changing the electoral law introduced in 1993. See also EIU (1999c: 15).
10 In all, 33 parties obtained licenses between 1992 and the end of 1999, but the net result of various splits and mergers was to reduce this number to 21.
11 1992 law exemption: at Article 26.
12 Article 14 of Law No. 32 of 1992.
13 Law No. 12 of 1992.
14 Under the 1993 law, press licensing decisions could be subjected to judicial review. The word "loopholes" was used by Samir Mutawi, the Minister of Information at the time, when interviewed about the amendments on Jordanian TV. He said these were necessary because many papers had taken advantage of "loopholes." He alleged that their excesses had "damaged relations with some Arab states, created a dark cloud ... [and] ... tried to incite sedition and fragment the homeland's social fabric" (*BBC Summary of World Broadcasts* 1997).
15 This analysis of the balance of opinion at that point is based on the author's interviews with media practitioners in Amman in November 1998.
16 Abdel-Raouf al-Rawabdeh, prime minister from March 1999, had argued as an MP in the summer of 1998 that journalists should not be legally bound to be accurate unless they are allowed access to information. Abdel-Karim Kabariti, Chief of the Royal Court, had made a start toward dismantling the Information Ministry during his time as prime minister in 1996. Nasser Lawzi, Minister of Information from March 1999, was associated with Kabariti's move for reform (Fairouz 1999a). Saleh Qallab, a former editor of the outspoken private daily, *Al-Arab al-Yawm*, replaced Lawzi in January 2000 (*Jordan Times* 2000). Kabariti resigned in January 2000, reportedly in frustration at the lack of progress toward reform (Fairouz 2000).
17 The law was ratified on 7 September and came into effect on 17 October 1999.
18 The provisions in question are contained in Articles 122, 132, 150, and 195 of the Penal Code.
19 Qattan belongs to Amnesty International and the Arab Organisation for Human Rights (Reporters sans Frontières 1999).
20 The 18 papers are: *Al-Majd, Al-Raseef, Al-Hiwar, Al-Diyar, Al-Mashreq, Shihan, Al-Bilad, Hawadeth al-Saa, Sawt al-Mara'a, Al-Haqiqa, Al-Hayat, Al-Sayyad, Abed Rabbo, Al-Liwa, Al-Sabeel, Akhbar al-Usbou, Al-Urdun*, and the English-language weekly *The Star*. In all, 40 licenses were granted in the period 1993–1997, including licenses for papers belonging to the newly legalized political parties. The total number of weeklies was 21 in September 1997 (Najjar 1998: 132).
21 The required capital is outlined in Article 7 of the 1997 amendments. The fines are outlined in Amended Article 50/1 (C). Content restrictions are outlined in Amended Articles 40 (a) and 50/1 (C).

22 Alert put out on 1 July 1999, by the International Freedom of Expression Exchange (IFEX) and others.
23 The withdrawal appeared to reflect a power struggle between the Royal Court, which ordered Petra to resume transmissions to *Al-Arab al-Yawm*, and associates of the prime minister, whose policies *Al-Arab al-Yawm* had criticized (Kamal 1999a: 15).
24 The Companies Law makes liquidation compulsory when a firm's losses reach 75 per cent of its capital.
25 www.cnn.com/WORLD/meast, 14 March 1999.
26 The French press freedom group, Reporters sans Frontières, said in a statement on 24 August 1999 that it had protested to King Abdullah about Barghouti's arrest and detention.
27 "Press institutions" are defined as printing presses, distribution agencies, publishing houses, study and research centers, and advertising bureaux. The relevant provisions are contained in Articles 18, 19, 25, 27, and 30.
28 The members who worked for government-owned papers were Abdullah Hassanat, chief editor of the *Jordan Times*, *Al-Ra'i* columnist Sultan Hattab, and Jihad Momani, a columnist with *Al-Destour*.
29 Dr Abu Jaber said he disagreed with the PPD's action (interview, Amman, 23 November 1998).
30 For discussion of programming by the Palestine Television Corporation see Associated Press (1999a). For discussion of Hebrew soundtracks see Reuters (1998).
31 Data from the ITU's annual *World Telecommunications Development Report*.
32 The large number of Jordanian university graduates trained in IT encouraged those involved in this initiative to compare Jordan's ambition with the achievements of a country like Ireland, which has come to serve IT companies from all over Europe (Mekki 1999).
33 For discussion of "seeking political gain" see Wiktorowicz (1999: 609–610).

References

Abdel-Rahman, Maha (1999) "Civil society against itself: Egyptian NGOs in the neo-liberal era." Paper presented to the Conference of the European Association for Middle East Studies, Ghent: Eurames, September.

Albrecht, Kirk (1996) "Jordan is talking politics online," *The Middle East*, June: 20.

Al-Quds al-Arabi (1997) report, reproduced in *Mideast Mirror*, 5 March: 16.

Al-Ra'i (1996) 30 May.

—— (1997) The Provisional Law (not numbered), 18 May. (See the *BBC Summary of World Broadcasts*, ME/2929 MED/20–22, 23 May 1997, for an English translation.)

Arabicnews.com (1998) "Jordanian government halts accreditation of Qatari satellite station," 5 November. Available at: http:// www.arabicnews.com.

Article 19 (1997) *Blaming the Press: Jordan's Democratization Process in Crisis* and *Memorandum on Jordan's Proposed 1998 Press and Publications Law* (London: Article 19).

Associated Press (1999a) report from Amman, 16 February.

—— (1999b) news report from Amman, 18 September.

Ayoub, Tareq (1999) "Al-Arab al-Yawm publishers cut capital to avoid liquidation," *Jordan Times*, 6 November.

BBC Summary of World Broadcasts (1997) ME/2923 MED/18, 20 May.

—— (1998) ME/3377 MED/6, 6 November.

Borger, Julian (1997) "Opposition attacks King Hussein's press clampdown," *Guardian*, 29 October.

Cable and Satellite Europe (1998) "Datafile: Transponder Watch," June.

Economist Intelligence Unit (EIU) (1999a) *Jordan Country Profile 1999–2000*, London: Economist Intelligence Unit.

—— (1999b) "A law on the independence of the judiciary is drafted," *Jordan Country Report*, 4th quarter: 16.

—— (1999c) "The opposition proposes changes to the election law," *Jordan Country Report*, 4th quarter: 15.

Eutelsat (1998) *Cable and Satellite Penetration Data*, mid-1998.

Fairouz, Ayeesha (1999a) "Government to tackle Jordan press law," *Middle East Times*, 28 March.
—— (1999b) "Mud-slinging signals press crackdown," *Middle East Times*, 23 July.
—— (1999c) "Jordanian editor released on bail," *Middle East Times*, 24 September.
—— (2000) "Cabinet reshuffle deals Jordanians bad hand," *Middle East Times*, 27 January.
Feuilherade, Peter (2000) "Censor-free zones?," *Middle East International*, 28 January: 13.
Hamdan, Dima (1999) "Two students arrested for attempting to launch anti-normalization site," *Jordan Times*, 27 October.
Hamzeh, Alia Shukri (1999a) "JPA rescinds decision to expel journalists who visited Israel," *Jordan Times*, 18 November.
—— (1999b) "Court freezes publishing house assets," *Jordan Times*, 4 December.
—— (1999c) "Journalist files lawsuits against JPA and Al-Ra'i," *Jordan Times*, 9 December.
—— (1999d) "Journalist files lawsuits against JPA and Al-Ra'i," *Jordan Times*, 13 December.
—— (2000a) "Cabinet approves 'free media zone' draft law," *Jordan Times*, 13 January.
—— (2000b) "Cabinet puts media free zone in final form," *Jordan Times*, 18 January.
Hamzeh, Alia Shukri and Henderson, Amy (1999) "Potential users of 'media free zone' demand guarantee of total freedom," *Jordan Times*, 3 November.
Hassanat, Abdullah (1998) "Impediments to Freedom of Expression in Jordan." Paper presented to the MacBride Roundtable on Culture and Communication in the Global Information Society, Amman, November.
Hattar, Saad (1999) "Etoum pledges 'tolerance' in dealings with press," *Jordan Times*, 18 October.
Henderson, Amy (1996) "Peace on the line," *Jerusalem Report*, 28 November: 42–43.
—— (1998a) "Democracy at a standstill–poll," *Jordan Times*, 13 June.
—— (1998b) "Lower House endorses press association law," *Jordan Times*, 30 July.
—— (1998c) "Press ponders future of investigative reporting after approval of draft law," *Jordan Times*, 10 August.
—— (1998d) "New government favors relaxed application of press law–minister," *Jordan Times*, 24 August.
Hourani, Hani (1999) "Jordanian civil society in the nineties," *Civil Society*, Vol. 8, Issue 87, March: 16–19.
Human Rights Watch (1997) *Jordan: Clamping Down on Critics* (New York: Human Rights Watch).
—— (1999) *The Internet in the Mideast and North Africa: Free Expression and Censorship* (New York: Human Rights Watch).
Hussein, Mohammed Ben (1999) "Government apologizes to MBC journalist after assault," *Jordan Times*, 13 October.
—— (2000) "Al Aswaq faces financial difficulties," *Jordan Times*, 27 January.
Jordan Times (1999) "Parliament pledges cooperation with government to achieve economic reforms, fight corruption," 11 November.
—— (2000) "Profiles of new ministers," 16 January.
Jordan Times staff (1999a) "Media restructuring committee discusses future of public media," *Jordan Times*, 1 November.
—— (1999b) "Editor, cartoonist to appear for second hearing on slander charges," *Jordan Times*, 14 November.
—— (1999c) "Human Rights Office to draft national plan," *Jordan Times*, 13 December.
—— (2000) "King to meet IT, media leaders in Davos," *Jordan Times*, 29 January.
Kamal, Sana (1999a) "Jordan: Democratic tests," *Middle East International* No. 605, 30 July: 14.
—— (1999b) "Abdullah the modernizer," *Middle East International*, No. 606, 20 August: 12–13.

Khouri, Rami (1997) "The Jordan government's imposition of the temporary press law was politically wrong," *Jordan Times*, 27 May.

Kramer, Gudrun (1994) "The integration of the integrists: A comparative study of Egypt, Jordan and Tunisia," in Ghassan Salamé (ed.) *Democracy without Democrats? The Renewal of Politics in the Muslim World*, London: I. B. Tauris: 200–226.

Mekki, Hassan (1999) "Jordan wants slice of regional IT cake," *Jordan Times*, 1 December.

Middle East Broadcast and Satellite (2000) Vol. 7, No. 1, January: 4.

Middle East Economic Digest (1997) 4 April: 7

Middle East International (1994) "Jordan's press in the new democratic atmosphere," 2 December: 19.

Najjar, Orayb Aref (1998) "The ebb and flow of the liberalization of the Jordanian press: 1985–97," *Journalism and Mass Communication Quarterly*, Vol. 75 (1), Spring: 127–142.

Official Gazette (1993) Law No. 10, 17 April.

Reporters sans Frontières (1999) *Annual Report: Middle East and North Africa*.

—— (2000) *1999 Annual Report for the Middle East: Jordan*, www.rsf.fr, January.

Reuters (1998) report from Amman, 20 October.

Robinson, Glenn (1997) "Can Islamists be democrats? The case of Jordan," *Middle East Journal*, Vol. 51, No. 3: 373–387.

Rugh, William A. (1987) *The Arab Press: News Media and Political Process in the Arab World*, revised 2nd edition, New York: Syracuse University Press.

Sakr, Naomi (1999) "Frontiers of freedom: Diverse responses to satellite television in the Middle East and North Africa," in *Javnost/The Public*, Vol. 6, 1: 93–106.

Snow, Peter (1972) *Hussein: A Biography*, London: Barrie and Jenkins.

Weiner, Jed (1997) "The Internet in Egypt, Jordan and the Middle East." Unpublished M. Phil. thesis, St Antony's College, University of Oxford.

Wiktorowicz, Quintan (1999) "The limits of democracy in the Middle East: The case of Jordan," *Middle East Journal*, Vol. 53, No. 4: 606–620.

Yorke, Valerie (1988) *Domestic Politics and Regional Security: Jordan, Syria and Israel*, Aldershot: Gower.

7

THE PARTIAL TRANSITION

Ukraine's post-communist media

Andrei Richter

Introduction

Political transition and media reform in Ukraine were initially induced by the decline and collapse of communist rule in the former Soviet Union. Ukraine formed a vital part of the communist system, and, as a result, the Ukrainian transition has been significantly influenced by the dynamics of this former alliance.

The initial period of Ukrainian media reform in 1991–1992 was marked by the passage of extensive new legislation related to media development. Since that time, Ukraine has established a broad set of laws that govern all aspects of media regulation, from print to broadcast and emerging technologies. In this process, the pressure of international organizations and various international treaty obligations (UN, Council of Europe, OSCE, WIPO, and so on) has contributed to the establishment of a model legislative structure. In fact, as far as the structure of the legislative framework is concerned, Ukraine has effectively covered its bases.

The implementation of this framework, however, has proved more problematic. The agendas of numerous political factions within parliament and government have prevented the unbiased implementation of these laws. State actors have consistently attempted to lure media to their side through a number of selective benefits. Political actors have made inappropriate use of legislation in order to control the newly developing broadcasting sector and assure their recognition and popularity among the electorate.

Political agendas have played into other areas of the media reform process as well. In particular, the Ukrainian government's policy of nationalism as a major vehicle for structuring and reinforcing national identity has led to severe restrictions on Russian media. State resources, both financial and other, have been biased in favor of nationally based information sources.

Finally, within the economic sphere, there has been a general push to privatize state and public property, including major publishing houses, television and film production facilities, and radio frequencies. Crucial elements such as relay transmission lines, modern publishing houses of scale, and major television and radio towers, however, have remained in the hands of the government.

Low levels of capital finance have led to an underdeveloped advertising market and limited ad profits. This, in turn, has made media beholden to various political and business interests calling into question whether Ukrainian media can report on events impartially. To date, media have demonstrated that they can be persuaded to take sides in a debate, especially during electoral periods when economically influential political and business powers use the Ukrainian media as their personal soapboxes.

Government subsidies and systems of tax relief have been structured in such a way as to favor the state-owned media over the private sector. Such elements present continued barriers to the development of truly free and independent media in Ukraine.

Overview of the media reform process

The process of media reform and democratic transition in Ukraine began in 1985 with *perestroika* (restructuring) and *glasnost* (openness), reform policies introduced by Mikhail Gorbachev in the USSR. The leadership of the Ukrainian Communist Party, then dominated by First Secretary Vladimir Shcherbitsky, attempted to limit the impact of Gorbachev's reforms, especially his acceptance of an increased amount of criticism in the Soviet mass media. As a result, critical coverage of the communist system was rare, either in Kiev publications or in Ukrainian broadcasts. Critical reporting did, nonetheless, filter through from Moscow-based mass media. Shcherbitsky's replacement in 1989 by Leonid Kravchuk, a politician more loyal to Gorbachev, marked the formal end of the "stagnation" period in Ukraine.

The *Supreme Rada* (parliament) was democratically elected for the first time in 1990 and included numerous nationalist and anti-communist deputies in its ranks. Following the failed Moscow coup of August 1991, the legitimacy of communist parties across the USSR suffered. Kravchuk, like so many other Soviet republic leaders, faced the dilemma of being ousted or heading the emerging nationalist group. He chose the latter.

A popular referendum held on 1 December 1991 confirmed Ukraine's declaration of independence of 24 August of that year. This decision paved the way to a formal break-up of the Soviet Union and to the subsequent formation later that month of the Commonwealth of Independent States (CIS), founded by Belarus, Russia, and Ukraine. December 1991 ended the *perestroika* period of liberalization in Ukraine and marked the start of the country's independent history.

The political independence that editors gained during *glasnost* was codified through legal measures, originally designed to legitimize *glasnost* policy. On 12 June 1990, the Supreme Soviet (the USSR's parliament) adopted a Statute on the Press and Other Mass Media.[1] The statute acknowledged the freedom of information and protected activity to seek, obtain, produce, and disseminate information, except where prohibited by other legislation. It also guaranteed the right to set up mass media outlets, to their ownership, use, and management and to the preparation, acquisition, and operation of technical devices and equipment, raw goods, and materials intended for the production and distribution of mass media products. This statute also banned all forms of prior censorship.

The situation, however, began to develop rapidly in ways unanticipated by the Communist Party. The 1990 statute demanded that all publications be officially registered by submitting documentation to a state registration authority. However, the statute expressly allowed anyone to be a "founder" and editorial staffs proceeded to register "founders" who were different from their old masters or even under their own names. The newly independent media refused to be subordinated any longer. At the same time, media space began to be filled with publications launched by enterprising editors or the *nouveaux riches*.

The next blow to Soviet structures in the media came in August 1991, when the Communist Party was officially banned and its property expropriated. This process gave birth to thousands of publications, re-registered as a result of the dissolution of the party committees. Some of the ex-communist papers, primarily the provincial ones, changed their names and eliminated communist references. For example, the words "*Kommunist*" (Communist), "*Pravda*" (Truth), or "*Sovetsky*" (Soviet) were eliminated from the titles. Others established editorial policies that differed from the Communist Party line. All became free of the central press structure as the governing party ceased to exist as a dominant force. As a result of this legislative development that put an official end to communism in the Soviet Union, hundreds of new publications hit the streets of Ukrainian cities and dozens of private broadcasters began transmitting uncensored programs (Kachkaeva and Richter 1992: 4).

Ukraine began drafting a constitution in 1994, a process that, too, has had an impact on the development of the mass media. Disagreement over reform of the executive branch and arguments about whether a presidential or a parliamentary system should be adopted brought the executive and the legislative branches to a standoff. This deadlock resulted in early presidential and parliamentary elections in 1994. The majority of seats within the new Supreme Rada went to representatives of the left: the Ukrainian Communist, Socialist and Peasants' parties. Leonid Kuchma was elected president and was able to gain consensus within the Supreme Rada regarding basic constitutional provisions concerning the future political structure of the country. A new Ukrainian constitution was adopted in 1996.

The Ukranian media legislative framework

Provisions introduced in the 1996 constitution act as the primary legal source governing media rights and freedoms. Article 15 forbids prior censorship. Article 34 guarantees freedom of thought, speech, and expression. Taken together, these two provisions serve as the basis for the development of a free and independent media system.

Ukraine's independence in 1991 ushered in a period of intensive law making. Ukraine was one of the few former Soviet republics to adopt the full troika of mass media laws on information, print media, and broadcasting, as envisioned by liberal Soviet thinkers such as Yuri Baturin, Mikhail Fedotov, and Nikolai Fedorov in the late 1980s.

The first of these laws was the 1992 Statute on Information.[2] It represented a major legislative step in interpreting freedom of expression under new political, economic, and social circumstances, providing a comprehensive statutory framework for structuring mass media in Ukraine. The statute formulated the rights of Ukrainian citizens to disseminate and receive information very broadly. It also provided legal grounds for information-gathering activities. In a sense, the information statute influences mass media regulation as a constitution impacts general lawmaking. The statute governs "informational relations that appear in all spheres of life and activity in society and the state while obtaining, using, disseminating and preserving information." However, it also restricts information flow under certain circumstances. For example, Article 46 states: "Information shall not be used to call for an overthrow of the constitutional order, a violation of the territorial integrity of Ukraine, or as propaganda for war, violence, cruelty, fanning of racial, national, religious enmity, or as instrument to violate human rights and liberties." The same article of the statute safeguards "state and other secrets stipulated by law" and "information regarding medical secrets, bank deposits, profits from enterprising activity, child adoption, correspondence, phone calls and cable messages, except when the law stipulates otherwise."[3]

The majority of media-related court cases in Ukraine are defamation lawsuits. A 1993 statute entitled "On Amendments to the Statutes and Regulations Concerning Protection of Dignity and Business Reputation" provided legal procedures that grant legal entities and private individuals the right to seek redress in the courts and instruct judges on how to award remedies of retraction or compensation for defamatory or inaccurate information.[4] State bodies have used this statute in particular against media outlets. While in 1993 there were 600 lawsuits on defamation, in 1997 their number increased by 2.6 times.[5] In comparison with other former Soviet republics, the amounts sought as compensation in defamation cases in Ukraine have frequently been unrealistically high, reaching levels of up to US$250 million. More recent statistics indicate that in 1999 more than 2,250 lawsuits were filed against Ukrainian newspapers for more than 90 billion hryvna (US$16.82 billion) in moral damages. That sum represents nearly twice the amount the national government planned to earn in 2000 (Associated Press 2000).

Editorial staff regularly lose such defamation cases. Often the accuracy of printed and broadcast information is difficult to prove either because the source cannot be divulged or because the individuals involved refuse to testify in court. The Arbitrazh (economic) courts have the authority to freeze bank accounts in advance of proceedings in order to secure financial compensation for moral damages, thus paralyzing production in news organizations. When media outlets lose defamation cases, they generally find themselves in an even more catastrophic financial situation than before (Lange 1997: 232).

The 1994 Statute on State Secrets is another item of legislation that has an impact on mass media.[6] According to its text, information pertaining to defense, the economy, foreign relations, state security, and the safeguarding of law and order are classified as state secrets. A list of items defined as state secrets was published on 17 August 1995. Dissemination of such information is considered criminal under the 1994 statute.

A statute on advertising was adopted by the parliament on 3 July 1996 and governs the creation, production, dissemination, and receipt of advertising within media as a whole. It introduces a blanket ban on advertising prescription medicines and addictive substances, in addition to prohibitions on the advertising of tobacco and alcohol products on television and radio (see below).

The Supreme Rada adopted a statute "On the Procedures of the Coverage of Activities of the Bodies of State Power and Bodies of Local Self-government in Ukraine by the Mass Media" on 23 September 1997.[7] In accordance with this statute, all government organs are to provide full information regarding their activities to the mass media.[8] Accordingly, media journalists are formally granted free access to all government information.[9] Under this legislation, the Supreme Rada adopts a decree at the first session of each sitting, detailing procedures of access and coverage of its meetings. However, the statute allows for only officially translated versions of documents to be published.

On 1 January 1998, a statute "On the State Support of the Mass Media and Social Protection of Journalists" entered into force.[10] Market information monopolies are prohibited in Article 10, which formally ensures diversity of media. The statute also regulates government subsidies, economic support to the media, and the social security of journalists. It establishes state-granted economic privileges for all mass media with the exception of erotic (pornographic) publications and programs, publications with more than 40 per cent advertising in a single issue or broadcast stations with more than 15 per cent commercials in their daily program, all mass media with more than 50 per cent foreign media contents, media established by international organizations or with participation of foreign entities, and media established by companies that also deal in newsprint production, publishing, or broadcast communication. Thus, if a particular media actor does not feature pornography, does not devote more than 40 per cent of printing space or 15 per cent of airtime to advertising and commercials, and does not reprint stories from foreign (such as Russian) mass media, then it is likely that the state will deem it to have social value and will offer economic assistance.

The statute on state support of the media introduces many types of indirect state benefits for mass media outlets. Among them are relief from tax obligations, customs duties, tariffs, rent, for the promotion of culture and education. The national budget now allocates a sum specifically for the support of the mass media. In 1998, this figure amounted to 182 million hryvna.[11] In 1999, it was 161 million hryvna. The statute also prohibits privatization of mass media organizations if they "are recognized by the Supreme Rada as leading in the sphere of informational activity" or if they are of "supranational importance."[12] Finally, the statute introduces a number of social privileges for journalists. These include the free use of municipal transportation or free rent, heating, and power for dwellings in the countryside. In general, most journalists and media outlets are aware of these benefits and make use of them.

Media reform by sector

Print media

Legislation

The most far-reaching legislation for print media since independence is the 1992 statute "On Printed Mass Media (the Press) in Ukraine," which was adopted by the Supreme Rada at the end of that year. The statute sets the legal framework for print media activity, guarantees broad press freedoms, and regulates the relationship among editorial staff, citizens, and other organizations and bodies.[13] For example, it specifies procedures for electing editors, provides the contents of the founding contract, sets the terms of retraction, and so on. It also sets the standard for subsequent legislation affecting print media.

As noted above, press market monopolization is prohibited under Article 10 of the 1997 statute "On the State Support of the Mass Media and the Social Protection of Journalists." Its specific press provisions stipulate that no person or legal entity can be "founder" or "co-founder" or control more than 5 per cent of all national or regional publications. Article 10 of the 1992 Press Statute, in turn, defines "control" to mean "the possibility ... of influencing the activity of a publication by material or financial means."[14] As a result, it presents an important barrier to large press conglomerates and formally promotes diversity of the press.

The two laws also prohibit foreign persons and legal entities from setting up publications.[15] Nonetheless, foreign involvement in the Ukrainian press media does take place. One illustrative example is of a Norwegian company which, through its Polish branch, in 1998 bought a controlling share of closed stock companies that run major newspapers such as *Vysoki Zamok* (Lvov), *Industrialnoe Zaporozhie* and *Panorama* (Zaporozhie).

Press diversity in Ukraine

In Ukraine, total newspaper and magazine circulation has dropped ten-fold since 1991. Just 20 per cent of the population regularly read newspapers and only five general interest papers have a circulation over 100,000.[16] Print media conditions have gradually worsened as a result of economic hardship and the growing dependence of media on government subsidies. Currently, only a handful of publications are financially independent of the state or of politically biased groups. These publications have gained economic independence through developing other businesses on the side or investing in various profitable business concerns, such as the construction, telecommunications, advertising, and service industries. These groups are often tied to factions in the Rada, or to major industrial and banking concerns, or simply united by loyalty to a particular politician. In turn, they tend to view media as tools for the political control of the public. Publications require sponsors in order to survive and economic support is provided mainly for political reasons. Quite often, the tone of newspapers begins to resemble that of its new owner or of the dominant political group within the new owner's sector of operations.

A number of publications run by ecologists, consumer protection societies, feminist groups, and professional associations have escaped this dilemma of economic control. Their funding typically comes from domestic sponsors and international foundations. Their readership, however, is comparatively small and static. Certain civic organizations, like the Kharkov-based "Human Rights Group," operate within the press sector, monitoring publications and publishing violations of journalists' rights. They are sometimes also contracted by Moscow-based human rights organizations, such as the Glasnost Defense Foundation.

Since independence in 1991, the demand for a Kiev-based national press has gradually given way to an interest in local news, practical information, entertainment, and day-to-day life. Opinion polls indicate that concern for world affairs or national politics has dramatically decreased in the past few years. The majority of Ukrainians, first and foremost, want to read about issues such as the cost of living or levels of crime. This is precisely the type of information that the local press provides. Topics of least interest to Ukrainians are ethnic issues, news concerning other post-Soviet republics (with the notable exception of Russia), and foreign policy. These are all topics that are prominent in the national press.

Such preferences have resulted in the relative stability of circulation levels for local publications in comparison with national ones. In 1993, local print-runs exceeded those of national publications, although this has been attributed to the popularity of tabloids that publish classified ads and television listings. Another purely economic explanation for the stability of local press is its comparatively low distribution costs.

Historically, the Moscow press has been very popular in Ukraine. Even in the post-independence atmosphere of 1992, 42 per cent of all newspaper subscriptions were to Russian-based ones. Subscriptions to Kiev-based newspapers represented only 23 per cent of the market, while Ukrainian local press accounted for 35 per cent of total newspaper subscriptions.[17]

In 1995, the state began limiting distribution and printing subsidies to Ukrainian newspapers alone, thus making Russian papers printed in Ukraine comparatively expensive. Furthermore, the government imposed a monthly tax of ECU160 on every kiosk that sold "foreign" (Russian) publications.[18] Some Russian publications escaped this tax by registering joint ventures and by adding "Ukraine" to their titles (for example, *Izvestia-Ukraina*, *Trud-Ukraina*, *Argumenti i fakty-Ukraina*). Still, according to some press reports, Ukrainian authorities believe that such registrations were mistaken and that "Moscow" newspapers should not receive Ukrainian legal status on the grounds that a high proportion of their contents are of Russian origin. If successful, this move will considerably limit the diversity of print media in Ukraine.

Another interesting issue is that of language in the press. In a country where approximately half of the population speak Russian as their mother tongue, the constitution recognizes only Ukrainian as the official national language. At the same time, Article 6 of the 1992 statute "On National Minorities" guarantees minorities the right to national-cultural autonomy, including the use of their native language and "the satisfaction of [their] needs in literature, art, and the mass media." The predominant languages of mass media are Ukrainian and Russian and, as a result, questions persist regarding the true diversity of this sphere. Occasionally, programs are broadcast in other ethnic minority languages such as Yiddish, Moldovian, Gagauz (Turkic), Hungarian, Greek, or Slovak, but these are mainly restricted to regional television and radio stations in the western border areas.

Barrier to print media development

Article 15 of the Ukrainian constitution, as discussed above, formally bans prior censorship. However, the executive branch of the state has strong influence over the media economy in general, and over the distribution of government subsidies or benefits among both private and state-owned press media. For instance, several presidential decrees have affected the competitiveness of private print media. State-owned or state-established publications are exempt from VAT. Further, print media established by the Supreme Rada, the cabinet of ministers, executive bodies or regional authorities also receive state subsidies, which are often substantial. Table 7.1 presents state budgetary expenditure figures on the media.

Compounding the disadvantages that unsubsidized publications endure is the fact that both printing and distribution are virtually governmental monopolies (Lange 1997: 248). Such conditions represent an unfair competitive advantage of the state-supported press over commercial publications. The latter react to these circumstances by cutting editorial expenses and the quality of reporting. However, they cannot raise prices due to fierce competition within the print media sector and low levels of purchasing power among the population. Thus presidential and governmental decrees that benefit the state-run press and the journalists working for it have an overall detrimental effect on the independent press.

It must be noted, however, that the state does provide other subsidies and financial relief to the press in general. Certain publications do not pay VAT on subscriptions and sales, can obtain low-interest loans, and receive exemptions on custom duties, rent, and communication tariffs.[19]

Finally, the Ukrainian judicial system characterizes another indirect but detrimental influence of the state upon the print media. For example, in 1998 Aleksander Gorobets, editor-in-chief of *Pravda Ukrainy*, was arrested for allegedly

Table 7.1 State budget expenditures on the mass media in Ukraine

	1998	1999	% change
	(million hryvnas)		
Television[a]	79.2	141.018	-11.9
Radio	80.8	n/a	n/a
Printed press	8.61	11.34	+31.7
Book publishing	5.7	5.145	-9.7
Other mass media	7.83	3.5	-55.3
Total	182.14	161.003	-11.6

Note:
a In the 1999 budget, television and radio lines expenditures were combined.

Source: *Zakonodatelnyi bulleten* 1999a: 13.

raping a member of the paper's editorial staff. The newspaper's editorial board circulated a statement expressing "astonishment and indignation at the provocative act against the newspaper editor-in-chief" (McCormack 1999: 297). The trial ended on 24 May 1999 with a verdict of guilty. The punishment was a seven-month prison term. As this had been the exact length of time served by Gorobets in detention, he was immediately released (*Zakonodatelnyi bulleten* 1999b: 8). Another case involved the editorial board of *Kievskie Vedomosti*, which was evicted from its rented premises on 13 October 1998. The pretext for the eviction was a ruling by the Kiev Arbitrazh (economic) court that invalidated the agreement between the newspaper's editorial board and the proprietor of the building. In the opinion of certain legal experts, the government orchestrated both of these acts in order to disrupt the operation of the opposition press. Such measures are not normally used against newspapers loyal to the state (McCormack 1999: 297).

Professional organizations

The largest professional print media organization in Ukraine is the Union of Journalists. There is also a Guild of Chief Editors of the Mass Media, a Crimean Union of Free Journalists, and other professional unions. In 1997, the 9th Congress of the Union of Journalists adopted a Code of Professional Ethics of the Ukrainian Journalist. The code states, "The main duty of a journalist is to facilitate citizens in their right to obtain up-to-date information." The Code consists of ten points in which journalists' ethical standards are set out. Some of these codes overlap with legislative norms. Violation of the Code by journalists may lead to a public censure or to a discussion of the incident at editorial staff meetings, at the primary branches of the Union of Journalists, and at the Councils of Professional Ethics. In practice, however, such responsibility has not been enforced.

Overview

The now mostly privatized print media are currently experiencing a crisis of survival and press analysts are alarmed at the shrinking number of Ukrainian language press publications. As of 1997, for instance, only 36 per cent of all publications were in Ukrainian. This is down from 60 per cent in 1992. The share of Russian language publications published in Ukraine, in contrast, had risen to 24 per cent in 1997, up from 6 per cent in 1992 (*Ukraina: informatsia* 1997: 744). It should be noted, however, that the remaining 40 per cent of publications were published in both Ukrainian and Russian. This evidence runs counter to the arguments of analysts who worry about the demise of Ukrainian language in the printed press. In fact, the above figures suggest that readers, even those who would not normally buy a Ukrainian language newspaper, have become gradually accustomed to reading stories in Ukrainian, which are intermixed with Russian stories. Commercial and political Ukrainian–Russian newspapers or TV channels represent an important means of acquainting Russian-speakers with Ukrainian language and culture.

Television and radio broadcasting

Legislation

Like print media, broadcasting was also influenced by the development of a new legislative framework. The first law impacting this sector was the 1993 Statute on Television and Radio Broadcasting.[20] This statute governs:

> Relations between subjects in the area of television and radio broadcasting without regard to the forms of property, aims of creation, and the titular activity of the participant television and radio entities, or the means of distribution of television and radio information, if their programs are directed for mass consumption.

It also lays out the main principles of broadcasting in Ukraine:

> Objectivity, truthfulness of information, competency, guarantee for citizens of a right of access to information, of free expression of their views and thoughts, securing of ideological and political pluralism, observance of professional ethics and universal moral norms by the radio–television entities.

Following the adoption of the 1993 Broadcasting Statute and its amendments, a special supervisory body was established to provide regulatory oversight of both state and non-state broadcasters. The Statute on the National Council on Television and Radio Broadcasting Issues dated 30 September 1998, No. 134–XIV, gave the council the right to issue broadcasting channel licenses to Ukrainian television and radio organizations. The statute created the procedures for frequency allocation.

Under this statute, the council is also empowered to impose penalties for breaches of this law or the individual license conditions. The penalties include warnings and fines of up to 25 per cent of the license fee. The council may appeal to the courts to withdraw broadcasters' licenses, and all decisions of the council may also be subjected to court review.

A separate 1995 Statute on Communication regulates the procedures for obtaining a technical license for the use of television and radio frequencies.[21] A licensed broadcaster may lease or buy frequencies, technical facilities, and the equipment necessary to produce and transmit its signal from the governmental Radio Broadcasting, Radio Communication, and Television Concern. The 1993 Broadcasting Statute does not prohibit license holders from owning transmitting facilities. New stations normally own video equipment, but studio premises are often leased from the state broadcasting companies.

Having taken care of the technical elements discussed above, a new broadcasting company may apply to the National Council on Television and Radio Broadcasting Issues for a license. In the application process, a new broadcasting company must provide detailed information including the name, address, and bank account number of the applicant, the name, emblem, call sign, and address of the company, the broadcaster's program concept, the language(s) of broadcasting, the expected area of transmission and audience size, the schedule and duration of transmission (including quota of original programs), the type and methods of information distribution (TV, radio, teletext, over-the-air, cable, satellite, and so on), and data about the power, location, and so on of the transmitter.

The application must be supplemented with the internal statute of the broadcaster. The primary term of the license is five years for over-the-air stations or ten years for cable or wire broadcasters. Broadcasting licenses are fee-based and issued by the ministerial cabinet. According to the Decree of the Cabinet of Ministers no. 392 of 5 June 1995, the fee is to be set at the monthly rent of a state-run transmitting facility (at that time it was approximately US$2,000). This fee is reduced by 90 per cent if the licensee is a state broadcaster. It is doubled if the broadcaster transmits more than 20 per cent foreign-produced programming and increases by five times if foreign programming comprises more than 35 per cent of air time.

A statute "On Copyright and Related Rights" was also adopted in 1993, which has important implications for the enforcement of copyright on private television.[22] It provides for protection against piracy and damages for victims of this offence, and safeguards artistic, literary, and scientific broadcasts. Most private television companies in Ukraine cannot afford to pay Western copyright charges, and since their popularity and, in some cases, their very existence depends on using pirated programming, the companies broadcast such programs despite the law. The 1996 Statute on Advertising (discussed above) that bans tobacco and alcohol advertisements on television and radio has also considerably curtailed revenue.

Other legislation having an impact on broadcasting media includes the 1997 Statute on the Procedures of the Coverage of Activities of the Bodies of State Power and Bodies of Local Self-government in Ukraine by the Mass Media. This defines the legal entities granted the right to use national state television and radio broadcasting channels under emergency conditions. They include the president, the chairperson of the Supreme Rada, the prime minister, the chairpersons of the Supreme Court and of the Constitutional Court. The statute also allocates 3 per cent of annual state television and radio broadcasts for the transmission of parliamentary proceedings, with the Supreme Rada's administration reimbursing state television companies for the cost of these broadcasts.

Connected to the reform of Ukrainian broadcasting law, an intriguing development took place toward the end of 1997. Following a debate between the Supreme Rada and the president over certain provisions of a new public broadcasting law, Ukraine finally adopted a statute providing a legal basis for the creation of a public broadcasting system.[23] The Statute on the System of Public Television and Radio Broadcasting came into force on 5 November 1997. It established the Hromadske Ukrainske radiomovlennya ta telebachennya (HURT, the Ukrainian Public Broadcasting Company) as an independent legal entity with the status of a nationwide unitary and non-profit mass communication system, owned by the Ukrainian people. Under this law, the Supreme Rada would approve HURT's internal statute and its program concept, and would take part in the creation of its governing bodies. HURT would be financed through license fees, procurement fees from government programming, commercial broadcasting activities, and other sources. Advertising would be phased out over time, but in the first year HURT would be financed directly from the national budget.

The declared goals of the new structure included:

- implementation of the system of public broadcasting as an informational guarantor of human rights for access to pluralistic information and provision for the existence of the independent media, publicly controlled, on the basis of provision of fair status to non-governmental television and radio organizations;
- provision of free access to national broadcasting channels to a broad range of local [...] television and radio organizations irrespective of their form of ownership, as well as representatives of political parties, civic and religious associations;
- preservation and propaganda of the best samples of the national culture and art, protection of national interests and national spirituality, development of respect for general human values and general societal interests in the sphere of information;
- realization of broad information support for various political and social movements that stand for the strengthening of the Ukrainian statehood.

(UCIPR 1997: 8)

According to the program concept, HURT would be granted seventy hours of weekly television broadcasting time and 140 hours of weekly radio airtime. HURT would be expected to produce 40 per cent of its programming in-house, to reserve another 40 per cent for productions supplied by regional companies, and to commit the other 20 per cent to foreign programming (UCIPR 1997: 8). Programming was to consist of 20 per cent equal shares of political and social programs, public affairs and educational programs, culture programs, special programs for children and young people, and entertainment and films.

It should be noted, however, that despite detailed legislation, public radio or television stations are not expected to commence broadcasting soon. State bodies currently refuse to provide frequency licenses, block financing of public broadcasters, and find loopholes that sabotage the formation of the numerous councils designed to oversee public broadcasting in Ukraine. The reason lies in the reluctance of the president and, therefore, of the executive branch to follow decisions made by the parliament.

In a separate vote on 15 January 1998 the Supreme Rada approved the membership of HURT's public council. As of September 2000, however, HURT had not obtained a frequency license from the National Council on Television and Radio Broadcasting Issues and was thus not broadcasting.

Broadcasting diversity

Four national television channels broadcast in Ukraine. They are UT-1, UT-2, Inter, and ICTV. Of these, the state controls only UT-1. In 2000, the channels reached 96 per cent, 92 per cent, 67 per cent and 42 per cent of the population, respectively.

"Radio Channel One" is the principal radio station in the country, broadcasting mainly news and current affairs. Radio "Promin" broadcasts short news bulletins every hour with musical programming in between, and is targeted at a youth audience. "Radio Channel Three" broadcasts radio dramas, music, and entertainment programs. In addition, there is a world service that broadcasts in Ukrainian, English, and in German for listeners abroad.

STATE TELEVISION (UT-1)

Since January 1995, national state-owned television and radio companies have run all national state radio and television channels. Derzhteleradio, the State Television and Radio Committee, controls the national companies and the state television and radio broadcasting companies of the twenty-four Ukrainian regions (*oblasti*). This committee is charged with the implementation of state policy for broadcasting media, under the supervision of the National Council on Television and Radio Broadcasting Issues (see above), disseminating information to broadcast media abroad, and running the Radio Broadcasting, Radio Communication, and Television Concern (RRT). The Ukrainian president appoints the committee's chairperson and those of the two national companies, and the former must be approved by parliament. The state committee also selects the heads of the regional television and radio companies, with the consent of local administration.

State television has become the focus of a struggle among branches of government. Since independence, the president and prime minister and the Supreme Rada have been fighting for control over national television. After 1995, however, the executive branch appeared to have won. From about that time, the executive ignored parliamentary decisions related to broadcasting and the president vetoed decisions he did not like.

On 29 September 1998, the president issued a decree that placed the State Committee on Television and Radio under the direct control of the cabinet of ministers rather than the ministry of information, established in November 1996 (Decree of the President 1998).[24] The Supreme Rada retaliated, and in a separate decree of the ministerial cabinet, dated 10 June 1998, the RRT was transferred from the supervision of the State Committee on Television and Radio to the ministry of information.

On 16 September 1998, the president countered with a decree "On Improvement of the State Administration of the Informational Sphere," which established a state stock company, Ukrainian Television and Radio (DAK Ukrteleradio). At the same time, it abolished the national television and radio companies. Finally, on 23 December 1998, the Supreme Rada appealed to the president to cancel the decree which it claimed was unconstitutional. A group of parliamentary deputies, headed by the chairperson of the parliamentary mass media committee, additionally requested the Constitutional Court to review the presidential decree. The Supreme Rada then attempted to pass a statute forbidding changes to legislation concerning the national television and radio companies. As of September 2000, these continue to function and are recognized by the president.

PRIVATE TV

Historically, Moscow-based broadcasting has been very popular in Ukraine. Even after independence, audience share for just one Russian television channel, Ostankino, was 60 per cent. Subsequently, in 1992–1993, all but one Russian television and radio channel were removed from the Ukrainian airwaves by the government. In 1995, Ukraine transferred Russian Public Television (ORT) to a different and weaker frequency, thus cutting its potential audience by 40 per cent.[26] The following year the frequency was assigned to Inter television, which originally kept the main ORT newscasts and prime-time programming. Inter, which retains Russian as its principal broadcasting language, has tended to reduce Moscow programming. Still, it remains the most popular channel in Ukraine.[27]

The ratio of Ukrainian to Russian language transmissions is approximately 60:40. Russian language programming dominates private television and radio. In contrast, Ukrainian is the principal language of state broadcasters. Since Russian state enterprises currently produce little new programming, at present Ukrainian broadcasts are dominated by re-runs of Soviet-era films and documentaries, and by interviews and talk shows where participants speak Russian, even when questions are posed in Ukrainian.

The cable television market has recently expanded its quality and variety. However, the archaic communications infrastructure and the poor state of the economy limit this market. Only about 8 per cent of households, nationwide, have cable access. An average cable operator in Kiev offers fifteen channels, including three national channels, approximately five local channels, and other international transmissions. Of the Western channels, CNN and Eurosport are the most widely received (*Kyiv Post* 1998). A 1999 joint decision of the Anti-Monopoly Committee and the Kiev city administration set a tariff of 1 hryvna a month for cable services offering up to twelve channels and 4 hryvna (approximately US$1) a month for up to twenty-four channels.

Radio

While television broadcasters have been targets of control by political and economic elites, radio has remained virtually unaffected by politics. This is primarily due to the fact that most stations broadcast only music. Ukrainian state-owned radio broadcasts over three national channels and also operates a world service, with a combined total of 94.5 hours per day. According to the 1993 Broadcasting Statute, a licensed broadcaster may lease the frequency and the technical facilities and equipment required from the RRT. The 1993 Broadcasting Statute also established the private ownership of transmitters. However, most television stations possess only primitive video equipment and lease both studios and transmitters from state broadcasting organizations.

Censorship in Ukrainian broadcasting

Events have been observed with regard to state television, which both experts and journalists have defined as "effective censorship." Early in 1996, the program *Pislyamova* (PostScript), of the production studio *Nova Mova* (New Speech), was taken off the air on UT-1 by a decision of the National Council on Broadcasting. The head of the studio, in an official statement, interpreted this act as revenge on the part of certain political players for his refusal to cut a report critical of their activities. Later, *Pislyamova* was again taken off the air on a number of occasions and on various television channels in spite of its high ratings and high professional standard.

At the end of 1996, the information program *Vikna* (Windows), disappeared from UT-2. This had been acclaimed as one of the best independent news programs on Ukrainian TV. The formal pretext for its disappearance was a problem in obtaining a broadcasting license by Studio 1+1. However, well before this happened, the producers were also under political pressure from state officials who attempted to influence the program's content, and exercised direct censorship of each program issue prior to its transmission.

According to observers, state control over the content of information programs is possible because there are loopholes in media legislation (McCormack 1999: 298–299). Although interference of state bodies in the activities of TV and radio broadcasters is prohibited by the statute "On Television and Radio Broadcasting," the same statute makes broadcasters responsible for the content of their programs.[28] During elections, the electoral law protects media from facing responsibility for statements made by candidates that may be libelous. Normally, however, media are legally responsible for all statements made by individuals when these statements are transmitted on air or in print. This has been given as one reason for requiring the hand-over of program tapes for previewing. State officials appeal to this particular clause when demanding the submission of information programs made by state channels for preliminary monitoring and subsequent revision.

Since Ukrainian politicians consider television one of the most important means of influencing public opinion, state interference tends to increase during election periods. This was certainly the case during the parliamentary elections of March 1998 and the presidential elections of October 1999. In preparation for the elections, President Kuchma launched a massive reorganization of media structures in late 1998. Kuchma established the joint stock Ukrainian Television and Radio Broadcasting Company by a presidential decree of 16 September 1998. By another decree of 29 September 1998, Kuchma placed two major organizations, the State News Agency of Ukraine (DINAU) and the State Committee on Television and Radio Broadcasting, under the direct control of the government.

Summary

Ukrainian media legislation envisions a pluralistic broadcasting system, with both state-owned and independent broadcasters.[29] Still, one of the provisions of the 1993 Broadcasting Statute describes state television and radio entities as "the foundation" of national broadcasting, thus creating a serious legal obstacle to any challenge of the state's predominance, at least at the national level. By law, those prohibited from holding licenses to own a broadcasting facility include foreign citizens, political parties, trade unions, and religious organizations, including subsidiary enterprises and organizations.

While the first independent broadcasting stations appeared only in 1990, by March 1993 there were already 499 private television and 343 radio companies, production studios, and channels. This is a record figure, not just in the former USSR, but in Europe, as well.[30] Some of these companies, however, exist only on paper, evidenced by the fact that the total broadcasting time by independent broadcasters (via cable, wire, and air) was just 800 hours per day.[31] This peak number of 842 broadcasters substantially decreased after 1993 as a result of a decline in audience interest, lack of advertising revenue, and increasingly enforced copyright protection. Further limitations were also placed on foreign investment in Ukrainian broadcasting. Foreigners could invest in broadcasting only if permitted to do so by the National Council on Television and Radio Broadcasting Issues, and any foreign investment was limited to a maximum of 30 per cent of a company's stock capitalization, donations and charity included. The National Council continues to oversee such foreign investment.

At the same time, Ukraine enjoys the second highest level of Western media investment within the CIS, next in order after Russia. This has resulted from the perceived profitability of Ukrainian television and radio and the growing volume of advertising in this sector.[32] In fact, many broadcasters (FM radio, national television, regional channels) have foreign partners (Lange 1997: 250). One example is the "1+1" group, broadcasting on UT-2, which is controlled by the British company, Central European Media Enterprises (CME). Another is Gala-Radio, which was founded by a US citizen. At a regional level, industrial firms provide some level of financial support to the broadcasting media. Such support, however, is mainly of a temporary character. Further, media outlets regularly change sponsors, which include major banks, energy concerns, and trade companies. The majority of commercial enterprises support media outlets for political reasons. These enterprises attempt to form links with political leaders who, in turn, will lobby for their interests. Direct returns on their investments are secondary.

Emerging technologies

According to local observers, Internet development in Ukraine has been hindered by a number of factors: the weak condition of telecommunications infrastructure, leading to delays and breaks in the line; the limited number of direct channels which can be used to access the world-wide information networks; the high tariffs imposed on use of the Internet (US$1.50–$3.00 per hour); and the limit of information resources on the Ukrainian part of the Internet.[33]

In spite of these factors, the Internet as a source of information has become much more important. This has been true even though Ukrainian platforms remain relatively underdeveloped in relation to Russian resources. This is significant because the intake of Russian books and periodicals into libraries has almost ceased since 1991 (McCormack 1999: 312).

A 1994 statute "On Protection of Information in Automatic Systems" currently regulates the functioning of automated systems (AS), defined by Article 1 of the statute as "systems that deal with automatic data processing and which include technical means of its processing (computing technology and communication), as well as methods and procedures, software."[34] The statute regulates relations between providers of information and AS, and their end-users. Further, it provides for the protection of information from unsanctioned access through AS. It also determines the role of the state in this field.

On 22 April 1998, the president approved a decree "On Certain Measures Regarding Defense of the State Interests in the Information Sphere." By this act, international transmission of data over the Internet was to be allowed only through a network of three operators (providers): Ukrtelecom, Ukrkosmos, and Infokom. Human rights groups objected to the decree and the public uproar provoked delegitimized the decree. More importantly, however, the original idea proved unworkable because of technical problems. Although the decree remains in place, it is ignored.

At the beginning of 1998, out of 264,000 computers operating in Ukraine, approximately 25,000 were connected to the Internet. In a European country of 50 million people, this is quite a low figure. In July 1997, there were approximately 350 servers located in Ukraine in addition to approximately 400 virtual Web-servers. In August 1997, 103 Internet providers operated in Ukraine. The vast majority were located in Kiev (22), Donetsk (13), Dnepropetrovsk (10), Kharkov (8) (McCormack 1999: 312). Partisan or political party affiliations within the new technological media have not been observed, to date.

The government has attempted to privatize sections of the telecom networks and operators to potential foreign investors. The main obstacle to this plan has been the parliament. For example, on 15 December 1998, Ukraine's Supreme Rada rejected government-proposed legislation that would allow the privatization of Ukrtelecom, the country's telecommunications giant. Deputies voted the bill unconstitutional. The state intends to sell off up to 30 per cent of Ukrtelecom. This telecom company has thirty-five subsidiaries and 738 branches throughout Ukraine, and employs 130,000 people. It is currently worth about US$10 billion. As a result, potential bidders have come primarily from the West.

Western telecom companies have also been active in telephone, paging, and other communication services. For example, the American company Metromedia has interests in the paging business in Dnepropetrovsk. Such foreign concerns have been sharply criticized both in parliament and in the press on the grounds of potential harm to national security. However, threats to foreign investment hamper modernization of communication lines, while high costs and the low purchasing power of the population have limited infrastructural development to major cities.

Assessment

The media in Ukraine have undergone a tremendous transformation over the past ten years, diversifying, expanding, and enormously improving professional and technical standards. Pre-publication censorship conducted by the communist authorities prior to 1990 no longer takes place. Nevertheless, media, in general, are dominated by political and commercial interests, which have led to almost total engagement by general interest press and broadcasting channels with one or another of the interest groups.

The majority of media statutes adopted in Ukraine are in line with European standards and have been structured in a manner appropriate to overall media development and freedom. They were adopted at early stages of transition when the government was concerned about the image of the newly independent state, was reluctant to irritate media, and was generally more concerned with military reforms, foreign relations, and privatization than with media control. As a function of these conditions, the president vetoed none of the early media bills and neither parliament nor the Constitutional Court challenged any of the media-related presidential decrees.

A code of professional ethics, on the other hand, is a vague notion for most Ukrainian journalists as for most of their colleagues in the CIS. The subject was strongly tied to the communist values and images that were thrown out with the communist regime. That journalists should be free of any corporate or governmental control is now the slogan of the day and codes of ethics exist in very few media organizations.

Much time will pass before a code of ethics again becomes "fashionable" or is demanded by the audience. One circumstance that may impose self-regulation on journalists could be the decision to enforce judgements in defamation cases won against the media. Though at present most of the winners are public figures, their widely publicized cases lead the general public to believe that suing and punishing unethical media is possible. Once legal suits become an imminent threat to press editors and proprietors, a code of ethics will likely once again come to the fore to create self-imposed limits, observed by "free" journalists.

Though in general media, especially in Kiev, offer more objective interpretations of events, favoritism in subsidies to the state-owned press is an ongoing problem for the print media market in Ukraine. The press currently operates on a very uneven playing field. The variety of publications and broadcasting media affiliated with different political interest groups, however, arguably offers a certain degree of plurality. Readers and listeners can at least choose which media they agree with or trust.

The most serious setbacks for Ukrainian media continue to take place in the political and economic spheres. State officials frequently interfere in the information sphere and abuse government data for political reasons, especially in the run-up to important elections. The practice of using the courts and the tax inspectorate to punish media for opposing the government has shown no signs of weakening over the past year and was, in fact, underscored during the presidential elections in October 1999.

The media, as business concerns, continually fail to bring in significant profits. Increased costs of media output have followed in the wake of marketization reforms, and private media are often indirectly penalized through the preferential economic treatment that the state media sector receives. Despite heavy losses and declining press circulation, however, there is little evidence of an imminent print media collapse.[35]

While many media outlets have attempted to reach a national audience, no quality newspaper or magazine can claim to have done so yet in Ukraine. The Russian (Moscow) press is still the leading quality press there and most of the popular Ukrainian print media reprint stories from their Russian counterparts. Under fully free market conditions, no national Ukrainian television or radio channel would be able to compete today with Russian broadcasting. One reason is the much poorer artistic quality of stories and programming originating in Kiev, let alone Poltava or Rovno. A Ukrainian observer has noted that it has become fashionable to criticize national television for its "hicksville image" (Kostenko *et al.* 1994: 151). Another reason lies in a shift from the image of Moscow as an oppressor, "consum[ing] Ukrainian wheat and sugar for free," prevalent in 1991, to an image of a beacon of relative, and therefore more feasible, economic prosperity, cultural influence, fashion trends, achievements in sports, etc.[36]

Together with the continued limitations placed on the Russian media, in conjunction with the gradual strengthening of the Ukrainian media, culture, and language, a political nation will be formed on Ukrainian territory.[37] One day, the "foreign press" will no doubt be overpowered and Ukrainian or Ukrainian-language broadcasting will be predominant. The problem, at that point, will lie in the ability of media to maintain high standards of pluralism, professionalism, and freedom.

Until recently, Ukrainian media defined themselves by the fact that they broke the limits of the uniform communist press. Their identity has been grounded in the instrumental role that they played in destroying communist models and images and in the fact that they were able to move beyond communism.

Currently, Ukrainian media have passed through the period of self-expression characteristic of *glasnost* and have entered into a commercial phase of development. Relapses to fierce anti-communist rhetoric are common only during election periods.[38]

Electoral campaigning has been the rare occasion on which the new Ukrainian media have revealed their level of influence. The Supreme Rada campaigns of February and March 1998 are one example. During campaigning, the media exercised its influence through selectively selling advertising spots, accepting money from political donors, and launching full-fledged media attacks. As observers from the European Institute for the Media noted in their preliminary report on the media coverage of the 1998 Ukrainian parliamentary elections, "the media did not fully discharge their obligations to the voters" and "were broadly unsuccessful in providing accurate and fair information on the political processes at work during the parliamentary campaign in Ukraine" (1998). Thus the media, even when in the national spotlight, failed to serve the public. Instead, they looked for financial and political incentives to represent (or misrepresent) the interests of important political and economic actors. As the Organization for Security and Cooperation in Europe (OSCE) has noted in its report on the 1998 parliamentary elections, "the lack of a truly independent media hindered an informed electorate. Most media entities were controlled by the government or by moneyed political interests" (1998).

Media legislation in Ukraine guarantees media freedom and autonomy and promotes pluralism. The presence of a broadcasting law and of regulatory broadcasting agencies is notable. They mark a positive exception to the laws and regulatory systems in other CIS republics. Certain ground rules, regarding the founding of a mass media entity, state registration, state support, and economic relief, are applied in actual practice. Meanwhile, mass communications legislation has laid part of the foundations for the development of the media in Ukraine. If its provisions are observed and enforced, Ukraine will possess one of the most politically independent media systems in the former USSR.

Still, at this stage of media reform process, problems are likely to occur. Ukraine, like Russia, is a country with a tradition of disregard for law, both on the part of the rulers and on the part of the ruled. In 1999, President Kuchma was proclaimed by the American-based Committee to Protect Journalists as one of the ten national leaders most detrimental to the free press. Ukraine must look for a larger compromise between the declared rights of citizens and realities of day-to-day life. Such a compromise must address the interests of government, private business, and individual citizens while also taking account of the country's national and international interests.[39] Ukrainian mass media legislation, in this narrow but important field, can serve as a kind of blueprint, recognized by all parties and establishing ground rules for compromise.

The task of constructing and strengthening democratic society, a prerequisite for real and lasting media freedom, is a process more difficult and consequential than that of overturning the previous communist machine. This goal represents the greatest challenge to Ukrainian journalists.

In this transitional period, both the state and legal institutions are, on the whole, too weak and incompetent to be truly effective. A well-functioning market economy, non-existent in Ukraine, is a prerequisite for the development of political democracy and for the economic freedom of non-state broadcasters and journalists. It is hoped that in the future, such a properly functioning market economy will provide the basis for a fully functional political democracy and that effective legal institutions and law-enforcement mechanisms will be established. Only then will media legislation be capable of defending freedom of speech in practice as well as in word.

Notes

1 Zakon "*O pechati i drugikh sredstvakh massovoi informatsii.*"
2 Zakon "*Pro informatsiyu,*" no. 2657–XII.
3 For texts of all Ukrainian statutes regulating mass media cited in this chapter, see *Ukraina: informatsia* (1997).
4 Adopted by the *Rada* on 6 May 1993.
5 The data are those of the Supreme Court of Ukraine. (*Zakonodatelny bulleten* 1998: 10)
6 Adopted by the *Rada* on 21 January 1994.
7 This law entered into force on 17 October 1997.
8 Government organs are understood as the Supreme Rada, the Office of the President, the cabinet of ministers, national ministries and departments, the Supreme Court, and the Constitutional Court.
9 With the exceptions itemized in the addendum to the 1994 statute "On State Secrets."
10 Zakon "*Pro derzhavnu pidtrymku zasobim masovoi informatsii ta sotsialnyi zakhyst zhurnalistiv,*" no. 540/97-VR. This legislation was adopted by the Supreme Rada and signed by the president on 23 September 1997.
11 1 hryvna was equal to US$0.60 in mid-1998 and US$0.25 in mid-1999.
12 Article 11.

13 The statute covers print media activity by defining the right to establish print media outlets, to operate such outlets, and to acquire and operate technical devices and equipment related to the distribution of print media products.
14 1992 Press Statute, Article 10.
15 News agencies are exempted.
16 They are *Silski visti*, *Holos Ukrainy*, *Uryadovy kurier*, *Robitnycha gazeta*, and *Kommunist*, all based in Kiev. For mass media statistics, see *Ukraina: informatsia* (1997: 754) and European Institute for the Media (1998).
17 For statistics on the popularity of the press in 1992–1994, see: Kostenko *et al.* (1994: 148–155) and Bebik (1994).
18 The tax was fixed in ECU by the act in order to avoid problems from inflation.
19 No support whatsoever is provided to pornographic or advertising publications or those founded with the participation of foreign entities. No support is provided for publications which have 50 per cent or more foreign (i.e. Russian) content.
20 Statute adopted December 1993. For a detailed analysis and the full text of this act, see Richter and Krug (1994: 3, 4, 14).
21 This statute was adopted by the Supreme Rada on 16 May 1995.
22 "*Pro avtorske pravo i sumizhni prava*," 23 December 1993, no. 3792–XII.
23 For a discussion of the Public Broadcasting Statute, see *IRIS* (1997, 1998: 10:12; 4:10).
24 The ministry incorporated several key bodies involved in media legislation and regulation. The minister of information, who was to be appointed by the president, was also to be a member of the cabinet.
25 Note that these companies have already been technically eliminated by the above presidential decree.
26 ORT was the last remaining TV broadcaster from Moscow.
27 This is proved by the fact that in 1997 Inter took 43% of the revenues from advertising obtained by all four national TV channels in Ukraine (Karaulshcikov 1998: 6–7).
28 Zakon "*Pro telebachennya ta radiomovlennya*," no. 3759–XII of 21 December 1993, Article 6.
29 In the form of private companies, joint stock ventures, or cooperatives.
30 The relevant figure for Russia was approximately 500 broadcasters. For Uzbekistan, only a handful. For Europe, see the number of television channels in Europe in *Statistical Yearbook* (1997: 140).
31 Broadcasters receive a 12-month grace period to begin transmission, which is why they often exist only on paper. See Interfax-Ukraine (wire service), 1993, 12 September.
32 The levels of advertising had doubled annually prior to the 1998 economic crisis.
33 Local observers include: Vladimir Natalchenko, editor of a media law and policy newsletter in Kiev, who provided information for the chapter on Ukraine in McCormack 1999. According to recent data, there are 186 publications of Ukrainian newspapers and magazines on the Internet, including 40 Ukrainian newspapers with virtually no useful search engines (*Ukrainskiy Media-Bulleten* 1999: 47–52). Available at: http://www.internetri.com.ua/
34 Zakon "*Pro zakhyst informatsii v avtomatyzovannykh systemakh*," 5 July 1994, no. 81/94-VR.
35 This view is supported by the authors of the analysis in a Kiev journal (Kostenko *et al.* 1994: 150).
36 In general, Russian artists are much more popular than Ukrainian artists.
37 This strengthening of the national identity can be achieved with government support.
38 As was the case in March 1998 and October 1999.
39 Relations with Russia represent one of the most crucial aspects.

References

Associated Press (2000) *Moscow Times*, 5 May.
Bebik, Valery (1994) "Ukrainski mas-media yak dzerkalo nashoi gromadskoi svidomosti," *Holos Ukrainy*, 2 November.
Decree of the President of Ukraine (1998) "On Amendments to the Decree of the President of Ukraine of 13 November 1996," no. 1061, no. 1075 of 29 September 1998.

Ellis, Frank (1999) *From Glasnost to the Internet: Russia's New Infosphere*, New York: St Martin's Press.

European Institute for the Media (1998) *Media Coverage of the Ukrainian Parliamentary Elections March 1998*, preliminary unpublished report. Used with permission.

IRIS (1996–1999) Monthly Bulletin of the European Audiovisual Observatory, Strasbourg.

Kachkaeva, Anna and Richter, Andrei G. (1992) "The Emergence of Non-state TV in Ukraine," *Canadian Journal of Communication*, Vol. 17: 4.

Karaulshcikov, Pyotr (1998) "Reklama na natsionalnom televidenii: nekotorye itogi goda," *Zakonodatelny bulleten dlya sredstv massovoy informatsii* (Kiev: Legal Newsletter for the Mass Media) no. 1: 2–3.

Kostenko, Natalia *et al.* (1994) "Ukrainian Mass Media and Freedom of Information," *Political Thought* (Kiev): 4.

Kyiv Post (1998) (weekly newspaper, Kiev, 16 October).

Lange, Yasha (1997) *Media in the CIS: A Study of the Political, Legislative and Socio-Economic Framework*, Dusseldorf: European Institute for the Media.

Lenin, Vladimir "What Is to Be Done" (written in 1902 as a plan for Communist revolution) in *Collected Works*, vol. 1. Moscow: Progress Publishers, 1967: 233.

McCormack, Gillian (1999) "Ukraine," in *Media in the CIS: A Study of the Political, Legislative and Socio-Economic Framework*. Second edition. Dusseldorf: European Institute for the Media.

Nahaylo, Bohdan (1992) "Ukraine," *RFE/RL Research Report*, Vol. 1, 39.

Organization for Security and Cooperation in Europe (OSCE) (1998) "Ukraine's Parliamentary Election," 29 March.

Post-Soviet Media Law and Policy Newsletter (1993–1999).

Richter, Andrei (1993) "Broadcasting Law in the Ukraine," in Kleinwachter, Wolfgang (ed.) *Broadcasting in Transition: The Changing Legal Framework in the Eastern Part of Europe* (Netcom Papers, 3, Leipzig: Medienstadt Leipzig e.V.).

—— (1998) "Media Regulation in Selected Countries of the Former Soviet Union," in Langham-Brown, Jo (ed.) *Media in Europe: The Yearbook of the European Institute for the Media*, 1998 (Dusseldorf: European Institute for the Media).

—— (1999) "Ukraina," in Monakhov, Viktor and Kandybina, Elena (eds) *Zakony i praktika sredstv massovoi informatsii stran SNG i Baltii* (Mass Media Law and Practice in the CIS Countries and the Baltics). (Moscow: Galeria).

—— (1999) "Ukraine," in Nikoltchev, Susanne (ed.) *Legal Guide to Audiovisual Media in Europe* (Strasbourg, European Audiovisual Observatory).

Richter, Andrei and Krug, Peter (1994) "The New Ukrainian Statute: A Commentary," *Post-Soviet Media Law and Policy Newsletter*, 7.

Statistical Yearbook (1997) Film, Television, Video and New Media in Europe. European Audiovisual Observatory. 1998 edition. Strasbourg.

UCIPR (1997) "Slicing the Media Cake," in *Research Update of the Ukrainian Center for Independent Political Research*, No. 94, 8 December.

Ukraina: informatsia i svoboda slova (1997) Kiev: Molod.

Ukraine's Parliamentary Election (1998). Report prepared by the staff of the Commission on Security and Cooperation in Europe. Washington, DC, 29 March.

Ukrainskiy Media-Bulleten (1999) Issue 3–4. (Ukrainian Media Bulletin) Kiev: European Institute for the Media.

Zakonodatelny bulleten dlya sredstv massovoy informatsii (Kiev: Legal Newsletter for the Mass Media) (1998), no. 2: 10.

Zakonodatelnyi bulleten dkya sredstv massovoi informatsii (Legal Bulletin for the Mass Media) (1997–1999), Kiev.

Zakonodatelnyi bulleten dlya sredstv massovoi informatsii (Kiev: Legal Bulletin for the Mass Media) (1999a), no. 1: 13.

—— (1999b), no. 5: 19.

Zakonodatelstvo i praktika sredstv massovoi informatsii (ZiP, Media Law and Policy) (1994–1999), Monthly Journal of the Moscow Media Law and Policy Centre. www.medialaw.ru

Zadvornyi, A. M. (ed.) (1997) *Ukraina: Informatsiya i svoboda slova* (Ukraine: Information and Free Speech). Kiev: Molod.

8

THE CURRENT STATE OF
MEDIA REFORM IN UGANDA

Ronald David Kayanja

Introduction

There are many factors that have hindered the establishment of independent media within Uganda. Demography is one. Over 80 per cent of Uganda's 22 million population are peasants living in rural areas and subsisting on agricultural production. At least fifty-six languages are spoken within an area of just 236,000 sq. km and only just over half of the population can read and write.[1] Although English continues to be the country's official language, those who speak it are part of the minority who have received a formal education.[2]

Infrastructural problems persist. Electricity is only available in a limited number of areas, resulting in a sparsely and unevenly distributed range of televised broadcasting throughout the country. The availability of newer, emerging technologies is all but non-existent in the country, with the exception of urban centers such as Kampala. The Acacia Initiative of the Canadian International Development Research Center (IDRC) has attempted to combat the problem by sponsoring the development of new "telecenters" in five districts of Uganda that will provide telephone, fax, electronic mail, and the Internet (Opoku-Mensah 1998). However, Uganda continues to have one of the lowest rates of telephone penetration in the world (with a national capacity of just under 70,000 lines).[3]

But perhaps most detrimental to independent media development is Uganda's authoritarian history. With dictatorial regimes in place for most of its post-colonial history, Uganda has suffered the deleterious effects of arbitrary rule: ethnic violence, numerous coups, military excesses, disappearances, and economic turmoil. Since 1986, however, the country has been on the road to recovery. The reform program introduced by the Museveni government has led to the institution of some elements of the rule of law, the development of media legislation, and the formal devolution of some degree of power to a popularly elected legislature. The election of 2000, while not yielding a shift in power, provided the visible formation of a significant opposition.

Consistent with these political developments, Uganda has moved from a state of continued authoritarianism to the preliminary stages of democratic transition. The tasks which now face the country in the development of free and independent media lie equally within the institutional, legislative, and economic spheres. The most urgent problem in the institutional sphere is the issue of the presidency, an office that remains largely unstructured, with no accepted mechanism for the peaceful transfer of executive power. It remains to be seen whether the Museveni regime will hand over power without a struggle and through the implementation of legal and institutional structures or whether another period of bloodletting and civil war will ensue with the president's departure.[4] The election of June 2000 was promising in this respect.

Difficulties also persist with a judiciary still beholden to the other branches of government. This issue, in particular, needs to be addressed in order to ensure an unbiased implementation of the nation's laws. Independent media require a judiciary strong enough to ensure that problems of "inappropriate utilization," where political leaders use existing legislation to undermine and blackmail media actors, are eradicated.[5] If media are to play a significant role in democratization, the popularly elected legislature must enact legislation that fosters the media sector in such a way as to allow it to fulfill both its watchdog role and its more substantive role of creating a public forum, which shapes both identity and the larger political debate.

Structural and economic problems in the polity as a whole make the fulfillment of such goals difficult. Reform goes hand-in-hand with the larger process of democratization currently underway, and if this were halted it is likely that political actors who would prefer that citizens remain uninformed would once again stifle media.

The colonial dimension: a prelude to dictatorship?

A former British colony, Uganda gained political independence in October 1962. The previous colonial regime was autocratic and, at times, resorted to crude force to undermine attempts at self-rule. As an element of that rule, the colonial government enacted stringent laws against the press and trade unions, while suppressing the nationalist intelligentsia.

Governing through decrees and ordinances that lacked popular legitimacy, colonial authorities often resorted to draconian and authoritarian legal measures to compel compliance (Kiddu-Makubuya 1991).[6] Only after the Second World War were even token concessions made, and in 1945 the colonial government nominated the first Ugandan legislative assembly (Legco). In 1958, elections were held to this assembly, representing the first move toward any form of democratic governance in Uganda's history.

As early as 1910, Uganda's colonial government enacted the first laws to control the press. The Newspapers Surety Ordinance No. 9 of 1910 and the Press and Censorship Ordinance No. 4 of 1915 were the earliest mechanisms. These laws imposed stiff penalties on any publication that violated the law. The Penal Code, sections 48, 52, and 53, set conditions and punishments for seditious publications. A publication was considered to be seditious if it incited hatred, contempt, or disaffection against the colonial government of Uganda, incited the general public to modify the government by unlawful means, or promoted feelings of hostility between different classes of the population.

Such laws were used by the colonial regime to suppress all manner of debate or dissent against colonial policies. Of the sixty-four newspapers founded in

Uganda between 1900 and 1962, only five remained at the time of independence. The colonial government had banned some papers, while editors of others were imprisoned on charges of sedition. Many of the remainder simply folded under the burden of hefty libel costs (Gariyo 1992: 90).

Prior to independence, Uganda had one of the best civil services south of the Sahara. Makerere University in Kampala, founded in 1922, was one of the first institutions of higher learning in sub-Saharan Africa. This tradition bore fruit in the period immediately after independence, when the country boasted a booming economy based on the export of agricultural raw materials. In the early 1960s, Uganda was comparatively successful among developing countries. The infrastructure was restored and developed, new industries sprang up, and social services expanded.

Still, in the wake of gaining independence, political corruption began to set in, complicated by the issue of ethnicity.[7] There were few examples or established institutions of democratic governance to build upon, and familiarity with democratic values such as compromise, constitutionalism, and tolerance was absent. This situation was exacerbated by the 1962 constitution, which created a quasi-federal system, further aggravating the existing ethnic divisions. The 1962 constitution institutionalized competing centers of power that constrained and threatened the amateur central government. Nationalist claims and secessionist tendencies that were intensified by the constitution's federal structure led to the country's first military coup in 1966. Idi Amin, the then Deputy Army Commander, led the coup that stormed the palace of Sir Edward Muteesa II, President of Uganda and King of the Buganda province.

A period of civilian dictatorship ensued after 1966, engendering waves of violence, murders, chaos, and economic collapse. Milton Obote headed the government from 1967 to 1971. Obote's administration had brought about the further erosion of the nation as rumors of state-inspired terrorism emerged. The Western world became increasingly disenchanted with the regime, which was showing signs of following a communist course (as was the case in Tanzania at the time). Western forces eventually assisted Idi Amin in overthrowing the Obote regime in 1971. The consequences were not favorable.

The Amin regime habitualized rule by presidential decree, outlawed parliamentary procedure, undermined the independence of the judiciary, and eliminated any remaining due process protections (Oloka-Onyango 1991: 4). Under Amin, the politics and economy of Uganda were ruined as the president handed key industries over to a clique of his Muslim and predominantly Nubian friends and foreign investors left. Journalists, playwrights, politicians, and academicians, meanwhile, died under mysterious circumstances.[8]

These initial post-independence governments deployed, with slight modifications, the draconian laws previously used by the colonial regime against the Ugandan press. The Newspapers Act of 1963 created the press censorship board, and the situation worsened when Amin issued a decree in 1972 that stated, *inter alia*, that the appropriate government official "may, if he is satisfied that it is in the public interest to do so by statutory order, prohibit the publication of any newspaper for a specified or indefinite period." This decree, which remained in force until 1995, was used by subsequent regimes to ban numerous newspapers.

Amin was toppled in 1979, but tribal and ethnic conflicts characterized the post-Amin era. Thus, from 1979 to 1986, Uganda had five governments, all of which involved the army to some extent. In fact, although hundreds of thousands of people died during the Amin regime, even more severe atrocities were committed under Obote when he became president for the second time and ruled from 1980 until 1985.[9]

The post-Amin governments in Uganda were harshly repressive toward media. Just after the fall of Amin, many newspapers began publishing articles critical of the new regime. This was thought to be the first opportunity for a truly free press to develop in Uganda. The new independence was to be shortlived. The Obote II regime was particularly hostile to the press. Those independent, critical voices on political, economic and social matters that emerged in the wake of Amin would not be tolerated, nor could state policies or corrupt functionaries be publicly questioned. Influential newspapers including *The Citizen*, *Economy*, *Aga Africa*, *Mulengera*, *Saba Saba*, *The Champion*, and *Weekly Topic* were all banned in 1981 (Gariyo 1993: 36).

Many journalists were also harassed and detained. The editor of the state-owned *Uganda Times*, Ben Bella Illakut, had to flee the country in 1981 after publishing a story about civilian massacres in Moyo. Anthony Sekweyama, editor of the Democratic Party's publication, *Munnansi*, was jailed under the Public Safety Act and freed only after the 1985 coup. Others like Drake Sekeba and Sam Katweere of *The Star* were detained in the mid-1980s for publishing stories alleging government corruption.

In 1986, following a protracted five-year civil war, Yoweri Museveni and his National Resistance Movement (NRM) came to power and, since then, have instituted a period of democratic transition. Elections were held at all levels in 1989, and a new constitution, based on wide grassroots consultations, was ratified by a constituent assembly in 1995. For the first time in Ugandan history, a president elected by universal adult suffrage and a relatively independent parliament was in place. The 1995 constitution, meanwhile, limited the powers of the president and guaranteed freedom of expression and media.[10]

Many consider the present atmosphere of relative tolerance to be a direct function of President Yoweri Museveni's personal charisma. A number of important institutional reforms have already taken place and are consolidating the basis for democratic development. A program of decentralization is underway where citizens will elect representatives from the village to the district level in the form of committees known as "local councils." This system has enhanced political participation, accountability, resolution of conflict, economic development, security consciousness, and the flow of information.

Other initiatives include the creation of an autonomous office of the inspector general, which has been founded to help curb corruption, and an independent human rights commission to serve as a government watchdog. Over 500 new NGOs have sprung up in the country since 1986 in fields as diverse as human rights, environmental concerns, women's interests, development, and orphan protection. Measures such as these constitute an indispensable revision and reformulation of institutional structures that support and promote the wider process of democratic reform.

When Museveni assumed power in 1986, Uganda's economy was in ruins. GDP had fallen by half since independence, while the population had more than doubled in size. Roads were impassable, hospitals lacked water and drugs, factories stood idle, and the countryside was ravaged by war (Brett 1991). Since 1989, however, the economy of the country has been growing by an annual average of 6.7 per cent, while the manufacturing sector is gradually expanding. Investors are becoming increasingly attracted to Uganda, the country's infrastructure has improved, and social services have been restored and repaired.

Such economic revisions contributed to the democratization process, with increased citizen confidence and regular economic relations among citizens. In spite of these impressive economic growth rates, however, the results in real terms have not yet been adequately and equitably translated into a better standard of living for the vast majority of the population. The annual average GDP per capita is still a paltry US$1,020, elite corruption is reportedly high, and the life expectancy is only 43 years.[11]

Since the advent of the National Resistance Movement (NRM) in 1986, however, political party activity has been severely curtailed. Political parties exist but are prohibited from supporting candidates or campaigning freely in the parliamentary or presidential elections because of a "no party" policy written into the constitution in 1995. Originally, the close regulation of political parties began in order to avoid the violent tribalism said to have sprung from pluralism under Amin and Obote. However, the opposition views this system as antithetical to democratic practices. The June 2000 referendum confirmed the "no party democracy" principles set forth in the constitution, but the surprising strength of an opposition suggested that Uganda was marking time for change.

Change may be in the offing, but at the turn of the century Uganda found itself burdened with a legislative structure largely unreformed and marred by its previous colonial and authoritarian heritage. Its institutions are weak and often dependent on the will of the president for their operation and sometimes for their very survival. Under such conditions, the rebuilding of a functional and binding institutional and legal structure represents the first vital step toward promoting media freedom and independence.

Ugandan media today

Museveni's NRM government came to power amid both chaos and the violent abuse of human rights. The new leaders, however, seemed to set a fresh example, especially on the international stage. They presented themselves as legitimate freedom fighters who observed fundamental human rights and made numerous commitments to continue protecting such rights. The record has, however, been uneven at best.[12]

The prolonged era of dictatorships in Uganda had made it difficult for both the public and media to identify the limits of responsible reporting and there was no established ethical practice. The interaction between government and newspapers and the early experiences of the press under the new regime were crude reminders of the traditional intolerance of dissent or criticism by the state, and a clear statement that Museveni's government's promises of protection of human rights were largely for foreign consumption rather than domestic policy.

Hardly two months into the new regime, Ndiwalana Kiwanuka, the editor of *Focus*, was charged with sedition following publication of an article on the army. In September 1986, *Weekend Digest* was banned for publishing a story concerning an attempted coup. Then in December 1986, Francis Odida of the *Sunday Review* was jailed for seven months for publishing stories on Alice Lakwena, the female leader of a militant opposition group.

In 1992, Lawrence Kiwanuka from *The Citizen* was arrested for publishing stories about Itongwa, an army officer turned rebel, and was continuously harassed until he eventually sought exile in Kenya.[13] In 1998 alone, there were fifteen cases of journalists being questioned by state security agents, arrested by police, often on trumped-up charges, or publicly threatened by political leaders. Press policy was consistent with other government measures: the Museveni government used a combination of coercive, legislative, economic, and co-optive measures in an attempt to underwrite state control.

However, over time, journalists managed to carve out their own space. Publications such as *Uganda Confidential* widened the scope of press freedom in the country with frequent revelations of corruption and the misdeeds of government officials. Bold coverage provided media with a much-needed boost of confidence. Still, certain newspapers have been attacked for reporting considered irresponsible. Political party newspapers like *The People* (Ugandan People's Congress) and *The Citizen* have, on many occasions, published undocumented stories about deaths in northern Uganda or about the corruption of public officials.

Coercion and general media legislation

The repressive use of law made its appearance early in the Museveni era. A Penal Code was instituted in 1988, designed to prevent media from publishing information regarding military installations, equipment, or supplies.[14] The law did not, however, stop the press from reporting about human rights violations, although self-censorship was evident. Opposition groups in Uganda increasingly used media to comment on the influx of Rwandan refugees into the Ugandan army. This prompted an amendment to the Penal Code, popularly termed the "Anti-Sectarian Statute." The intention of this revision was two-fold. In the first place, it attempted to build a unified country after the decades of conflict. In the second place, it aimed at silencing anti-Rwandan groups.

Further aspects of this legal control have included occasional misuse of libel and sedition laws in dealing with media.[15] These colonial sedition and criminal libel laws are still on the books and have been increasingly used by the Museveni government. The 1994 US State Department annual Human Rights Report stated, "the government [of Uganda] restricted freedom of speech by publicly harassing opposition leaders and the media through short term detention and legal actions on vague sedition charges."

A forum for revisiting the legal setting for government media regulation occurred about four years after the Museveni government took office. The first draft of a new Press Law was produced in 1990, but its content was vehemently opposed by media organizations that had allies in the National Resistance Council, the country's legislative body at that time. A compromise was reached and a new Press and Journalists Statute came into force in July 1995. This new Press Law repealed certain earlier restrictive laws, specifically the Newspaper and Publications Act and the Press Censorship and Correction Act. Other measures, such as the hefty bonds that had been previously required in order to establish a media outlet in Uganda and prior censorship requirements for publications were also abolished. As a result, there are currently no legal provisions in Uganda under which a newspaper can be banned. The new Press Law also simplified the process of newspaper registration.

The Press Law provides for the establishment of a media council, reflecting the view at the time the law was passed that journalists often operated irresponsibly, outside any code of ethics, and required oversight. As envisaged, Uganda's media council is meant to censor films, videotapes, and theatrical productions. It is also meant to take disciplinary action against journalists, promote their ethical behavior, and facilitate "the flow of information." Journalists have tended to view the council as a statutory body specifically introduced to restrict media.

Because of the complexity of its objectives and composition, the council wields little influence in its own right. The information minister has the power to regulate the operations of the media council.[16] The secretary of the council must be a senior public servant in the ministry of information, and he appoints eight members out of thirteen. This structure ensures that the council is under the control of the government.[17]

The council also has the function of regulating entry into the journalistic profession. It issues annual certificates to journalists without which they may not practice. This power has allowed the government to exclude those who are too critical and displease them from the profession. The Press Law also established an organization for journalists, the National Institute of Journalists of Uganda. The institute is entrusted with the responsibility of training journalists and seeking to enhance professional standards. Membership is restricted to university graduates of the journalism or mass communication fields (see below).[18]

While the principles in the 1995 constitution (see above) are not, as has been indicated, faithfully observed, a certain degree of progress has been made in Ugandan media law reform. Freedom of expression and the press is now codified in the nation's basic law. The new Press and Journalists Statute, although problematic, eased entry by new publications and eliminated some significant censorious practices. Most important, the law has removed the legal justification for banning media publications. On the other hand, problems of "inappropriate structuring" and "implementation" are still rife and need to be dealt with before Uganda's media can function fully and independently.

Co-opting media

In addition to the legislative controls discussed above, government has also attempted to co-opt the press through a series of informal measures. Because Ugandan journalists' sensationalist writing style was attributed to inexperience and lack of training, a degree course in mass communication was established at Uganda's Makerere University. Although the degree was said to be designed to produce "responsible" journalists, it instead ensured an institutional homogeneity among the nation's journalists. Its graduates have now permeated most Ugandan media outlets. Without diversity in journalistic education, it is unlikely that government manipulation can be prevented. President Museveni has also used informal contacts to keep the media closer and friendlier to the leadership. One such technique involves regular press dialogues instituted between President Museveni and the leading Ugandan editors. As Onyango-Obbo, editor of *The Monitor*, states:

> [S]uch conversations would be off the record. Museveni would then proceed to discuss a wide range of issues, including some that were not legitimate off-the-record material [...] seeing editors whose publications are rabidly anti-Museveni laughing with him at dinner, then seeing nothing about what was discussed in the papers, led some readers to believe that the opposition and independent journalists were double-faced.[19]

(Onyango-Obbo 1999c).

Museveni has played host to journalists at his family farm and at military operation areas. Poorer journalists have been provided with state jobs or with scholarships to study abroad. A small clique of preferred journalists has also been brought together into an informal body that advises the government on press relations. Other reporters who formerly worked for the opposition or independent press have been given promotions at the state-owned daily, *The New Vision*. When taken together, these efforts have functioned as a more or less successful campaign of co-option.

Government has also practiced informal control through its allocation of state advertisements and through its dismissive attitude *vis-à-vis* certain publications. In 1993, government banned all state departments from advertising in independent or opposition media. This was a heavy blow to poor or young newspapers, which depended on revenue received from state advertising.[20] Even after the ban was lifted in 1997, many investors, eager for government favors such as tax holidays, made it a practice not to advertise with opposition or independent media.[21] Consequently, funding has remained low in this sector, constraining further growth and development.

The opposition papers have been consistently denied access to information. Government sources leak valuable leads to the state-owned press while opposition papers are ignored. The government has also developed other modes of isolating journalists who publish critical pieces. This tends to decrease journalists' credibility in the eyes of the public. Cumulatively, these factors underlie the decline of independent print circulation and many independent papers folded. In fact, only three daily newspapers are currently published in Uganda, far below the thirty dailies of the late 1980s.[22]

Printed press

Press diversity

The print medium in Uganda has gradually failed since the advent of a private press, which was allowed to emerge in 1986. At its zenith, Uganda's press sector, both private and state-owned, was comprised of a total of thirty newspapers. Ten of these were daily publications, and included *Ngabo*, *The Star*, *Munno*, *The New Vision*, *Mulengera*, *Economy*, and *Focus*.[23] In addition, the government established four regional local language newspapers: *Rupiny* for the north, *Bukedde* for central Uganda (formerly known as the province of Buganda, now part of the districts of Kampala, Mpigi, Mukono, Masaka, Kalangala, Kiboga, Rakai, and Mubende), *Etop* for the east and *Orumuri* for the west.

The Ugandan print media field is quite fluid, with new papers constantly emerging and disappearing from the scene. At the end of 1999, however, only two English dailies, the state-owned *The New Vision* and the independent *Monitor*, and the state-owned regional papers were published regularly. *The New Vision* and its sister papers in the regions operated under a corporation with a board of directors directly appointed by the information minister. They enjoy a daily circulation of approximately 30,000 copies. *The New Vision* was founded soon after the advent of the NRM government, replacing the *Uganda Times*, which had been the state-owned newspaper of earlier regimes.

Since 1986, a government-appointed British editor, William Pike, has run *The New Vision*.[24] Pike has been able to maintain a balanced editorial policy and has published many articles critical of the government, a phenomenon previously unknown for a state-owned paper. Indeed, on several occasions, Pike has appeared in court over articles with which the government disagreed.[25] He has exercised a limited degree of editorial independence and has possibly made *The New Vision* the country's leading daily. The articles that appear have recently often shocked Uganda's population, once unfamiliar with even mild criticism of the government from its state paper. Onyango-Obbo, editor of *The Monitor*, comments:

> Unlike past government newspapers, *The New Vision* [does] not frequently tell lies or give unbridled support to all government actions: it could tell half or three quarters of the truth. More importantly, if the government [gets] itself into a scandal, it [*The New Vision*] never wait [s] for the opposition and independent media to give the story first.
>
> (Onyango-Obbo 1999a)

The other Ugandan daily is *The Monitor*, an independent English-language paper started in 1992 by *The New Vision* journalists who had fallen out of favor with the state. This is now Uganda's only independent daily publication with an average circulation of 29,000 copies. The paper attempts to be analytical without being overly critical of the government. It also combines political and economic analysis with human interest and entertainment articles.

Aside from *The Monitor*, other independent newspapers, most of which publish weekly, have a circulation of fewer than 5,000 copies. It is mainly struggling journalists and political party activists who own the independent print media. Although the private sector is small, it is likely to be more prominent in the non-print media business in the future. Economic players active in the country's newly developing private sector have few clear business incentives for investing in print media due to current limitations, but more opportunities may be present in radio and television.

The establishment of state-owned regional papers has been aimed primarily at bringing state propaganda in local languages to the semi-literate populations in the regions. They have attempted to fill the information vacuum in the absence of a rural press. Some of these rural populations, especially in the north and the east, have been traditionally antagonistic toward the central government and the intention is that through a careful use of local print media, popular opinions can be formulated and channeled to the advantage of the regime. Apart from the Agha Khan Foundation, which owns the Kenyan-published *East African*, there are no foreign private sector interests active in the Ugandan print media sector.

The general downward trend within the print media can, then, be attributed to many of the factors already mentioned. The government has levied high taxes (VAT at 17 per cent) on newsprint, making newspaper production expensive. Second, as mentioned above, government banned all state departments from advertising in the independent and opposition newspapers in 1993, a policy that left its mark even though now abandoned (Onyango-Obbo 1999a). In addition to the high degree of illiteracy, Uganda's population, rural and poor, is difficult to reach efficiently. In certain cases, newspapers have taken two days to reach their destination because of the poor transportation network. Even the few people who can read are not likely to be able to afford a daily newspaper that costs UGX600.[26]

Fourth, many opposition papers have discredited themselves. At the start of his rule, President Museveni was very popular throughout a large section of the population. The opposition papers, failing to assess correctly the mood of the times, wrote numerous sensationalist stories and leveled blunt abuses at the president and his government. Additionally, many of the stories printed were inaccurate. The popularity and circulation of such papers gradually dropped.[27]

Surviving newspapers, nevertheless, continue to set the media agenda. They raise important political issues that are then transmitted by the electronic media in news broadcasts. Kampala newspaper editors also frequently comment on political issues on television and radio programs. Having only one independent newspaper in Uganda is, however, a severe threat to press freedom. In addition, the editors of the independent *Monitor* are arguably too closely linked with the government and lack the level of independence that could be desired.

Print organizations

During the period of transition, media associations have been lobbying the government for media reform and development, and have met with some success. The Ugandan Newspaper Editors and Proprietors Association (UNEPA) has regularly held meetings with the president regarding current press issues and concerns. In one such meeting, the president directly called upon the police to stop the "weekend arrests" of journalists.[28] The Ugandan Journalists Association (UJA) has also played a key role in the formulation of the Press and Journalists Statute of 1995, and in producing alternative positions that were presented to the legislature for consideration. The Ugandan Journalists Safety Committee (UJSC) has played an advocacy role by calling attention to various infringements of press freedom. The UJSC has produced an annual report detailing instances of harassment, intimidation, or suppression of the press. Together, these organizations have been putting up a spirited fight against the misuse of sedition and criminal libel laws and the registration of journalists.

The Ugandan press and its relationship with civil society

Years of authoritarian rule have prevented a strong civil society from flourishing in Uganda. Various ethnic, religious, and minority groups, however, have had some influence on media performance since democratic reforms began.

An example of a group's influence on the press is that of the Catholic church, which printed *Munno* since colonial times, closing only in the mid-1990s. Even without the newspaper, the church has continued to be influential in agitating against various "immoral publications," including magazines such as *Spice*, *Secrets*, and *Chic*, which appeared in 1997 and often included pictures of near-nude women. As a result, the circulation of these magazines dropped, editions now appear irregularly, and the content is "lighter" than was originally the case.

Women's groups have also played a key role in shifting the focus of Ugandan print media. Since the advent of the NRM government, increased attention has been paid to gender equality in politics, education, and employment opportunities. Women's activists comment critically whenever a woman is depicted negatively in the media, and voice outrage to instances of rape and abuse. Activists for child protection, the environment, human rights, and the disabled have also importantly influenced media content. There have been more articles in papers addressing such issues, as a result (for example, see Muto (1999: 1) [about human rights] and Mucunguzi (1999: 1) [about homosexuality]).

Makerere and other new universities have also played a significant role in the development of the press. The columnists at many daily newspapers have been educated at university.[29] However, Uganda still lacks worthwhile media analysis from pre-Amin academics.[30] Slowly a new generation of academic analysts is developing, including Joe Oloka-Onyango, Tamale Ssali, and Salie Simba Kayunga.[31]

Print media summary

The early years of Museveni's NRM government, between 1986 and 1991, represented a honeymoon period for newspapers with increased space for press expression. With the advent of private television and radio, people's taste changed. The circulation of many papers declined and those still in print present a balance between political news and entertainment. Media space, especially in print, has shrunk considerably in Uganda, not as a result of government suppression, but from a combination of financial and social factors.

Broadcasting media

During the recurrent violent changes of government that Uganda has experienced since 1962, radio has played a strong role. Army officers or civilian dictators used Radio Uganda to announce their new government at the start of each coup because that channel was the only means of mass communication accessible to the whole country. Because of the association between radio and power, no regime had contemplated the liberalization of this broadcasting medium. Finally, in 1990, the then information minister Paul Etiang made a new policy statement to parliament, announcing that private radio and television stations would begin to operate.

Since this time, the broadcasting media sector has expanded apace. The period following Etiang's policy statement prompted a mushrooming of private FM radio and television stations. Prior to this, no legal framework on the registration and transmission of radio and television broadcasting existed in Uganda.

Legislation

The development of the broadcasting sector, following Etiang's statement, prompted the passage of the 1996 Electronic Media Statute. The parliament passed this legislation partly in response to clashes between certain radio stations, like the Baganda nationalist CBS FM, and the government.[32]

The legislation established a broadcasting council to license all radio and television stations. The licenses are renewable annually and it is illegal to operate without one. This means that a broadcaster's operations can be halted by a decision not to renew a license; there is no such annual re-licensing requirement for print media. Stations are also expected to register with the media council, established by the 1995 Press Law.

The broadcasting council consists of twelve members; the information minister appoints seven (including the chairman). The remainder is made up of senior civil servants. Article 10 (5) of the Electronic Media Statute stipulates that the information minister may give policy directions to the broadcasting council, to which the council shall comply. The broadcasting council's functions include control and supervision of broadcasting activities, the setting of ethical broadcasting standards, arbitration in cases of dispute, and advising government in broadcasting issues.

There are numerous problems with the Electronic Media Statute. The broadcasting council duplicates many of the functions that could be better handled under a more coherently formulated media council. It also creates conditions that can result in government suppression of broadcasting in a country already tainted by authoritarian rule. Further, the statute directly conflicts with the Ugandan Communications Act of 1997, which assigns the role of allocating radio and television spectrum to a Uganda Communications Commission.[33] In effect, having three separate bodies is unnecessary.

Additionally, the Electronic Media Statute is lacking in content and overall guidance on the use of broadcasting for development. Together with the United Nations Development Program (UNDP) and UNESCO, the information ministry has worked out policy proposals that are currently under debate. These proposals include, among others, regulations on local versus foreign programming content, the balance between entertainment and educational programming, and mechanisms for the production of local educational broadcasting materials.

Broadcasting diversity

Within the overall broadcasting media structure and until the sector's liberalization in 1992, Radio Uganda (RU) and Uganda Television (UTV) were sole broadcasters, operating directly under the information minister.[34] By 1986, however, radio media were decentralized.[35]

Low literacy levels, poor infrastructure, and traditions of oral culture have made radio the ideal tool of mass communication in Uganda. Starting out with two private radio stations in Kampala in 1992 (Capital 91.3 FM and Sanyu 88.2 FM), Uganda now boasts twenty-five FM stations, which have revolutionized the radio industry. Those interested in international news now have direct access to the BBC. Others can listen to local news and entertainment.

Radio stations depend on private sector advertising for their survival. The proliferation of FM stations in such a small economy has meant that traditional financial methods such as advertising are inadequate to support all radio broadcasting concerns. This makes the fear of collapse real.

There is one state-owned television channel. Most of the private channels broadcast mainly popular American films, soap operas, and comedies.[36] They also transmit news but reach, at most, half the country where electricity is available. The first independent television station, Cablesat (CTV), was founded and owned by Ugandan businessmen. It began its operations in 1992 by relaying CNN broadcasts and American, British, and Australian soap operas. Together, they cover an average radius of 100km around Kampala. The exception to this range is the state-owned television channel (UTV), which reaches more than half the country.

The new independent television stations provide a challenge to the state-owned broadcasters. First, state-owned stations possess obsolete technical equipment. Second, they are badly managed due to the imposed civil service structure that is not oriented toward targeting talent. Finally, because of poor remuneration, low staff morale is endemic and many state employees have left for positions with the new private stations that offer higher salaries.

In light of these problems, there have been transformations within state-owned broadcasters. Previously, UTV broadcast only in the evenings. In reaction to the twenty-four-hour transmissions of the private television companies, UTV now begins its broadcasts at 1:00 p.m. daily. Screen designs, content, and the presentation of news programs have all changed. A wider variety of foreign broadcasts have been included to allow the station to compete favorably in the liberalizing environment. In addition, in the late 1990s, it was agreed that Radio Uganda and UTV would be restructured into the Ugandan Broadcasting Authority, which would serve as a public service broadcaster with increased autonomy.[37]

The process of liberalization has also affected radio broadcasters. RU has established two FM stations, Star and Green, which transmit in the same formats as private FM stations: news updates, music, and a few talk shows. Nevertheless, both UTV and RU remain thoroughly under state control through the information minister. The state treasury appropriates all revenue generated by UTV and RU. State broadcasters must face the arduous process of annual budgetary allocation to finance their operations.

All barriers to foreign investment and radio and television station start-ups have been formally lifted in Uganda. The only restriction that remains is that legal entities must be residents of Uganda (although not necessarily citizens) or must be registered locally. Foreign investors who utilize local companies to circumvent such provisions in fact own many independent television concerns.

In contrast to the print media, radio and television broadcasters have not exhibited the same diversity of political opinion. Under the "no-party" or "one-party" regime, political party activity is limited. Given the prolonged periods of dictatorship, political parties have not had the chance to develop and establish themselves. Parties have lacked adequate finances to sustain radio or television production. However, some opposition politicians have taken advantage of the new independent FM stations to put forward their positions on crucial national issues.

Second, people appointed by the government staff the broadcasting licensing councils. Even if political parties were to have resources adequate to establish television or radio concerns, they would find obtaining a frequency very difficult. This, especially, represents an important element of state control.

However, though most private radio stations do not generally invest in their own news service and "download" news from the daily papers, FM radio stations have made key political actors in Uganda more accountable through live talk shows where ordinary people ask critical questions. Local newspaper editors have become household names as they frequently provide commentary on current political and economic issues in radio programs. Indeed, the FM stations have arguably widened people's participation in Uganda's political debates to a greater extent than any other media (Musoke 1999; Kajoba 1999).

One noteworthy radio station is the Central Broadcasting Service (CBS), owned by Bagandan investors and run as a mobilization tool for the Buganda kingdom. This is the first radio station thus far to have openly opposed the state. Although of all post-independence governments, President Museveni's administration appears to be most sympathetic to the Baganda, it has not met the Baganda's key demands.[38] During the 1995 constitutional negotiations, the Baganda, as had happened in 1962, voiced their demands for federal status. The government rejected the demands as secessionist. Since that time, the Baganda have formed part of an opposition to the government.

In 1996, the government introduced a new Value Added Tax (VAT). Partly because it was new, but also owing to its poor implementation by revenue officers, this tax was unpopular among the Ugandan business community. CBS's producer, Mulindwa Muwonge, used the radio station to mobilize businesses to boycott in opposition to the VAT. Business in Kampala came to a standstill as businessmen refused to open shops. Muwonge was arrested on charge of sedition, but was later released. CBS's agitation over the 1998 Land Act provides another cogent example of opposition to government organized over the airwaves.[39]

CBS FM has also continuously acted as a watchdog over government. It presents news about human rights infringements by state operatives, and championed the cause of the people of Masaka who were forced to do military service and undergo politicization. CBS FM's persistent treatment of the story forced the government to make a formal apology to the Masaka people in May

2000. In addition, people are able to put forward their points of view in its programs, especially to express dissatisfaction with the government. In retaliation, the state has established an FM station, Star, to try to neutralize CBS FM. Star FM broadcasts in Luganda and has a pro-Baganda tone, and the government hopes it will supplant the more recalcitrant CBS.

The internationalization of broadcasting media

In Uganda today, both the BBC and CNN can be viewed on independent television stations. The establishment of relay FM stations for the BBC and CFI and the relaying of BBC broadcasts over several FM stations (Capital Radio, Sanyu Radio, and VOT) has also meant that increasing numbers of people can more easily access this information.

Television broadcasters that offer twenty-four-hour service such as Light House Television (LTV) present mainly US religious programs with some local programming and all M-net (pay TV) programming is foreign. WBS broadcasts only thirty minutes of local news, some local soap operas, and a talk show accounting for a total of three hours of local production. Other television stations also carry mainly foreign programs. This is primarily due to the prohibitive expense of local television production.

Only state-owned television broadcasts a variety of local programming including news, farming programs, political propaganda such as the regular presidential programs, and school educational programs. Radio stations provide little local content. Except for stations like Simba FM and CBS FM which broadcast in Luganda and the rural FM radios like VOT, Radio Rukungiri, Radio West, the urban stations have styled their productions on British and American FM systems with similar formats.

On the other hand, there have been efforts to diversify the radio and television broadcasting throughout the region of southern Africa. Worldspace Corporation and International Television Network Ltd is the parent company of Sanyu FM and has recently agreed to broadcast Sanyu FM over its satellite digital audio system for the whole region (*BBC Monitoring World Media* 1998). They have also signed a contract with SATELLIFE to launch a public health channel in Uganda, Kenya, Zimbabwe, and Ethiopia (*Africa News* 2000). This channel is aimed at assisting medical professionals in Africa.

Cross-media tendencies in print and broadcasting media

Two major Ugandan newspapers, *The New Vision* and *The Monitor*, are seeking ways of combining radio and print into one package. *The New Vision*, which has been state owned, is soon to be sold. One key contender for its purchase is its editor-in-chief and general manager, William Pike, also a shareholder in one of Uganda's leading FM stations, Capital Radio.

The Monitor has also purchased a radio operating license and has come to an agreement with the powerful Nation Media Group of Kenya, owned by Agha Khan. This agreement is aimed at a partnership that will see the Nation group investing more money in *The Monitor* and helping it start a radio station. If the partnership and its plans are successful, it will mark a fundamental transformation of the media industry in Uganda. There have also been recent indications that the IPP Media Group, owned by the Tanzanian media mogul, Reginald Mengi, has begun investing in the Ugandan media.[40] IPP has a number of newspapers and radio and television stations across Tanzania.

Other aspects of media crossover include Ugandan newspapers that have increasingly exploited the Internet to cater to expatriates who subscribe to the major daily newspapers online.[41] The papers have also used new technologies such as e-mail for delivering stories, comments, and articles.

Film and other media

The Amin regime dealt a severe blow to the budding film industry in Uganda. In the 1960s, the information department ran an established film unit that produced 16-inch films on health, education, and various social issues that were then screened in rural areas using film vans. In 1972, Amin declared an "economic war" and banned all foreign films on the grounds that they contained "imperialist propaganda." As a result, Uganda currently has no capacity for film production. Only since 1996 have new cinema halls started to operate.[42] Currently, there are four in Kampala.

With the demise of film, local theater came to prominence. Ugandans, because of their oral culture, were fascinated by local drama. The Amin era saw a peak in drama production and many plays depicting the changes in Uganda were produced. However, as Amin began to oppress and execute theater personalities, the theater industry became extremely cautious. The first known playwright and actor murdered by Amin was Byron Kawadwa who, in 1973, produced a play titled *Oluyimba Lwa Wankoko* (A Song of Chicken), which depicted high-level corruption. Other actors like Robert Sserumaga went into exile.

The Museveni government has generally provided a freer atmosphere for theater groups. Most productions deal with current events and characters are representative of leaders of the day. The 1995 Press and Journalists Statute, discussed above, states that the media council should censor all plays and music for public consumption, but it does not establish the criteria for this censorship. To date, however, the media council has not taken up its censorship role.

Many plays have been used for political agitation, campaigns against corruption, and reflecting popular disenchantment. One of the most prominent actors and playwrights in Uganda today, Alex Mukulu, has produced critical plays such as *Wounds of Africa* and *30 Years of Bananas*. Production of the latter coincided with the thirtieth anniversary of Uganda's independence. Characters depicted various Ugandan heads of state, including the current president, and pointed out their flaws. Museveni himself attended a showing. Afterward he stated that he would work hard not to be like former leaders.

Government links in with theater groups through the National Cultural Center, under the cultural ministry. The center is, however, grossly underfunded. Government took theater, as a whole, very lightly until the early 1990s when studies showed that AIDS campaigns could be brought to the public effectively through local drama groups. Government, with the help of donor organizations, subsequently commissioned drama groups to produce plays and music about the AIDS virus. Substantive messages came from the AIDS Control Program in the health ministry. Currently, many international organizations such as UNICEF, UNFPA, DANIDA, and others are utilizing theater groups in their child welfare, water and sanitation campaigns, and HIV/AIDS prevention projects. Drama is thought to be more effective, especially for the rural population, since people are able to identify more easily with local characters and messages in their own languages and settings.

Given the limited number of film cinemas, thousands of makeshift video projection halls have sprung up in all the urban centers. According to the 1996 Electronic Media Statute, these halls are to be licensed by the broadcasting council and the media council must censor all videos. Because these laws are new and the video halls are numerous, such regulations have had no effect to date. Instead, video operators gain access to the latest films that have normally been licensed to local villages or parishes, thereby circumventing government controls. In addition, the health and agricultural departments have procured video and film vans with the support of donors. These vehicles take educational films and videos to rural areas as part of their campaigns.

The key milestone in the use of performing arts as a communication media came in 1990 when the popular Ugandan musician, Philly Bongoley Lutaaya, first publicly announced that he had contracted the HIV/AIDS virus. In the early 1990s, the stigma was so great that even though there were over 6,000 cases of AIDS reported in 1989 and 1990, and 10,235 in 1991 no one wanted to talk about it (UNAIDS and WHO 2000). The Ugandan AIDS Control Program used Lutaaya's celebrity status to rally a campaign program around him. Prior to his death in 1991, he produced a documentary titled *Born in Africa* that showed how AIDS had destroyed his life, and made an appeal for a change in social behavior. He also produced a record titled "Alone and Frightened," which has become a theme song in the anti-AIDS campaign in Uganda and in other African countries.

Emerging technologies

The UN has recently acknowledged that Africa is lagging far behind the current information technology age (UNDP 1999: 61). This is primarily due to the poverty of the continent and high levels of illiteracy. In Uganda, access to the Internet is still very low, with millions of people lacking basic computer knowledge. Most have never seen a computer.

As discussed above, Uganda has one of the lowest telephone penetration rates in the world. As of July 1995, the Ugandan Post and Telecommunications Corporation had installed capacity of just under 70,000 lines and had approximately 42,000 subscribers. The telecommunications industry has been expanded and liberalized with the entry of two companies, Mobile Telecommunications Network, a South African based company, and CelTel Uganda, a Ugandan–American concern, recently licensed to operate. MTN has already installed 90,000 lines, while CelTel installed over 35,000 lines in 1999. These companies, however, operate mainly in Kampala and other prosperous urban areas such as Masaka, Jinja, Mbarara, and Entebbe, and a large percentage of the population outside these areas lacks access to basic telephone services.

By the end of 1999, Uganda had nine Internet service providers, up from two in 1996, and an estimated 5,200 Internet service subscribers (*BBC Summary of World Broadcasts* 2000). These included schools, companies, NGOs, and international organizations. In Kampala, three Internet cafés with a capacity of twenty people each have been established. It is mainly students, foreign visitors, and international residents who visit these.

There are several small pilot initiatives currently under way aimed at widening knowledge of computers among Ugandans. IDRC of Canada is working closely with UNESCO on a pilot project at Nakaseke, 40 kilometers outside Kampala, to establish a Community Tele-Center. The center provides library and educational services to a community of over 10,000 predominantly illiterate people. In addition, it houses a collection of videos, newspapers, and e-mail services. Community participants are trained in Internet use to further their own education. With the support of UNDP, the Ugandan National Chamber of Commerce has established ten district private sector promotion centres.[43] Here business people are taught how to use Internet information to improve their businesses.

Internet service providers fall under the 1997 Ugandan Communications Act, but they are required to register with the authorities as a result of provisions of the Company Act of 1965. To date, there has been little government interest in controlling the Internet. This has been mainly because it is still a budding sector, but also because most government functionaries have not yet "discovered" the Internet. The Museveni government has established several web pages to explain its policies, but these have been unprofessionally executed. Whole documents, like budget speeches, are uploaded onto the World Wide Web and various other documents, including the Uganda constitution, have also been put up. Other government departments, among them the Ugandan Tourism Board, have attempted to create web pages to provide information on Uganda's ecology.

Certain political groups within Uganda have begun to utilize the Internet to their advantage. One such group is the notorious Lord's Resistance Army (LRA), a rebel group that regularly abducts children in northern Uganda, forcing them to fight the government.

For the majority of Ugandans, it will be a long time before Internet access is widespread. First, the hardware is expensive. A personal computer costs the equivalent of a Ugandan medical doctor's salary for one and a half years . If the government were to waive import taxes on computer equipment, this would most likely assist technological development. Second, 80 per cent of all Internet websites are in English. In Uganda, only those who have had more than twelve years of schooling understand English. With a basic literacy rate of just 55 per cent, the majority of Ugandans would not be able to use the Internet even if connected.

Finally, Internet use requires an efficient telecommunications infrastructure. In Uganda, government has left this to the private sector, which has failed to lay adequate ground lines. When Senegal privatized telephone services, operators were required under their licensing agreements to install public telephones in 50 per cent of rural villages with populations over 3,000 by the year 2000. In the Philippines, mobile phone operators are required to install 400,000 landlines in poor communities within five years. The Ugandan government could implement such requirements to improve telecommunication and computer access.

The government also needs to build capacity to use the Internet by installing connections at schools, by putting local content on the Web, and by designing locally decipherable web pages. Further, in poor countries such as Uganda, community telecenters are a good way of bringing emerging media technology to rural areas. As such, greater levels of financing should be devoted to their development.

Media reform and civil society

Civil society in Uganda has been consistently suppressed by numerous autocratic regimes since colonial times. Ugandans started forming cooperative organizations as far back as 1910. Trade unions also attempted to organize in the 1940s. All of these groups were either "tamed" through legislation or banned outright. Finally, in the 1990s, civil society has begun to evolve with groups forming in the fields of women's emancipation, workers' solidarity, human rights, and business or manufacturers' interests.

When the NRM government came to power in 1986, it introduced local government reform based on "resistance councils" (now called local councils). These consist of nine-person committees from village to district level, each democratically elected by the people in that locality. Committees have also been granted certain judicial powers in their areas, for settling disputes and resolving conflicts. These committees have worked extremely well in giving people an opportunity to participate in their own governance and people can now deliberate more freely on issues that pertain to their locality and to the country as a whole.

Government began affirmative policies for women in the mid-1980s. Radio and television stations, as a result, started broadcasting women's programs, while newspapers increasingly gave space to women's issues such as domestic violence, rape, and inequalities in employment and education (Kameo 2000; *The New Vision* 2000). Organizations like Action for Development (ACFODE) and the Ugandan Media Women's Association (UMWA) spearheaded these campaigns. They produced magazines and newsletters on women's and children's issues. Newspapers now have children's pages and special columns by women.

Journalists themselves have formed more than twenty associations.[44] These groups respond whenever one of their members falls victim to the repressive state machinery or when they disagree with proposed media laws (*The New Vision* 1998). Some influential groups, like the Ugandan Newspaper Editors and Proprietors Association (UNEPA), raise issues with the president and parliament and this has on occasion created an atmosphere that is more conducive to flourishing media.[45]

Recommendations

Uganda's political situation has significantly improved since the transition began in 1986. In spite of civil conflicts in the north and west of the country, the democratization process is still on course. It is increasingly likely that Uganda will soon have a multi-party democracy, but even now the power of participation has been assured through popular elections and local government reforms. A sense of political accountability has also developed, a situation in which media have played crucial roles. However, popular participation is limited in a country where nearly half the population is illiterate and where poor infrastructure makes it difficult for citizens to communicate. This lack of infrastructure has also had an adverse effect on the development of a rural press.

The present government has repealed a number of oppressive media laws. However, sedition and criminal libel laws are still used to intimidate journalists. Furthermore, laws requiring the annual licensing of journalists, the need for qualifications to practice, and the threat of a partisan media council all run counter to the traditions of a free media society. Such laws should be repealed or amended.

In addition, the country still needs to develop a courageous, independent, and assertive judiciary that will make decisions in the area of media, even if these decisions have a negative impact on the government. Some papers have closed because of the excessive costs incurred in libel suits. There have also been cases where specific judges have been assigned to cases involving journalists. This is hardly a characteristic of an impartial judiciary.

In the wake of broadcasting liberalization, state-owned radio and television stations have been neglected. An independent public authority should be established to revitalize the services provided by Uganda Television and Radio Uganda. In addition, access to such public media should be guaranteed for all political groups legally existing within the country.

One good example where mandated access to government media is successful is that of South Africa. An independent media commission set up in 1994 monitored the broadcasting transmissions during the presidential elections to ensure that every political party had equitable access to the South African Broadcasting Corporation. In the same vein, this author believes that owners of private broadcasting stations, knowing that they are using a public resource (namely, the airwaves), should respect minimum standards of program content in order to maintain national unity and the culture of the country. Self-regulatory frameworks might be introduced to ensure that such provisions are accounted for.

The 1995 Ugandan constitution provides both media and the general public with freedom of access to government information. A separate law that would operationalize this provision has not, as yet, been formulated. This freedom of access to information would not only facilitate media development, but would also ensure that government actions were more accurately reported. Such a provision should, therefore, be given priority.

While the establishment of a media council may prove a benefit, it should be composed of media representatives, the judiciary, the general public, and public figures who command respect rather than government-appointed members. The current formulation of the media council leaves loopholes for practitioners in the event of a less tolerant regime. Further, although the present National Institute of Journalists of Uganda (NIJU) represents an attempt by government to "help" journalists organize themselves, government's involvement reduces the institute's credibility.

The composition of the broadcasting council needs to be more reflective of the electronic media industry as a whole. Members of the Uganda Broadcasting Association, owners of stations, and members of the Uganda Broadcasters' Forum, the broadcasters, should, therefore, be more highly represented on this council.

Finally, as discussed above, there cannot be media development without overall development within a country. The poor infrastructure, low levels of education, and inadequate incomes all constrain the development of a free media in Uganda. As government tackles the more difficult task of general development, certain measures exist, such as tax breaks on newsprint or subsidization of certain independent publications (as currently practiced in some Scandinavian countries) that could lead to the faster evolution of free media. To achieve this end, government must understand that free media are essential to the good governance of the country. This point does not yet appear to be understood by all leaders in Uganda.

Notes

1 Literacy (defined as age 15 and over, can read and write), in Uganda was estimated at: total population: 61.8%; male: 73.7%; female: 50.2% in 1995 (*CIA World Factbook* 2000).
2 According to www.unicef.org in 2001 the school enrolment ratios were: Primary school (gross) male 129, female 114; Primary school (net) male 92, female 83; Secondary school (gross) male 15, female 9. Available at: http://www.unicef.org/statis/Country_1Page180.html.
3 In December 1997, however, Mobile Telecommunications Network (MTN) was awarded the "second operator's license." MTN now also offers cellular services, which breaks the monopoly of CelTel, a company that has been the sole cellular provider in Uganda for three years. According to the terms of the license, MTN must install 89,000 new lines within a period of five years.
4 At the moment, although elections take place in Uganda, they do so within a "one-party" system of rule. As a result, voter choice has remained largely constricted.
5 Discussed in Chapter 1.
6 Kiddu-Makubuya is a minister in the current government and a former student of Makerere University's Law Faculty.
7 See the discussion of the impact of Baganda nationalism on Uganda's development, below.
8 It is estimated that over 500,000 people were murdered during Amin's regime, most of whom were members of the elite whom he suspected of conspiring against him. Makerere University's Vice-Chancellor, Prof. Frank Kalimuzo, Archbishop Janan Luwum, and playwright Byron Kawadwa have been among the prominent victims.
9 This second regime is known as Obote II.
10 Article 29.1.a provides freedom of expression and media. Article 41.1 states that every citizen has a right of access to information in the possession of the state or any other organ or agency of the state except where the release of the information is likely to prejudice the security or sovereignty of the state or interfere with the right to privacy of any other person. Article 42.2 provides that parliament shall pass laws prescribing these classes of information as well as the procedure to obtain such information. (To date no such law has been passed.) Article 67 (3) provides that "all presidential candidates have an equal right of access to state-owned media in order to present their political programs." Article 67 (4) states that parliament is to work out modalities for the use of public resources (including media) during elections. With reference to Article 67, however, the accepted practice has been to use state-owned newspapers for government propaganda and mudslinging, as evidenced in the 1996 presidential elections. In the referendum of 2000, under the watchful eye of international monitors, use of the press to reflect different views was improved.

11 Per capita estimate from 1998. Figures from 1999 Photius Coutsoukis: http://www. photius.com/wfb1999/uganda (viewed on 8 August 2000).

12 International opinion has been that the existence of media as watchdog and the presence of non-government organizations are most likely to reduce further government abuses. For a description of human rights violations see the US Department of State's 1999 Country Report on Human Rights Practices (US Department of State 2000).

13 *The Citizen* is affiliated with the Democratic Party.

14 Penal Code No. 9, 1988. At this time the government was faced with rebellions in the north and east and also reported army misbehavior.

15 One of the most controversial cases took place in 1990 and involved three journalists who were arrested for "defaming a foreign dignitary" under legislation dating back to the colonial regime.

16 Article 47 (1) of the Press and Journalists Statute of 1995 provides that "The Minister may, on advice of the Council, make regulations for the better carrying into effect the provisions of the statute." Given the way the council is appointed, this article gives the state an entry point to control the working of the press.

17 The ministryt of information comes under the jurisdiction of the office of the president. It houses the National Institute of Journalists of Uganda and media council.

18 The Press Law contains an addendum with a code of conduct for journalists.

19 Charles Onyango-Obbo is one of the most influential journalists in Uganda. He is editor of *The Monitor*, the leading independent daily, and a key commentator on political issues in Uganda.

20 Government departments accounted for 70% of all advertising revenue, prior to privatization in 1997.

21 The ban on state advertising was lifted with the implementation of privatization reforms in 1997.

22 Compare Tanzania with at least fifteen dailies.

23 Among these, *Munno* was published by the Catholic church, the two weeklies *Munnansi/Citizen* and *The People* belonged to the DP and UPC political parties respectively. *The New Vision* is the state-owned press and in 1992 journalists established an independent daily, *The Monitor*.

24 Pike was the first to report on the operations of Museveni's bush war in central Uganda for a British newspaper, *The Observer*, in the early 1980s.

25 In 1992, William Pike and Didas Bakunzi of *The New Vision* were arrested and briefly detained for publishing an article about the release of Islamic fundamentalists, the Tabliqs.

26 This figure converts to approximately US$0.40.

27 Onyango-Obbo described an interesting incident: "When *Shariat*, about four years ago, called President Museveni an adulterer, murderer and a mad man, it thought it would sell highly in Gulu where the government is unpopular. However, it got the shock of its life when it sold only five copies in this town where the government is most hated. The government paper, *The New Vision*, in contrast sold 300 copies on that issue" (1999a).

28 Sometimes, in an attempt to stifle media, journalists are arrested on Friday evenings in order to have them jailed and harassed for at least two days before courts open on Monday morning.

29 Some examples include Austin Ejeit's *Take or Leave It*, Karooro Okrut's *The Long View*, and Professor Karasco's *Education Viewpoint*.

30 Professor Mazrui, Wadada Nabudere, Yash Tandon, Apolo Nsibambi and Akiiki Mujaju.

31 Joe Oloka-Onyango is an associate professor in the Faculty of Law, Makerere University, Kampala. Tamale Ssali is a lawyer and lecturer in the Faculty of Law, Makerere University, and has published many books on gender issues. Dr Salie Simba Kayunga is a lecturer in the Department of Political Science, Makerere University, and is the author of *Uganda National Congress and the Struggle for Democracy: 1952–1962* and *Islamic Fundamentalism in Uganda: A case of the Tabligh Youth Movement*.

32 One example of these clashes took place in 1996 when a Central Broadcasting Service (CBS) presenter Mulindwa Muwonge was arrested by police for "inciting the public" against the newly introduced Value Added Tax (VAT).

33 The Uganda Communications Act, 1997, establishes the Uganda Communications Commission, whose functions include Article 5(b) "to monitor, inspect, license and regulate communications activities"; and section (c), "to allocate and license the use of radio frequency spectrum and to process applications for the allocation of satellite orbital locations." Certainly its mandate extends beyond broadcasting, but it has duplicated license roles with the broadcasting council and media council. A synchronization of the work of the three bodies is desirable.

34 Radio Uganda (RU) was founded by the colonial government in 1954. Uganda Television (UTV) was founded after independence in 1963.

35 The reach of RU transmissions had been reduced to only a few areas in the west and central regions where once it had transmitted to the entire country in 25 languages. UTV, too, transmits to less than half the country.

36 There were seven private channels at the time of writing. These include the state-owned Uganda Television (UTV); WBS, owned by a local businessman; LTV, a Christian station broadcasting mainly US religious programs; Channel TV, owned by a Ugandan/Asian millionaire, Madvani; STV, formerly Sanyu Television and now owned by a South African conglomerate; and M-net Africa, the only pay-television station, owned by South Africans and relaying the BBC, Supersport, and Movie Magic.

37 The merger has already begun. In September 1999 the newsrooms of UTV and Radio Uganda were merged (*The New Vision* 1999b).

38 For instance, the Museveni government has restored the traditional Buganda kingdom.

39 In 1998, police questioned Mulindwa Muwonge over remarks he made regarding the Land Act of 1998. Since colonial times the Baganda have had a separate land ownership system that encouraged a few landlords to own large parcels of land (*mailo*). This practice reduced many people in Buganda to mere squatters. The government wanted to alter this, but the *Kabaka* (King) of Buganda also owns 9,000 square miles of land granted to him by the British colonial rulers. This had been turned into public land by the post-independence governments. The Baganda, however, demanded the land restored and their unique ownership system retained in the new law, and used CBS radio to campaign for these measures. At one point, President Museveni himself participated in one of the radio programs, explaining the government's position and calling presenters of this radio station to the state house for briefing.

40 Mengi has received licensing from Uganda for his TV and radio network to begin broadcasting in Kampala (Mwamunyange 1999).

41 For example, *The New Vision* is online at www.newvision.co.ug and *The Monitor* at www.monitor.co.ug.

42 Note that the 1996 Electronic Media Statute mandates licenses for "operating a cinematography theater or a video tapes hiring library" as well as using, selling or transferring possession of television.

43 They are located in Mbale, Moroto, Bushenyi, Nebbi, Lira, Busia, Masaka, Fort-Portal, and Kabale.

44 United Journalists Association is an example.

45 The UNEPA criticized some provisions in the Referendum and Other Provisions Bill 1999 because they considered them restrictive (*New Vision* 1999a).

References

Africa News (2000) "Africa-at-Large; WorldSpace, Satellife Create First Public Health Channel," 22 May.

Associated Press (1999) "First East African Broadcasting Network in Offing," *The Associated Press Business News*, 30 July.

BBC Monitoring World Media. (1998) "WorldSpace Signs Deal with Private Ugandan Sanyu-FM," 6 May.

BBC Summary of World Broadcasts (2000) "Rise in Number of Internet Service Providers and Telephone Users," 4 March, Saturday. Source: PANA news agency web site, Dakar, in English, 24 February 2000.

Brett, Edward A. (1991) "Rebuilding Survival Structures for the Poor: Organizational Options for Reconstruction in the 1990s," in Holger Bernt Hansen and Twaddle, Michael (eds), *Changing Uganda: The Dilemmas of Structural Adjustment and Revolutionary Change*. London: J. Currey; Kampala: Fountain Press; Athens: Ohio University Press; Niarobi: Heinemann Kenya.

CIA World Factbook (2000) Washington DC: Central Intelligence Agency. Available at: http://www.cia.gov/cia/publications/factbook/geos/ug.html

Gariyo, Zie (1992) *The Press and Democratic Struggles in Uganda: 1900–1962*. Kampala: Center for Basic Research.

—— (1993) *The Media, Constitutionalism and Democracy in Uganda*. Kampala: Center for Basic Research.

Kajoba, Amos (1999) *The Monitor* – Kampala "Uganda: FM Radios Bring on the Good Life," *Africa News*, 28 November.

Kameo, Elizabeth (2000) "Uganda: Acholi Top Domestic Violence List Report," *Africa News*, 12 July.

Karugire, S. R. (1980) *A Political History of Uganda*. Nairobi: Heinemann.

Kasoma, F. P. (1997) "The Independent Press and Politics in Africa," *International Journal for Communication Studies*. Vol 59, Number 4–5.

Kiddu-Makubuya (1991) "The Rule of Law and Human Rights in Uganda: The Missing Link," in Holger Bernt Hansen and Twaddle, Michael (eds). *Changing Uganda: The Dilemmas of Structural Adjustment and Revolutionary Change*. London: J. Currey; Kampala: Fountain Press; Athens: Ohio University Press; Niarobi: Heinemann Kenya.

Mamdani, Mahmood (1976) *Politics of Class Formation in Uganda*. Kampala: Fountain Publishers.

—— (1993) *Pluralism and the Right of Association*. Kampala: CBR.

Mucunguzi, Julius and Agencies (1999) "Women Writers Urged," *The Monitor*, 17 November: 1.

Mugaju, Justus (1996) "The Historical Overview," in Mugaju, Justus (ed.), *Uganda's Age of Reforms: A Critical Overview*. Kampala: Fountain Publishers.

Musoke, Isabirye (1999) *The Monitor* – Kampala "Uganda: Too Much Politics on FM Talk-shows," *Africa News*, 3 February.

Muto, John (1999) "Ono p'Lajur" (in Gulu) "Investigate More NRM Abuses – Mao," *The Monitor*, 25 November: 1.

Mwamunyange, Joseph (1999) "Dar Broadcaster Sets the Stage for East African Onslaught," 4–10 August, The East African Section: regional. Available at http://www.nationaudio.com/News/EastAfrican/020899/Regional/Regional7.html

Ogbondah, C. W. (1997) "Communication and Democratisation in Africa," *International Journal for Communication Studies*. Vol 59, Number 4–5.

Oloka-Onyango, Joe (1991) *Armed Conflict, Political Violence and the Human Rights Monitoring of Uganda: 1971 to 1990*. Kampala: CBR.

Onyango-Obbo, Charles (1999a) "To Cry or Not Cry for the Independent Press," *The Monitor*, Kampala, 24 July.

—— (1999b) "Press Fortunes Hit Rock Bottom," *The Monitor*, Kampala, 27 July.

—— (1999c) "Uganda Press: Beating the Odds," *The Monitor*, Kampala, 28 July.

Opoku-Mensah, Aida (1998) "Technology-Uganda: The Rich Can Afford – But what about the poor?," *Inter Press Service*, 5 August.

Republic of Uganda (1995) *Constitution of the Republic of Uganda*. Kampala: LDC.

—— (1995) *The Press and Journalists Statute*. Entebbe: UPPC.

—— (1996) *The Electronic Media Statute*. Entebbe: UPPC.

—— (1997) *The Communications Act*. Entebbe: UPPC.

—— (1997) *The Movement Act*. Entebbe: UPPC.

—— (1999) *The Referendum and Other Provisions Act*. Entebbe: UPPC.

The New Vision (Kampala) (1998) "Uganda: UJA Rejects Act," *Africa News*, 30 October.

—— (1999a) "Uganda: Media Appeals on Referendum," *Africa News*, 22 May.

—— (1999b) "Radio Uganda, UTV Merge Newsrooms," sec: News, Documents, and Commentary, 2 September.

—— (2000) "Uganda: Women Want Domestic Violence Law This Year," *Africa News*, 1 February.

Uganda Journalists Safety Committee (1998) *Annual Report, 1998*. Kampala: UJSC.

UNAIDS and World Health Organization (2000) *Epidemiological Fact Sheet on HIV and Sexually Transmitted Diseases: 2000 Update*. http://www.unaids.org

United Nations Development Program (UNDP) (1999) *Human Development Report 1999*. New York: Oxford University Press.

US Department of State (1995) Uganda Human Rights Practises: 1994. Released February.

—— (2000) 1999 Uganda Country Report on Human Rights Practices. Released by the US Department of State: Bureau of Democracy, Human Rights, and Labor, 25 February. Available at: http://www.state.gov/www/global/human_rights/1999_hrp_report/uganda.html

9

THE DISENFRANCHISED VOTER

Silences and exclusions in Indian media

Nilanjana Gupta

Introduction

India is an extraordinary case for examining the relationship between media structure, media law reform, and the expansion of a democratic ideal. India's media reflects a colonial heritage, the influence of the country's period of political neutrality, its interest in socialist models, and, now, the major impact of globalism, free market tendencies, and the winds of capitalism. India is a case where the media structure, new policies, and their implementation determine the extent of government control over the information space, the validation or strengthening of various languages, regions, or political groups, and the way in which information shapes participation. Ultimately, the structure and uses of media influence how individuals perceive themselves as citizens, and, therefore, the extent to which democratic aspirations become meaningful to them.

This chapter concentrates on four Indian mass media sectors: print, film, broadcasting, and new media. The print media sector has historically played a significant role in Indian society since the colonial period. This section focuses on problems associated with redefining democratic institutions following the break from British rule. The film industry is perhaps the most thriving media sector in India. Here, the relationship between the government and the market is distinctly different. Broadcasting media, until recently, have been entirely controlled by the state. The changes in this sector will be examined. Finally, the development of new forms of media, including direct-to-home broadcasting systems and the Internet suggests that the role of the state in media is currently undergoing a transformation.

Historical overview

India gained independence from British rule on 15 August 1947.[1] The largest legacy of colonial rule has been India's political and legal system. India's 1949 Constitution incorporated most of the provisions of the 1935 Government of India Act. The constitution declared India a sovereign republic of secular, socialist, and democratic aims. It also established a parliamentary government and granted universal, adult suffrage. Certain fundamental rights, such as freedom of thought, expression, belief, faith, and equality of gender were guaranteed.

However, the constitution also included a unique set of economic and social rights that served to signpost the direction the country was to take. The centralized broadcasting system inherited from the British period was transformed into the radio structure for the new government. It was a vehicle, from the very beginning, to shape national identity, and to help in economic development and was not necessarily constructed as a vehicle for freedom of speech.

The Republic of India is a federal union of twenty-five states, six centrally administered union territories, and a capital area. Two official languages, Hindi and English, were chosen from among the eighteen recognized languages and the more than 100 different dialects spoken in the country. Elections have taken place at regular intervals and power has changed hands between the government and the opposition, another signpost of an established democracy. Numerous political parties with differentiated ideological positions have also developed; many have been organized on the basis of language, religion, and caste. Democratic rights such as the right to vote, freedom of expression, of religious beliefs, and other rights guaranteed by the constitution have been enforced during most of the post-independence period.

India's problems have been more subtle. While guaranteeing democratic rights, the democratic system has not been able to ensure the fulfillment of the basic needs of millions of its citizens. One-third of the population of almost 900 million live below the poverty line and do not have access to basic education, healthcare, housing, or food. While healthcare, literacy, and other human need indicators reveal that living standards have improved since independence, the process has been an extremely slow one. India's GDP per capita (purchasing power parity, US$) is 2,077 (United Nations Development Program 2000).[2] Literacy is also growing, but at a very slow pace. According to the latest census figures, the literacy rate rose from 48.56 per cent in 1981 to 52.19 per cent in 1991. The gender ratio shows that the male literacy rate is 64.20 per cent while that of women is only 24.88 per cent (Parikh 1997).

Because of the compelling need for economic development, media policy in India has been closely connected to it. India's economic growth has been steady but not remarkable. While each citizen is constitutionally entitled to vote, economic poverty undermines this legal right by limiting the political awareness needed to inform active and conscientious citizens and voters. This was especially the case during the immediate post-independence period (1948–1960) when the powerful and hegemonic Congress Party was unhesitatingly voted to power in most states and in the capital. Over the years, radio and television have assisted in the process of making democratic options available to citizens by raising political consciousness and narrowing the gap between the literate and the illiterate. In election after election, illiteracy has been less and less a barrier to conscientious and enlightened voting.

In the history of India since independence, legal and constitutional rights were suspended only during the state of emergency declared by the then Prime Minister Indira Gandhi in 1975–1977. That period was notorious for many reasons. The government began a program of "forced sterilization" of poor males in an attempt to implement population control targets. Repressive measures were utilized against trade unions and the various communist parties. The police, the army, and the ruling Congress Party colluded in an attempt to clamp down on the political left in the state of West Bengal, and media were particularly affected by censorship. Using Article 359 of the constitution, the state of emergency suspended fundamental constitutional rights such as the freedom of expression, and broadcasting systems were used for government propaganda. Film and theater, too, faced political control and gradually developed mechanisms of self-censorship to cope with these constraints.

It is an indication of the strength of democracy in India that this period was brought to an end in 1977 by a general election. Today, circumstances have changed. The growth of regional political parties, caste-based parties, and other group-based parties has forced the dominant Congress Party to share power with other sections of society. Coalition politics has been the inevitable result.

For the first forty years after independence, the Indian economy was conceived as a "mixed economy," where the state played a significant role in the economic development of the nation alongside market stimuli. The envisaged structure has been reflected in India's bifurcated media system. While radio and television broadcasting have long remained in state hands (with a continuing government monopoly over terrestrial broadcasting only recently relaxed for radio), the press, cinema, theater, literature, music, and other art forms have, to a large extent, been relegated to the market.

Government intervention in the arts has been confined to encouraging "high" art or commercially non-viable production such as art cinema, classical music, or folk art. This policy has led to a very lively and complex cultural dynamic where commercially driven cultural production and socially motivated, message-oriented programming have existed side by side. Thus, the commercially based Indian press is very influential and commercial cinema has flourished, while state-controlled radio and television remain the most influential media in the country as low literacy levels make many other media inaccessible to large sections of the population.

One direct result of the state's investment in higher education and research has been the creation of a large middle class of technical and scientific professionals. The middle class is the major consumer of culture in India as well as the economic foundation on which the cultural market survives. Expansion of the middle class drives change in the media, just as the media itself has helped build and reinforce this growing sector of the population.

India's democratic framework has also provided the necessary atmosphere for the development of a thriving cultural scene that is in marked contrast to the situation in much of the developing world. A state policy of protectionism has contributed to the guaranteed development and viability of the Indian press, though the policy of excluding foreign investment in Indian newspapers has come under question. Indian cinema has been successful in creating a distinct identity for itself. The large number of regional languages and the development of Hindi as a pan-Indian language, however, have complicated this success. Strong regional trends have occasionally acted against the development of Hindi-based culture.

The current transformation of media in India is a consequence of a new set of economic policies. As of the 1990s, the Indian economy has experienced a "liberalization" with less government intervention in licensing or restrictions on imports, alongside lower government spending on social welfare issues such as education, housing, and so on. Liberalization has formed part of a new economic mantra that also includes globalization and privatization. This policy shift has coincided with the advent of satellite broadcasting, new computer publishing technologies, the Internet, and the growth of sizeable international media conglomerates.

As Chapter 1 suggests, any definition of democracy is certain to be contentious. The Indian experience illustrates the limitations of trying to define democracy merely by procedural and legal-institutional indicators. The constitution guarantees the independence of the judicial review and the rule of law, and the executive and judiciary are reasonably well insulated from each other. Although the president appoints judges of the supreme and high courts, the terms and conditions of service are directly regulated by the constitution. Dismissal is only possible with the approval of both houses of parliament. However, if a definition of democratization also includes citizen empowerment and access to legal redress irrespective of economic condition, so that each individual enjoys material conditions that enable the exercise of her constitutional rights, Indian democracy still has a long way to go.

Practically speaking, the legal system remains inaccessible to many ordinary citizens. Numerous reasons underlie this inadequacy. However, the two most important factors are low literacy rates and the resulting low level of awareness of legal rights and an extremely slow and costly legal system. In terms of women's rights, for example, there are laws in place to protect women from social inequalities including marriage dowries and sexual harassment in the workplace. However, very few women are aware of these rights because their literacy level is low.

Because the legal system is slow and costly, large institutions and corporations are given an unfair advantage over individual citizens who are limited by their resources. In the case of defamation suits where large publications have dragged cases out for years, most people have become too intimidated even to file a complaint. Often, the political-legal system serves to protect the interests of the socially powerful. This structural inequality has led to a general mistrust of the judicial system and an increasing tendency toward vigilante action, especially in the cultural arena.

Numerous religious and regional tensions also continue to exist. A consequence is specific legal restrictions aimed at reducing sectarian violence. Broadcasters are proscribed from relaying material that may increase such violence by a code that is applicable to all programs broadcast, whether by private producers or public. India was the first country to ban Salman Rushdie's novel, *The Satanic Verses* in reaction to protests by certain Muslim groups. Some fundamentalist Hindu groups have attacked cinema halls, exhibitions, or other cultural locations in order to terrorize artists or their distributors. Such tactics have often led to an atmosphere of fear and self-censorship. The legal system, including the police and judiciary, has proved unable to prevent such incidents, although many were recorded on camera.

Indian law has been notoriously slow in reacting to new circumstances, illustrated in its lack of response to the new media technologies such as satellite broadcasting, video recording and viewing, dubbed Hollywood films, the

Internet, direct-to-home broadcasting, and so on. Thus, a curious situation obtains where new technologies are being introduced without any legal framework. While the current legal framework at least theoretically allowed some measure of recourse (as illustrated by the cases below), a highly ambiguous and undefined situation now exists in many media areas.

The print media in India

Legislation

The colonial period left enduring marks upon the Indian legal system. As a result, an examination of pre-independence media legislation should assist in placing contemporary events in context.

The earliest publication in India was the *Bengal Gazette*, better known as "*Hicky's" Gazette*, which began publishing in Calcutta in 1780. Its relationship with the colonial authorities was contentious right from the very start. Warren Hastings, then governor general, prosecuted the journal for publishing scandals concerning him. J. A. Hicky was given a one-year prison sentence, fined Rs 2,000, and a further Rs 500 was awarded to Warren Hastings in damages. Nonetheless, the *Bengal Gazette* continued to publish until a satirical piece on Hasting's conduct of the Oudh war caused him to seize the gazette's typesetting equipment.

Meanwhile, other publications ensured state support for themselves through publishing government notices free of charge and by running stories favorable to the administration. In May 1799, a level of legal control was introduced when a set of publishing regulations were put in place.[3] These regulations effectively introduced pre-publication censorship to India. This continued in various forms, among them the film certification process (discussed below).

The "mutiny" or first war of independence in 1857 changed the relationship between the British colonists and India's native population. For the first time, a marked difference became noticeable between the attitudes toward the administration in the English-owned and in the Indian-owned newspapers, as independence campaigners began to recognize the potential of the press. Many campaigners, including the activist and social reformer Keshab Chander Sen who took over the *Indian Mirror*, began to realize the need for a vernacular press. He established the *Sulab Samachar* with a circulation of 4,000, very high for the late nineteenth century. The paper proved a powerful medium for the propagation of the ideals of the proprietor.

The English language *Amrita Bazaar Patrika* was established in 1868, and was more interested in politics than in profit. Lord Canning introduced the Control of the Press Act as an emergency measure following the mutiny to contain the damage done by such publications. Soon afterward, the Vernacular Press Act (1908) was designed to monitor the many local newspapers that had strong nationalist biases.

Censorship of the press became even more stringent during the First World War with the passage of the Defense of India Act. This act provided for the screening of news considered useful to the enemy and for the omission of prejudicial reports. In general, however, the colonial administration and the indigenous publishers ordinarily negotiated compliance by resolving contentious points among themselves. As the main inspiration behind the Satygraha movement, Mahatma Gandhi firmly believed in the power of the press to influence the views of the population. To promote his ideas, he founded two newspapers, one in English and one in Hindi. As the popularity of Gandhi's movement grew, there were fears of more stringent government laws. However, an All India Newspaper Editors' conference in 1940 negotiated with the government and a code of conduct was developed in opposition to the ad hoc arrangement that had previously been dominant.

Much of post-independence media development in India was based on the framework set down by the British. No specific mention of the rights, privileges, or responsibilities of the press was made in the 1949 Indian constitution. During the constituent assembly debates, Dr Ambedkar, as the main framer of the constitution, justified this omission by arguing that the press was to be considered as merely another medium used by individuals or citizens to express their views.[4]

As a result, the constitution guaranteed all citizens the "liberty of thought, expression, belief, faith, and worship" and this provision was considered to apply equally to the press. Article 19 of the constitution concerning "freedom of speech" was, however, qualified by the "reasonable restrictions" clause covering eight areas: the sovereignty and integrity of India; the security of the state; friendly relations with foreign states; public order; decency and morality; contempt of court; defamation; and incitement to an offence.

These exceptions soon gained significance when both the central government and respective state governments began to utilize them to muzzle the press. There were a number of attempts made by the government at various levels to impose press censorship in the 1980s. During this particularly turbulent period, there was a surge of secessionist region-based terrorist activity in various parts of the country. The governments retaliated with legal measures such as the Special Powers (Press) Bill in Jammu and Kashmir and the Defamation (Press) Bill that strove to control publication content in these regions. Each of these laws, however, failed as a result of opposition from political parties and other pressure groups throughout India. No cohesive nationwide press act has been passed to date.

All publications are required to register with the Indian Newspaper Registrar under the Press and Registration of Books Act of 1867. An annual report is published to make the registry data available. The registrar is also responsible for allocating supplies of newsprint, recommending the import of printing machinery, and issuing entitlement certificates for small publications to purchase newsprint from the authorized paper mills. The 1962 Newsprint Control Act formalized this control over the allocation of newsprint.

Because of the shortage of newsprint, the allocation of this scarce commodity has become a key indirect method of state press control. This practice, established during colonial rule, continued after independence. However, the general policy of state press control has been repeatedly and successfully challenged in a number of cases. In the 1962 *Sakal Papers* vs. *Union of India* case, the Supreme Court considered the validity of the 1956 Newspaper (Price and Page) Act that had sought to regulate print price and quantity of pages. The court declared the act void, as it would affect the circulation of newspapers and thus indirectly curtail freedom of circulation. In the 1972 *Bennett, Coleman & Co.* vs. *Union of*

India case, the newsprint policy of the central government was challenged under the same argument. Under the new regime of liberalization, however, the import of newsprint has been deregulated in the 1992 budget and such control is no longer possible.

Other efforts to redress the colonial legacy were also made. A Press Laws Inquiry Committee was set up in 1948 to consider the validity of legislation under the Indian Penal Code. Eventually, four acts were repealed in 1951: the Press (Emergency Powers) Act, the Foreign Relations Act, the Indian States (Protection against Disaffection) Act and the Indian States (Protection) Act. The rest remain in force.

On the recommendation of the First Press Commission, the Press Council of India Act was passed in 1965 and the Press Council of India was established in 1966. This council is charged with ensuring the freedom of the press, while maintaining and raising press standards through the development of a code of conduct. It hears complaints against press and government. However, it is only empowered to recommend and not to act. Its membership consists of thirteen journalists, six management representatives, one news agency representative, three private citizens, and five members of parliament. This body has its own code of conduct, which is not, however, binding. As a result, redress for code of conduct infringements has often proved inadequate.

Diversity

In 1993, 33,612 newspapers and periodicals were published in India. The ownership patterns are demonstrated in Table 9.1. Of the owners there, the most important are the joint-stock companies, which account for 38 per cent of the total number of newspapers circulated.

In 1997, the number of publications increased to 41,705. Although an accurate breakdown is not available, it is estimated that nearly one-third of the total circulation consists of newspapers and periodicals owned by individuals. There are a few large publishing groups of which the most important are Bennett, Coleman & Co. (also known as the *Times of India* group), the Express Newspapers, the *Hindustan Times* group, and the *Ananda Bazaar Patrika* group. While these large publishing houses dominate the market, the ownership patterns suggest a wide diversity of publication type, ranging from news-based publications to women's magazines, children's magazines, and the publications of political parties, religious bodies, social organizations, and so on.

Table 9.1 Ownership patterns of newspapers and periodicals in India, 1993

Individuals	24,474
Societies and associations	4,162
Firms and partnerships	1,449
Joint-stock companies	1,502
Central and state government	713
Trusts, cooperative societies, educational institutes, etc.	1,312

Source: Indian Ministry of Information and Broadcasting, 1994.

One of the important features of Indian media is the prevalence of family connections. For instance, the Birlas, the Tatas, the Goenkas, and the Jains are key big business families also able to dominate the private press in the country. Thus, the press is generally biased toward big business and the political leanings of these families are reflected in the overall editorial policy of the publication groups, although the control is not very tight or obvious.

The total circulation of newspapers and periodicals in 1997 has been estimated at 105,708,191. Because of the relatively high price of these items in India compared to per capita income, however, the readership per copy is very high and is usually considered to average more than five persons. In 1997, the three newspapers with the highest circulation were the *Hindustan Times*, published in English, with a circulation of 540,919; the *Times of India*, also published in English, and with a circulation of 530,504; and *Ananda Bazaar Patrika*, published in Bengali, with a circulation of 490,765.

According to figures available for 1996, in the 39,149 publications in that year, 100 different languages were used. Most publications appeared in Hindi: a total of 15,647, of which 2,004 were dailies and 7,799 were weeklies. The second language was English with a total of 5,912, of which 320 were dailies and 749 were weeklies. Following these were the Urdu, Bengali, Marathi, and Tamil languages. The smallest number was in Kashmiri, which had only one weekly, followed by Konkani, which had no daily newspapers and a total of only five publications.

State involvement

There is no direct financial involvement of the state in the print media. Of the 33,612 publications registered in 1993, only 713 were published by central or state governments and these were generally used for the dissemination of information on the activities of government departments. Their readership comprised less than 1 per cent of the total.

However, state advertising in newspapers and magazines is one important facet of indirect government financing. Of the 3,300 publications monitored in 1993, approximately 350 received 75 per cent or more of their income from government sources. Naturally, due to their meager resources, smaller publications were dependent to a greater degree on government advertising. Of the "small newspapers" category, it is estimated that 31 per cent of the revenue comes from the state. For large newspapers, these sources comprise less than 18 per cent of total revenue. Some, however, consider this policy to be a positive step in ensuring the survival of small publications that fail to be commercially viable as a result of language or subject matter. The indirect state subsidization helps such publications to survive and adds to the overall diversity of Indian print media.[5]

In general, the judiciary has consistently upheld the "Right to Information" clause in the Indian constitution and has often ruled against the government in such matters. There have been several lawsuits brought by individuals that have had serious repercussions. One important case in the 1950s was that of Dr Ram Manohar Lohia who was arrested for making speeches against the government of Uttar Pradesh over its decision to raise taxes, exhorting people not to pay. He was arrested under the Uttar Pradesh Special Powers Act. The Supreme Court ruled in 1960 that this arrest was unjustified, as the plea to boycott taxes could not be construed as coming under the "reasonable restriction" list in the constitution. It also declared the act unconstitutional and therefore void.

During the state of emergency, in addition to the suspension of constitutional rights (discussed above), a number of other laws such as the Maintenance of Internal Security Act, the Conservation of Foreign Exchange and Prevention of Smuggling Activities, and other legislation were misused to harass and imprison political and other critics of Indira Gandhi's regime. Then in 1976, Indira Gandhi's government passed the Prevention of Publication of Objectionable Matters Act, which was used to harass the press through the use of pre-publication censorship. Such censorship had previously only been used during certain periods of the British Raj.

Interest groups

Several bodies exist to represent the various interests involved in print media. These include the Indian Language Newspapers Association (1941), the All India Federation of Working Journalists (1951), and the Press Guild of India (1965) which looks after non-union press concerns.

A government-appointed wage board undertakes wage negotiations. These organizations have protected the interests of various groups within the media such as the workers and journalists. While legislation is in place to protect both journalists and private citizens, such laws are often inadequate in application. Recently, there have been cases of journalists and publishers being harassed by local interest groups. Laws seem to be inadequate in providing security to journalists who probe into crime and the nexus between politicians and criminals.

Similarly, the legal recourse offered to citizens is extremely lax and few, if any, defamation cases are actually concluded to the defendants' satisfaction. A case in point is the defamation brought by Professor Biplab Dasgupta, then a member of parliament, who sued *The Telegraph* for a story that suggested he was involved in financial scams. This case is still in the courts after more than fifteen years. As a result, the press is not overly concerned with accuracy and most publications suffer from a lack of credibility.

None of the major political parties has direct control over any of the major publications in the country, but several newspapers express quite clear political biases, resulting from their relationship with the ownership groups. Some political parties, such as the various communist parties, have their own daily newspapers. In certain states such as West Bengal and Kerala, these publications enjoy very high circulation figures of over 150,000 copies daily.

The Indian press and civil society

Social biases have been perpetuated by the fact that the majority of media professionals in India belong to the privileged groups in society: they are male, urbanized, and Hindu, (usually from the higher castes). Only recently has this traditionalist bias begun to change. The increased role of women in journalism has been significant, especially in the English language press. It is still too early, however, to assess whether this shift has had any enduring impact on the gender biases of the medium.

While the legal system has, in general, upheld the cause of the freedom of the press in India, it must again be emphasized that low literacy levels among the population naturally limit the reach of print media. In addition, the relative predominance of the urban centers is reflected by the fact that of the 3,740 publications considered in the Indian Newspaper Registrar's 1994 annual report, 28 per cent were published in four metropolitan cities: Delhi, Calcutta, Mumbai (formerly Bombay), and Chennai (formerly Madras). The report also indicated that English was the most common language of publication. Nineteen per cent of publications were issued in other state capitals in Urdu and Kannada, while 23 per cent were published in small towns and union territories where Hindi and Malayalam were the most widely used languages of publication.

Even in the large cities, there is a distinct difference in style, subject matter, and approach between the English language papers and the regional language newspapers. While the former are, broadly speaking, more concerned with national and international issues, the latter are more interested in local and emotive issues.

The fact that the cost of newspapers and periodicals is beyond the means of most of the population further undermines the press in India. However, a related issue is that newspapers, being mainly privately owned and therefore profit-oriented, cater to the middle or upper classes. Issues of concern to the impoverished and unempowered are conspicuously absent in publications. Rural India, especially, is neglected. Thus, while on the one hand, the Indian press is relatively vital and free, the commercial nature of the press deprives the majority of Indian citizens of true access to the medium.

Overall, however, the role of newspapers has been a positive one in the functioning of democracy in India. There is a tradition of investigative journalism in the Indian press, although it is not as strong as it could be. The publication and ensuing scandal of the Bofors gun deal that Rajiv Gandhi, then prime minister, was supposed to have finalized with kickbacks from the Swedish manufacturers going to Swiss bank accounts led to his defeat in the 1989 elections. The caste-dominated oppression in certain rural areas of Bihar and Madhya Pradesh has also been brought to public attention by the press. The economist Amartya Sen has cited the press as a very important factor in the prevention of famines in post-independence India.

Broadcast media in India

Legislation and state involvement

The 1885 Indian Telegraphy Act provided government with the power to control all matters related to the telegraphic services. This act remains in force and currently interprets the concept of communication very liberally. Another item of legislation affecting broadcasting is the 1935 Government of India Act, which contains provisions for the collection of license fees. Also in 1935, All India Radio was created as a monopolistic broadcasting entity. In contrast to print media and despite pressure from all sides, the state has maintained control over the broadcast sector.

India is one of the few democracies in which terrestrial broadcasting has been wholly within the monopoly of the state. Only since 1999 have private radio licenses in major cities, few in number and containing news restrictions, been permitted. The state has been responsible for funding and setting up the huge network of hardware necessary for national broadcasting. Especially significant has been the launch of the INSAT satellite series that has provided India with the technology necessary for the development of the medium.

In the 1950s and 1960s, when the role of the state was oriented toward fulfilling public service goals of "education, enlightenment, and entertainment," several rural education programs were initiated to provide updates on the latest agricultural innovations. The state promoted radio information dissemination by supplying villages with free radios and by encouraging community listening. This scheme proved a moderate success. Overall, however, affluent farmers were generally the ones who benefited, as they could implement the schemes suggested. These experiences have led to the conclusion that information dissemination should be tied into other government initiatives, such as loan facilities and irrigation so that benefits can reach their target audiences of poor peasants.

The habit of government censorship in the broadcasting sector has been difficult to negate. In 1968, an All India Radio (AIR) Code (later extended to the television body, Doordarshan) was evolved through discussions with all of the recognized political parties. This code closely followed the Indian constitution's Article 19 provisions, but also included clauses that prohibited "attacks on political parties by name" and "hostile criticism of state or the center."

The government has also consistently been unable to pass new laws to cope with emerging technologies such as cable and satellite broadcasting. This failure has led to an extremely anomalous situation where the terrestrial television network is controlled by the state, but private satellite channels have practically free entry into India. The Prasar Bharati Act, originally passed by the government in 1990, was aimed at providing autonomy for the state-run Doordarshan telecasting and All India Radio networks. However, these aspects of the act were largely neglected for years as it was ignored and some aspects of it were revived only in 1997, when the "Third Front" government of anti-Congress and anti-Bharatiya Janata Party forces was in power.

Some reforms have been introduced as part of the process of legislative modernization, even though the comprehensive bill itself was foundering. A 1996 Broadcasting Bill was introduced in parliament by the short-lived Third Front government. The bill has become the focus of debates centering on issues like "cultural imperialism," "privatization in place of social commitment," and the entry of foreign channels. Because of the controversy surrounding the bill, the current government is resorting to alternative avenues to address some of the more vital and perhaps more controversial issues. For example, a Union Cabinet decision has been taken to allow uplinking facilities for Indian broadcasters and a similar decision is pending before the cabinet to allow the same facilities for foreign broadcasters.

A Cable Television Networks Regulation Act was also passed in 1995 through which all channels follow a program and advertising code. It is mandatory for cable operators to carry Doordarshan 1 and 2 on particular bands. The legislation is aimed at addressing new areas of broadcasting. However, one contentious issue is that of foreign ownership of channels. There exists a strong lobby that is trying to restrict the privilege of broadcasting to companies with Indian stakeholders ostensibly to protect Indian culture.

Several of the private channels carried on cable are foreign owned. Of these, the biggest player is Rupert Murdoch's STAR network. However, there is a definitional problem about the term "foreign" because all channels technically broadcast from outside India as uplinking facilities are as yet not freely allowed in India. The Broadcasting Bill is expected to address such concerns.

Several court cases have been filed regarding the broadcasting regulatory structure and the government's refusal to allow private broadcasting stations into India. All have been turned down, usually under the justification of national security. The most significant case was the Hero Cup decision based on a complaint filed against the government's decision to retain Doordarshan's monopoly over telecast rights when the programming included the much-desired and significant cricket tournaments in 1995.[6]

This case went to the Supreme Court, which used the opportunity to rule on far more than coverage of significant sporting events. The court virtually ruled that legislation must be formulated to ensure that the government takes steps to end its broadcasting monopoly. The ruling was an explicit recognition of the role of the right to receive and impart information on the nature of media and their relationship to the democratic process. The Broadcasting Bill was a direct result of the Hero Cup ruling. Other significant cases included challenges to the in-house censorship policy of Doordarshan.

The need for further legislation is clear. Several factors, including the uncertain coalition politics of recent years, however, have prevented the government from taking a stand on contentious issues. Proposed legislation follows international models, but not coherently. Rather, they are mixed and matched.

Structure

Television and radio are, without doubt, the most important media in a developing society such as India's where illiteracy and poverty remain high. All India Radio reaches 97.3 per cent of the population while television covers 87 per cent. Television was late in coming to India, and government policy was slow to extend the medium to the remote regions of the country. Although there are no figures available on the number of radios and transistors in use, the number is very large indeed. The number of television sets now in India is estimated to be anywhere between 55 and 60 million.

Of these, 20 million have cable and satellite connections. A factor often overlooked in considering media contribution to pluralism and independence is the mode of producing programming. In the case of Indian broadcasting, originally, the radio and television bodies, Akashvani and Doordarshan, produced all their programming in-house and controlled all broadcasts. At that time, they were exclusively funded by the state. Gradually, however, these networks have become commercialized. Not only do they rely on advertising, they now lease broadcasting time to private producers. In AIR, the FM band is leased out to private operators. Leasing time does not necessarily lead to a high degree of diversity. In fact, strict rules exist concerning what can be broadcast. In addition, allegations of corruption on the part of bureaucrats in charge of allocating program space have made the process suspect.

Radio remains an instrument for creating a national identity, for development purposes, and for education. It is the most accessible medium for the majority of Indians and remains the most popular medium in rural areas. AIR administers, centrally, quantitative goals concerning coverage or education on key issues (such as encouragement of home building, or sanitation). It is the responsibility of the station in the field to determine that the prescribed issues receive the amount of attention determined by the administration. It may well be that the very importance of radio as a medium for information and development accounts for the government's reluctance to alter it to a public service model and provide it with greater autonomy, or to have large-scale corporations determine what should be broadcast there and when.

As indicated, the decade from 1991 to 2001 has been a transforming one for television, which is becoming increasingly popular. Since 1991, private satellite channels beamed from outside India have been available through cable-based networks in India. Large dishes pick up signals and then transmit them to individual households via cable. The entire network is in private hands. The largest, STAR, has channels which are estimated to reach 18 million homes. The next largest and most successful is the Zee Network owned by Subhas Chandra. There are many other players in this market, ranging from low-cost one-person outfits with extremely low budgets to international channels like CNN, CBS, ABC (Australia Broadcasting Corporation), and others. As private broadcasting is not yet officially permitted, these channels all broadcast from outside Indian territory.

The impact that these events in television have on the process of democratization is not yet clear. Certainly, the growth of cable and satellite channels has meant an increase in regional programming and programming in languages other than Hindi and English, thus strengthening the voice of democracy. The proliferation of strong regional stations will undoubtedly have consequences for loyalties, identities, and attitudes toward the state. The proliferation has consequences both for the extent of state power and for the perception that the state can manage the products carried on the various new technologies.

While satellite and cable television have shown rapid growth over the past five years, their viewership still lags far behind that of Doordarshan. This is partly because of the mostly urban and Westernized orientation of the satellite/cable programming. The STAR World Channel screens exclusively English language programs made outside India and is estimated to be available in around 7,171,000 homes. However, these are the same channels that attract the largest advertising revenues. Certain of the satellite channels, especially Hindi and some regional language channels, are doing well financially, even though they may have much lower viewer levels.

Concerns about internationalization, however, have been voiced. They are made at two levels. Those who hold traditional values, especially religious values, object to many consequences of modernity, and satellite channels can be made into markers of foreign taste, corruption, and the debasing of deeply felt habits of acting and representation. First, the objections are directed at broadcasts of "Western" programs, largely American, but also British and Australian. These are, in general, not very popular. Niche channels such as sports, news, educational, and children's, are relatively more successful, but only among a very small percentage of viewers.

Second, even though Indian programming itself has long shown evidence of modernity, somehow its packaging and delivery by foreigners (or significant Indian broadcasters using the new technologies) via satellite makes the process more objectionable. Concerns about the destruction of Indian values are couched in different tones: namely the confusion of Indian history and culture by adapting or fusing it with Western programs. The Indianization of international programming where items such as news, soap operas, game shows, or horror films are adapted and modified through dubbing or subtitling is often objectionable. On the other hand, many broadcasters feel that international production values and schemes adapted to local tastes have been a great success. For example, the program "Wheel of Fortune" has been adapted to Hindi film trivia in the Hindi language.

The availability of Pakistani television channels in India has presented another interesting challenge to ideas of free expression. During times of great crises with Pakistan, the government has attempted to black out these channels. However, given the diffuse nature of new media technology, control and policing have become extremely difficult to maintain. During 1999, the minister of information issued an order barring any cable operator from redistributing Pakistani Television. Further, the dominant Indian ISP "voluntarily" terminated its connection with the server that delivered one of Pakistan's significant daily newspapers to Indian Internet users. National security, fear of attack, or a potential war footing has often been a characteristic of the Indian government consciousness and this was not the first time that such security considerations affected media policy.

One of the most significant influences of encroaching private media is that it has forced Doordarshan and AIR to compete with the private channels on their terms. In some ways, this has been positive and caused the revamping of news programs. However, the abandonment of socially motivated programming creates concern. The commercialization of the state networks has led to an emphasis on providing programming aimed at urban middle classes rather than the general population.

Broadcasting and civil society

The centralized structure of broadcasting media has led to a monolithic media entity that limits the expression of the political, social, and cultural diversity of Indian society. Although state media broadcast various religious events or use newscasters from different ethnic backgrounds, these are generally token gestures and radio and television remain heavily biased toward Hindi, north Indian culture and is Delhi-centric.

As a result, popular protests have dogged state television from a variety of angles. Political opposition groups have protested the manipulation of television by the currently ruling party and have demanded individual state channels. Religious groups have demanded that their festivals be covered. Language-based protests have been organized against what is perceived to be the imposition of Hindi as the dominant language. In more recent times, groups have protested certain programs and advertisements, claiming that they have resulted in children's death or serious injury as a result of copycat actions.

Various methods have been developed by different pressure groups to enforce ethical codes on private channels in the absence of any existing legislative framework. Private channels have generally censored their own programming rather than brave public opinion following a number of protests concerning sex, drink, vulgar language, and other issues on television. One notable incident concerned a comment made on a STAR Plus talk show deemed to be derogatory to Mahatma Gandhi. A series of protests resulted, including one within the parliament. In response, STAR decided to take the program off the air.

Film media in India

In certain ways, film is significantly more important than any of the other media in India. Numerous commentators on India, academic and other, have considered the film industry, especially the Hindi, as the true creator of an Indian consciousness. Hindi films have unified national audiences that are otherwise deeply divided by class, language, caste, and religion. Where state radio and television failed to create a cohesive Indian consciousness, the commercial market seems to have succeeded.

India produces the largest number of feature films in the world, the majority of which are financed privately. In 1993, 812 full-length feature films were produced and an overwhelming number were in Hindi. Films are also produced in all the major languages of India. The state's most significant role in this sector has been its practice of pre-screening censorship. The Indian Cinematograph Act, initially passed in 1918 and subsequently modified, founded film censor boards that are active in the three major urban centers, Chennai, Calcutta, and Mumbai. In 1997 alone, the censor board screened 697 Indian and 191 foreign films: 888 films in total.

The Central Board of Film Certification is appointed directly by the state. There are also six other regional offices with their own boards. These censor boards appoint advisory panels that screen films, normally selecting educators, film critics, journalists, and social workers to these positions. There also exists a system of appeal to the Film Certification Appellate Tribunal in New Delhi.

The political and moral criteria used to censor Indian films have been a source of ongoing contention. Recently, the controversies have centered on the issue of "morality," rather than politics. One nationwide controversy involved Hindu fundamentalist groups vandalizing cinema halls screening the film *Fire* for its depiction of a lesbian relationship. Major controversies have erupted over the depiction of sex and nudity in films. The censoring of Stanley Kubrick's *Eyes Wide*

Shut, however, was more complicated. It turned on the fact that the film used Sanskrit religious shlokas that were viewed as derogatory to the Hindu religion.

Such circumstances have led to the development of an atmosphere of self-censorship. This was illustrated in the case of the film *Bombay* where the censors and boards were scared to clear it for fear of the reaction of the Shiv Sena, a regional group with an aggressively Hindu agenda that was in power at the time in Maharashtra. Amitabh Bachhan, a high-profile actor and well-connected businessman who then held discussions with Bal Thackeray, the leader of the Shiv Sena, produced the film. Bachhan personally assured Thackeray that there was nothing objectionable in the film and when Thackeray cleared it, the censors did the same and no protests arose.

Another significant role played by the state is as film financier, a role that stems from the Film Finance Corporation formed out of the S. K. Patil Film Enquiry Committee Report of 1951. This led to the development of a state-sponsored "New Indian Cinema" in opposition to the commercial film industry. Neo-realist, author-based cinema came to be heavily supported by the state and Mrinal Sen, Basu Chatterji, Shyam Benegal formed part of the "art cinema" alternative that state sponsorship made possible. This body was later transformed into the National Film Development Corporation (NFDC) (1980) and its objectives have also changed over time from its role as financier, to a more comprehensive role in the film industry, including the import and export of films. Individual states have also provided subsidies for film production in regional languages.[7]

The state has recently officially declared film an industry. This will guarantee rights for thousands of film employees and will also enable producers to approach legitimate funding sources, such as banks. It remains to be seen, however, whether this will in any way change the corrupt nature of current funding mechanisms.

Indian film and theater have always "plagiarized" stories, concepts, and modes of representation at all levels. However, the stories are often transformed in profound ways so that it is extremely difficult to label this process a simple "internationalization" of content. In fact, Indian films are now being exported. The main target has been the expatriate Indian community, but other countries in Asia and Africa are also importers of Indian films. At the same time, the new technology of dubbing Hollywood film not only into Hindi but also into regional Indian languages has led to the creation of a huge new market for Hollywood products. Powerful film-making associations have viewed this development as a threat to their hegemony, but to date they have taken no steps to curb the practice.

Indian media and civil society

Unlike some of the other countries assessed in this book, after independence, India has had a lively and well-entrenched tradition of democracy in which the various media segments have played significant roles. Radio and television, despite government control have proved particularly vibrant.

These media have, sometimes purposely and sometimes inadvertently, been the source of information and knowledge for the underprivileged, particularly the illiterate population in India. Audiences from low-income backgrounds tend to utilize these media as their primary information sources. In contrast, middle- and upper-class audiences tend to treat state broadcasting media as sources of entertainment alone. Thus, the less privileged prefer the informative but dull Doordarshan news broadcasts or the "bulletin board" style of AIR to the more attractively packaged foreign news channels or even STAR news. Any further study of media and democratization in India would focus on these disparate impacts of particular technologies. They would focus, too, on the relationship of media to development and of development to democracy.

Even serials and soap operas provide lessons in linguistic accent, clothing styles, and other outward indicators of class. Surveys have repeatedly shown the usefulness of these media for communicating information on basic issues such as hygiene. One of the best documented and most successful campaigns on radio and television was designed to inform mothers about providing proper rehydration to their children in the form of a salt, sugar, and lemon drink if they suffered from dysentery. Research into the use of agricultural innovations has found that many farmers are introduced to new seeds, fertilizers, and other developments through AIR programs. These circumstances highlight the possibility that media could be effectively used to promote social causes. Such efforts could, in turn, lead to a more meaningful level of democracy than the purely procedural one now in place.

The use of broadcasting for these purposes can be contrasted with profit maximization as a standard. That motivation certainly exists within the commercial media sector, but it is increasingly true for the government sector as well. As a result, social responsibility is neither expected nor found in these media. The press, in particular, remains largely uninterested in social issues. The general reaction of the national and local press during the Mandal crisis was to take up a practically unanimous anti-quota stance.[8] The personnel and audience of the press are all, with few exceptions, from the higher and privileged castes. Therefore, it came as no surprise to find the press taking such a stand.

Similarly, during the communal tensions and riots surrounding the Babri Masjid issue in which a mosque was ultimately destroyed by a group of Hindu Right fanatics, the role of the press was far from ideal. Certain local newspapers, especially in the Hindi language, were found to have deliberately inflated the number of Hindus killed in the ensuing violence. English language newspapers were less blatant, but their pro-Hindu biases were apparent. Rather than acting as impartial observers and neutral commentators, the press openly sided with the powerful community against the minority Muslim community.

Cross-media tendencies

Such social problems as the ones discussed above are aggravated by cross-media tendencies, which are extremely high in India. Only the most important will be discussed here. The print media is quickly adjusting to the Internet by publishing online editions of its publications. Many newspapers and magazines have been quick to take up this innovation. However, because of a lack of efficient software and the elite bias of the new medium, such innovations have been largely limited to English language publications. Recently, magazines like *i.t. – Information*

Technology have started including CDs with computer games and software as part of their content.

Most significant developments, however, have occurred among the commercial cinema, music, radio, and television sectors. Radio was the first medium to realize the power of film music when private channels and Radio Ceylon forced AIR to begin broadcasting such entertainment. While the advent of television was initially perceived as a threat to the huge film industry, actual circumstances proved to be quite different. Most of the popular shows on television relate to films in some manner. Either they show clippings of the song and dance sequences, or they hold competitions where the participants sing film songs, or there are film-based quiz competitions. Thus, television has become dependent on the film industry to a large extent. This is also reflected in the number of film channels available in Hindi and in regional languages. Both the private television industry and the Doordarshan have launched such channels. This influence has not been wholly one-sided. While television has harnessed the popularity of the film industry, Indian cinema has also profited from the exposure that television has provided.

As may be inferred from even this sketchy description, many benefits have been accrued from such cross-media holdings. The larger publishing houses, such as Bennett, Coleman & Co. or the *Ananda Bazaar Patrika* group, have entered the news and entertainment television markets. There are also large conglomerates, such as Living Media, which publish the most widely read magazine in India, *India Today*. The group also produces television shows, including the most popular news magazine show, *Aaj Tak*. This program, in particular, has established a reputation of investigative journalism. The group runs a music sales industry under the banner, Music Today, they own an art gallery in Delhi that hosts established and new artists, and they run a television magazine, *TV Today*.

Under current circumstances, considerable advantage is to be gained by cross-media consolidation because of the opportunity to capture the market. In the early phases of post-independence democracy, the role of the state was much more significant in the area of broadcasting. Private enterprise was limited to a few hours on a single radio channel and all television programming was produced by the state. Thus, little scope for cross-media ownership existed.

In the print media, technological innovations have allowed the larger houses to expand their operations throughout the country by publishing several editions simultaneously from different cities and in different languages. In some cases, this has led to a monopolistic tendency as large, national newspapers dislodge the local independent papers. For example, *The Statesman*, a Calcutta based paper is now also published from Siliguri, a town in the north of Bengal.

Within the film industry, the state's role has been relatively clearly demarcated from that of private producers. The state produced documentaries for propaganda and information dissemination and it was mandatory for all cinema halls to screen these before their regular feature films. In addition, the NFDC sponsored the serious art cinema that became distinguished from commercial cinema. Now, with the emphasis on profit generation in the state administration and the cut-back of subsidies at all levels, such support has been diluted.

In recent years, the tendency has been for consolidation between the various segments in the media landscape. Thus, a likely scenario is the emergence of a smaller number of larger players who will each control vertical segments of the market. These issues need to be considered in context of the larger shift in the role of the state since the triad of Liberalization–Privatization–Globalization remains the signpost for economic development in India. To understand the implications of these economic policies for media, the state's role in the development of the new media, especially the Internet, should be considered.

Emerging media technology

The case of the Internet poses some fundamental questions regarding the nature of democracy in India. In a country where the number of computers available is still extremely low in comparison with the population size, the number of software professionals in this sector is disproportionately high. Thus, the anomalies and disparities that exist in Indian society are magnified when the range is extended to consider literacy and Internet-competency. In this context, a simple procedural definition of democracy seems inadequate. Although every Indian has one vote, the level of information disparity is so wide that the meaning of this right is severely limited.

Official government policy for developing the Internet infrastructure also reveals a second transition that India is undergoing from a "mixed" economy with a socialistic ethos to a "liberalized" economy. During debates surrounding the development of television in the late 1960s and early 1970s, there existed rhetoric of its public service aspect and its educational potential. The Satellite Instructional Television Experiment (SITE) represented an attempt to utilize television for the social purposes of primary education, primary health awareness, scientific methods of agricultural cultivation, and campaigns against undesirable social attitudes such as the neglect of female children.[9]

By the 1990s, however, government policy had shifted toward the development of Internet for only the elite sections of society. The goals and targets are commercial rather than social. A publicity brochure for Videsh Sanchar Nigam Limited (VSNL), India's exclusive provider of international telecommunication services and its only Internet gateway, carries a chairman's message that makes no mention of social objectives:

> Today, we at VSNL are proud to roll out a world-class telecom and IT infrastructure which is poised to meet the need of an economy on the fast track, connecting people to people and country to country – anytime, anywhere, cost effectively and efficiently.

VSNL provides a range of telecommunication services that include global mobile personal communications by satellite, Internet, e-mail, and so on. The Indian government holds a 52.9 per cent stake in this company. Following the onset of economic liberalization in India, state shares were divested on the European and Indian markets and financial institutions like the United Trust of India bought up most of the shares. At present, all Internet connections run through VSNL and the company has been granted a monopoly until 2004. Internet connectivity only began in 1995. By October 1999, there were 273,999 connections to VSNL directly and yet more to the ISPs. The total is estimated to be approximately 333,000 connections.

Another developing technology that is raising concern is the direct-to-home (DTH) broadcasting system. DTH satellite broadcasting and other entertainment options such as video viewing necessitate familiarity and inclination to Western and English language culture. These factors combine to create a new dividing line between the privileged classes and those less privileged.

Among other reservations voiced about DTH is the possibility of political propaganda from unspecified enemies, usually implying Pakistan or China, the prevalence of uncensored sex, or unbridled Westernization. There is a fear that DTH might bypass the state's control over what individuals are able to view. The proposed Broadcasting Bill may encompass some aspects of this new technology, but probably not for long.

There are similar reservations cited concerning the lack of monitoring of the Internet. During border skirmishes with Pakistan at the end of the 1990s, the government banned reception of PTV, the Pakistani national television channel that is very popular among Indians. It also tried to jam Internet editions of Pakistani newspapers. However, Internet users with even basic computer knowledge soon learned to bypass the block. This information was then communicated via the Internet to anyone who was interested in receiving Pakistani media.

The problem of monitoring is reflected in the government's recent Information Technology Plan. Clause 101 envisions "an Information Security Agency on the national level to play the role of Cyber Cop," while clause 103 specifies that "Cyber infractions shall be addressed within the legal framework of the Ministry of Justice and Company Affairs." Lack of legislative structures in this sector, however, has prompted the government to refer disputes to the Telecom Regulatory Authority of India. In response, an Electronic Transaction Act has been passed in cabinet to regulate e-commerce in India.

A few examples of attempts by the state to democratize the new media should be noted. For example, there was much media hype concerning the Janmabhoomi initiative launched by Andhra Pradesh's chief minister. Under this scheme, the state government would pay 70 per cent of the costs of setting up infrastructure connecting rural Andhra Pradesh to the Internet. It was envisaged that this scheme would improve rural administration, ensure better implementation of rural development schemes, and provide for quicker settlements of land-related and other disputes. Thus far, however, the scheme has not proved very popular among the villagers of the state, who were expected to carry 30 per cent of the costs.

While the development of the Internet and other new media technologies raise questions about internal inequalities within India, they highlight increasing global inequalities. Far from creating an equal world, new media may have further contributed to its bifurcation. The level of Internet technology in India is very low in comparison with that of developed countries.

In addition, new media have created a ghettoization of labor. The "bodyshopper" companies who hire Indian software professionals illustrate this point. By saving on wage costs through hiring Indians who are willing to work for less than their Western counterparts, such companies are able to ensure remarkable profits. Indian software developers are also hired at comparatively much lower salaries than in Western nations, much like the poor garment manufacturers of Bangladesh or Korea. Thus, at a global level, new media work against prospects of equal communication.

Conclusion

The media sector is a particularly thriving part of Indian society. The lack of a responsive legal structure or framework, however, decreases levels of oversight. The state continues to maintain an extremely powerful position toward media though that position is being increasingly challenged by the very nature of new media. Often, however, the lack of sound legal systems and procedures has made producers wary of antagonizing powerful groups within society and has led to an unhealthy practice of self-censorship.

In addition, an overall mistrust of the judicial system persists at a general level. The current prime minister has urged judicial reforms in a country where hundreds of thousands of cases remain unaddressed. Justice deferred is justice denied and many people fail to file cases as a result of a lack of resources, economic and physical, required to conclude a case.

Legal reform thus needs to be geared toward the establishment of a legal system that would ensure both formal and actual rights, as guaranteed by the constitution. Rights must be publicized and social conditions created so that citizens perceive the legal system as being on their side, rather than on the side of the powerful. Over the last five years, judicial activism has moved the state in this direction. The Supreme Court ruling that led to the framing of the Broadcasting Bill is one example.

New media legislation also needs to be formulated and action must be taken to ensure that radio and television retain their previous social role as providers of public service. The state's change in policy orientation is most noticeable within new media. In accordance with the directives set by the World Trade Organization, new media are being treated as technologies rather than means of communication, in possession of social possibilities and responsibilities. By using the term "information technology" when framing policy guidelines and objectives, the issue of the content is effectively-sidelined.

For the Internet and other new media to be useful and accessible to the majority of Indian citizens, the current approach must be drastically modified. A technology that is establishing yet another set of privileges for an already privileged section of society should be reassessed. The theoretical potential for using new media in implementing social change is immense, but has thus far been neglected. Certain features of these media inherently encourage accessibility, creativity, and exposure to information and experiences that would otherwise be restricted. These aspects, however, have been consistently less explored and developed than the new media's potential for e-commerce.

Communication technologies need to be used to communicate. The existence of free and independent media cannot be a goal, in itself, if it remains a synonym for privately owned, profit-based media. Neither can the heavy hand of the state ensure true democratization of society or media. The elaboration of a media policy, together with an attendant legislative framework that would support and encourage true democratic rights for all citizens, is a challenge that all nations interested in aspects of media, democracy, and change must accept. Only this will ensure the creation of a truly democratic global society.

Notes

1   British rule in India can be divided into two eras. The first was the result of commerce-driven battles fought by the East India Company as the trading corporation became a ruling power. It was only in 1858, after the Sepoy Mutiny in 1857 (also known as the First War of Independence) that the British government assumed power, in place of the East India Company. India achieved independence on 15 August 1947. However, the division of the region into India and Pakistan marred this achievement. Part of Pakistan is today the independent state of Bangladesh. The bitterness surrounding the events of Partition has left deep scars on the psyche of all three nations and is the source of much sub-continental tension.

2   Also see mapsofindia.com for a map of the per capita income of each state in India. "Per capita income of states 1997–1998: Quick estimates." Available at: http://www.mapsofindia.com/maps/india/percapitaincome.htm

3   The regulations were: (1) every newspaper printer was to print his name at the bottom of the paper; (2) every newspaper editor or proprietor was to deliver his name and place of abode to the secretary to the government; (3) no paper was to be published on a Sunday; (4) no paper was to be published without previous inspection and authorization by the secretary to the government; (5) the penalty for breaking the above regulations was immediate deportation to Europe.

4   Thus, he concluded, "[T]he press has no special rights which are not to be given to or which are not to be experienced by the citizen in his individual capacity. The editor of a press or the manager are all citizens and therefore, when they choose to write in newspapers, they are merely exercising their right of expression, and in my judgment therefore, no special mention is necessary of the freedom of press at all."

5   The state has, however, occasionally used such indirect financing to influence the editorial policies of newspapers and magazines. In 1952–1953, the state stopped advertising with the *Times of India* as a result of its criticism of the government.

6   *Secretary, Ministry of Information and Broadcasting* vs. *Cricket Association of Bengal* (1995) 2 S.C.C. 161.

7   The state levies a fairly heavy entertainment tax on cinema attendance that can be as high as 40 per cent of the ticket price and varies from state to state. However, this is often waived in the case of films that are deemed to have a "social value." In some states, in order to attract viewers, this tax is not levied on regional language films.

8   In the period 1989–1990, India was rocked by the government's recommendation that seats and posts should be reserved for the so-called backward castes and tribes.

9   SITE extended over a huge area in rural India covering 2,400 villages and was a television-based development program designed to provide inputs for agricultural, social, health-related improvements. The experiment lasted from 1 August 1975 to 31 July 1976.

Bibliography

This list includes suggestions for further reading as well as material specifically cited in the text.

Baruah, U. L. (1983) *This is All India Radio*. New Delhi: Publications Division, Ministry of Information and Broadcasting.

Basu, Tapan *et al.* (1993) *Khaki Shorts and Saffron Flags*. New Delhi: Orient Longman.

Chatterji. P. C. (1991) *Broadcasting in India*. New Delhi: Sage.

Desai, Ashok V. (1972) *Economic Aspects of the Indian Press*. New Delhi: Press Institute of India.

Gupta, Nilanjana (1998) *Switching Channels: Ideologies of Television in India*. New Delhi: Oxford University Press.

India 1990: A Reference Annual (1991). New Delhi: Publications Division, Ministry of Information and Broadcasting, Government of India.

India 1999. New Delhi: Research, Reference and Training Division, Ministry of Information and Broadcasting, Government of India.

India's Gateway to the World (1999). Mumbai: Videsh Sanchar Nigam Ltd.

Indian Ministry of Information and Broadcasting (1994). Press in India: 38th Annual Report of the Registrar of Newspapers for India. New Delhi: Publications Division, Government of India.

Kulshreshtha, Sudhir (1995) *Fundamental Rights and the Supreme Court*. New Delhi and Jaipur: Rawat Publishers.

Manorama Yearbook (1999). Malayala Manorama: Kottayam.

Natarajan, S. (1962) *A History of the Press in India*. Bombay: Asia Publishing House.

Parikh, K. S. (1997) *India Development Report*. New Delhi: Oxford University Press.

Rajadhyaksha, Ashish and Paul Willeman (1995) *Encyclopaedia of Indian Cinema*. New Delhi: Oxford University Press.

Stanhope, Leicester (1823) *Influence of the Press in British India*. London: Publisher not given.

Universities Handbook (1997). New Delhi: Assocn of Indian Universities.

United Nations Development Program (2000) *Human Development Report*. New York: Human Development Report Office. Available at: http://www.undp.org/hdro/

www.askallindia.com/infotechdesk/art2.htm (consulted 29 November 1999).

10

MEDIA IN TRANSITION

The case of Poland

Karol Jakubowicz

Much of the writing on democratic transitions seeks to capture the essence of the relationship between media change and social change and to develop a general framework for analyzing it. However, there is currently no unanimity in the literature on the relationship between mass communications and social change. The issues of whether mass media lead or follow change, whether they mirror or mould society, and whether they should be conceptualized as agents of social change or of the status quo are yet to be resolved.

In general terms, the goal of media transformation in Central and Eastern Europe has been the creation of free and democratic media. This process has encompassed the evolution of media systems from unity to diversity as well as the birth of a "fourth estate" of media, no longer serving as the mouthpiece of government but rather as a check upon it. At a minimum, this process requires democratization, demonopolization of the media, autonomization, decentralization, and professionalization of journalists.

Processes of media change are, of course, dependent in transitional societies on changes in key areas of social life, as reflected in Table 10.1.

Media autonomy, or independence, cannot be achieved until media have become disentangled from state and political institutions and become structurally

Table 10.1 Process of social change impacting on media change

Depending on Political factors, the media can	*Politics, economy determine whether the media can*	*Economy, market mechanisms favor or hinder*	*"Cultural change" is required for*
Become liberalized Become pluralistic and open Become deregulated Promote the professionalization of journalists	Gain autonomy Decentralize Diversify in content Address minority groups Internationalize	Abolition of media monopoly Commercialization Concentration Globalization	Depoliticization of media Institutionalization of rule of law Definition of and service to the public interest Development of public opinion The media to serve as impartial watchdogs

free of inhibiting forms of economic, political, or other dependency. However, it is hardly possible for the media to fulfill their watchdog role, reporting objectively upon and potentially exposing the abuses of government or of the larger political or economic establishment, if media or journalists themselves are in any way tied to or dependent upon those they are meant to oversee. This is where journalistic professionalism comes into play.

Media independence therefore depends on external independence of media organizations, internal independence of editorial staff, personal/professional independence of media practitioners, and both management and journalists. External organizational independence amounts, in very general terms, to the freedom to establish and operate media outlets without legal, political, or administrative interference or restraint and without external pressure or interference from public authorities, governments, private interest groups, or individuals.

Internal independence can be defined as "independent editorial work," "the work of collecting, editing, and publishing information conducted within the framework of editorial aims that are articulated and adopted by the professionals involved," or as the "internal independence of editors and journalists from interference by owners, publishers and managers." In other words, internal independence depends on a freedom from internal interference whereby owners, publishers, managers (who might themselves enjoy external independence) limit or constrain journalistic independence through the nature of their relationship with the editorial staff. Certainly, absolute internal independence is hardly possible, but editorial staffs determined to protect their autonomy can achieve significant advantage.

The personal/professional independence of media practitioners signifies both their impartiality and detachment from social, political, and economic interests in their performance of journalistic duties and a sense of high professionalism and dedication to journalistic ethics. Professionalization of journalists should be understood both as the promotion of journalistic skills and as "collective professionalization," a process in which a profession develops a service ideal, code of conduct, and a specific professional organization dedicated to enforcing and implementing this service ideal and protecting the autonomy and standing of members of that profession. This service ideal concerns service to the general public rather than to media owners and managers or to political or economic interests. While a fully developed media system should be pluralistic, allowing different media representing various shades of opinion, in the unique circumstances of systemic transition, the first priority should be assisting the public in making sense of the dilemmas of transformation and in finding their bearings under these new circumstances.

Of all aspects of media transformation, the redefinition of journalism has been particularly difficult to achieve in transition societies. The shift from advocacy and propaganda orientation to impartial reporting and state watchdog functions has proven particularly elusive. Many journalists lack the training, detachment, professionalism, and indeed will to be truly independent. As a result, they often confuse audiences by offering partisan, tendentious, and therefore conflicting reports or analyses of developments in their societies.

Apart from this, personal/professional independence may be non-existent at the individual, group, or media institutional level for several reasons.

- The professional self-definition of media practitioners who, guided either by their political views or by their understanding of journalism as a role of social and/or political leadership, subordinate their professional activities to promoting a cause or the interests of certain political groups or other organizations.
- The owners, managers, and editors may direct journalistic staff to take sides on social, political, and other issues, to support one view while dismissing others, causing a lack of internal independence.
- The entire newspaper or station may be controlled by outside interests and used for outside purposes, causing a lack of external independence.

Media independence can be portrayed in three levels. These are:

- external independence: possible without internal or personal/professional independence;
- internal independence: impossible without external independence; and
- external and internal independence: meaningless without personal/professional independence.

As demonstrated by these levels, the onus lies squarely with editorial staffs to maintain their own personal/professional independence. Without this, all the legal and institutional measures to safeguard media independence are just an empty shell. Conversely, even without the formal safeguards of media independence, editorial staffs determined to preserve their personal/professional independence can make a significant difference.

The irony of the situation in many Central and Eastern European countries – as the new century began – was that, given the willingness of some media managers and journalists to play the political game, safeguards of external and internal independence developed in those countries often protected bad rather than good media performance. Laws alone cannot guarantee media independence. These must be accompanied by a political culture of democracy and by the ability of public opinion and civil society to make politicians and the administration accountable for any violation of that independence. Otherwise, the use of numerous formal and informal, legal or extra-legal measures will continue to bring pressure to bear on media.

Even given a favorable political and economic context (and this is rare enough), change in Central and Eastern Europe is also "cultural." Without the emergence of a political culture of democracy and civil society (including acceptance of the rule of law, democratic procedures, and market practices) and a different value system (individual freedom rather than collectivism; human rights and civil liberties rather than respect for authority; citizenship rather than submission to authoritarianism), change elsewhere will be incomplete. It is such cultural change, a change of social consciousness, which takes a particularly long time to develop.

Accordingly, it is only the consolidation of democracy (a process to which the media naturally contribute in a slow and gradual way) that will create the prerequisites of a democratic media system. These prerequisites include:

- the existence of civil society and an independent public sphere;
- an established role for public opinion in public life;
- a willingness to depoliticize important areas of social life;
- some accepted notion of the public interest;
- trust in and acceptance of public broadcasting regulation to serve public interest;
- the emergence of journalistic professionalism based on a notion of public service.

Another precondition of media development is the existence of a free market and economic growth. Otherwise the development of a private, advertising-financed media sector is very difficult. Media can be independent only if they are financially successful. Meanwhile, most post-communist countries can at best be described as latent media markets, characterized by a lack of growth opportunities for large-scale media organizations because there is insufficient start-up capital and an inadequate volume of advertising to finance such endeavors; lack of favorable conditions for media concentration; low interest on the part of foreign investors, further impeding private media development; and an inadequate economic base for the development of new technologies.

Therefore, consideration of the prerequisites of media independence should cover not just the manner of financing media but also the general economic environment. Under circumstances where economic reform is going badly, the advertising-driven process of media pluralization will need a long time to take effect. This is especially true of broadcasting since a small and relatively poor market cannot sustain numerous specialized broadcasting outlets. Commercial broadcasting, especially locally financed and managed, is only starting up in such markets and it will take a long time for new companies to accumulate capital enabling them, should they want to do so, to introduce narrow-cast channels and finance them as they slowly become established. Finally, minorities are, in many cases, either too small or too poor to be attractive to commercial broadcasters.

An assessment of media reform during the period of democratization naturally depends on the definition of the process of media reform as well as its goals. A normative/prescriptive approach will proceed from the assumption that the process will end once the desired result has been achieved. Such is the case with those, for example, which seek changes of social power relations (in the media and in general) and the realization of a radical program of civil society empowerment, both in a general political and a communicative sense.

Thus, Sparks points out that a model of civil society empowerment, as originally espoused by dissidents, has failed to take hold in Central and Eastern Europe. Rather, a "standard model," which leads to the empowerment of new political and economic elites and entails a mixture of paternal and commercial systems, has taken hold (Sparks 1998: 127). Similarly, Splichal concludes that an "Italianization" of media, typified by strong state control of the media, pronounced political partisanship, close integration of media and political elites, and a lack of consolidated and shared professional ethics among media professionals, has taken place in Central and Eastern Europe (Splichal 1994). However, he also argues that while the situation is stable in Italy, it may be transitory in the new post-communist democracies.

Given that the normative/prescriptive approach has not proved particularly fruitful in determining criteria for ascertaining whether transition is complete, an analytical approach might, instead, be opted for. One possibility is to adopt a comparative perspective. For example, Johnson has predicted that by the time Central European countries become serious candidates for membership of the European Union, "their media systems will be virtually indistinguishable from those of today's Western Europe" (Johnson 1995: 164). Along the same lines, Lukosiunas provides the following answer to the question "Is the transition over?":

> One may probably say that the first phase of the transition – which included the disruption of the Soviet media system and emergence of the new structure of the media which is capable of integrating Western journalistic practices and is ready to be integrated into the structures of Western media businesses – is over, and the next stage – which is to find its place and voice in united Europe – has just started.
>
> (Lukosiunas 1998)

The application in Poland: transition

In the Polish case, it is difficult to determine what the criteria of assessment should be. It is clear that media reform has fallen far short of the original Solidarity ideal of "media socialization," or the direct social control of, and ability to speak through, mass media. On the other hand, the more modest goal of approximation to Western media models may have been achieved in Poland, with all the weaknesses this type of media system implies. If the minimum criteria for qualitative change and media freedom are applied (i.e., whether the processes of economic reform, democratization of the media, demonopolization, autono-mization, decentralization, and professionalization of journalists have been completed) in an examination of Poland's ongoing transition then the result is a mixed verdict.

Between 1989 and 1993, Poland was ruled by a succession of governments with their roots in the opposition trade union, Solidarity.[1] The general election of 1993, however, brought defeat to the post-Solidarity parties and returned power to the former communists in the form of a coalition between the SLD (the Democratic Left Alliance) and the PSL (the Polish Peasants' Party).[2] This was followed in 1995 by an even more stunning event: a narrow victory in the presidential election for Aleksander Kwaśniewski, leader of the Social Democratic Party, the SdRP, and one-time communist official, over Lech Wałęsa, the legendary Solidarity leader and the country's first democratically elected president.[3]

The 1997 general election ended in victory for Akcja Wyborcza Solidarność (AWS), a right-wing alliance of some fifty political groupings.[4] The four reform initiatives launched by the subsequent right-wing government have produced so much dissatisfaction (largely as a result of the inefficient way in which they have been introduced) that the current government enjoys very low popular support.[5] "Political capitalism," where certain sectors of the economy are directly or indirectly politically controlled, has become even more acutely prevalent than was previously the case.[6] Meanwhile, the 300 political parties that mushroomed after the transition began in 1989 have been reduced to four major contenders and a handful of marginal ones.[7]

Throughout these political changes and since Solidarity's symbolic victory over the communist regime in 1989, Poland has faced a dual transition process that has involved economic reform as well as political democratization. The role of the Polish media in this process has been one of response and "trend-following" rather than of "trend-setting." However, important inroads have been made in its reform. In the political sphere, legal and institutional mechanisms of control have been dismantled.

The first fundamental economic reforms were based on a strict monetarist and neo-liberal economic strategy. The reform program was formally inaugurated on 1 January 1990 and came to be popularly known as the "Big Bang" reform, as it was a shock to the economy.[8] Inflation soared, production dropped, and unemployment rose. With time, however, the therapy began to reap rewards. In 1998, only three post-communist countries (Poland, Slovenia, and Slovakia) had a level of GDP higher than their pre-1989 level. Only in Poland, however, did GDP rise by more than 20 per cent.

Media were restructured within the newly developed system of market competition. As a result, the state's financial hold over media was significantly limited. Nonetheless, many hybrid and intermediate forms of economic ownership still existed. Administrative control of the economy as well as state interventionism was prevalent and favored by both left- and right-wing parties. There was, as the new century started, still too much direct and indirect political control over certain segments of the economy. Different authors have described the resulting political and economic system as either "political capitalism" or "democratic socialism" (Sasińska-Klas 1996).

The second branch of the reform, democratization, has affected primarily public service broadcasters in the media, both in the method of appointment and in the composition of their governing bodies. Democratization has been influenced by certain regulations requiring public service broadcasters to provide access to various strands of political opinion, to promote the free expression of opinions, and to contribute to the free formation of public opinion. Though residual control exists in certain media sectors (evident in the National Broadcasting Council difficulties discussed below), on the whole, the Polish media have developed an external independence from the state. However, democratization of media has been inadequate. Pluralism of content has remained insufficient and many social groups have been deprived of media that spoke on their behalf. There have been few regulations providing for social access to media, and regulations have related primarily to political access. There has been an attempt to create a third category of "social" or "civic" broadcasters that would promote pluralism in public debate.[9] This effort has been only partially successful, as most broadcasters fitting this category have been based in religious broadcasting.

In addition to increasing pluralism, the goal of promoting civil society was part of the democratization effort. Citizen participation in public life is a hallmark of civil society and a test of the freedom enjoyed by individuals to influence the decision-making process affecting their lives. However, what has emerged to date has been not a civil society but a "political" society (Korbonski 1994). According to Grabowska, the early transition period failed to allow a civil society to emerge because of the "authoritarian" style of post-Solidarity parties (Grabowska 1995). That failure fueled indifference in society, already discouraged by the lack of progress in solving the country's problems and by the interminable power struggles. Many people have opted out of public life.

Kurczewska, Staszyńska, and Bajor have concluded that the full development of civil society was prevented in Poland by the fact that a weak society was interacting with a weak state (Kurczewska *et al.* 1993). Civil society was weak, in part, as a result of two factors. On the one hand, the number of new organizations and associations was inadequate to meet social needs. On the other hand, the expectation that "the state would provide," satisfying the needs of society, was still very much ingrained. In 1997, only 19 per cent of the population felt that they could influence events in the country and only 25 per cent felt they had an impact upon events in their own community (Kolarska-Bobińska 1998).

The examination of the demonopolization process is the next step in exploring Poland's media independence during the transition. The dismantling of the state publishing conglomerate RSW (see below) and the passage of the Broadcasting Act (1992), followed by the licensing of commercial radio and television stations (beginning in 1994), effectively demonopolized the Polish media (Ustawa 1993). While politicians have continued to try to control the media (especially the public service broadcast media), their emancipation from political control is quite advanced. Amendments to the press law adopted in 1989 and 1990 removed all political controls. Private media were free from any association with politicians unless they chose such involvement. Public service radio and television were also, at least fitfully, well protected against outside interference.

However, in view of the continued political influence upon public service broadcasting, the lack of impartiality throughout many important print media, and the political affiliations of both editors and journalists, autonomization was more doubtful. In consequence, Polish national newspapers were described as approximating the European model of a "pluralistic system of party-oriented newspapers," with particular newspapers committed to promoting sets of political interests or views (Burnetko 1995). Local newspapers tried to maintain a level of impartiality in this context.

The process of decentralization was both planned and spontaneous. On the one hand, there was a grassroots emergence of local and regional newspapers and periodicals in large numbers. On the other hand, in broadcasting, this decentralization came about through the administrative transformation of public service broadcasters in 1994. This process divested local Polish Radio studios to independent regional radio stations and turned regional Polish Television (TVP) production centers into full-fledged regional stations with their own program services. Also, the licensing policy of the National Broadcasting Council led to the emergence of a large number of local commercial radio stations and some local commercial television stations.

Decentralization made considerable progress but, especially in the print media, the process of concentration began to regain power as larger chains swallowed up many local newspapers. The resulting consolidation of editors often reduced independence and the ability to cover local developments fully. Local radio largely retained its local character, despite links with regional and national chains that promoted economies of scale. Local commercial television relied heavily on bought-in material and had little ability to finance extensive in-house production. Regional public service radio and television programming, however, played an important role in decentralization.

Besides economic reform, democratization, demonopolization, autonomization, and decentralization, professionalization is also crucial for ensuring free media. While some elements of professionalization were apparent in Poland, the tradition of journalism as politics by other means dies hard.

> Journalists – the great majority of whom were committed politically – have been far from objective. The "civic attitude" inherited from the past [when under the communist system one had to take sides in the struggle between communism and democracy] led editors and journalists to do their utmost to promote the cause of their own political camp and its version of reality, rather than to inform objectively and provide a cold and dispassionate (such an attitude was wholly out of the question) analysis of the situation. As a result, the Polish press market has become dominated by politically affiliated journalism masquerading as objective. That was particularly obvious during election campaigns.
>
> (Żakowski 1996: 205)

Many journalists voluntarily represent partisan political viewpoints out of a conviction that their civic responsibility requires them to promote what they personally consider to be the best political course for the country. Professional skills have, on average, remained relatively low. The issue of media professionalism is one area that still needs to be developed if media in Poland are to become truly free and independent. This will also determine their ability to participate in and perhaps promote the ongoing processes of democratic competition and participation, the keys to democratic consolidation.

Zbigniew Brzeziński, the Polish-American political scientist and politician, has identified (1994) three main phases of transition in post-communist countries, which are outlined in Table 10.2. By these criteria and in light of the conflicting evidence for the economic reform, democratization, demonopolization, autonomization, decentralization, and professionalization, at the turn of the century Poland was, but only in some respects, well into its third phase.

The way in which various factors discussed in this section have played out within each of the media sectors will be examined in greater detail below.

Table 10.2 Three phases of post-communist transition

Stage1 (1–5 years): the breakthrough

Political goal – transformation: introduction of rudimentary democracy, free press, an end to one-party rule, development of early coalitions promoting change.
Economic goal – stabilization: elimination of price controls and subsidies; end of collectivization; early, haphazard privatization.
Legal regulation – elimination of arbitrary state control over all areas of life.

Stage 2 (3–10 years): change takes hold

Political goal – transformation to stabilization: new constitution, electoral law, elections, decentralized local government, stable democratic coalition, and new political elite.
Economic goal – stabilization to transformation: banking system, small and medium-scale privatization, demonopolization, and emergence of a new business class.
Legal regulation – legal regulation of ownership and business.

Stage 3 (3–15+ years): emergence of stable democratic order

Political goal – consolidation: emergence of stable political parties; a democratic political culture takes root.
Economic goal – steady economic growth: mass privatization, emergence of capitalist lobby and private enterprise culture.
Legal regulation – emergence of an independent judiciary and a legal culture.

Source: Brzeziński (1994).

Media in Poland at the turn of the century

Print media and its legal background

One important facet of print media freedom, especially with regard to the countries of Central and Eastern Europe, is the degree to which the press was removed from the overt political or economic control of the state. At the point of transition in 1989, there was no question that print media should be fully liberalized and, except for certain isolated cases, post-1989 governments generally followed this policy. In light of this, the independence of those newspapers and periodicals that survived and became established in the competitive market was underpinned by their ability to finance both operations and growth from advertising revenue. The swift development of an advertising market based on rapid economic growth was an important aspect of the establishment of free and independent print media in Poland.

Deregulation

To date, Poland retains its 1984 press law. However, amendments passed in 1989 and 1990 eliminated all constraints on the press. These changes to the law replaced licensing requirements for newspapers and periodicals with registration by the courts. As a result, there were no restrictions on the establishment of private newspapers or on their distribution.

In contrast, however, the amended 1984 press law was inadequate for dealing with new circumstances within the press market, including the presence of foreign capital, media concentration or monopolization of ownership, lack of transparency of ownership, journalistic working conditions, access to information, abuse of journalistic freedom, and so on (Kononiuk 1999). Without satisfactorily addressing these factors in subsequent amendments, the problem of print media concentration remained a distinct possibility.

In April 1990, a special law abolished censorship. Previous to that, in March 1990, another law initiated the dismantling of RSW "Prasa-Książka-Ruch," a huge state publishing conglomerate, formerly controlled by the Communist Party, that served as a control mechanism over print media. Other measures eliminated licensing of printing equipment. The state monopoly over press distribution was abolished in 1988, and a new customs law of 1989 eliminated controls on printed material brought into the country. These measures formed the core of the deregulation of Polish print media.

The law that dismantled RSW ushered in an important stage in the post-communist transformation of the print media in Poland. At its peak, RSW employed nearly 100,000 people and controlled the majority of newspapers and periodicals, all bookshops, and the entire press distribution system. It also incorporated major printing facilities, and some book publishers, as well as news and photographic agencies. Under the 1990 law, the prime minister appointed a liquidation commission to divest all publications and other property and, in the meantime, to manage the assets of the conglomerate. It completed its job by September 1999. When appointed, it assumed control of 178 newspapers and periodicals. Of those, it sold 104, turned seventy-one over to staff cooperatives free of charge, and returned three to the control of the state treasury.[10]

With certain exceptions, the activities of the liquidation commission were the major instance of state involvement in the Polish print media. Under the left-wing government of 1993–1997, state funds were used to support the establishment of a news magazine and a cultural weekly (both subsequently folded). In turn, since the right-wing government returned to power, the ministry of culture used its modest funds to support periodicals with right-wing tendencies. Otherwise, practically all print media were in private hands with no direct government influence.

State control over the major government-owned newspaper of the communist era, *Rzeczpospolita*, also effectively ended during the period of decentralization.[11] In September 1989, the new Solidarity government gave up control and 49 per cent of the stock was sold to Hersant, a French publisher. A Polish state company retained 51 per cent. In 1995, however, Hersant bought another 2 per cent, gaining a total of 51 per cent. This holding was purchased in 1996 by Orkla Media, a Norwegian company, and as of 2000 the state was a minority partner with no effective power to influence the newspaper's editorial policies.

Finally, under a law adopted in 1997, the Polish Press Agency (PAP) gained statutory status (Ustawa 1997b). The statute required the PAP to provide reliable, impartial, and comprehensive information. It also prohibited the agency from falling under the control of any political or economic groups. In 2000, the agency was wholly owned by the state, but under the 1997 legal provisions, up to 49 per cent of its stock was to be sold.[12] The state was to retain 51 per cent of the shares, thereby exercising control over the agency. This translates into a certain measure of political control, but not any real control over information reaching the media or the public, since all other national and international news sources were freely available.

In short, since 1989, there has been more deregulation than new regulation of the print media. The many attempts to draft a new press law have failed. Existing print media legislation has imposed practically no constraints, but by the same token would allow for print media monopolization (potentially limited by competition law), as it contained no safeguards against media concentration. Subsidization and other mechanisms of state economic influence over the commercial print media have been absent.[13]

Freedom of expression and its limits

In 1992, Poland ratified the European Convention for the Protection of Human Rights and Fundamental Freedoms.[14] Article 10 of the convention sets the European standard for the protection of freedom of expression. Article 54 of Poland's new constitution contains a shorter version of this provision: (1) Everyone shall have the right to express their opinions as well as to receive and impart information. (2) Pre-publication censorship of the media of social communication and the licensing of the press shall be banned. A statute may require the licensing of radio or television stations. In addition, Article 14 of the new constitution reads: "The Republic of Poland guarantees the freedom of the press and of other means of social communication" (Konstytucja Rzeczypospolitej Polskiej 1997). By these two measures, freedom of expression had been formally enshrined within Polish law.

Other pertinent legislation included a new criminal code, which entered into force on 1 January 1998 and contains generally liberalized provisions on freedom of expression (Ustawa 1997a). Nonetheless, Polish human rights advocates maintained that the criminal code was not fully synchronized with European standards, particularly with the case law of the European Court of Human Rights.[15] Human rights groups also asserted that remaining limits to freedom of expression found in this legislation were excessive and disproportionate. Politicians, officials, and businesses used the criminal code to "protect their good name." In certain cases, courts issued temporary injunctions, banning publication of stories or information gathered regarding a particular person or company. Such actions were decried as a form of censorship.

Further, Article 23 of the Polish civil code states that individual personal rights such as honor are protected by civil law irrespective of the protection afforded by other legislation. Article 448 of the civil code reads:

> In case of violation of personal rights, the court may, in addition to ordering actions required to redress the offence, adjudge in favour of the injured person an appropriate sum of money as damages for the wrong he/she suffered, or at his/her request adjudge an appropriate sum of money in favour of some social purpose specified by him/her.
>
> (Ustawa 1996)

Thus, injured persons may potentially claim high damages, maliciously bankrupting newspapers found guilty of such practices. Abused by politicians, individuals, or companies, this provision could have a chilling effect on the press; however, the courts have refrained from awarding punitively high damages in such cases.

In this connection, the State Secrets Act (1982) allows for the prosecution of citizens who publish or otherwise disclose state secrets (Ustawa 1982). Human rights groups have criticized this law on the grounds that it restricts the right to free speech. Article 5.1 states: "The obligation to keep state secrets is binding upon everyone who has come into the possession of such information." Through this act, civil servants, military and security personnel, journalists, and all other citizens are duty-bound not to reveal state secrets and may be prosecuted for doing so. Journalists could be refused information by civil servants or public officials on this basis and there is no judicial recourse available to verify claims that a civil servant is protecting a state secret.

The new criminal code, however, has further regulated the protection of journalistic sources. The code grants news sources absolute protection, except in cases involving national security, murder, or terrorist acts. Statutory provisions are applied retroactively if their terms are beneficial to the accused. Journalists who refused to divulge sources prior to the new code's enactment could avoid sanctions by invoking "journalistic privilege."

Poland has accepted a wide range of international obligations in the field of human rights that importantly influenced the press. The country is signatory to the International Covenant on Civil and Political Rights (1976), including its first Optional Protocol, which came into force in 1992.[16] Further, it has accepted the right of individual petition as of 1 May 1993, as well as the jurisdiction of the European Court of Human Rights in all matters concerning interpretation and application of the convention.

In its capacity as a participating state in the Organization for Security and Cooperation in Europe (OSCE), Poland has accepted many additional international commitments.[17] These include the 1975 Helsinki Final Act, the 1990 Charter of Paris for a New Europe, the 1990 Copenhagen Document, and the 1994 Budapest Document.

On international norms, Article 91 of the Polish constitution stipulates:

> (1) An international treaty, once it has been ratified and published in the *Dziennik Ustaw* (Official Gazette), shall constitute an integral part of the Polish legal framework and shall be applied directly, unless its implementation requires the adoption of a statute. (2) An international agreement, once it has been ratified, shall take precedence over a statute, if it cannot be reconciled with the statute. (3) If an international agreement founding an international organisation and ratified by the Polish Republic so determines, the legislation passed by that organisation shall be applied directly and shall take precedence over Polish statutes where they cannot be reconciled.
>
> (Konstytucja Rzeczypospolitej Polskiej 1997)

Thus, any international agreements to which Poland has acceded form part of the country's legal framework and directly impact the Polish media.

Implications of the legal structure

On balance, the Polish legal structure has effectively deregulated the print media over the course of the past decade and has ensured that it is free of both political and state economic control in its ownership structures. Officially and effectively, print media content has also been deregulated and removed from political or state economic interference. International norms and conventions have further buttressed commitment to print media freedom and independence in this area.

In terms of freedom of expression, however, areas of "inappropriate structuration" have persisted. Although such mechanisms have not been implemented, their presence has constituted a clear mechanism through which political control could re-emerge to threaten print media autonomy.

Print media diversity

A second important aspect of print media freedom and independence is the creation of a diverse media space. Following the depoliticization of the print media and the collapse of hundreds of new titles established by political parties, trade unions, and various organizations after 1989, private enterprise was the sole remaining force in Poland within the print media market.[18]

In 1998, the press in Poland included seventy-six daily publications and 195 weeklies. The degree of concentration in at least one sector of the press market was indicated by the fact that the total print-runs of general interest daily newspapers amounted to 2.5 million copies on weekdays and almost 5 million copies on weekends in the third quarter of 1998. Of the daily circulation of 2.5 million, nearly 1.6 million (that is, 61 per cent) were published by three press groups: Polskapresse, controlled by Neue Passauer Presse of Germany, Agora SA, and Orkla Media AS, a Norwegian company.

The liquidation commission of the RSW conglomerate admitted in its final report that it had failed to create a press system accurately reflecting the pluralism of Polish society. However, the assumption that it could do so while undertaking privatization of the conglomerate at the same time was unrealistic. The commission neither had the power to set up newspapers nor could it support papers facing extinction in order to promote press pluralism. Given the tendency toward media concentration, the almost total deregulation of the press, and the absence of barriers to foreign direct investment (in expectation of accession to the European Union), there was little the commission could do to promote diversity once newspapers and periodicals were privatized and market mechanisms took over. As a result:

> The dailies in most cases speak for and are addressed to the intelligentsia. There is no really national newspaper or periodical that the largest social group, that is, the workers, could call their own. Even left-wing newspapers are those of the left-wing intelligentsia. Also small businessmen, regarded as the core of the "new Polish middle class," have

no press of their own [. . .] It is debatable whether the farmers recognize
any newspapers as really speaking for them.

(Jerschina 1994: 13)

As elsewhere in Central and Eastern Europe, though no state-owned print
media survived in Poland, other titles inherited from communist times survived
into the new era, while new titles found survival very difficult.

Another aim of the liquidation commission during privatization and the lifting
of restrictions on foreign ownership was to prevent the overall takeover by
foreign (especially German) capital. When foreign offers to buy publications were
considered, preference was often given to French over German capital.[19] In the
process, the Polish press market was de-concentrated and undercapitalized to
such an extent (with most privatized titles becoming separate companies) that
many publications became ripe for takeover and found it hard to compete with
new foreign publications entering the Polish market. Among the ninety leading
publishing houses analyzed in late 1998, foreign owners wholly or partly
controlled forty-one. Of these, fifteen had exclusively foreign owners.[20]

Although ostensibly diverse, the Polish print media sector faced the possibility
that press pluralism based on liberalization and market competition would be
undermined by the lack of measures to address private or corporate
concentration. Particularly important to this process was the influx of foreign
capital that was in a better position to compete for media space. Therefore, in the
long term, media freedom and independence may shrink rather than expand.

Broadcasting media in Poland

The legal background

At the end of the 1990s, the 1992 Broadcasting Act was still the major piece of
legislation regulating broadcasting in Poland (Ustawa 1993). This law established
the National Broadcasting Council as the main regulatory authority. In
consultation with the prime minister, it was charged to formulate general state
policy in the broadcasting sector but remained effectively outside governmental
structure. The council was made up of nine members who held office for six years
and could not be reappointed.[21] They directly elected their own chairman and
were barred from holding either political party office or parliamentary seats.

The Broadcasting Act determined the status of public broadcasters, the
licensing of commercial broadcasters, the programming obligations of public and
commercial broadcasters, advertising and sponsoring, registration of
retransmission of program services by cable operators, and the collection and
distribution of broadcasting fees.

Licensing was a special administrative procedure based on the Broadcasting
Act and the administrative procedural code. The license authorized program
distribution as well as televised text communications. In the licensing process, the
council evaluated the type of proposed programming, the applicant's ability to
make the necessary investment, the share of the broadcaster's own programming
in transmission time, and past observance of broadcasting regulations. The
council was obliged to examine the overall position of the applicant within the

mass media market, refusing the license if the applicant held a dominant position. This assessment was to include the press market and programming production. The council also determined the licensee and the conditions of the license. The president of the council issued the formal licensing decision, which could be contested before the Supreme Administrative Court.[22]

Articles 15 and 18 of the Broadcasting Act determined content requirements. The most significant, in 2000, was the domestic production quota, which may not be lower than 30 per cent of the annual transmission time according to Article 15.1. The exact amount of domestic production for specific types of program services was determined by the Broadcasting Council Regulation of 22 September 1993 (*Dziennik Ustaw* 1993b). The quotas were differentiated and ranged from 60 per cent for nationwide public television program services to 35 per cent for program services transmitted via cable or satellite. The independent production quota stood at 10 per cent of annual transmission time and affected all broadcasters according to Article 15.2. Finally, the broadcasting council, under authority of the Broadcasting Act, introduced a European production quota.[23]

The act also stated that the broadcasting council chairman must register retransmission of program services by cable systems if they meet formal requirements determined by the Broadcasting Act and the council's regulations concerning registration procedures, model registers, and registration fees (*Dziennik Ustaw* 1993a). Under must-carry regulations, the cable operator was required to introduce the program service in the following order: (1) national public program services; (2) regional public program services; (3) commercial domestic program services available in a given area; (4) foreign broadcaster programming and domestic programming not available in the area.

The Broadcasting Act also made the following provisions for the allocation of national broadcasting airtime. Under Article 21, public broadcasters monitored appearances of political party representatives in their programming and sought to preserve a rough balance corresponding to that particular party's performance in the previous elections. Under Article 22, the president, prime minister, and speakers of the Sejm (parliament) and Senat (senate) could request airtime for an occasional address to the general public. In Article 23, the National Broadcasting Council issued a regulation instructing public broadcasters to transmit programs devoted to the discussion of current issues with the participation of the main governing and opposition parties. Pursuant to Article 24, public broadcasters were to allot free airtime to candidates in presidential, general, or local government elections, under rules laid down in acts of parliament. The State Electoral Commission supervised their performance in this respect.

Licenses were granted under the act in Article 35 to Polish citizens or legal entities resident in Poland. Companies with foreign shareholders could be granted licenses if foreigners controlled less than 33 per cent of opening capital or stock in the company and the initial agreement or statutes of the company specified the following: (a) Polish resident citizens constitute a majority of the directorate and management boards of the company in question; and (b) foreign legal entities or entities controlled by them control less than 33 per cent of votes in meetings of partners or in general meetings of shareholders. In other words, outright foreign ownership and control of Polish broadcast media was prohibited by law. Some stations did, however, have foreign co-owners, as will be discussed in further detail below.

Nevertheless, given the size and commercial attractiveness of the Polish broadcasting market, some television stations chose "delocalization," establishing themselves in other countries in order to evade the Polish ownership restrictions and production quotas and take advantage of a more liberal local broadcasting environment (for instance, with regard to European quotas). For example, Wizja TV established itself in the United Kingdom where, among other things, it has not been obligated to comply with the European quota. However, in the year 2000 Wizja TV applied for Polish licenses both as the operator of a digital satellite platform and as the broadcaster of two original channels offered on this platform (Wizja 1 and Wizja Sport). This meant that it had decided to subordinate itself to Polish jurisdiction and by all accounts intended to move its operations to Poland.

Delocalization led to a debate in Poland over whether to raise the cap on foreign capital involvement in anticipation of accession to the European Union, when all limits to European capital have to be eliminated. Such a policy may encourage "delocalized" broadcasters to relocate themselves in Poland. For political reasons, however, such changes were rejected by parliament in 1998.

In autumn 1999, the government submitted another set of Broadcasting Act amendments to parliament; again they proposed that caps on foreign capital involvement be increased. The proposal was for the limit to be raised to 49 per cent for terrestrial broadcasters and to 100 per cent for satellite and cable broadcasters. Some commentators believe that this is a direct result of lobbying by Wizja TV, which has both satellite channels and a large cable operation. However, parliament rejected any changes, though it is aware that no limits on foreign capital involvement can remain once Poland has joined the European Union.

In terms of political infringements, if public broadcasters deviate from political impartiality or neutrality, they do so either because of the political leanings of particular program makers or because of the composition of their governing bodies, and not as a result of direct outside political interference. Nevertheless, certain problems did persist in the implementation of the Broadcasting Act. In particular, successive Polish presidents and governments have been loath to accept the independence of the National Broadcasting Council or of a public service broadcaster, generally. Attempts have been made to interfere in (TVP) operations and to curtail its independence.

In 1994, President Wałęsa dismissed the chairman and two other members of the council for granting a national commercial television license to an applicant he disfavored.[24] The Constitutional Tribunal later ruled that the president had acted without legal authorization. Consequently, the Broadcasting Act was amended to provide for the direct election of the council chairman by its members, instead of by presidential appointment. Measures were also introduced to prevent recall of council members.

Another instance of political interference occurred in January 2000 when the chairman and one of the Polish Radio board members were dismissed. Both had been Polish Peasants' Party (PSL) representatives who apparently displeased their political masters. The party forged a coalition in the supervisory board to have the two dismissed and replaced with other PSL appointees. This coalition brought together representatives of the PSL, their previous coalition partner, the Sojusz Lewicy Demokratycznej (SLD), and the AWS.[25] The rationale behind the AWS's collusion lay in that party's need for the PSL's support in promoting an AWS parliamentary candidate to a public post. This deal was widely condemned as a political game of musical chairs with no concern for the public interest.

The ministry of telecommunications and its agencies, which collaborate with the National Broadcasting Council in the allocation of frequencies and in determining technical aspects of station operations, too, have often delayed procedures in order to complicate council operations. Since no legal mechanism existed to control the National Broadcasting Council, governments made every effort to marginalize it and to limit its influence.

The finance minister and later the state treasury minister have occasionally dismissed supervisory board members or entire boards, even though such actions are without legal basis.[26] Since corporate law also governed public service broadcasters, ministers have invoked its provisions to dismiss members in spite of a constitutional tribunal ruling that members of these supervisory boards should not be recalled during their three-year terms.

Since 1997, the state treasury minister has tried to stop TVP from entering the digital television field. The general meeting of shareholders has, for example, passed a resolution instructing the management board not to establish thematic digital channels. The management board, in turn, has taken the matter to court, requesting that the resolution be dismissed.

Having no other recourse to influence TVP development or to alter its governing bodies, the treasury minister has considered the possibility of liquidation, with the appointment of a liquidator to run the state broadcaster. To date, however, this action has not been taken.

As the new century began, however, a new attempt by the government to change TVP's status and method of financing appeared possible. These measures were ostensibly to depoliticize the broadcaster, but in reality they served to weaken it. The plan, spelled out in draft amendments to the Broadcasting Act prepared for the state treasury minister, called for ownership rights to TVP and Polish Radio to be transferred to state universities, with some shares also to be held by local government bodies and the ministry of culture. The shareholders, the state treasury minister, the National Broadcasting Council, and the employees would appoint members of the supervisory boards. Board members would be appointed by the universities, with one person each to be appointed by local government bodies and by the culture minister.

Under the proposal, one national channel would have been closed to advertising, but would have been compensated by commercial television levies that would have been channeled into a fund used to commission or buy programming for TVP in line with its public service mandate. After two years, this programming would then become freely available to stations contributing to the fund. The stations would also have been granted access to TVP's archives. The proposal, however, remains highly controversial.

Under the structure at the time of writing, public broadcasters were financed from both license fee revenue and advertising. There were practically no state subsidies for public service broadcasters, apart from funds earmarked by the ministry of education for educational programming on the national channels. Private broadcasters were financed entirely from advertising revenue.

Plans were being mooted that would involve state companies as shareholders in a new production company, Telewizja Familijna (Family Television), which would operate a nationwide Catholic television channel. The company license was held by the Franciscan brotherhood, which previously operated the local channel, Niepokalanów TV. Niepokalanów TV programming was to be transformed into a satellite-to-cable channel and existing and future terrestrial frequencies were to be taken over by Telewizja Familijna. This process was to be financed by a number of state companies (from the copper, oil and power industries to the state insurance company) and two foreign media corporations whose identity has not yet been disclosed. One is reportedly European, the other American.

A former media adviser to the prime minister developed this project. Given the significant role played by Radio Maryja in mobilizing support for the right-wing AWS during the 1997 election, this project may also be interpreted politically as a way of countering the perceived influence of TVP.[27] When media revealed this project, however, a number of state firms indicated uncertainty as to whether they would indeed invest in the new station.

In addition to the domestic Broadcasting Act, there are a number of international agreements and conventions which affected the audio-visual sector, for example, the Europe Agreement establishing an association between Poland and the European Community, the European Convention on Transfrontier Television, and international copyright conventions.

The general parity of Polish broadcasting regulations with the European Convention on Transfrontier Television resulted largely from the adoption and implementation of the Broadcasting Act. Polish regulations also generally comply with the requirements contained in the European Union's Television Without Frontiers Directive of 3 October 1989.[28] A comparison of the main areas of European and Polish broadcasting regulation indicates that only a few domestic regulations need amendment to harmonize with European standards.[29]

Broadcasting diversity

(TVP) is a public service broadcaster composed of a corporate center in Warsaw that, in 2000, employed approximately 4,200 people and twelve regional stations that employed approximately 2,600 people. TVP broadcasts on two nationwide channels (Channel 1 broadcasts twenty hours a day and reaches 97 per cent of Polish television viewers; Channel 2 broadcasts seventeen hours a day and reaches 96 per cent of viewers) and a satellite channel, TV Polonia, targeted at Poles living abroad.[30]

Under the Broadcasting Act, the nineteen public broadcasters founded in January 1994 functioned as single-person joint stock companies of the state treasury.[31] The state treasury minister, whose powers were considerably limited, especially in comparison with commercial companies, represented the state in the company's general assembly. Despite their formal status, public service broadcasters were controlled neither by parliament nor by the government. The general assembly was legally prohibited from influencing programming content.

Also, it appointed only one out of nine members of the public radio and television supervisory boards; the National Broadcasting Council appoints the remaining eight. The public broadcaster supervisory boards appointed their own boards of management.

These and other measures limited or precluded any direct interference into the operation of public broadcasters by the state. However, because the process of appointing members of the respective supervisory bodies (National Broadcasting Council, supervisory boards, and management boards) was unavoidably political and their composition was sometimes politically lopsided, such indirect interference provoked prolonged controversies and politicized public debate concerning their role and performance. As it happens, political opponents of the government of the day have controlled TVP since 1994.[32]

The main commercial television station was POLSAT, whose main terrestrial channel covered some 69 per cent of the country's territory and potentially reached 80 per cent of the population.[33] It was unashamedly commercial and entertainment-oriented in its approach. It also had a second satellite channel and was in the process of launching its own digital platform that would include digital thematic channels. This was the third digital platform launched in Poland.

POLSAT acquired 51 per cent of Baltijos TV and reportedly planned on buying into Latvian and Estonian television stations.[34] There are reports of POLSAT's possible interest in the cable television market. The possibility of its buying out the Dami company which operates cable systems serving some 110,000 subscribers across fourteen towns has been cited (Siemieniec 2000). POLSAT also operated what may be termed an "incipient" digital satellite platform, known as Cyfra POLSAT, composed of six thematic channels, available via cable or via decoders distributed among members enrolled in its pension fund. Plans were announced which called for these and other channels to be put on a digital satellite platform in 2000.

The second most influential commercial station was TVN, a sub-national station, owned exclusively by ITI Holdings, a Polish–Irish concern, following CME's sale of its stake to its former partner.[35] TVN reached some 13.5 per cent of the territory and potentially 30 per cent of the population.

Next, mention must be made of RTL7, a delocalized satellite channel, owned in 2000 by CLT which uplinks from Luxembourg.[36] Another sub-national Polish station has been TV 4, owned by a consortium of Polish businessmen, which covered 9.3 per cent of the country's territory and potentially reaches 16 per cent of the population. Canal Plus Polska, which broadcasts a terrestrial encoded pay-TV service, was also an important player in the Polish broadcasting market. Its owners were Canal Plus France (33 per cent), Polcom Invest Poland (36 per cent), ACTV (20 per cent), and Bank Handlowy (11 per cent).[37] Canal Plus Polska covered 7.3 per cent of the country's territory and could be received by 27.4 per cent of the population.

In estimating the geographical reach of all of these broadcasters, it must be noted that some 30 per cent of Polish households received cable television and approximately 19 per cent had satellite dishes by 2000. As a result, broadcasting via satellite could extend its reach quite considerably. It was with these viewers in mind that foreign broadcasters launched either new satellite channels or made Polish-language translations of popular Western programming (including

Eurosport, Planete, Animal Planet, Discovery, Travel, National Geographic, Fox Kids, Hallmark, TCM).

Wizja TV, a digital bouquet licensed in the United Kingdom and beamed to Poland via satellite, primarily pursued such developments. This conglomerate was owned by the American firm, @Entertainment, which also controlled PTK, a cable television system with nearly a million subscribers across many parts of Poland. Both were then sold to the Amsterdam-based United Pan Europe Communications NV (UPC), 62 per cent of which is owned by United International Holdings Inc. in the United States.

Market shares of commercial broadcasters in 1998 are presented in Table 10.3. As noted, public broadcasters controlled 53.7 per cent of the total Polish market share. Within a decade of transition, however, the private market was able to capture 46.3 per cent of the market. This represented an important achievement in the development of a media free market in Poland.

On public service channels, foreign programming accounted for nearly one third of broadcasts. In the first half of 1999, foreign programming accounted for 32 per cent of airtime on TVP1 and 31 per cent on TVP2. The origins of this programming are given in Table 10.4.

Foreign programming constituted a much higher share of airtime for commercial broadcasters: 60 per cent on TVN and Canal Plus and some 74 per cent on Nasza TV. Foreign films accounted for 48 per cent of broadcasts on TVP in the first half of 1998. Across three commercial stations the category accounted for 78 per cent of all broadcasts.

Cable broadcasters also made a strong showing in the Polish market over the last decade of transition. The National Broadcasting Council issued some 250 licenses to cable television operators. Many of these cable channels provided local news in addition to general entertainment, thereby offering their subscribers an alternative news source.

Table 10.3   Market shares of TV channels in Poland, 1998

Channel	Market share (%)
TVP1	30.4
POLSAT 1	24.7
TVP2	18.0
TVN	5.8
TVP: regional stations	5.3
RTL7	3.6
TV Polonia	1.5
Polsat 2	1.5
Nasza TV	1.4
Others	7.8

Source: National Broadcasting Council.

Table 10.4 Foreign programming on national broadcasting channels in Poland, 1998

TVP1 (%)		TVP2 (%)	
US	53	US	40
UK	13	UK	21
France	7	France	9
Australia	5	Australia	5
Italy	5	Canada	3
Other	17	Other	21

Source: TVP.

Radio broadcasting diversity

Broadcasting diversity has been an issue for Polish radio at the beginning of the twenty-first century, also. In the process of transforming the old Radio and which had been controlled by the Communist Party into public service broadcasters, was separated from TVP. broadcast across four national channels, one external channel, and seventeen regional public radio channels. Each of these seventeen stations was a separate state-owned company, with governing bodies and systems of ownership and management identical to those of national public service television broadcasters.

There were two commercial radio stations that broadcast nationally, Radio Zet (Warsaw) and RMF FM (Kraków). Radio Zet had a geographical coverage of 80 per cent and reached 90 per cent of the listening population. Its musical programming was described as "adult contemporary/European hit radio." The station devoted 25 per cent of airtime to news and current affairs. In 2000, two private individuals held 62 per cent of its stock and Europa Development International, France, held the remaining 38 per cent. RMF FM, in contrast, covered 86 per cent of the country's territory and reached 79 per cent of the population. Its service was also available via satellite in some European countries and in parts of the United States. News and current affairs accounted for 14 per cent of its airtime and its musical format was described as "contemporary hit radio, adult oriented rock, and classic rock." Kraków Foundation for Social Communication was its owner. Radio Maryja, a Catholic radio network run by the Redemptorist Fathers was another important private broadcaster, with a geographical coverage of 63 per cent and reaching 74 per cent of the population. It devoted up to 50 per cent of airtime to strictly religious programming and some 15 per cent to news and current affairs. It appealed to an older, more conservative and traditional-minded audience and, having proved increasingly capable of influencing public opinion, was very influential as the spokesperson for this social group. In addition, there was a Catholic radio network of twenty-three stations operated by individual dioceses that devoted part of their airtime to programming provided by the production house Radio Plus, both operating under the auspices of the Roman Catholic church. Some twenty other local Catholic stations also broadcast regularly.

Apart from the large number of private local radio stations owned by a variety of individuals and companies, there were also a few regional or sub-regional radio networks, including Radio WAWA, owned by its Polish founders and Modular Investment Ltd, Ireland; Radiostacja, co-owned by the Polish Scouts and Group P4, Norway; and Tok FM, a news-and-talk station owned by a number of Polish and foreign companies.

The Polish public service radio broadcasters owned a much higher proportion of market share than was the case with television. On average, 73 per cent of the Polish population listens to one of the "Polish Radio" stations in a given week. Yet individually, the most popular commercial stations, RMF FM and Radio Zet are, respectively, only 3.5 per cent and 11.4 per cent behind the national average of listener numbers. The case can be argued that true quantitative diversity has been achieved in Polish radio broadcasting. Commercial radio broadcasters have been able to attract audience and finance at levels that ensure their competitiveness with the Polish national radio broadcasters.

The Polish broadcast media and civil society

In public opinion polls, Polish Radio Plc and Polish Television Plc were at, or close to, the top of the list of public institutions that enjoyed the greatest credibility among the general public in 2000. Right-wing politicians, unhappy with the political composition of the governing bodies of these institutions (dominated by representatives of the left), accused them of a left-wing bias. The broadcasters' news and current affairs programs, however, adequately reflected the broad diversity of political opinion in Polish public life.

The commercial and private broadcasting media, too, represent a wide diversity of interests. Purely commercial broadcasters do not usually devote much time to news or current affairs programming and tend to steer away from taking political sides. Some radio stations have been co-financed by local governmental bodies and could be susceptible to their political influence, depending on the composition of those bodies. In contrast, the church-affiliated radio stations usually tend to represent a right-wing audience.

A number of organizations, both civil and professional, have formed around issues in the broadcasting media. Recently, for instance, the Association for the Protection of Viewers and Listeners became active in Poland. Founded mostly by Catholic activists, its main focus was to combat sex, violence, and pornographic materials in broadcasting, especially on television. In February 1999, in cooperation with the National Broadcasting Council, television broadcasters concluded their own professional agreement entitled "Friendly Media." This agreement comprised a set of rules for protecting minors against violence, sex, and pornography in the broadcasting media.

Polish Television has developed its own code of professional practice for reporters and journalists working for news, current affairs, and documentary programs. This code had its own board, elected from among employees, which administers the code. A similar system obtains for .

As a result, although not overwhelming, the level of activity within the civil society and professional sectors of broadcasting media has been noteworthy. As civil society as a whole develops, it is anticipated that such activity will gradually increase, perhaps helping to shape the broadcast media in Poland.

Media reform, democratization and civil society

Under the communist system, the emerging civil society clearly desired freedom of speech and free media. Solidarity representatives at the historic April 1989 roundtable between representatives of this popular grouping and the communist regime voiced such demands. Their agreement paved the way for liberalization of the press, but allowed the authorities to maintain control over broadcasting. The demise of the communist system was necessary for true media freedom.

A primary role has been played by those involved in the underground press and "Solidarity" radio during the martial law period (1981–1983). Following 1989, they contributed to planning media reform, developing new media, and encouraging a new journalistic style – both for good and bad. Their clear political commitment and combative style of journalism (viewed as politics by other means) have impeded media differentiation to some degree. The current lack of differentiation is now less the result of administrative or political control over the media than of the political orientation of media owners and their staff.

Since the collapse of communism, public opinion has followed developments in the media with considerable interest. It has also expressed its views (via the media themselves and public opinion polls) regarding the turn media reform has taken. However, civil society in Poland was still weak at the time of this research. It had relatively little active influence on the legislative process or on systemic changes in the media. The majority of activity in the 1990s took in the political sphere, which was largely the result of calculations by political actors. The market conditions prevailing in the Polish media, however, often left the final verdict to the consumer. For instance, a great number of party and trade union publications that emerged after 1989 soon went out of business, having failed to win the interest and support of the public. The numerous journalistic and media professional associations sought to make their voices heard in the process of media change, but their inability to present a united front weakened their hand and reduced what influence they might have had.

Yet media contributed to a slow process of civil society maturation. Print media in Poland has been financially successful on the whole and not dependent on state authorities for funding. Therefore, the press has been able to perform its watchdog function (all the difficulties of investigative journalism notwithstanding) and gradually bolster public confidence in the fact that politicians and state officials are not immune to criticism and must answer for any mistakes or abuses. There have been spectacular public cases of cabinet ministers and other officials being dismissed or resigning following press exposures of their wrongdoings.

This process contributed to a re-establishment of the balance between the state and civil society, which is indispensable in order for civil society to operate properly. Following a period of state and political party omnipotence, civil society began, though slowly, to reassert itself, and this is due in large part to media.

Theoretical approach and assessment

The picture presented by this discussion indicates that Poland proceeded quite far under certain assessments of the media reform process during the 1990s. Demonopolization and decentralization were largely achieved and both institutionally and economically, the Polish media found themselves freer and more independent than they have been throughout much of the twentieth century.

At the conclusion of the decade, other issues, however, still begged resolution if this progress was to be maintained. These have included the danger of consolidated corporate economic control over the media and the lack of media professionalization, an aspect closely tied into the development of Polish civil society. The Polish media, as a profession, must relinquish political ties and the partisan nature of the relationship with the state and with Polish society that developed over the course of communist rule. Otherwise, media will inevitably remain the tool of various political and economic interests, rather than a neutral commentator.

The course that the Polish media reform takes in the future, whether in support of further democratization or against democratic development, is yet to be seen. The foundations that have been laid, however, provide a stable base for future growth.

Notes

1 Tadeusz Mazowiecki was prime minister from 12 September 1989 to 14 December 1990. Jan Krzysztof Bielecki who served from 12 January 1991 to 27 October 1991 followed him. Jan Olszewski took over on 23 December 1991 and held office until 4 June 1992. Finally, Hanna Suchocka took up the prime minister's post on 11 July 1992 and was defeated in a vote of no confidence on 28 May 1993, bringing about new parliamentary elections later that year. Two prospective prime ministers also failed to form governments during this period, Bronisław Geremek in November 1991 and Waldemar Pawlak in June 1992.
2 The SLD (Sojusz Lewicy Demokratycznej) represented a grouping of nearly thirty political parties and movements, led by the Social Democratic Party of the Polish Republic (Socjaldemokracja Rzeczpospolitej Polskiej or SdRP), formed after the dissolution of the Polish Communist Party (Polska Zjednoczona Partia Robotnicza or PZPR). The PSL is a successor to the United Peasant's Party (Zjednoczone Stronnictwo Ludowe or ZSL), one-time client of the PZPR and an integral part of the system of government in communist times.
3 The SdRP is the leading partner in the SLD coalition (see note 2).
4 Akcja Wyborcza "Solidarność" (Electoral Action "Solidarity").
5 These reforms have been targeted at administration, education, healthcare, and pensions.
6 For a discussion of the concept of "political capitalism," see Sasińska-Klas (1996).
7 These four players include the AWS, the SLD, the PSL, and the UW (Unia Wolności or Freedom Union).
8 This reform encompassed placing strict limits on public spending, including pay rises in the public sector, raising interest rates, limiting bank credits, creating internal convertibility of the Polish currency, liberalizing foreign trade, liberalizing pricing structures, and privatizing the economy.
9 Broadcasters in this category serve groups or communities overlooked by public service or commercial broadcasters.
10 The commission gave preference to groups emerging out of "Solidarity" which represented a wide spectrum of political orientations. It also allowed the SdRP

(successor to the former Communist Party, see note 3) to buy out some former party newspapers. Periodicals turned over free of charge to cooperatives were made possible by the above-mentioned law.

11 This was, itself, a rarity at a time when most newspapers were controlled directly by the Communist Party.

12 The treasury minister appoints the supervisory board that in turn appoints the managerial board.

13 The ministry of culture does, however, provide financial support to a number of non-commercial cultural periodicals, a few on an ongoing basis and the rest through competitive grants.

14 This convention came into force on 19 January 1993. See http://www.coe.fr/eng/legaltxt/5e.htm

15 According to these human rights advocates, inconsistencies include: Article 133: "Whoever publicly insults the Polish Nation or the Republic of Poland shall be subject to the penalty of deprivation of liberty for up to 3 years;" Article 135.2: "Whoever publicly insults the President of the Republic of Poland shall be subject to the penalty of deprivation of liberty for up to 3 years;" Article 137.1: "Whoever publicly insults, destroys, damages, or removes an emblem, banner, standard, ensign, flag or other symbol of the Polish State shall be subject to a penalty of a fine, limitation of liberty or deprivation of liberty for up to 1 year;" Article 226.3: "Whoever publicly insults or degrades a constitutional organ of the Republic of Poland shall be subject to the penalty of a fine, limitation of freedom or deprivation of freedom for up to 2 years;" Article 226.1: "Whoever insults a public functionary or a person called upon to assist him, in the course or in connection with, the performance of official duties, shall be subject to the penalty of a fine, limitation of liberty or deprivation of liberty for up to 1 year;" Article 256: "Whoever publicly propagates fascism or any other totalitarian state system or incites to hatred for reasons of nationality, ethnicity, race, religion or against non-believers shall be subject to the penalty of a fine, limitation of liberty or deprivation of liberty for up to 2 years;" Article 257; "Whoever publicly insults a group of people or an individual person by reason of their nationality, ethnicity, race, religion or for having no religious affiliation, or for these reasons does bodily harm to another person, shall be subject to the penalty of deprivation of liberty for up to 3 years."

16 http://www.tufts.edu/departments/fletcher/multi/texts/BH498.txt

17 Previously the Conference on Security and Cooperation in Europe (CSCE).

18 At the end of 1991, there were an estimated 2,000 press titles in Poland, 1,300 of which had first appeared between 1989 and 1991.

19 Six dailies were sold to the French company, Hersant.

20 Foreign investors involved in those ninety publishing houses come from Germany (eight companies), Switzerland (four), the Netherlands (three companies), the United States (two), Italy (two), Norway (one) and France (three companies with shares in one publishing house).

21 Four members are appointed by the Sejm, two by the Senat, and three by the president.

22 Radio licenses are issued for a maximum of seven years while television licenses are granted for up to ten years.

23 Reception of domestic and foreign programming, intended by broadcasters for the general public, is free by law. There are no legal instruments that can be used to prohibit or restrict the freedom of reception of all available program services.

24 The president had previously directly appointed all three, himself.

25 Sojusz Lewicy Demokratycznej (Democratic Left Alliance).

26 The finance minister originally represented the state treasury in general meetings with public service broadcaster shareholders. The Broadcasting Act describes the manner of appointment, but says nothing about the eventuality of dismissal.

27 Radio Maryja is a nationwide Catholic radio network.

28 http://europa.eu.int/comm/dg10/avpolicy/twf/newinten.html

29 1. Freedom of reception and retransmission is guaranteed constitutionally. Article 1.2. of the Broadcasting Act (hereinafter "BA") and by-rules on unconditional registration of retransmissions in cable networks that meet the requirement of must-carry rules and basic technical standards address this area in national law.

2. Provision of information by broadcasters meets with European standards upon the institution of a regulatory authority endowed with necessary instruments for the authorization of broadcasters (BA, Articles 21–26).

3. Polish regulations are compatible with the Convention and the EU Directive as regards (Annex I provides a table which juxtaposes provisions of the EU Directive with corresponding Polish legal provisions).

4. Content requirements: (a) Pornography (Criminal Code, Article 173; BA, Article 18.1), (b) Violence (BA, Article 18.1.2.; Broadcasting Council Regulation 1995/20/108 (details principles of dissemination of programming likely to impair physical, mental or moral development of children), (c) Protection of children (BA, Article 18.3; Broadcasting Council Regulation 1995/20/108), (d) Fair presentation of facts, free formation of opinions is supported by constitutional freedom of speech, Press Law regulations (Article 12.1.1) determining journalists' obligations concerning gathering and using materials for publication and BA, Article 21 on reliable information and promotion of unconstrained development of public opinion (however, this applies to public broadcasters alone).

5. The Press Law guarantees the right of reply (chapter 5).

6. Cultural objectives – support of independent producers is addressed in BA, Article 15.2 and in license obligations pertaining to own programming production of broadcaster.

Advertising: (a) General advertising requirements are defined by BA, Article 16 and in the Broadcasting Council Regulation on the principles of advertising in radio and television programs, 1993/204/44 (hereinafter "BCR-93"), (b) Duration of advertising is regulated by BA, Articles 16.2–3, (c) Direct offers to the public are regulated via BCR-93, (d) Form and presentation of advertising (as defined via BA, Article 16 and by BCR-93), (e) Insertion of advertising is regulated by BA, Article 16 and by BCR-93, (f) Advertising of particular products is often more stringently regulated in Poland than in the EU, (g) Protection of minors is secured by Article 16 of the law on unfair competition. Administrative instruments are, however, lacking.

7. Sponsorship: Identification of sponsors is regulated by BA, Article 17.1; Prohibition of sponsor influence over programming content is provided by BA, Article 17.2; Prohibition of sale promotion through sponsoring is contained in BA, Article 4.7 and in the Broadcasting Council Regulation concerning the ban on sponsoring particular program items and particular methods of sponsoring, 1993/91/423 (hereinafter "BCR-93b"); Prohibition of sponsorship by persons manufacturing products, prohibited by BCR-93b.

There are no respective regulations in the following areas or the existing ones are insufficient for harmonization with EU standards: (a) Identification of broadcasters in the program service – there is no broadcasting regulation on this subject, although the problem is resolved on the grounds of voluntary identification; (b) Access to major events – no broadcasting or press regulation cover this, although it is possible to construe the Act on Counteracting Monopolistic Practices in a way which counteracts prohibition of such access; (c) Cinematographic work transmission – due to a lack of broadcasting regulation, the legal protection of producers' rights plays a major role; (d) Definition of "teleshopping" – can be construed from existing regulation, but will be included in new amendments to the Broadcasting Act; (e) Support for European works – the National Broadcasting Council has not yet issued a regulation introducing a European production quota; (f) Definition of EU works – will be included in this regulation. Progress in areas (e) and (f) have been halted by negotiations concerning Poland's accession to the OECD, even though the National Broadcasting Council was ready to move ahead. Once the terms of Poland's accession have been worked out and Poland has been admitted, it will be possible to return to these issues.

30 TV Polonia is on the air twenty-fours hour a day and is seen in Europe, Israel, North Africa, and Kazakhstan via the Eutelsat II F6 13E-Hot Bird satellite and in Canada and the United States in the DBS system via the Orion Atlantic and ECHOSTAR III 61.5W satellites.

31 TVP, "Polish Radio" and seventeen regional public radio stations.

32 TVP was restructured into a public service broadcaster on 1 January 1994.

33 Wholly owned by its founder, a Polish businessman.
34 Baltijos TV is a Lithuanian television station.
35 CME is an American company that had invested in numerous media groups throughout East Central Europe.
36 With the US Universal Studios as co-owner at one point.
37 ACTV is owned by Agora, a company that also owns Gazeta Wyborcza and a number of radio stations. Bank Handlowy is one of Poland's leading banks.

References

This list includes suggestions for further reading as well as material specifically cited in the text.

Alexander, J. C. (1981) "The Mass Media in a Systemic, Historical and Comparative Perspective," in E. Katz, T. Szecsko (eds) *Mass Media and Social Change*. London and Beverly Hills: Sage Publications.
Androunas, E. (1993) *Soviet Media in Transition. Structural and Economic Alternatives*. Westport, Conn.: Praeger.
Balcerowicz, L. (1995) *Socialism, Capitalism, Transition*. Budapest: Central European University Press.
Barnowski, M. (1999) "Stany przedprocesowe" [A Step away from Litigation], *Press*, No. 12.
Bazyler, M. and Pomar, O. (1994) "An Analysis of Mass Media Law in Belarus." Paper prepared for a conference on "The Law of the Press and the Process of Democratization," Minsk, 3–5 May 1994.
Brzeziński, Z. (1994) "Polska scena obrotowa," *Polityka*, No. 44, 29 October.
Bubnicki, R., Rotkiewicz, M., Sadecki, J., and Usidus, M. (1994) "Niemcy przed wszystkimi" [Germans über Alles], *Rzeczpospolita*, 24–25 September.
Budapest Document. Available at: http://heiwww.unige.ch/humanrts/osce/new/budapesttoc.html
Burnetko, K. (1995) "Media a wybory: egzamin, jednak, zaliczony. Z Walerym Pisarkiem rozmawia K. Burnetko," *Tygodnik Powszechny*, No. 50, 10 December: 36.
De Fleur, M. L. and Ball-Rokeach, S. (1982) *Theories of Mass Communication*. White Plains, NY: Longman.
Downing, J. (1996) *Internationalizing Media Theory. Transition, Power, Culture. Reflections on Media in Russia, Poland and Hungary 1980–1995*. London: Sage.
Duch, R. M. and Lemieux, D. H. (1986) "The Political Economy of Communications Development." Paper presented at the ICA Conference, Chicago.
Dziennik Ustaw (Official Gazette) (1993a), No. 79, pos. 375.
—— (1993b), No. 90, pos. 456.
Dziki, Sylwester *et al.* (1998) *Katalog mediów polskich* [Directory of Polish Media] (Kraków: OśrodekBadań Prasoznawczych): 417.
Filas, R. (1999) "Dziesięć lat przemian mediów masowych w Polsce (1989–1999)" [Ten Years of Mass Media Change in Poland (1989–1999)], *Zeszyty Prasoznawcze*, No. 1–2: 30–58.
Glinski, P., and Palska, H. (1997) "Cztery wymiary społecznej aktywności obywatelskiej," in H. Domański and A. Rychard (eds) *Elementy nowego ładu*. Warsaw: Wydawnictwo IFiS PAN.
Grabowska, M. (1995) "Civil Society after 1989 – Rebirth or Death?," in E. Wnuk-Lipiński (ed.) *After Communism. A Multidisciplinary Approach to Radical Social Change*. Warsaw: PAN.
Hamelink, Cees J. (1996) "Media Regulation and Media Independence. Towards a Model Regulatory Regime." Amsterdam: Center for Communication and Human Rights (ms.).
Helsinki Final Act. Available at: http://www.house.gov/csce/finalact.htm
Hollifield, Ann (1993) "The Globalization of Eastern Europe's Print Media: German Investment During the Post-Revolution Era." Paper presented to the 1993 conference of AEJMC, Kansas City, Missouri, 14 August.
Jakubowicz, Karol (1997) "Freedom of Speech in Poland: An Evolving Concept," *The Global Network. Communication and Society in Eastern Europe*, No. 8: 23–52.

—— (1990) "Solidarity and Media Reform in Poland," *European Journal of Communication*, Vol. 5, Nos. 2–3.

Jakubowicz, K. and Jędrzejewski, S. (1988) "Polish Broadcasting: The Choices Ahead," *European Journal of Communication*, Vol. 3, No. 1: 91–112.

Jerschina, J. (1994) "Zwierciadło elit: Etos i profesjonalizm," *Rzeczpospolita*, 29 October.

Johnson, O. V. (1995) "Mass Media and the Velvet Revolution," in J. Popkin (ed.) *Media and Revolution: Comparative Perspectives*. Lexington: University Press of Kentucky: 220–231.

Kasprów, R. (1999) "Wielkie wojny wirtualne" [Great Virtual Wars], *Rzeczpospolita*, 22 December.

Kasprów, R. and Zalewska, L. (1999) "Z nędzy do pieniędzy" [Rags to Riches], *Rzeczpospolita*, 8–9 May.

Katz, E. (1981) "Epilogue: Where Do We Stand?," in E. Katz, and T. Szecsko (eds) *Mass Media and Social Change*. London: Sage Publications.

Kofman, J. and Roszkowski, W. (1999) "Po upadku wieży Babel," *Rzeczpospolita*, 21–22 August.

Kolarska-Bobińska, L. (1998) "Nowa mała stabilizacja," *Polityka*, 21 February: 30–32.

Kononiuk, T. (1999) "Refleksje wokół prawa prasowego," *Forum dziennikarzy*, X–XI.

Konstytucja Rzeczypospolitej Polskiej. Text ratified by the National Assembly on 2 April 1997. Available at: http://www.sejm.gov.pl/prawo/konstytucja/kon1.htm

Korbonski, A. (1994) "Civil Society and Democracy in Poland: Problems and Prospects," in A. Bibic, and G. Graziano (eds) *Civil Society, Political Society, Democracy*: 215–230. Ljubljana: Slovenian Political Science Association.

Król, K. (1999) "Nowa elita," *Wprost. Intermedia*, 12 September.

Kunczik, M. (1984) *Communication and Social Change*. Bonn: Friedrich–Ebert–Stiftung.

Kurczewska, J., Staszyńska, K., and Bajor, H. (1993) "Blokady społeczeństwa obywatelskiego: czyli słabe społeczeństwo obywatelskie i słabe państwo," in A. Rychard and M. Federowicz (ed.) *Społeczeństwo w transformacji. Ekspertyzy i Studia*. Warsaw: PAN.

Lukosiunas, M. (1998) "Is the Transition Over?," *Mass Media Law and Practice. Latvia, Lithuania, Estonia* (Baltic Edition of *Mass Media Law and Practice Bulletin*, Moscow), Issue 6, July. Available at: http://www.medialaw.ru/e_pages/publications/zip/baltic/vil106-1.html

McQuail, D. (1987) *Mass Communication Theory. An Introduction*. London, Newbury Park, Beverly Hills, and New Delhi: Sage Publications.

—— (1994) *Mass Communication Theory. An Introduction*. London: Sage Publications.

Matys, M. (1999–2000) "Solorz na każdy temat" [Solorz on Every Subject], *Gazeta Wyborcza*, 31 December–2 January.

"Poland. Country Report on Human Rights Practices for 1998," Washington: US Department of State. Available at: http:\\www.state.gov\www\global\human_rights\1998_hrp_report\ poland.html, 5 September 1999.

"Prawo vs Media" [The Law vs. The Media] (Warsaw: Centrum Monitoringu Wolności Prasy. Available at: http:\\www.freepress.org.pl, 3 September 1999.

Procesy własnościowe i koncentracja w środkach masowego przekazu [Ownership Trends and Concentration in the Media]. Report by a panel appointed by the prime minister (Warsaw: The Prime Minister's Chancellery), 1999, mimeo: 38.

Pysiewicz, W. (1999) "Operatorzy kablowi zdobędą pieniadzą," *Puls Biznesu*, 9 December.

Report of the Special Rapporteur on the promotion and protection of the right to freedom of opinion and expression, Mr Abid Hussain, on the mission to the Republic of Poland (1998). Geneva: Commission on Human Rights, E/CN.4/1998/40/Add.2.

Rosengren, K. E. (1981) "Mass Media and Social Change: Some Current Approaches," in E. Katz and T. Szecsko (eds) *Mass Media and Social Change*. London: Sage Publications.

Sasińska-Klas, T. (1996) "Społeczeństwo polskie w transformacji-dylematy przejścia od monocentrycznego ładu społecznego do demokracji," in G. G. Kopper, I. Rutkiewicz, and K. Schliep (eds) *Media i dziennikarstwo w Polsce*. Kraków: OBP.

Schöpflin, G. (1995) "Post-communism: A Profile," *Javnost/The Public*, II(1): 63–74.

Siemieniec, T. (2000) "Dami może trafić w ręce Solorza" [Dami may fall into Solorz's hands], *Puls Biznesu*, 6 January.

Sparks, C. (1998) (with Anna Reading), *Communism, Capitalism and the Mass Media*. London: Sage Publications.
Splichal, S. (1994) *Media beyond Socialism: Theory and Practice in East-Central Europe*. Boulder: Westview Press.
Staniszkis, J. (1995) "In Search of a Paradigm of Transformation," in E. Wnuk-Lipiński (ed.) *After Communism. A Multidisciplinary Approach to Radical Social Change*. Warsaw: PAN.
Sulejewski, A. (2000) "Agora powiększyła swoją bazż radiową" [Agora Extends its Radio Empire], *Puls Biznesu*, 13 January.
"Ustawa z dnia 14 grudnia 1982 o ochronie tajemnicy państwowej i służbowej" (Statute dated 14 December 1982 on the Protection of State and Official Secrets) (1982) *Dziennik Ustaw* (Official Gazette), 18 December 1982, No. 40, pos. 271.
"Ustawa z dnia 23 sierpnia 1996 r. o zmianie ustawy – Kodeks cywilny." (Statute dated 23 August 1996 on Changes to the Civil Code of 23 April 1964) (1996) *Dziennik Ustaw* (Official Gazette), 27 August 1996, No. 114, pos. 542. Available at: http://www.abc.com.pl/serwis/du/1996/0542.htm
"Ustawa z dnia 29 grudnia 1992 roku o radiofonii i telewizji" (Statute dated 29 December 1992 on Broadcasting) (1993) *Dziennik Ustaw* (Official Gazette), 1993, No. 7, pos. 34. Act amended 1995, No. 66, pos. 335 and 1995, No. 142, pos. 701.
"Ustawa z dnia 6 czerwca 1997r. Kodeks karny. (Statute dated 6 June 1997. The Criminal Code) (1997a) *Dziennik Ustaw* (Official Gazette), 1997, No. 88, pos. 553. Available at: http://www.abc.com.pl/serwis/du/1997/0553.htm
"Ustawa z dnia 31 lipca 1997 r. o Polskiej Agencji Prasowej" (Statute dated 31 July 1997 on the Polish Press Agency) (1997b) *Dziennik Ustaw* (Official Gazette), 15 September 1997, No. 107, pos. 687. Available at: http://www.abc.com.pl/serwis/du/1997 /0687.htm
Westley, B. (1973) "Communication and Social Change," in G. Zaltman *et al.*, *Processes and Phenomena of Social Change*. New York: John Wiley and Sons.
Whiting, G. C. (1982) "How Does Communication Interface with Change?" in E. M. Rogers (ed.), *Communication and Development. Critical Perspectives*. Beverly Hills: Sage Publications.
Żakowski, J. (1996) "Etyka mediów," in G. G. Kopper, I. Rutkiewicz, and K. Schliep (eds) *Media i dziennikarstwo w Polsce*. Kraków: OBP.
Zwierzchowski, Z. (1999a) "Kto ma w domu komputer," *Rzeczpospolita*, 14 September.
—— (1999b) "Polska w sieci," *Rzeczpospolita*, 18 November.
—— (1999c) "Pole teleinformatycznych możliwoęci," *Rzeczpospolita*, 15 April.

11

MEDIA REFORM IN URUGUAY

A case study in mature transition

Roque Faraone

Introduction

In many ways, Uruguay typifies the category of states at the late or mature stage of democratic transition, presenting the entire panoply of relationships between stages of democratization and media reform. Uruguay currently possesses both a viable executive and a legislature. The holders of these offices have been democratically elected for the past fifteen years. Further, the popularly elected government has developed effective power to govern. There are no limits to electoral competition and all parties are permitted freely to put forward platforms and candidates.

Additionally, there has been a significant shift in the composition of the ruling elite and the former regime leaders have been all but replaced by a new group of (relatively) professional political actors. Freedom of expression and various civil liberties are effectively guaranteed in the majority of cases and information sources are free of direct state control. Although the impartiality of the judiciary is sometimes questionable, this branch of the government is characterized by increased professionalism. Uruguay's transition to democracy has reached maturity.

Media reform has paralleled Uruguay's transition to democracy. A number of questions arise from a consideration of these dual processes. In the first place, are the transitions toward democracy and in media intertwined or independent of each other? To the extent that there is interconnection, what is the direction of causality? Specifically, does the general process of democratization promote developments within media and do media reforms advance the general transition to democracy and the developments of democratic norms? Moreover, if these processes are related, to what degree do they approximate the general theoretical model of media reform stages set out in Chapter 1? These are some of the questions that this chapter will endeavor to address.

It begins with a brief overview of the democratic transition and its relation to the media reform process in Uruguay. This first section addresses the application of a "stages of transition" approach to assess the role of particular measures of media reform in the overall process of (re)constructing democratic institutions. Each media sector is then examined to assess its particularities and its relationship to general developments within the country's media landscape. The final section evaluates the relation of Uruguay's current media profile to the general theory of media reform in societies in transition.

The media reform process

The transition to democracy in Uruguay began with the end of military rule in 1984 and was marked by an "internally pacted" transition. This pact allowed certain (but not all) relevant actors to negotiate acceptable terms of transition and led directly to a peaceful post-authoritarian settlement. Uruguay's experience with liberal political practices in the years prior to the accession of the military to power meant that substantive legal, institutional, and economic questions had been extensively addressed earlier in the country's history.

As a result, at the point of transition, media were in need of legal, institutional, and economic fine-tuning, rather than fundamental restructuring. Yet, while ensuring a peaceful transition in the short term, the pacted nature of the process left certain scars and "reserve domains" within the country's institutional structures, most notably the military, which filtered into and affected media freedom and independence.

Legal–institutional questions

Throughout its history, Uruguay has had a small population of some 3 million, which has been highly integrated in its ethnicity, language, and religion.[1] Partly as a result, in 1910–1915 the Uruguayan government was able to construct and stabilize liberal political practices resembling those of European countries at that time. Constitutional reforms undertaken in 1919 established universal male suffrage by secret ballot and a system of proportional representation in the national parliament, as well as the formal separation of power between the Catholic Church and the Uruguayan state. Regular parliamentary and presidential elections commenced in 1924, which encompassed significant legal guarantees for the citizenry and in 1938 the franchise was extended to women.

Political parties operated openly during this period and elections were both orderly and free of significant fraud. Further, in 1919–1933 and 1951–1965, the two majority parties (representing 90 per cent of the popular vote) shared executive power in a council based on the Swiss model. Consensus between the two ruling parties was generally broad and the formal separation of powers, which was guaranteed by the constitution, was, on the whole, effectively enforced. Until the imposition of military rule in 1973, the only exception to democratic government from this point was a period of civilian dictatorship between 1933 and 1942, led in the first instance by Gabriel Terra, which was principally the result of the 1929 worldwide economic crisis (Faraone 1972).[2] A functional legal and institutional democratic framework was therefore in place in Uruguay for most of the twentieth century.

During the period between 1919 and 1973, print and later broadcast media remained free from censorship.[3] However, the press was, in the early stages of its development, affiliated to one of the two main political parties, and consequently there existed both pro-government and opposition presses.[4] Government refrained from any interference in the publications of its opposition. Radio broadcasting was introduced in Uruguay in the early 1930s and expanded beyond the capital to include local stations by the mid-1960s.[5]

During the same thirty-year period, print media reached their zenith with daily publications reaching nearly 500,000 copies in a population of barely 2.5 million. There was extensive freedom of speech (within the limits of the law – see below) except in the authoritarian period between 1933 and 1942. The competition between newspapers depended largely on sales rather than on advertising. This led to a press independent of political or economic forces, which acted as a vehicle for information dissemination and popular discussion (Faraone 1960).

Since about 1967 television has gradually become the most widespread medium, followed by radio and the press. A fundamental aspect of media reform, however, has been that for all media sectors, legislative frameworks were created well before the coming of the authoritarian military regime in 1973. This is discussed in more detail later.

Article 29 of the 1919 Uruguayan constitution guaranteed "freedom of speech" and "the free communication of thoughts" without prior state censorship, leaving it to the law to determine the particular punishment to be applied "in the event of abuses."[6] These provisions were applicable to all media sectors, and arose from a tradition of the rights of the citizen *vis-à-vis* the government.

Initially, the government placed no restrictions upon the press, the most important means of communication at that time. During the period of civilian dictatorship (1933–1942), however, Uruguay developed its first press legislation, which was largely used to stifle media.[7] This law was later amended on several occasions, most recently in Law 16,099 of 1989. This included a registration requirement, an obligation to publish official statements, and recognition of a right to reply. The Supreme Court (*Suprema Corte de Justicia*), upheld this legislation as constitutional on a number of occasions.[8]

In 1928, Uruguay introduced legislation regulating the newly developing radio sector. When television was introduced in 1956, this medium, too, was regulated through Decree No. 23,941 of 7 June 1956 *de Estaciones de televisión* (on television stations).[9] The text of Law No. 8.390 *de Estaciones radioeléctricas transmisoras* (on radioelectric transmitter stations) of 28 January 1928 was short. It obliged broadcasters to ask for governmental authorization for registration, gave preference in terms of time and technical conditions to official transmissions, and forbade immoral communications.

In the beginning of television, only its technical aspects were addressed. It was felt that the 1928 law was sufficient to cope with any technical developments and new legislation was not adopted until 1977, during tthe military regime.

In general, the concept of the rule of law and particular incarnations of this system were already well established in Uruguay before the advent of authoritarian rule in 1973. Specific media legislation (which dealt with technological developments up until that time) was already in place and a wider institutional structure, which included a normal legislature creating the laws, an active judiciary that ruled on their constitutionality, and a bipartisan represented executive, who sought their implementation, had already been developed.

Socio-economic problems and an adverse international situation

In addition to creating this legal/institutional framework in the early part of the century, Uruguay had also addressed substantive socio-economic questions. For most of the first half of the twentieth century and until the 1960s, a socio-economic policy that today could be defined as "social-democratic" was successfully applied to housing, education, healthcare, and culture. Education policy, for instance, resulted in a dramatic decline in illiteracy over a sixty-year period, from 50 per cent in 1900 to just 8 per cent by 1960. In addition, the nation's private economic sector was already well developed and established by this time.

In about 1955, however, all Latin American economies suffered the impact of liberal economic policies promoted by international organizations, notably the International Monetary Fund (IMF) (Couriel and Lichtensztejn 1969). These policies reduced local economic protectionism and, as a result, jeopardized established social-democratic practices, particularly in education and social welfare.[10] This tendency was furthered by the collapse of import-substituting industrialization and the extended period of economic stagnation that followed (Finch 1991: 207–208). A change of government in 1959 facilitated the application of external economic guidelines, and consequently, the 1960s witnessed social and economic changes that altered many of the features of the previous years of prosperity.[11] In light of constricting economic resources, private business interests became increasingly unwilling to maintain the social-democratic practices that had been developed.

Trade unions, which had developed rapidly in the early 1940s as a result of continued growth in the urban economy, stressed their claims for the reintroduction of previous salary levels and other social measures. Students and teachers made similar demands while becoming increasingly militant. Opposition groups became radicalized to a much greater extent than previously. Uruguay's first unified trade union, the Convención Nacional de Trabajadores (CNT), was formed in 1964. At the same time, the economy began to deteriorate and the state could not find solutions adequate to maintain the previous standards of living.

Some have claimed that the deterioration of the traditional governmental consensus was also a function of Uruguay's particular institutional structure. The peculiar electoral system that was devised produced extreme party factionalism within the Blanco and Colorado parties.[12] In addition, "the personalist nature of political leadership and the divided executive impeded the process of policy formation" (Finch 1991: 208–209). The political and legislative structures were in dire need of revision.

In 1966, elections were held which resulted in the victory of the Colorado y Batallista faction, led by a retired army officer, Oscar Gestido. Constitutional reform was the principal issue in these elections, stemming from the widely held interpretation of economic stagnation as a direct result of the collegiate executive system. The constitution was modified to restore a presidential executive in an attempt to adapt political institutions to an adverse economic situation and provide a strengthened leadership, but within an already established tradition of political liberalism. The constitutional amendment did not, however, prove to be a solution, and the economic, political, and social circumstances further deteriorated.

Jorge Pacheco Areco, a political unknown acting as vice-president to Gestido, took office following Gestido's sudden death in November 1967. From June 1968, Pacheco imposed an almost continuous state of emergency, which permitted him to govern with limited opposition. His first action after taking up the presidency was to close down two newspapers and to suppress certain left-wing political groups. Further, Pacheco used the state of emergencies to "arrest trade union leaders, prohibit assemblies, and censor the press" (Finch 1991: 215).

In spite of these preventative measures, inflation continued to rise, while labor disputes and economic unrest increased. Very small groups of urban guerrillas, such as the Movimiento de Liberación Nacional-Tupamaros (MLN-T), which originally participated only in protest action, became more prominent. Meanwhile, political life continued to be highly divided among the various subgroups within the two political parties, which displayed no internal cohesion except when coming to electoral agreements.

In 1968, a semi-dictatorial period began. The president ruled practically without parliament, which was unable to maintain the balance of power prescribed by the constitution. The opposition press suffered severe attacks in the form of unlawful closures and temporary restrictions based on constitutional emergency rules intended for extreme circumstances such as a state of war.

A number of publications were either closed down or discontinued: the dailies *Extra*, *De Frente*, *Ya*, *La Idea*, *Ahora*, *El Popular*, *Democracia*, and the weekly *Marcha* (Paris *et al.* 1997). In some circumstances, parliament voted to nullify the official acts taken against publications, but could not sustain such resistance. In fact, the weakness of parliament was fully realized in 1970 and 1971 when, after it had voted to lift emergency measures, it was overruled by the president who immediately reimposed these measures.

Until mid-century Uruguay was pursuing a transition away from colonial rule (which ended in 1828) and had succeeded in establishing a number of democratic and partially market-oriented legal, institutional, and economic structures. As a result, Uruguay at this time could be considered to have been at least at a late stage of primary transition, to use the terms from Chapter 1. Inappropriate structure (that is, a divisive political party system, a constitution not sufficiently well established to resist abuse by a newly introduced presidential branch, and so on) coupled with economic deterioration and social unrest, however, led to a period of backsliding which eventually resulted in the accession in 1973 of a military authoritarian regime.

However, because the rule of law was firmly established by this point, when power was seized by the military, this was done on legal grounds.[13] Moreover, many aspects of the legal system were respected during the authoritarian regime. Ironically, such attention to law and legality would eventually bring about the regime's downfall twelve years later.

The military dictatorship (1973–1984)

In 1973, having completely dismantled the incipient guerrilla movement, the army took advantage of legal circumstances and the disrepute of political institutions that had been unable to solve the economic crisis to gain complete control of government. It did, however, allow the president, who had been elected in 1972, to keep his position.

A very rigorous and repressive regime was imposed, with absolute control over education and media, which proscribed all political activity and maintained strict control over citizens' social life. Over the course of its rule, the military government imprisoned approximately 50,000 people. During the twelve years of this regime, however, the military dictatorship modified itself. At first, it attempted to set up an authoritarian government for an indefinite period of rule. Later, possibly as a consequence of external pressures, a return to civilian life was attempted through certain political parties that, nonetheless, initially remained entirely dependent on military power.

In 1977, the military regime amended the 1956 broadcasting law (Law No. 14,670) replacing the phrase "public service" with "of public interest." The change reflected a move away from concern for a public forum to a more corporate-driven philosophy where media entities were in the right as long as they kept the public's interest in mind. In short, media were no longer required to serve the public as they had been in the past. The 1977 law regulated content, advertising time, and other elements with the aim of avoiding a concentration of station ownership in the hands of a few people, but none of these extreme measures was enforced during the dictatorship. Individual stations, however, engaged in extensive self-censorship. After 1985 and the end of the military dictatorship, the legislation still obtained though most regulations on content were eliminated and limitations on advertising time were not applied. Because the military government rarely enforced the 1977 law it was easy to go back to the older, softer ways once 1984 brought a return to civilian governance.

Television grew in social importance over time and the military, free of political opposition, used it as their favorite instrument of ideological control. The military leadership received help from the major television stations in the effort to ensure ideological control.

In an attempt to formalize the military's power, a plebiscite aimed at approving a new constitution was organized in 1980 and, most likely in order to legitimate this referendum, the government uncharacteristically authorized the broadcasting of debates on the adoption of the proposed constitution. However, since the Uruguayan electoral system ensured the secrecy of voting (and since the military regime respected this provision), the results of the plebiscite were revealed to be adverse to the regime.[14] Even in the absence of legally recognized political parties and a truly free press, the traditions of political liberalism were still alive. As Finch has stated, "The fundamental reason for the withdrawal of the military from power was the continuing strength of Uruguay's democratic tradition and the acquiescence of the military itself to the authority of the ballot box" (Finch 1991: 224). This fact, coupled perhaps with renewed external pressures, led to the search for ways of "returning the army to the barracks," a claim that some military sectors were beginning to make.

In 1982, the military government declared that authorized political parties (the left was excluded) should elect a new president and parliament. Simultaneously, there was a monetary collapse, which caused the population to question the economic acumen of the military government. From that point on, it was possible to detect signs of exhaustion in the dictatorship, the culmination of which were the 1984 negotiations paving the way for the return to power of an elected civilian government.

Some weekly publications directed by political figures who had not collaborated with the dictatorship began to circulate at this time (*Opinar*, *El Correo de los Viernes*, *Aquí*). Censorship, however, could not be directly attacked unless one was prepared to risk one's liberty (Faraone 1987). Having been systematically persecuted and having changed their names, trade unions also began a process of reorganization. They subsequently formed the federation Plenario Intersindical de Trabajadores (PIT or Inter-Union Workers' Plenary). This group organized a demonstration that was held on 1 May 1983 (Workers' Day), ten years after it had been last commemorated.

Beginning of the reform process toward democratization

On 20 May 1983, the military held discussions with political parties (excluding the left) to negotiate terms for the return of power to civilian hands. These negotiations, however, proved problematic. Although the military experienced much external pressure to step down, it was divided as an institution on how to devolve power to a civilian government. It was also fearful that the reinstatement of a civilian regime might lead to the prosecution of army personnel for the systematic violation of human rights (murders, tortures, and disappearances) for which the army was responsible as an institution. Numerous political prisoners remained in military custody and certain political leaders and entire parties were still banned.

The military government had also distorted the country's institutional framework. It had created a ministry of justice, which was able to limit the power of the Supreme Court of Justice. Military justices were also able to increase their power.

Civilian political leaders, on the other hand, lacked cohesion and legitimacy as opposition leaders since many of them had either taken part in the regime to some degree or had tolerated the previous period of institutionalized state terrorism. The opposition's task lay not in wresting power from the military but rather in seeking to negotiate the transition from authoritarian to democratic rule. The most delicate part of the negotiations for the opposition was to avoid derailing the process by making demands that would be considered too extreme. Civilian leaders were eager to return to power and most of them were ready to accept nearly any conditions.

As a result, the pact concluded between the military and the civilian leaders did not encompass all political parties, but all parties agreed to it. It provided for the release of political prisoners, the scheduled resumption of elections (although some political leaders were barred from participating), a change of name for the communist party, and the reinstatement of various civil liberties, including the freedom of the press. In some manner, although not sufficiently explicit or documented, an amnesty for military members who committed or ordered human rights crimes during the dictatorship seems to have been agreed to in the negotiations (involving participants with very different power shares). In this regard, the case of Uruguay closely mimicked the transitional processes in other Latin American countries.

The negotiated agreement to transfer power was in keeping with the country's political traditions. Civil wars during the nineteenth century and other seemingly insoluble problems often ended in negotiations that left many loose ends. Such was the case with the internally pacted transition; although initially ensuring a peaceful abdication of power to the opposition, it left many legal and institutional traces of the authoritarian regime.

In particular, the agreement left the role of the military unresolved. Such an ambiguity would impact the development of media in Uruguay, limiting their freedom and autonomy. For instance, high-ranking military chiefs frequently made public statements in the press on the favorable role of the armed forces toward democracy during the transition. These were political statements forbidden by the constitution, but the civilian government remained silent on the matter. Media owners, on their part, interpreted this ambiguous situation in prudential terms and continued to publish.

Re-establishing a civilian government was not an easy task. One of the first steps taken by the new executive on his first day in office was to abrogate all rules instituted by the previous regime that restricted the freedom of press. The parliament also repealed some restrictions introduced during the military dictatorship that had been framed as law. Other measures, for instance limitations on time and content of television advertising, remained valid, but neither were applied.

Elections to install a civilian government were held in November 1984. The continuing overlap between the emerging civilian government and the military regime remained evident. A few days prior to the November elections, the military government ruled that the National Directorate of Communications, thus far under civilian control, would be reassigned to the ministry of defense. With this action, the military demonstrated their belief in the significant influence wielded by media. Moreover, this development reflected quite clearly the sensitive and contentious nature of the relationship between the country's mass media and the emerging democratic regime.

As soon as parliament re-opened, a bill proposing the return of the Directorate of Communications to the civilian sphere was passed unanimously by one of the parliamentary chambers.[15] When the bill reached the second chamber, the executive announced his dissent; consequently, those parliamentary members of the president's party voted against the bill. However, the majority of the chamber voted in favor and the bill was passed. The executive then vetoed the bill and there were insufficient votes to overrule that veto. It was clear that the military had demanded that such a vital instrument of communication control was to be left under their control.

Tension between the military and the civilian population had not ceased and this was reflected in the media domain.

Media in Uruguay today

Print media

Legislation

In addition to the 1966 constitutional provisions and the law on communication and information, which specifically govern the printed media, other legislation also forms part of the environment in which Uruguayan print media law operates.[16] The Criminal Code, which was first ratified in 1933 at the start of the civilian dictatorship of Gabriel Terra and which is still extant, defines libel and slander as criminal.[17] In addition, the communication and information law, discussed above, while also covering broadcasting (with regard to content), sends an ambiguous message to the press. On the one hand, the law introduces protection of professional secrecy in article 1 and an improved right to reply in article 7, which serve to increase the freedom and independence of print media. On the other hand, it criminalizes offences committed through media (committing a crime on air or knowingly disseminating false information with serious consequences, and so on) in article 19 and libel and slander committed by media in article 28.

Local press is protected to some degree by two special press laws. Law No. 12,802 extends limited tax exemptions to local publications.[18] Law No. 13,641 provides state subsidies for local publications, based on a set of defined criteria.[19] Although these pieces of legislation are conceivably open to manipulation by the state, thus far they have not been implemented in any political manner that would suggest governmental control.

As is apparent, although some elements of Uruguayan press law are conducive to overall media freedom, other provisions work in the opposite direction and need to be further restructured.

The role of the state in print media

In the past, the Uruguayan state offered print media companies tax exemptions, allowed the duty-free import of press-related products and, above all, failed to demand strict compliance with regard to their social security contributions. In 1996, however, the government suspended tax exemptions on the import of newsprint through a budgetary law causing a number of publications to fold.[20] Further, the government issued a Decree 241/96 in June 1996, which continues to require the authorization of the government in order to import newsprint. Both of these economic measures have, to some extent, limited the diversity of this media sector.

The state bureaucracy also plays a certain role in influencing the print media's operation by facilitating the pro-government print media while hindering the opposition counterparts. This has happened with regard both to the provision of information and to the allocation of paid advertising by state departments, ministries, or state-owned economic enterprises, of which there are several in Uruguay.[21]

Press diversity

Only the Montevidean daily press has nationwide circulation. There are five morning papers, which are the only ones circulating at a national level. *La Juventud* represents a small political faction of radical orientation and does not offer substantial general information. Of the other four, two have very low circulation rates of between 2,000 and 5,000 copies per day (see Table 11.1).

As a result, only two Uruguayan publications have substantial influence: *El País* and *La República*. *El País* is the most comprehensive paper because of its varied information. It also boasts the largest circulation and is recognized as an establishment paper, both politically and economically.

La República is a poorer, opposition-influenced tabloid, enjoying approximately one-half of the circulation of *El País* on weekdays. Currently it is experiencing economic difficulties and is predominantly politically sensationalist, rather than providing information on crime or accidents.[22] The government has shown hostility toward this paper to the point of lodging a legal suit against its director and editor-in-chief. The suit resulted in the imprisonment of two of the paper's journalists, but the courts later overturned the verdict. This case, to some degree, has underscored the effectiveness of the judicial branch *vis-à-vis* the executive with regard to the print media.[23]

Private print media offer little political diversity. Most newspapers are favorable to the government with only slight shades of criticism. *La República*, *La Juventud* and the weekly *Brecha* are the only publications that voice critical positions. They have, therefore, been classified as "opposition" or independent papers. *Búsqueda* is a quality publication targeted primarily at business people. In practice, this publication represents the government's most respected supporter.

Table 11.1 Circulation of publications in Uruguay, April–June 1999

	Thousands of readers	
Dailies	Daily (average)	Sunday
El Diario	1.2	0.8
El Observador	22.8	28.9
El Pais	66.3	343.9
La Juventud	0	0.4
La Mañana	2.1	0.4
La República	34.0	54.4
Últimas Noticias	17.8	15.4
Weeklies		
Brecha	17.9	
Búsqueda	20.8	
Posdata	14.1	
Tres	8.8	
Noticias	9.1	
Manos	2.5	

Source: Market and Opinion Research International (MORI)

Posdata and *Tres* are illustrated weeklies with varied reporting and some relatively independent political information.

La Mañana still maintains links with one of the two traditional political parties in Uruguay.[24] *El País*, in turn, maintains links with the National Party. *El Observador* has a Catholic conservative bias with no obvious party links. *Últimas Noticias* is owned by the Unification Church of the Reverend Moon, but it is a light, generalist tabloid without evident party connections. *La República* appears to have some association with the Frente Amplio party, but it frequently allows other political party leaders space to voice their opinions.[25] This particular daily ran the campaign for the repeal of the impunity law at its own cost and has often publicly denounced military arrogance. The range of papers available thus indicates that there is a sufficient diversity of opinion presented within Uruguayan print media.

Broadcasting media

Legislation

The 1977 law on radio diffusion, as discussed above, currently governs television and broadcasting.[26] With the return of a civil regime in 1985, privately owned TV, which had remained active even during military rule, gradually regained a critical and controversial style, although within a framework somewhat marked by self-censorship. Given that no judgment had been passed on television's obsequious attitude to the dictatorship, as was also the case with newspapers that had failed to provide resistance, TV continued quietly to adapt to the new circumstances.

The role of the state in broadcasting media

The Uruguayan state has limited its role in television broadcasting to exempting the private television channels from different types of taxation while maintaining ownership of one official state channel (Channel 5) using very limited budgetary resources. The output of Channel 5 is of mediocre quality. It commands only a 5 per cent share of total TV audiences, although it has been broadcasting since 1963. Originally, it carried no advertising, but in 1965 it was by law allotted a percentage of state agency advertising, against the wishes of private broadcasters. Here again, the state's economic influence was notable. The state follows a financial policy that does not regulate private advertising or airtime and invests little in the state-owned television channel.

Legal restrictions to broadcastings include certain minor provisions, not enforced, on "correct" language and socially acceptable behavior on the state channel. One regulation allows the executive to require state television and radio stations to transmit specific broadcasts simultaneously. These are generally presidential, ministerial, or other official government statements. The president has discretionary powers to make use of this simultaneous broadcasting resource, but the opposition has never been authorized to do so. The procedure is infrequently used, however, since the memory of military misuse still persists.

No regulations exist which require private television channels to broadcast state messages, but a law was passed in 1998 that regulates the access of political parties to the state television channel.[27] When the bill was being considered, private channels objected. They discussed the issue with legislators, offering to implement a self-regulation policy, and arrived at a formal agreement with the two political parties in government.[28] This instance quite clearly reflected both the importance and the negotiating power of the private sector within the larger broadcasting media framework in Uruguay.

Broadcasting diversity

Approximately 42 per cent of Uruguay's population lives in the capital, Montevideo. If the suburbs that have access to Montevideo's television broadcasting are included, its reach extends to 60 per cent of the population. In addition, local relay stations exist which transmit some of their own programming. Thus, the three private Montevideo channels have a joint audience share of over 95 per cent.[29] In general audience-viewing terms, although levels vary from one program to another, the three private channels may be considered to enjoy equal popularity (Pallares and Stolovich 1991). As has already been mentioned, the state regulates neither programming nor advertising.

The three channels have come to informal mutual agreements that significantly reduce competition. They jointly purchase soap operas and divide successful programming equally among themselves. They have agreements not to broadcast sporting events that may reduce the number of spectators in stadiums. They synchronize evening news broadcasts and advertising slots, which are made to coincide in order to neutralize the effects of switching channels. Channel surfing will only result in finding advertising on the other two channels. Agreements between the private channels used to be even broader (Gabay 1993). It is likely that such agreements include other aspects related to advertising and ideological control.[30]

The three private television channels have traditionally been strongly progovernment in their orientation. Since the opposition has gained one-third of electoral support, however, the stations have allowed some moderate or slightly eccentric opposition leaders to broadcast. They receive less time than the amount devoted to government coalition leaders.

Laws forbidding concentration, as discussed above, are not enforced. In the mid-1990s when broadcasting had reached near total coverage, the broadcasting industry began to invest in cable and subscription-based television. In response, the government invited tenders and decided of its own accord to allot cable broadcasting licenses in Montevideo to a consortium formed by the three private TV channels (García 1994).

Of approximately twenty radio stations in Montevideo, three belong to the state, two run political programs open to the opposition, and the remaining fifteen have varied programming, but offer little access to the opposition. In general, state radio broadcasting is almost exclusively music oriented, and therefore unsuitable to political manipulation. The remaining private stations offer considerable diversity of entertainment in the FM range.

As a result, although formally free in terms of equal legal treatment, in practise the established broadcasters are privileged in their organizational continuity and, somewhat less frequently, by the preferential treatment accorded them by the government. If true broadcasting diversity is to be achieved in Uruguay, questions of collusion and self-censorship need to be addressed to a greater degree.

Interest group involvement in broadcasting

The most influential media interest group today is Uruguay's National Broadcasting Union (Asociación Nacional de Broadcasters Uruguayos (ANDEBU)). This body brings together the owners of private television channels and radio stations. The group broadcasts a five-minute simultaneous radio transmission every day, at noon, and during 1999 it allowed the president of the republic free weekly use of this slot, presumably as a personal favor.

The president made use of this time slot to speak favorably of his government administration. The leaders of other political parties were not granted the same opportunity. However, the president does not speak specifically about his own party but about the government entrusted to him, and since the party which gained the second highest number of votes in the most recent election participates in this government, it has abstained from criticism.

ANDEBU exerts a very strong influence over the parliament as well. It has persuaded legislators not to regulate private broadcasters. Its affiliates are effectively able to control broadcasting access (report by Juan Martín Posadas, *La República*, 28 November 1991). The union has also been able to influence print media and many key papers have become "speakers" on its behalf. The influence of broadcasting's economic actors remains significant under such circumstances, underscoring the continued importance of the economic dimension in Uruguay's media reform process.

Emerging technologies

New media technologies did not make inroads in Uruguay until the advent of civilian rule after 1984. In 1990, the Universidad de la Republica set up the first Internet connection to Bidnet through a Chilean node. During its time, it connected sixty e-mail users, but ceased operations in 1991 for technical reasons.

The number of Internet users has recently undergone an extraordinary expansion. According to official data from August 1998, 205,000 of a population of 3 million are estimated to have access to the Internet (*Busqueda*, 19 November 1998). However, the data do not discriminate between "Internet access" and "e-mail access." Empirically, e-mail use has spread significantly, while the more expensive use of the Internet is unlikely to have grown as much. Reliable membership figures for certain Internet servers agree with this interpretation.[31]

The Uruguayan émigré communities in countries that have easy access to electronic communications have had a positive influence on the rapid growth of the number of new technology users. By the existence and activity, such expatriate technology users have encouraged their relatives in Uruguay to acquire the electronic means to communicate.

Although systematic studies in this media sector are yet to be undertaken, it is likely that these new forms of communication will result in a more timely introduction of advanced democratic practices that may eventually have an influence on higher-level changes. In particular, the deterioration of the national press coupled with its high costs is shifting many people's demand for information to the arena of electronic information. There, citizens have access to both national and international press. In turn, this process contributes to the growth of an internal public forum. The risk of growing commercialization of the Internet, however, has become increasingly apparent in Uruguay.

Cross-media analysis

In a media environment dominated by commercial television, followed by radio broadcasting and finally by the print media, the issue of the freedom of communication has grown more complex. Broadcasting media produce more ephemeral messages, undocumented in most cases, which offer little opportunity for reflection. Acting within a market media system, broadcasters depend exclusively on advertising for their revenue. The original 1928 broadcasting law did not address advertising. The 1977 broadcasting law, issued during the dictatorship, was constructed along the same lines. Although sections of the 1978 decree fixed advertising limits, they have never been rigorously enforced. As a result, Uruguay's legislative structure fails to offer the necessary guarantees for a fully independent media system to flourish. This highlights another instance of inappropriate structure with regard to media law.

Low average national incomes, high print media prices, and the expansion of television have all contributed to a decline of print media.[32] In 1960, approximately 500,000 newspapers were printed daily for a population slightly over 2.6 million. Currently, only 60,000 to 70,000 copies are printed daily for a population exceeding 3 million. With the advent of civilian rule, media censorship has ceased and political life has been revitalized. However, the drop in printed press circulation levels indicates that socio-economic factors are possibly more influential than political ones in determining media development.

Running parallel to this dual process of television expansion and press contraction, radio broadcasting has gradually increased its audience share. It represents a cheap medium for which receiving equipment was already available in large quantities and which continues to enter the market at very low prices. Many who previously read newspapers changed their habits after the fall of the military dictatorship and began listening to the radio for access to different opinions. In addition, recent evidence presented to parliament by the state television channel authorities indicates that audience share has risen from 3 per cent to 5 per cent since state television began to transmit sports programs not previously covered (Servicio Oficial de Radiodifusion y Espectaculos (SODRE) 1996; José L. Guntin in *Búsqueda*, 24 July 1997: 18).

Hardly any state financial investment has been made in media during the transitional period. This is attributable to several factors:

- the general decline of state income;
- the lack of political interest in expanding state activities in this area; and

- the pragmatism of most political leaders who adapt to a reality in which the power of the state is somehow linked to the power of television.

It is possible to say with certainty that the concept of an effective, publicly defined, public service media function does not exist in Uruguay. As discussed, one state television channel does exist. However, the state does not regulate content when state broadcast time is privately subcontracted. Private media actors have construed their state licenses as absolute ownership and the state acquiesces in this attitude.[33]

There is one significant exception to the lack of a public voice, but it also demonstrates the paradoxes of competition with a concentrated, advertising-supported set of competitors. State-run Channel 5 broadcasts an evening news program at approximately the same time that the evening news is shown on the three private channels. Comparatively, the state news program excels, mainly because it contains much less advertising than the other three. It also broadcasts relatively less sports information than the commercial channels. This is because commercial channels purchase this very popular type of information while the state channel cannot afford it. Lastly, private channels devote more time to crimes and accident reports because they send out broadcast vehicles to the scene. Financial constraints prohibit the state channel from covering such news items extensively. Consequently, some would say that by avoiding crime and accidents, considered more sensational, state news reporting gains in quality, but loses audience.

The significant overlap of different media sector influences in the transition from military dictatorship to democracy masks whether television, radio, or print media may have played a more decisive role in the process. Once the military regime allowed open criticism, the first opening took place in the press with the appearance of new weeklies. These functioned as public vehicles for equally new political groups which led a moderate political discussion process that was tolerated by the military. There was practically no clandestine press or radio.

Toward the end of military rule, once a certain level of opposition had already been allowed, audiotapes also began to circulate containing political messages recorded by opposition leader, Wilson Ferreira Aldunate.[34] Broadcast media, more commercial than political, continued to be more sensitive to self-censorship. Similar self-censoring tendencies also appeared within the daily press.

In Uruguay, media did not initiate the democratic transition. Rather, media reform accompanied and followed the democratization process. To this day, the "public forum" that these processes created continues to censor itself, particularly with regard to the role the military played during the twelve years of dictatorship and the privileged position the military continues to enjoy today.

Assessment

It is possible to gauge media performance during the continuing transition to democracy in Uruguay by focusing on certain significant events. Two, in particular, will be discussed: the Berríos affair and the CNN affair.

The Berríos affair

In 1992, it became known that a Chilean biochemist, Eugenio Berríos, who had worked for the Chilean army's secret service in their attempts to manufacture a lethal gas, could be summoned as a witness in the conspiracy case connected with the assassination of Orlando Letellier in Washington DC.[35] The threat of his potential testimony caused him to lose the confidence of the Pinochet regime. Presumably for that reason, Berríos took refuge in, or rather was taken to, Montevideo, in semi-secrecy. There he was placed under the "protection" and "guard" of Chilean and Uruguayan military officials. On 15 November 1992, Berríos managed to escape and presented himself to police at a seaside resort near Montevideo. He was terrified and asked for protection, claiming that, "Pinochet had ordered his assassination" (*Brecha*, 11 June 1993: 5).

The moment his request was registered, two Uruguayan army officials appeared at the police station. They identified themselves, stated that they were in charge of Berríos's protection and took him away. This event and news of Berríos's subsequent disappearance were published in the press and a scandal ensued. In response, the ministry of the interior removed the head of the police department in the district where the particular police station was situated (*Brecha*, 6 June 1993).

All senior army officers joined together to protect the commander-in-chief of the army, publicly stating that they would all refuse to replace him in the event of his dismissal following the scandal. After the controversy over military impunity in 1986, this event constituted a new case in which there had been conspiracy with other national armies and in which deprivation of freedom or kidnapping had been committed without fear of being held to account. Parliament investigated the case, as did the courts. After some time and with the appearance of a letter in Italy presumed to have been written by Berríos (later proved to be a forgery), the case was closed.

In 1995, a body was washed up on a beach and the subsequent investigation, slow despite parliamentary pressure, revealed it to be that of Eugenio Berríos. Since the murder had taken place after the "transaction" between the executive and the military agreed upon when the kidnapping was made public, the judiciary was faced with the problem of investigating a homicide, while parliament would have to look into the subversion of law by the military. Both parliament and the judiciary, however, buried the issues.

What was the role played by media in the face of these significant events? All media addressed them, but in most cases under a *fait divers* view, they merely described the events and stripped them of all institutional meaning. Only *Brecha* and, to some extent, *La República* provided an institutional analysis of the events. It was as if the country had two distinct systems of social communication. The majority system practiced self-censorship or a conspiratorial silence with regard to the status quo, which the political and military powers continue to impose, and a small minority addressed the matter freely. The events also served to further highlight a continued lack of true independence in media from political and military forces.

The CNN affair

In November 1997, Channel 4-Montecarlo suspended a newsreader for having made public an interview with an industrialist who criticized the nation's economic situation following immediately after another interview with a senior state official who had praised it; apparently a professional mistake. The journalists' union issued a declaration denouncing "government pressures." The presidential press secretary denied any government interference and countered by saying that "when there were pressures, they had originated in Atlanta [CNN's headquarters]" (Faraone 1998). Up to this point, several media had covered the controversy between the journalists' union and the presidential official, in general providing the two versions of the story but never taking a stand on the matter.

A few days later, *Brecha* issued a vigorous denial on behalf of CNN. When CNN had interviewed the president-elect Julio María Sanguinetti in 1994, it had questioned whether pressures on media would continue under his second presidency, as had been the case with his first presidency under press secretary, Walter Nessi. The president replied that, naturally, they would not and further, that he was not aware of any previous state pressure on media. CNN claimed that Channel 4 had suppressed this question and that CNN, linked to Channel 4 by contract, had demanded that the interview be broadcast in full the following day. In a parallel personal letter, the CNN representative added very negative comments about Uruguay's freedom of information (*Brecha*, 19 February 1997).

Certain papers, *El Observador*, *Posdata*, *Tres*, and *El País* among them, included some coverage, but avoided critical comments concerning the government (*El Observador*, 17 December 1997; *Posdata*, 19 December 1997; *Tres*, 19 December 1997; *El País*, 17–18 December 1997). All of these papers, in addition to *Búsqueda*, remained conspicuously silent regarding the CNN letter. It was an extraordinarily revealing and unique event in the process of the democratic transition: a foreign source, unable to affect the status quo, denounced a form of censorship that also revealed connivance between a very important Uruguayan medium and the government, over which a general silence prevailed.

These examples indicate there are still significant barriers to the freedom and independence of media in Uruguay today. Possible explanations for this state of affairs are threefold. In the first place, media may be too closely associated with the two institutional forces to be effectively able to execute their watchdog role over state power. A second explanation may be that media have not yet been able to overcome their fear of governmental institutions, which twelve years of military dictatorship have instilled, to be able to be fully critical and investigative in their operations.

A final explanation is socio-economic and lies in the fact that open criticism of certain topics and areas may be seen to be economically detrimental, as a result either of direct government sanctions or of consumer pressure. This last factor is especially crucial in a small country where competition within a small market often forces compliance. Nonetheless, the evidence suggests that the freedom and independence of media at this stage of Uruguay's transition lie clearly in the domain of media itself.

Recommendations and conclusions

The above analysis indicates the ways in which media reform in Uruguay has been intertwined with the general process of democratic political transition. Throughout the post-1984 period, a discernible pattern has emerged. During the initial stages of democratic reform, Uruguay was primarily concerned with restructuring the legal and institutional framework within which the media operates. On the whole, since the country had a relatively viable tradition of democratic rule before the onset of military rule, many legal-institutional issues had been addressed earlier. Nonetheless, issues of inappropriate structuring and inappropriate utilization continued to arise during the primary and secondary stages of transition.

Certain legal questions in Uruguay still require attention. Most notably, constitutional modifications need to be introduced in order to cope with developments in television broadcasting. Further, Uruguay needs to be brought into line constitutionally with new legal doctrines incorporated into the Pact of San José de Costa Rica and other international agreements to which the country has acceded, particularly where the right to information is concerned. This situation, especially, has caused conflict among legislative reformers.

In addition, the state currently tolerates anti-competitive behavior and continues to exert only a weak legal control over television. Parliament should have the power to regulate the discretionary use of a simultaneous broadcast space on radio and television by the executive. It should also be able to guarantee broadcast time to all opposition parties. Enacting these several measures would result in political leaders being less dependent on the power of television than they are at the moment.

An additional problem is that the military continues to exert a degree of influence, both direct and indirect, over media. This is one reason why most media actors support the civilian government and try not to attack or criticize the underlying military power. In a certain sense, such actions defend media autonomy. Such military "reserve domains" represent a particular obstacle that may be specific to previous authoritarian military regimes and, as such, may represent a barrier to other cases within this general categorization.

Aside from these reservations, however, to date legal-institutional questions impacting the media have been for the most part settled. Issues of legal and institutional structure having matured, questions of economic structure and its relation to media freedom continue to be debated, although Uruguay's media structure has, for the most part, been relegated to free market mechanisms. In Uruguay, as elsewhere, questions have arisen regarding whether the free market, without regulatory intervention, allows media to perform its democratic functions.

Media owners often maintain that a media market free from state censorship naturally selects the best information and that society requires no additional legal protection. Clearly, however, such a framework has led to the dominance of the broadcasting media, which exhibits strong tendencies of collusion and ignores certain social responsibilities. As a result, the question of a public service medium is one that needs to be addressed more directly if the quality of Uruguayan media is to improve. Price structures within the print media also need to be reviewed in order to halt the decline of this medium.

Finally, the issue of media professionalism has been highlighted in recent years and current media problems center on aspects of the investigative acumen and the willingness of the profession to openly criticize the regime or other influential political and economic actors. While legal and even economic aspects of the media reform process have been put in place, professional attitudes within media have proved more difficult to inculcate.

The Uruguay case also suggests, counter to widely held views, that the specific causal relationship between media reforms and the transition to democracy is open to question. Media reforms may be the product of pre-existing political reforms rather than major contributing factors to the transition itself. Besides, and also somewhat counter to general views, a mature stage of democracy can exist without a mature media. By any criteria of what a democratic media should achieve (elitist model, pluralist model, or complex democracy model), the media reform process in Uruguay has fallen short.[36]

Media practitioners fail to act as effective watchdogs or to provide a public forum for the development of participative democratic ideals. As a result, establishing effective media that contribute to sustained democratic institutions remains difficult. Self-censorship, the overwhelming relationship of government to the industry, and the level of concentration and interconnectedness within media itself are all factors that limit their role in the democratic developments at hand.

In the final analysis, both the legal-institutional and economic structures that have been put into place within the Uruguayan media system shift the balance of necessary reform to the media sectors themselves. Since the law does not bar media from being open and critical, practitioners must now develop an internal professionalism that will allow them to achieve their goals. For true freedom and independence, media must begin to exert their own power. As a result, although certain legislative and economic fine-tuning is necessary, the primary questions of media self-empowerment in Uruguay clearly characterize the system during its late or mature stage of transition.

Notes

1 The ethnic composition of Uruguay is 88 per cent European, 8 per cent mestizo, and 4 per cent black or mulatto. Sixty-six per cent of the population profess the Roman Catholic faith, while 30 per cent classify themselves as "other" (i.e., none of the major world religions). The official state language is Spanish, but Portunoal and Brazilero are also widely spoken. Also, nearly half of the population is concentrated in the metropolitan area around Montevideo, the Uruguayan capital.
2 Importantly, Terra justified his dictatorial rule through the passing of a new constitution in 1934, reflecting the importance of continued legal legitimacy. However, "the new constitution was approved by little more than half the electorate, with the opposition factions of both parties abstaining" (Finch 1991). A new constitution failed to be passed until the year following the collapse of the *terrista–herrerista* alliance in 1941.
3 Radio since 1928 and TV since 1956.
4 The Colorado Party and the National (Blanco) Party.
5 Between approximately 1933 and 1966, the expansion created over 20 stations in the capital alongside middle-wave local stations in other cities.

6 Art. 166: "Communication of thoughts by words, private papers, printed matter, or whatever means, is completely free of pre-publication censorship, leaving the author, printer, or broadcaster responsible, according to the law, for abuse." See the 1947 constitution.

7 Law No. 9,480 of 28 June 1935 *de Imprenta*.

8 In spite of Supreme Court decisions, there were several important judgments on the application of Law 16,099. See *Brecha* (12 May 1993); *La República* (25 June 1996); *El País* (17 October 1996); and *Búsqueda* (27 May 1999: 53; 23 September 1999: 35).

9 NTSC, of the United States of America. Fixed by decree (unnumbered) of 6 August 1954, applied in 1956, together with Decree 23.941, of 7 July 1954.

10 For a full analysis of the development of social-democratic trends in Uruguay, see Finch 1991.

11 The *herrerista–ruralista* faction of the Blanco Party that emerged victorious in the 1958 elections seized upon these measures. The success was more the result of the anomalous Uruguayan electoral system than of a coherent policy platform.

12 The more conservative landowners usually support the National (Blanco) Party, while the Colorado Party has generally had a more liberal urban base.

13 In a strict sense, the coup d'état happened in two stages: in February 1973, the military imposed a Council of National Security not established by the constitution. Parliament, however, formally *accepted* this action in April. Then, in June, the president was able to dismiss parliament without calling new elections.

14 Fifty-seven per cent of the population voted against the plebiscite.

15 Parliament was dismissed on 27 June 1973 and reinstated on 15 February 1985.

16 Law No. 16,099 of 3 November 1989 *Comunicaciones e informaciones*.

17 Law No. 9,155 of 4 December 1933 *Código Penal*, Art. 333 and 334.

18 Law No. 12,802 of 30 November 1960.

19 Law No. 13,641 of 29 July 1965 *de Empresas periodísticas*. The criteria include the amount of information published in a particular edition, the number of people employed by the publication, the age of the publication, its frequency and circulation rates, and whether the publication prints its own editions.

20 The budgetary law was Law No. 16,736 of 5 January 1996.

21 An example of the impact of this partisan bureaucracy is reflected in *La Mañana*'s appeal in August 1999 to the members of the Colorado Party holding government posts to help the financially struggling paper by promoting official advertising in its pages.

22 Political sensationalism accords with Uruguay's particular civic features. Information on crime or accidents is normally provided in the evening papers.

23 See Federico Fassano, "10 Años de Multitud," *La República*, 10 October 1998, p. 498.

24 The Colorado Party, particularly its most conservative sections.

25 The Frente Amplio is a political party of opposition.

26 Law No. 14,670 of 23 June 1977 *de Radiodifusión*, with a regulating decree 734/1978. In 1985, the civilian government revalidated this law and its accompanying regulating decree. Certain sections of this legislation, however, have been subject to revision.

27 Law No. 17,045 of 14 December 1998 *de Partidos políticos con representación parlamentaria*.

28 This incident showed just how dependent lawmakers are on television broadcasting.

29 The three Montevidean channels are Channel 4 (Montecarlo), Channel 10 (Saeta), and Channel 12 (Teledoce).

30 In this sense, ideology is an internally consistent set of ideas or values that individuals or groups choose to implement.

31 Based on official figures obtained from officers at Chasque, a non-profit organization Internet server.

32 In Uruguay, a newspaper costs $1.50 on weekdays and $2.50 on Sundays. The *New York Times*, in contrast, costs $0.60 on weekdays and its readers have much higher incomes compared to Uruguayans.

33 See statements of President Julio María Sanguinetti in the press: *Búsqueda*, 14 September 1995, p. 10; *Búsqueda*, 28 February 1998, p. 27; *Búsqueda*, 19 November 1988, p. 44.

34 Wilson Ferreira Aldunate was a presidential candidate who had received the largest number of votes in the 1971 elections, but who had lost to Juan Maria Bordaberry on

the basis of the Uruguayan electoral system that gave victory to the *lema* (party) that had received most votes.
35 Orlando Letellier was Chile's foreign affairs minister during the socialist government of President Salvador Allende Gossens (1970–1973).
36 See Chapter 1 for an exposition of these three models of democracy and their implications for media reform.

Bibliography

Alvarez, Luciano (1990) *Medios de Comunicación y Trampas a la Democracia: Ensayos Sobre Comunicación y Democracia*, Claeh-Humanitas, Montevideo and Buenos Aires.
—— (1993) *La Casa Sin Espejos: Perspectivas de la Industria Audiovisual Uruguaya*, Claeh-Fin de Siglo, Montevideo.
Alvarez Ferretjans, Daniel (1985) *La Prensa en el Período de Transición*, El Libro Libre, Montevideo.
Backer and McKenzie (ed.) (1996) Dictamen sobre el marco jurídico de las telecomunicaciones en la República Oriental del Uruguay. Poder Ejecutivo (unpublished).
Blengio Brito, Raúl (1984) *La Libertad de Expresión*, Banda Oriental, Montevideo.
Blixen, Samuel (1998) *El Vientre del Cóndor*, Virus, Barcelona.
Couriel, A. and Lichtensztejn, S. (1969) *El F.M.I. y la Crisis Económica Nacional*, FCU, Montevideo.
Faraone, Roque (1960) La Prensa de Montevideo, Faculty of Law, Montevideo.
—— (1972) *El Uruguay en que Vivimos*, Arca, Montevideo (4th edn).
—— (1987) *De la Prosperidad a la Ruina*, Arca, Montevideo.
—— (1998) *Televisión y Estado*, Cal y Canto, Montevideo.
Fassano, Federico (1998) "10 Años de Multitud", *La República*, Montevideo.
Finch, Henry (1986) "The Transition to Civilian Government in Uruguay," *Third World Affairs*.
—— (1991) "Uruguay since 1930," in Leslie Bethell (ed.) *The Cambridge History of Latin America, volume 8: 1930 to the Present*, Cambridge University Press, Cambridge.
Gabay, Marcos (1993) Informe para el Grupo de Trabajo de la Universidad (unpublished).
García Rubio, C. (1994) *Lo que el Cable Nos Dejó. Televisión para Abonados, Comunicación y Democracia en el Uruguay*, Edición de la Pluma, Montevideo.
ICD (1988) *Mass Media-La Guía*, ICD, Montevideo.
Ministerio de Defensa Nacional (1994) *La Política Nacional de Comunicaciones*, Edición de la Secretaría Central del Ministerio, Montevideo.
O.I.T.–F.I.S.E., Uruguay 1973–1978, Syndicat National de l'Enseignement Supérieur (FEN), Paris.
Pallares, L. and Stolovich, L. (1991) *Medios Masivos de Comunicación en el Uruguay: Tecnología, poder, y crisis*, CUI, Montevideo.
Paris, B., Faraone, R. and Oddone, J. (1997) *Cronología Comparada de la Historia del Uruguay, 1830–1985*, Universidad de la República, Montevideo.
Rama, Claudio (ed.) (1992) *Industrias Culturales en Uruguay*, Arca, Montevideo.
Rodriguez Perdomo, M. and Bastón Maio, C. (1991) *Marco Jurídico y Formas de Gestión en Telecomunicaciones*, FCU, Montevideo.
SODRE, audience, Chamber of Representatives, doc. 415/96, 18 September 1996

Laws and decrees

Constitucion de la República Oriental del Uruguay del Año 1918 (1947), Librería Universitaria, Montevideo.
Decree No. 23,941 of 7 June 1956 *de Estaciones de televisión*.
Decree No. 30,966 of 27 January 1966 *de Televisión*.
Law No. 8,390, of 28 January 1928 *de Estaciones radioeléctricas transmisoras*.
Law No. 9,155 of 4 December 1933 (*Código Penal*).
Law No. 9,480 *de Imprenta* of 28 June 1935.

Law No. 13,641 of 29 July 1965 *de Empresas periodísticas*.
Law No. 13,349 of 29 July 1965 *de Rendición de Cuentas*.
Law No. 14,422 of 21 October 1975 *de Telecomunicaciones*.
Law No. 14,670 of 23 June 1977 *de Radiodifusión*.
Law No. 15,691 of 24 December 1983 *Disposiciones sobre publicidad y comercialización de cigarrillos, cigarros y tabaco*.
Decree 445/1988 of 5 July 1988 *Horario de protección al menor*.
Law No. 16,099 of 3 November 1989 *Comunicaciones e informaciones*.
Law No. 17,045 of 14 December 1998 *de Partidos políticos con representación parlamentaria*.

12

CONCLUSION

Monroe E. Price and Beata Rozumilowicz

Our objectives in this book have been somewhat instrumental. We set out to learn how media developments and changing media structures interact with the processes of rendering a society more or less democratic. Our Holy Grail of inquiry has involved determining whether there is a causal effect between liberalized media and a democratic society, and as happens in most religious searches, reaching a final destination is elusive. How can we tell whether, as is so widely assumed, media reform is a necessary condition of democratization, or rather, whether free and independent media are merely attractive, superb, and even justifying products of an already liberalized society? Does media reform promote democratization or is the existence of healthy and independent media merely a consequence or sign of a society that is already on the way toward greater democratic practice? Indeed, it may be that the two processes, media reform and democratization, are mutually exclusive with little or no effect of one upon the other.

In the end, we come back to the theory of "stages" of transition, the approach set forth in Chapter 1. For us, based on our reading of the case studies, no grand theory or overwhelming conclusion can be drawn. If the case studies illustrate anything, it is that the relationship between media reform and political transition is best considered as retail, not wholesale, as narrow and functional rather than dramatic and overarching. Certain adjustments in media structure and behavior at political stages in a country's history tend to move that polity in the direction of greater recognition of democratic norms. The extent to which change in media can further democratic tendencies is tied very much to a complex set of factors about the particular society. Those within and those without a state who seek to effect change may not be able to use media transformation as a tool for democratization, or they may not have the resources and capacity to intervene and obtain the changes in media structure and function that will enhance or render positive political changes more stable.

In addition, "globalism" may imply a lessening in the applicability of old generalizations. The existence of independent media does not necessarily mean that they will perform a meaningful critical function, since, to a considerable extent, commercialism can displace the checking function of media. Furthermore, the existence of information from outside may reduce pressure to create a domestic critical voice. In that respect, the existence of the Internet

254

could, ironically, alter the impetus or demand for state responsiveness to democratic voices.

Perhaps the best that can be achieved is that some sort of diagnostic capacity can emerge and the diagnostic is the best opening for the instrumental. Thus, from a pragmatic or programmatic standpoint, there is a major need for determining whether our preferred model of stages – pre-transition, primary transitional, secondary transitional, and late or mature – is useful as a guide to understanding the practicalities of media reform. The utility inheres because the model of "stages" in our study, has the potential for determining what kinds of interventions in media reform, whether through development of law or other changes, are most fruitful for enhancing democratic values in the society at large.

The relationship between social change and media reform

We start with the perspective set forth by Karol Jakubowicz in his chapter on Poland. He argues that there

> is currently no unanimity in the literature on the relationship between mass communications and social change. The issues of whether mass media lead or follow change, whether they mirror or mould society, and whether they should be conceptualized as agents of social change or of the status quo are yet to be resolved.

There is one additional complication. Media independence, or, rather, media autonomy, is often said to condition the capacity of media to perform the particularly desired functions of social change. And, as Jakubowicz has put it in his chapter, "Media autonomy, or independence, cannot be achieved until media have become disentangled from state and political institutions and become structurally free of inhibiting forms of economic, political, or other dependency." But this Habermasian ideal is precisely that – an ideal. The capacity of a press institution to function without reliance on any source of power in a society is almost impossible, especially in an immature democracy. Autonomy that is relatively indifferent to tangible government support may only be able to develop in a well-formed democracy, and only in appropriate economic circumstances can advertiser-supported or publicly supported media find some space for independence.

Table 10.1 (p. 203) in Jakubowicz's chapter seeks to demonstrate the social circumstances necessary for demonopolized and autonomous media.

Note that in his formulation, certain key determinants of the function of media are said to be products of cultural change, not direct variables of economic or political factors. Whether or not media serve the checking or "impartial watchdog" function, in this view, is not a result of the competitive structure of the market or even of the nature of the political system. In any specific context, media might be rendered more plural, autonomous, and demonopolized, but still not serve as developer of public opinion or as a critic of government. On the other hand, as a matter of likelihood, the cultural change necessary to produce effective media is far less probable if the political and economic factors that produce a liberalized, autonomous, and demonopolized media are not present.

If it is true that only cultural change produces publicly interested media, then how does that deep sense of need and performance become embedded in a society? The case studies in this book broach the idea that overt political change can alter the structure of media, rendering them more competitive and less dependent on the state without producing media that furthers democratic transitions. The Uruguay study, for example, finds that the absence of an effective public broadcasting service can impair political debate, even where there is a nominally competitive, autonomous broadcasting system. The rise of a critical capability, through the Internet, in China has occurred in spite of an absence of overt political encouragement. The case studies of Ukraine, Uzbekistan, and Indonesia underscore the difficulties encountered in encouraging a culture in which the media function responsibly, contributing to a public sphere through a professional corps of journalists and a discerning reading, listening, and viewing public.

Neither law nor economic structure necessarily produces a media-led enlightenment. The relationship of media change and political change is particularly marked in the so-called transition societies. In the cases of Ukraine and Poland, for example, we can see how dependent, at least at the early stages, media are on political developments. Formal steps to incorporate the trappings of media independence and autonomy are feasible, even without major modification in the political system. But the environment for a responsible and effective media requires change and time.

One might ask how the existence of an ideal, articulated as a right (for example, the right to receive and impart information) functions within this framework. The public articulation of a goal of media autonomy might, itself, have an influence on the cultural factors, because the public could expect or demand a deregulated, plural, professional media in a watchdog role. If that is the case, it is important to emphasize efforts by international press organizations and training groups to encourage this thinking in journalists, politicians, and the public at large. In a sense, this process is institutionalized in such entities as the Freedom Forum, the World Press Freedom Committee, or NGOs like Article 19. On the other hand, one might try to distinguish those factors relating to the market that arise within a society (demand, for example, for advertising space as a condition for a media less reliant on government), from those factors that arise from outside the society (the consequences of opening to global media) in order to discern the true role of outside organizations in comparison with the cultural setting.

One can look at the Jakubowicz chart from an additional perspective: the two central columns mark the capability of political and economic factors to affect change. Short-term interventions are possible in these areas. The two columns on either side deal with more deep-seated, cultural, or long-term expectations where investments toward change are more problematic but equally essential. The chart demonstrates the need to understand the interplay between political, economic, and cultural influences on the capacity of media to contribute to democratic processes.

Of course, the hope is for a cumulative effect. Even the beginnings of media autonomy have consequences that may be aggregating. Once potentially critical media exist, the capacity of political leaders to backtrack and reverse the democratizing aspects of a transition is limited. For example, demonopolization of broadcasting media structures in India creates more plural sources of authority, with diverse claims for the national agenda. India becomes a more mature democracy as it is socially and politically more difficult for the government to reimpose an emergency, close down papers, and intimidate journalists. In 2000, despite remaining a one-party system, Uganda became a more mature democracy after a referendum that empowered an opposition and opposition media. These steps made it more unlikely that the regime would abuse or coerce journalists. Technology is often conceived of as a more autonomous factor, with the Internet rendering its democratizing influence regardless of government policy. Here, too, the case studies show that the impact, even of technology, is fettered or affected by numerous circumstances that are the consequence of government action and sometimes of law.

On the other hand, the case studies reinforce the relationship between the existence and nature of markets and media independence. The line may not be bright between "controlled" and "market" economies. The Uganda case study notes that government control of advertising funds can in effect be media management where there is not a thriving independent economy. The India study, in its treatment of the rise of cable television, suggests that the existence of public demand and an emerging consumer society, though lacking specific legislative authorization, led to a media system that competed effectively with the government terrestrial broadcasting monopoly. The Poland study argues that, even in a society with a strong market economy, broadcasting media may reflect the public's cultural views on whether or not a strong public service monopoly should be sustained. Autonomy and liberalization may be a function of changed political attitudes, demonopolization a function of changing economic circumstances, transformation a function of the idea of public service, and the journalistic profession an agent of cultural change.

Most of the case studies in the volume emphasize the necessity of change in the profession, a kind of re-education for a differentiated role to impact society. To be sure, circumstances such as an increased demand for reliable, objective, and impartial news will have their own market-based impact. Enacted requirements of fairness or responsibility will influence journalistic behavior. As Jakubowicz writes in his chapter, the media cannot serve its watchdog role "if the media or journalists themselves are in any way tied to or dependent upon those they are meant to oversee." The Jakubowicz test is harshly absolute in a world with many grays and informal and (sometimes) respectable ties between the media and power. Versions of what Miklos Haraszti has called "the velvet prison," journalistic bias that is the consequence of government favoritism, are too common to dismiss even in the most advanced societies. If this cannot change through the presence of competition, then it must through "cultural" forces within the society itself or technical assistance and support from outside sources.

The desirability of journalistic professionalization seems fairly universal across types or stages of society. In Cambodia, there was the need for attention to journalism training in order to develop the media and a civil society in post-conflict situations where a pre-existing generation had been all but eliminated. In Kosovo or Bosnia, where journalistic practices were shaped by conflict, the potential of journalism to reignite conflict in advance of moving to a more stable and more democratic society seemed the most popular aspect of journalism. At times, the search for "professionalization" has veered into arguments for controlling the appointment of those who hire and train journalists. In Poland, as well as in other transition societies of Central and Eastern Europe, many of the "media wars" were over just such questions of control. In countries at a later stage of the transitional process, it is common to focus on the self-regulatory process by which a profession develops a service ideal and code of conduct. Such a code is reinforced by a specific professional organization dedicated to enforcing and implementing this service ideal. A specific notion of independence inheres in these codes. It is here, often, that autonomy includes independence from the publisher or even, in its most radical formulation, from an editor. The ambiguities are captured in this phrase, simple on the surface, but fraught with complexity, from Jakubowicz, "This [professional] ideal concerns service to the general public rather than to media owners and managers or to political or economic interests."

In his chapter Andrei Richter traces the rise and fall of various models of professional ethics, concluding that, in Ukraine's transition phase, a code of ethics is but a vague notion for most Ukrainian journalists. Ethics had previously been strongly tied to communist values and images and the code was thrown out at the end of the communist regime. Codes were signs of ethical behaviour, but also elements of control. The rejection of an ethical code is part of an important feature of post-communist transitions, namely the idea of being free of constraint. As Richter reports, that "journalists should be free of any corporate or governmental control is now the slogan of the day and codes of ethics exist in very few media organizations." But, given economic realities, slogans do not frequently govern behavior.

Jakubowicz describes a cultural mandate, independent of any political or economic force, for journalists and places a special responsibility on them. In describing the meaning of professionalization for journalists, Jakubowicz contends:

> Professionalization of journalists should be understood both as the promotion of journalistic skills and as "collective professionalization," a process in which a profession develops a service ideal, code of conduct, and a specific professional organization dedicated to enforcing and implementing this service ideal and protecting the autonomy and standing of members of that profession. This service ideal concerns service to the general public rather than to media owners and managers or to political or economic interests. While a fully developed media system should be pluralistic, allowing different media representing various shades of opinion, in the unique circumstances of systemic transition, the first priority should be assisting the public in making sense of the dilemmas of transformation and in finding their bearings under these new circumstances.

This context-based duty is a new (and perhaps unappealing) burden. Many journalists lack the training, detachment, professionalism, and indeed will to be truly independent. As a result, they often confuse audiences by offering partisan, tendentious, and therefore conflicting reports or analyses of developments in their societies.

Surveying the case studies, one might, identify those where cultural aspects that influence elements of journalistic independence and professionalization are particularly evident. In Jakubowicz's analysis, one impediment to his concept of "independence" is the professional self-definition of media practitioners who "subordinate their professional activities to promoting a cause or the interests of certain political groups or other organizations." The idea of journalistic subordination to a cause is especially true in those contexts in which media are organized along party lines, or where the political power structure induces journalists, consistently, to take a pro-authority perspective. In post-conflict Bosnia, the Office of the High Representative found that the alignment of television stations exactly along party and ethnic lines was especially disruptive of the peace process and the transition to democracy. In post-Soviet Russia entire newspapers and stations are reportedly controlled by outside interests and oligarchs run newspapers and broadcasting entities to further other business interests.

Professionalization may include the long-term shaping of attitudes toward free media. Naomi Sakr, in her study of Jordan, cites Abdullah Hassanat, of the *Jordan Times* for the proposition that universities and newspapers did not "create a breed of free-minded intelligentsia capable of defending the country at crucial junctures" (1998). Upholding an ideal of internal independence may just mean that when the owners are committed to specific positions and uncommitted to objectivity and impartiality, they should be tempered by a counterforce of journalists. Journalists may have to fight to ensure they retain the right to take radically different views from the owners, managers, and editors of the publication.

In Jakubowicz's view, the onus is squarely on editorial staff to maintain their own personal and professional independence and make media independence real. It is not law, but individual responsibility that is central to this theory. Jakubowicz concludes that barring this situation, "all the legal and institutional measures to safeguard media independence are just an empty shell. Conversely, even without the formal safeguards of media independence, editorial staffs determined to preserve their personal/professional independence can make a significant difference."

The relationship between modes of media and stages of society in transitions to democracy is relevant. According to Jakubowicz, democracy itself, though to some extent aided by the media must, in the end, become consolidated in order to "create the prerequisites of a democratic media system." The specific elements of such a consolidation of democracy are the existence of civil society and an independent public sphere; an established role for public opinion in public life; a willingness to de-politicize important areas of social life; some accepted notion of the public interest; trust in and acceptance of public broadcasting regulation to serve public interest; and the emergence of journalistic professionalism based on a notion of public service. Unfortunately, these are characteristics not always found in democracies, even if they are consolidated and mature. Elements of globalization and enhanced competition are often at war with the idea of a publicly accepted notion of public interest or heightened aspirations for professionalization of journalists.

The relationship between social change and media structure

What emerges from this analysis and the case studies is a picture of a complicated relationship between the political system and media structure. One piece of the puzzle is the causal way in which political and economic developments help determine the nature of media. A relevant investigation for our study would be the analysis of what altered functioning of the media in a society underwrites or reinforces the society's democratic tendencies. More plural, autonomous, demonopolized media are more likely in societies that have become more mature in their democratic tendencies. Instrumentally more significant, at least from the perspective of this book, is whether remolding media relates to the refashioning of society. Here, again, our conclusion is that minor implications, but no sweeping claim of causation, can be made. So complex are the conditions for media that enhance democratic values that one has to look outside media for the creation of those conditions.

In his study of Uruguay, Faraone questions the causal relationship between media reforms and democratic transitions. Studying the record in that country, he concludes that media reforms are the product of pre-existing political reforms rather than major contributing factors to the transition itself. He demonstrates that media in Uruguay have fallen short of what a democratic media should be.

> [They] fail to act as effective watchdogs or to provide a public forum for the development of participative democratic ideals. [...] Self-censorship, the overwhelming relationship of government to the industry, and the level of concentration and interconnectedness within media itself are all factors that limit their role in the democratic developments at hand.

Only in a few specific instances in the case studies does the existence of an active and involved media system cause a direct change in political structures. Yet one's intuition is that there is some relationship between the two. The "stages" approach, developed at length in Chapter 1 and reiterated here, assists in understanding the causality of media reform in connection with political change. The stages are not necessarily sequential, there is no inevitability about moving from one stage to another in a linear fashion, and "backsliding" is not only possible, but also frequent.

Changes in media structure have different meanings and implications at different stages in the political process. During a pre-transition stage, finding the right moment in which the introduction of plural voices can be a critical lever for change is a useful art form. In that stage, the use of international broadcasting, such as the Voice of America or the BBC World Service, has been particularly effective in facilitating change. One can say that during a stage of primary (or even secondary) transition the existence of liberalized media has a particular function. The availability of a more plural opportunity for diverse voices, with a stake in a more democratic society, itself acts as a brake on political backsliding.

The case studies took the shape they did because of such a "stage" approach for determining the relationship between media reform and political reform. It was important, in the process of developing the case studies, to ask the country experts to analyze the conditions, and the legal-institutional and socio-cultural aspects that contribute to the formation of an "enabling environment" for the development of free and independent media in new democracies. We asked them to clarify the role media reform has played in the initial shaping or consolidation of democracy in the country under study. There were specific areas of the role media reform plays that would be subjected to particular scrutiny. These included the most crucial legal-institutional reforms within the media sector that have promoted the development of free and independent media during the period of democratic transition and the important socio-cultural changes in the media sector that promoted the development of free and independent media during the period of democratic transition.

In the process, many of the authors provided an account of the milestones of the democratization process in the country since the beginning of transition. They sought to identify simultaneity between these political milestones and changes in media structures. To provide guidance as to causality or influence, the authors sought to identify the impact that the legal framework had on the process of media reform during the period of democratization. The authors also, in most cases, sought to distinguish between the varying traditions of law and regulation of print and electronic broadcasting. This included examining the role of the state as regulator and financier or owner. They looked at the management aspects of state-owned media and the state's allocation, if that is what occurred, of national media space for political competition. It was important, as well, to look at the introduction of private enterprise owners within the print and broadcasting industry.

Media internationalization

One quite important area in the analyses was whether voices and funds from outside a country influence the processes of democratization within. The United States government, after the conclusion of the NATO campaign in the Federal Republic of Yugoslavia, invested in a "ring around Serbia" to bring the Voice of America and other sources of information to the people of Serbia. NGOs invested in voices of independence. In many instances, the foreign influence is commercial or commercially based, as happens when CNN or Sky News is added to a local mix. There may be a special effectiveness to these measures of intervention at specific moments in a transition because they empower the opposition. The availability of newspapers from abroad, the use of foreign agencies in a contribution to local media, and, in an era of globalization, the receipt or retransmission of foreign (or now global) radio and television stations may also affect local media or empower opposition.

International principles also played their part, sometimes as a formal aspect of conditionality, sometimes as an informal element of conformity to widely accepted norms. Naomi Sakr's study of Jordan points to the fact that that country committed itself to upholding the right of freedom of expression "regardless of frontiers" in the International Covenant on Civil and Political Rights, but it also made ample use, at least under the regime of King Hussein, of the ICCPR provisos that allow certain restrictions in the interests of respecting reputations, protecting national security, and safeguarding public order, public health, and morals.[1] Sakr noted that under the Hussein regime it was very difficult for foreign media to establish themselves. The government's Press and Publications Department controlled the entry of foreign publications into the kingdom, though that control was increasingly open in its exercise. Recent liberalization has occurred partly as a result of recognizing the influence of technology. Previous attempts to ban the entry of London-based, pan-Arab dailies, notably *Al-Quds al-Arabi* and *Al-Hayat*, had not prevented would-be readers from accessing these papers' websites. In India, adherence to human rights conventions and absorption of international principles into the state constitution allowed the Indian judicial system virtually to compel increased diversity in the nation's broadcasting media.

The influence of civil society upon the media

Ultimately, any study of the relationship of media to political change must discuss the role of civil society and the public sphere. It is difficult to identify precisely the role of citizen groups or associations in the processes of encouraging transition, and, in addition, to link those impulses to the existence of independent media, but certain of the case studies explore such connections. Poland may be the outstanding example of a transition in which civil society found its own media, which then enhanced the potential for change. In China, a civil society may be developing around new media technology with the potential that such a movement has a long-term impact on political institutions.

In other states, the influence of ethnic groups (either minorities or majorities) upon media and media reform processes must be studied. Although it may not have been highlighted in the case studies, it has often been suggested that institutions such as universities and journalism schools contribute to the process of media reform, and that such contributions have their reflection in the stability of political change.

Without question, the increase in activity of NGOs has altered the landscape of political transformation. Organizations such as Internews grew from mere ideas in the early 1990s into sprawling empires a decade later, moving from transition to transition and encouraging the growth of an independent broadcasting sector as a lynchpin of stabilizing change.

The Jordan study questions the evidence behind the Western belief that civil society growth will ensure greater pluralism and the freedoms of association and expression. Sakr states, "Interest groups may well seek freedom of expression for themselves but not for others." In Russia, as elsewhere, civil society meant the growth of fringe groups, and in Rwanda efforts to encourage independent media unintentionally included the funding of radio entities that later propagated effective incitement to genocide. Cumulatively, however, the assertion of rights, even selfishly, will usually yield a more open society.

The emergence of new technology

Without question, the emergence of new technologies, including the Internet, provides an entirely new chapter in the relationship of media reform to democratization. New technologies provide a new mode of shaping a public sphere and possibly reshaping notions of what constitutes appropriate democratic governance. But the relationship between these new technologies and political transitions is not obvious or one-dimensional.

In a sense, given the fairly obvious assumption that the Internet can be an effective tool for furthering a broad human rights agenda, one issue is the nature of the infrastructure for information distribution. This includes how extensive it is, how information is distributed, what are the nodes of access. It may well be that the Internet, on some critical questions, is largely a device for more intimately connecting elites or opinion makers, rather than a technique for becoming a medium for large-scale participation in the political process. It may, on the other hand, be a means of enlarging the capacity of formerly excluded national elites for entering into an international debate.

The case study of China underscores how important the Internet is in forming a new stratum of political involvement. Against such restrictive measures as government-mandated registration of users, access, and service providers, "the establishment of a national firewall to prohibit access, and the utilization of Internet surveillance technologies," the Internet has developed on the black market as a source of national technological pride. As Chan and Qiu summarize the matter, if "the past speaks for the future, technological developments such as the Internet and satellite television will boost media liberalization in China."

The Internet is important in examining the relationship between media reform and political transition for another reason. More than other media technologies (although this assumption must constantly be questioned), the Internet depends on decisions that are built into the system – technical codes, rather than political regulation. Professor Lawrence Lessig, using a United States-centric descriptor, calls this a division between East Coast Code and West Coast Code. To the extent that the Internet, as a medium of organization, of reinventing the world, is a function of West Coast Code, of algorithms and engraved software chips, the nature of the political process existing above it becomes less relevant. A related question – from a corporate viewpoint as well as a governmental one – is what technical decisions render the use of Internet for political reform more or less likely? Political transition, as it affects the nature of democratic institutions, may be facilitated through technological change.[2] Whether these changes occur (and with what consequences) may have to do with ease of anonymity, potential for access to archival material, and a plethora of identifying characteristics of message transmission.

In the age of particularized, more personal media, other aspects of architecture will determine the contribution of the medium to political reform. Because of the exact path of transmission from computer to computer, the shape of the Internet may have implications for traceability and jurisdiction that influence empowerment of individuals and groups. For example, while the

Internet is a tool for the human right to receive and impart information (as compared to its use to advance other substantive agendas), there has also been concern for the power of the state, where necessary in a democracy, to protect national security, territorial integrity, the rights or interests of others, and public morals. China, the United States, and the United Kingdom, among many other states, have identified potential abuses, characterized as terrorism or cyberwarfare, and seek to impose regulations that allow monitoring and prevention of them. Barring a complete rejection of the aspirations of various governments (including that of the United States) to come to grips with these questions, it remains necessary to consider how most "solutions" to the ostensible question of terrorism have implications for the structure of the Internet that affect its use for human rights purposes. How these questions are resolved will affect the capacity of the medium to alter and affect political structures.

Too seldom is there an understanding of the relationship between media, the health of local languages, and the nature of political transitions. While the human right to receive and impart information is well recognized, the privilege of exercising that right in one's own language is less well rooted or documented. Political structures (and, as a consequence, their transformation) may be a function of the power of languages, and the power of languages may be a function of the nature of media. In Ukraine, in the era before the Internet, language on broadcasting media was closely calibrated, with consequences for the large minority of Russian speakers. As the Internet develops, language mapping will have similar consequences. The Internet may, passively, be an instrument for revitalizing some languages (and diasporas which rely on them) and for weakening others. Modes of political organization and a sense of participation will be altered by the resultant pattern of language usage.

As the Internet becomes a greater and greater factor in the distribution and processing of information, calibrating its penetration will become increasingly important. Furthermore, just as the nature of intermediaries for information in the traditional world of broadcasters and newspapers was a factor in its political impact, the same will be true on the Internet. A great deal of attention has to be paid to refashioning modes of wholesaling and retailing critical information. Otherwise, rather than reducing the so-called "digital divide," a phenomenon of dumping information or flooding information may occur. Attention has to be given to democratizing modes of access, simplifying navigational devices, and creating new intermediaries that help define local needs and assist in the sorting and filtering that makes information useful rather than overwhelming.

Stages and appropriate steps for international aid and media reform development

We return, finally, to the stages of transition, laid out in Chapter 1. As already mentioned, the very word "stages" might be somewhat misleading in that it intimates a sequence, as if Act I is automatically followed by Act II, rather than the other way around. It is impossible, in an era of optimism, not to look for progression. The theory implies that, ordinarily, a transition follows a pre-transition stage, and a secondary transition follows one that is primary. This may not be the case. "Shock therapy" in the post-Soviet period could be said to have been an effort to accelerate the movement from pre-transition to secondary transition. In some contexts, such as Indonesia, an almost violent upheaval and radical reorientation was characterized by efforts, perhaps unsuccessful, to move, almost without a pre-transition to an advanced structure for media in a democratic society. In China, elements of pre-transition and consolidation appear almost simultaneously. The case study of India also provides examples, such as the announcement of the Emergency, where transitions are suspended. And in Bosnia-Herzegovina and other post-conflict areas, the international community enforces media control precisely for the purpose, ostensibly, of facilitating political reform.

Evidence goes both ways on the progressiveness of stages. As Naomi Sakr writes of Jordan, ironically, the Press and Publications Law there at the end of King Hussein's reign was effectively less liberal than the one in force at the start of it. Despite some relaxation of the law in 1999 and the promise of a "free media zone," the overall thrust of change after 1993 was to restore and even increase curbs on free speech. On the other hand, in Uganda, the liberalization of the media under the Museveni regime, however inconsistent, helped support the idea that an opposition could be effective, and that opposition then made its mark in the Referendum of 2000 (although Uganda remains a one-party country).

In China, Deng Xiaoping's "socialism with Chinese characteristics" allowed the beginning of a "three-part reform program consisting of the responsibility system, the transition to a commodity-based economy, and an opening to the international economy." As Chan and Qiu demonstrate, the beginning of market liberalization and international trade promoted an expansion in media genres and encouraged advertising, variety, "predictability and stability," and "professionalism among journalists," although certain restrictions still remained. This process occurred in the absence of democratization.

To be sure, then, there must be a certain degree of caution about the use of "stages" as a firm guide to understanding the relationship between media law reform and institution of democratic practices. Still, as a point of reference, it is possible to turn to the stages themselves to see what can be gleaned from the case studies and other material about incremental efforts characteristic of each of them.

Pre-transition stage

For the pre-transition stage, Chapter 1 indicated several possible steps where media reform may have direct implications for political development.[3] These include "attempting to persuade the regime to recognize an opposition" and "providing constructive media infringement critiques." These steps are generally the kinds of approaches taken by external forces, whether by USAID or others, contemplating modes of intervention. It is not necessarily the view from within and does not pretend to provide all the answers. From our studies (and other sources), we can identify a number of examples of the kind of pre-transition intervention that we have hypothesized.

The heavy investment in international broadcasting during the Cold War is emblematic of a pre-transition strategy. The establishment of Radio Free Asia, whether effective or not, was designed as a pre-transition mode of intervention in

China, Burma, and elsewhere within its remit. Renewed information focus on Iraq and through the Voice of America and RFE/RL is also part of this process. Clandestine support for an emerging opposition in Poland, through the purchase of printing presses and other modes of reproduction and circulation of their views, is an example of pre-transition intervention by an external power in the extension of a sphere of influence and exercise of democratizing methodologies. The insistent efforts of certain NGOs like Internews in the post-Soviet period and equivalent organizations involved in media monitoring in Uzbekistan, with critiques of executive actions, could be perceived as part of a pre-transition strategy from outside donors. Finally, the United States debate over most-favored-nation policies in China, establishing some measure of negotiation or conditionality for participation in international benefits (however these negotiations are concluded), stands within this cohort of efforts.

Primary transition stage

For the primary transition stage, the steps suggested or observed – primarily external steps – among others things, included "analyzing other legislative media models, analyzing how emerging economic legislation will impact the development of media, and consulting with experts." These modes of intervention in the primary transition phase are couched, again, in the form of steps by external agencies, such as NGOs and their government funders. They could be restated to describe pressures and desires that arise from within a society, but they would then have a different dynamic.

The studies of Poland, Ukraine, Uganda, Uzbekistan, and Indonesia all contain elements from this aspect of primary transitions. For example, Richter notes that the majority of media-related court cases in Ukraine are defamation lawsuits, and that state bodies have frequently used the defamation statute against media outlets. He also points out that in comparison with other former Soviet republics, "the amounts sought as compensation in defamation cases in Ukraine have frequently been unrealistically high, reaching levels of up to US$250 million." Although interference of state bodies in the activities of TV and radio broadcasters is prohibited by the statute "On Television and Radio Broadcasting," the same statute makes broadcasters responsible for the content of their programs (Zakon 1993: Article 6). In addition, although the state (executive and legislative branches) is prohibited from direct intervention, the legal system (including judicial process) can be used to punish broadcasters when they violate the law.

The chapters on Ukraine, Indonesia, Poland, Uganda, and Uruguay, among others, discuss the role that control of state resources, including spectrum and newsprint, can have in the transition phases, particularly the primary transition. In each case, the extension of subsidies may become vital to sustaining media, but this mode of intervention also involves the dangers of backsliding and recurrent state control. To counteract this tendency, the Open Society Institute has developed the notion of awards as incentives for investigative reporting. Internews furthered a technique of providing equipment to innovators at individual stations that demonstrated promise of sustainability.

Faraone points out that even relatively advanced transitions require this kind of maintenance in the face of pressures from such institutions as the military. He also concludes that Uruguay needs to incorporate the legal doctrines of the Pact of San José de Costa Rica and "other international agreements to which the country has acceded, particularly where the right to information is concerned" into the constitution before real progress can continue. In some primary transitions, there are rudimentary infrastructural requirements. As Ronald Kayanja writes about Uganda, demographic factors such as the availability of electricity, telephones, and computer centers limit the sustainability of media.

Secondary transition stage

For those societies – if they can be so categorized – that are in a more advanced or secondary stage of transition, a somewhat different set of actions within the society might take place, often, as well, supported by international governmental and non-governmental agencies.

These would include, among other things, holding seminars and training conferences for both politicians and journalists, establishing networks of media professionals that may lead to more systematized and institutionalized cooperation between those working in similar fields, and encouraging increased foreign investment in order to bring a measure of independence to various media sectors that suffer from an inadequate domestic economic base.

Jakubowicz stresses the importance of a free market to media enhancement. "Otherwise the development of a private, advertising-financed media sector is very difficult. Media can be independent only if they are financially successful." Consideration of the prerequisites of media independence should cover not just the manner of financing media but also the general economic environment. In circumstances where economic reform is going badly, the advertising-driven process of media pluralization will take a long time. This is especially true of broadcasting since a small and relatively poor market cannot sustain numerous specialized broadcasting outlets. Commercial broadcasting, especially that which is locally financed and managed, is only beginning in such markets, and it takes a long time for new companies to accumulate capital enabling them, should they want to do so, to introduce narrow-cast channels and finance them as they become established. Minorities are, in many cases, either too small or too poor to be attractive to commercial broadcasters.

Late transition stage

During the late or mature stage, the model suggested "establishing international 'awards' or honors, linked to financial support for paradigm media performers, [...] creating international training institutes for media regulators in transition societies, [and] building or financing libraries and technical assistance units, which can provide the basis for intellectual development and innovation," among other steps. In a fairly mature and consolidated democracy, attention is paid to these areas merely as a matter of maintenance of the status quo and directionality.

In the introductory chapter to their recent book of essays, *De-Westernizing Media Studies*, James Curran and Myung-Jin Park deplored the "self-absorption and parochialism of much Western media theory." The problem, for them, was the method for a necessary process of correction. They wished to avoid an American-developed list of corrective processes and formulaic summaries of media reform. Instead, their technique was to "set a global exam paper," to be given to media academics.

As we have indicated in our introduction, we have taken, quite independently, a similar approach, although with very different questions. Their inquiries were: "How do the media relate to the power structure of society? What influences the media, and where does control over the media lie? How has the media influenced society? What effect has media globalization and new media had on the media system and society?" (2000). Throughout the Curran and Park book, there runs the idea that the world had never been as dichotomous as was thought to be true during the 1950s and that the distinction between market and state is not as clear. Their interrogatories also were designed to bring more perspective to issues of globalization and the now-ancient debate over cultural imperialism and media independence.

The inferences we have sought to draw are similarly based on a combination of case studies, analysis of the literature, and a collection of experience. Additionally, our goal has been to enhance the comparative approach and to provide a context in which the idea of "media reform" can be more meaningfully analyzed. All case studies – even those that have the perspective of many of the authors included here – are really in the nature of snapshots. The processes of change can overwhelm their simplified mode for the capture of time. Drawing on a number of such case studies, in a wide variety of settings, and by establishing and testing a theoretical framework, we have sought to compensate for this inevitable problem. The very nature of media reform is changing as technology alters. The very nature of democratic practice is changing as well. As a consequence, the relationship between the phenomena of media reform and political reform has an incalculable dynamic.

Notes

1   For the provision "regardless of frontiers" see Article 19 (2) of the ICCPR. For the other ICCPR provisos see Article 19 (3).
2   Though again this remains to be examined, the Internet is capable of revolutionizing access to information. For example, it may provide a new way of learning about political candidates or increasing candidate access to voters.
3   See Chapter 1 for outline of possible steps.

References

Curran, James and Park, Myung-Jin (eds) (2000) *De-Westernizing Media Studies*, London: Routledge.
Hassanat, Abdullah (1998) "Impediments to Freedom of Expression in Jordan," paper presented to the MacBride Roundtable on Culture and Communication in the Global Information Society, Amman, November.
Zakon "*Pro telebachennya ta radiomovlennya*", no. 3759–XII of 21 December 1993, Article 6.

INDEX